The Politics of Baseball

ALSO BY RON BRILEY

*Class at Bat, Gender on Deck and Race in the Hole:
A Line-up of Essays on Twentieth Century
Culture and America's Game*
(McFarland, 2003)

The Politics of Baseball

Essays on the Pastime and Power at Home and Abroad

Edited by RON BRILEY

McFarland & Company, Inc., Publishers
Jefferson, North Carolina, and London

LIBRARY OF CONGRESS CATALOGUING-IN-PUBLICATION DATA

The politics of baseball : essays on the pastime and power at home and abroad / edited by Ron Briley.
    p.   cm.
  Includes bibliographical references and index.
  ISBN 978-0-7864-4129-7
  softcover : 50# alkaline paper

  1. Baseball — Social aspects — United States. 2. Baseball — Political aspects — United States. I. Briley, Ron, 1949 –
  GV867.64.P65   2010
  796.3570973 — dc22   2010001186

British Library cataloguing data are available

©2010 Ron Briley. All rights reserved

No part of this book may be reproduced or transmitted in any form or by any means, electronic or mechanical, including photocopying or recording, or by any information storage and retrieval system, without permission in writing from the publisher.

Cover illustration ©2010 Dynamic Graphics

Manufactured in the United States of America

McFarland & Company, Inc., Publishers
  Box 611, Jefferson, North Carolina 28640
    www.mcfarlandpub.com

Table of Contents

Introduction (Ron Briley) — 1

PART ONE:
BASEBALL AND DOMESTIC POLITICS

1. Baseball and Ballots: Players and Politicians (John A. Tures) — 9
2. The Baseball Evangelist Throws Out John Barlycorn: Billy Sunday and Prohibition (Wendy Knickerbocker) — 25
3. Red Press Nation: The Baseball Rhetoric of Lester Rodney (Scott D. Peterson) — 38
4. Bob Dole and the Brooklyn Dodgers (Raymond I. Schuck) — 57
5. Are We There Yet? Major League Baseball and Sexual Orientation (Lisa Doris Alexander) — 71
6. Professional Baseball Wages in the Era of Integration (Michael J. Haupert) — 82
7. Sam Jethroe's Last Hit (N. Jeremi Duru) — 99
8. The Church of Detroit Baseball: American Civil Religion and Willie Horton at Comerica Park (Joshua Fleer) — 111

PART TWO: THE DIPLOMACY OF BASEBALL AND THE INTERNATIONAL GAME

9. The Nationalist Pastime: The Use of Baseball to Promote Nationalism Globally (Russ Crawford) — 125

10. More Than a Game: Baseball Diplomacy in World War II and
 the Cold War, 1941–1958 (BRYAN C. PRICE)   141

 11. Exporting the Horsehide American Dream: The Hidden Side
 of Nicaraguan Baseball (ROBERT ELIAS)   157

 12. The Politics of American Colonialism Through the Lens of
 Major League Baseball Academies (JESSICA SKOLNIKOFF and
 ROBERT ENGVALL)   171

 13. Recognizing — Not Just Rooting for — the Home Team:
 Nationalism and the Taiwanese Name Dispute at the 2006
 Baseball Classic (GLEN M.E. DUERR)   183

 14. Bud Selig's Use of "Smart Power" (ROBERT F. LEWIS)   195

 15. Commodore Selig: The Importance of Japanese Baseball Players
 in Major League Baseball (MATHEW J. BARTKOWIAK and
 YUYA KIUCHI)   212

 16. Major League Baseball, Welcome Back Veterans, and the
 Rhetoric of "Support the Troops" (MICHAEL L. BUTTERWORTH)   226

 About the Contributors   241
 Index   245

Introduction

As a young man growing up in a conservative community in rural west Texas, I was admonished by my parents to avoid such controversial topics as religion and politics—as if these two were mutually exclusive. Initially, I paid scant attention to this wisdom, but as I attended college and became increasingly politicized (even joining Students for a Democratic Society), I realized that maybe it would behoove me to heed the advice of my mother and father if I ever wanted to go home again. Accordingly, when visiting Childress, Texas, in the late 1960s and early 1970s and a former classmate or relative would bring up the Vietnam War, the civil rights movement, women's rights, or anything to do with the counterculture, I would immediately try to change the subject by interjecting, "How about those Astros." Surely I could find safe ground with friends and relatives in the national pastime of baseball and my favorite team, the Houston Astros, who entered the National League as the Houston Colt .45s when I was in the seventh grade. The Houston franchise and baseball always comforted me during the difficult days of adolescence.

Rather than discuss the prison revolt at Attica, perhaps we could, instead, have a great debate over the merits of artificial turf or the concept of a designated hitter. Alas, I discovered that baseball offered no respite from the burning questions of the day: there was a lot of discussion about the reserve clause and the hypocrisy of owners who talked about free enterprise but operated in a restrictive and controlled labor market, among other topics. I found myself in heated conversations defending black players such as Dick "Richie" Allen and Curt Flood for their courage in confronting racism and the baseball establishment. And, of course, I loved the Oakland A's. I recognized that the Oakland players were not really representative of the counterculture and that their beards and mustaches were grown in response to monetary incentives offered by owner Charley Finley, who perceived the facial hair as a marketing device.

Nevertheless, I could not help rooting for the somewhat disheveled Oakland club against the well-groomed Big Red Machine from Cincinnati. The 1972 World Series pitted the freaks against the straights, and the freaks won.

Pursuing the study of baseball in graduate school as a scholarly endeavor only confirmed my countercultural instincts that the national pastime was a reflection of and not an escape from the American political scene. Major League Baseball (MLB) — the baseball establishment, to use the vocabulary of the 1960s — often presumes to speak for all constituencies through the voice of the baseball commissioner, who purports to place the best interests of the game above selfish motives of profit and greed. This perception of MLB fits well into the Aristotelian tradition of politics based upon the goal of achieving what is best for the shared values of the community. Of course, whether MLB seeks the common good or simply to maximize the market potential for ownership is another question and moves us into the definitions of conflict emphasized by other political philosophers. Thomas Hobbes perceived politics as an activity in which interest groups act rationally for self-preservation, while Karl Marx perceived politics as the class struggle. Max Weber broadened Marx's definition, describing the political process as the struggle for power.

The essays in this collection owe more to the perceptions of Hobbes, Marx, and Weber than to Aristotle, focusing from various academic disciplines upon the issues of power and who wields it, and for what purpose, within the institution of organized baseball. A variety of concerns are addressed, including the broad issues of racial and sexual orientation discrimination in addition to the role played by baseball on the world stage in regard to fostering patriotism, colonialism, and globalization. Nevertheless, there are still numerous questions such as gender discrimination and the economic and community politics of stadium construction which require exploration. Thus, the collection is representative rather than comprehensive in suggesting the degree to which the baseball diamond, far from being a refuge from the political arena, is contested terrain. Some would have us believe that baseball, and sport in general, represents a meritocracy in which issues of political power and discrimination fail to intrude. The essays included in the collection persuasively argue that baseball reflects the larger political culture in which issues of economic power, social class, race, and sexual orientation matter a great deal.

Part One of this book emphasizes the politics of baseball on the domestic front. In the first essay, "Baseball and Ballots: Players and Politicians," John A. Tures concentrates on the careers of 34 owners, players, umpires, and executives in the political arena. Tures concludes that the baseball connection served most of these candidates well. But most were involved with baseball decades ago, and Tures speculates that labor controversies and enormous financial rewards reaped by today's players leaves them disinclined to seek elected office. Tures does not elaborate upon ideological preferences, but the more recent examples he incorporates into his essay seem to suggest that the baseball politicians incline toward conservatism.

One former player entered the political arena via religion. After a baseball career in the 1880s with the Chicago White Stockings, Pittsburgh Pirates, and Philadelphia Phillies, Billy Sunday (his real name) became a crusading evangelist against demon rum. In "The Baseball Evangelist Throws Out John Barlycorn: Billy Sunday and Prohibition," Wendy Knickerbocker argues Sunday employed baseball rhetoric and his athletic past in revival meetings to promote prohibition. Advocating a muscular Christianity, Sunday argued that Jesus was the ticket for individual salvation, while prohibition was the cure for society's ills.

The connections between the ills of baseball and the larger society were pursued on the political left by Lester Rodney as sports editor for the communist *Daily Worker*. In an astute comparative analysis of Rodney's 1947 (his first year as sports editor for the *Daily Worker*) rhetoric with that of John Kieran and Roscoe McGowen of the *New York Times*, Scott D. Peterson in "Red Press Nation: The Baseball Rhetoric of Lester Rodney" discusses telling differences in the treatment of issues such as racial integration and player grievances with ownership. While Kieran and McGowen toed the party line in supporting the baseball establishment, Rodney challenged both the status quo and baseball mythology.

Rhetorical analysis is also the concern of Raymond I. Schuck who focuses, in "Bob Dole and the Brooklyn Dodgers," on a quote from 1996 Republican candidate for president Bob Dole. Dole congratulates Hideo Nomo for throwing a no-hitter for the Brooklyn Dodgers, apparently forgetting that the Dodgers moved to Los Angeles after the 1957 season. Critics were quick to pounce on the Kansas senator for being out of touch with contemporary America. Schuck considers the strong reaction to the slip-up and argues that it mattered because baseball is part of the national community with which a successful candidate is expected to connect.

Sexual orientation, however, is a topic which many baseball players and officials, as well as politicians, seek to avoid. While some players such as Brad Ausmus and Mike Mussina have stated that they would have no problem playing alongside an openly gay teammate, Lisa Doris Alexander wonders whether baseball is ready for a gay athlete. In "Are We There Yet? Major League Baseball and Sexual Orientation" she examines the homophobic comments of John Rocker, Ozzie Guillén, and Julian Tavárez, as well as Commissioner Bud Selig's rather timid response to these statements, concluding that most players, along with baseball leadership, remain uncomfortable with issues of sexual orientation. Alexander asserts that it will take a "queer" Jackie Robinson to shatter baseball's prejudices toward gay athletes and citizens.

The last three chapters of Part I focus on issues of race from a black and white perspective. (The emergence of Latino and Asian ballplayers in the major leagues is addressed in the final section of Part II, on baseball diplomacy and globalization.) In his economic analysis of baseball wages in the era of integration, "Professional Baseball Wages in the Era of Integration," Michael J. Haupert determines that the wages of ballplayers in the 1930s and 1940s, whether in the Negro Leagues or the major leagues, exceeded those of both white and black manufacturing workers. Haupert concludes that there is little evidence of salary discrimination against black players after baseball integration. He adds, however, that since the first black major leaguers were older, having been shut out of so-called organized baseball for years, their time frame for earning top wages was shorter than for similar white athletes.

Haupert's arguments fit well with N. Jeremi Duru's "Sam Jethroe's Last Hit" regarding the short major league career of Jethroe, who at age twenty-eight earned National League Rookie of the Year honors with the Boston Braves in 1950. Due to his rather advanced age, Jethroe's skills began to decline during his third season with the Braves, and he was dealt to the Pirates. During the 1954 season, Jethroe was demoted to the minor leagues—before attaining the four full years of major league service necessary to qualify for a pension. After suffering personal and financial setbacks in his life after baseball, Jethroe, alleging racial discrimination, sued Major League Baseball for his pension. Jethroe's case was dismissed, but Duru argues that the ballplayer's litigation may serve as an example for remedial legislation addressing the long term effects of racial discrimination both on and off the playing field.

The final essay on race relations considers the impact of hometown hero Willie Horton on racial issues in Detroit. Horton is the only non–Hall of Fame Tiger to be memorialized with a statue at the new home of the Tigers, Comerica Park. Although Horton certainly enjoyed a distinguished baseball career, Joshua Fleer, who argues in "The Church of Detroit Baseball: American Civil Religion and Willie Horton at Comerica Park" that baseball functions as a civil religion in the United States, maintains that Horton was included primarily because of his efforts to head off further racial violence in Detroit during the troubled summers of 1967 and 1968. In honoring Horton, the ball club acknowledges its commitment to ending racial discrimination. Fleer considers the extent to which this symbol of reconciliation reflects the reality of conditions in the Motor City.

Part Two of this collection reflects the growing interest of scholars in the international ramifications of baseball as both a marketing tool and an instrument of American foreign policy. In the leadoff essay, "The Nationalist Pastime: The Use of Baseball to Promote Nationalism Globally," Russ Crawford discusses baseball as a tool to promote nationalism, pointing out that in the late nineteenth century the game was crucial in the assimilation of immigrant populations within the United States and in fostering an American sense of identity abroad. Crawford demonstrates that other nations have also embraced American baseball to serve their own purposes. During the Meiji Restoration in Japan, for instance, baseball was a vehicle for modernization, and in Cuba it was a sign of cultural independence from Spain.

Baseball diplomacy during the Second World War and early years of the Cold War is examined in Bryan C. Price's "More Than a Game: Baseball Diplomacy in World War II and the Cold War, 1941–1958." Describing what he terms the "pedestalization" of the sport by the press and organized baseball, Price argues that in the post-war period the United States government used baseball to promote democracy and American values by introducing the game in occupied Germany and Italy, in addition to restoring baseball in Japan.

While Price perceives baseball diplomacy as essentially benevolent, Robert Elias insists, in "Exporting the Horsehide American Dream: The Hidden Side of Nicaraguan Baseball," that in Nicaragua the game was used to galvanize the population in support of the American-backed Somoza family dictatorship. But baseball proved to have appeal in Nicaragua across ideological lines and was also adopted by the leftist Sandinistas during the civil war of the 1980s. As a participant in the Baseball for Peace program in Nicaragua, Elias maintains hope that baseball may still provide a degree of unity for the people of Nicaragua.

Colonial exploitation in Latin America is also examined by Jessica Skolnikoff and Robert Engvall in "The Politics of American Colonialism Through the Lens of Major League Baseball Academies." Skolnikoff and Engvall argue that rather than perpetuating the American dream, baseball academies further economic and cultural imperialism. In the final analysis, only a tiny fraction of those attending the baseball academies will be able to establish major league careers, and those who do enjoy success in the United States must abandon indigenous styles of play and conform to American standards.

As Glen M.E. Duerr argues in "Recognizing—Not Just Rooting For—the Home Team: Nationalism and the Taiwanese Name Dispute at the 2006 Baseball Classic," some countries have, to varying degrees, remade the game in their own image. The Americans and Japanese brought the game to Taiwan, and baseball has become an important component of cultural life on the island, as is evident in the success enjoyed by Taiwanese teams in the Little League World Series. Duerr focuses his attention, however, on Taiwan's relations with the People's Republic of China. Competing against the Chinese in the 2006 World Baseball Classic (WBC) Taiwan claimed a degree of international recognition for its desire to be accepted as a sovereign nation outside of the "two China" policy pursued by the United States.

The globalization of baseball involves the increasing use of what Robert F. Lewis terms "soft power" in "Bud Selig's Use of 'Smart Power.'" Borrowing a concept from Joseph S. Nye, Jr., Dean of the Kennedy School of Government at Harvard, Lewis argues that Major League Baseball has evolved from the employment of hard power (e.g., the reserve clause) to soft power marketing such as the WBC to establish its niche in both domestic and global markets. The Nye model suggests that soft power is often smart policy, emphasizing more co-optive solutions. Lewis astutely analyzes this concept through an examination of baseball commissioners from Kenesaw Mountain Landis to Bud Selig. Lewis concludes that Landis was the exemplar of the hard-power tactician with his unilateral rulings, while Selig uses the soft approach with an emphasis on globalization and markets.

Globalization also draws the attention of Mathew J. Bartkowiak and Yuya Kiuchi in their study of Japanese ballplayers, such as Ichiro Suzuki and Daisuke Matsuzaka, in major league baseball. In "Commodore Selig: The Importance of Japanese Baseball Players in Major League Baseball," the authors assert that the growing presence of Japanese players in the United States constitutes a march of transnational capitalism and a cultural exchange in which the Japanese athletes provide economic benefits for American clubs but shortchanges Japanese baseball and culture. As they demonstrate, globalization is not always the economic leveling process some advocates claim.

The final essay, "Major League Baseball, Welcome Back Veterans, and the Rhetoric of 'Support the Troops,'" is a provocative argument by Michael L. Butterworth in which the author analyzes the rhetoric employed by Major League Baseball in its Welcome Back Veterans (WBV) campaign. While acknowledging that honoring veterans is a laudable goal, Butterworth asserts that the WBV program is hardly apolitical as the rhetoric of Commissioner Selig suggests. Instead, the program associates patriotism with militarism, legitimizing the so-called War on Terror and invasion of Iraq by equating memoralization of 9/11 with honoring veterans of the Iraq War — establishing a link between 9/11 and Iraq that was disproven by the 9/11 Commission.

I would like to thank the scholars who contributed to this work highlighting the politics of baseball. Size limitations prevented the publication of several fine submissions, but this work does not constitute the final word on the contested diamond. Rather, these pieces should encourage further research on baseball and fundamental questions about power and authority.

Finally, I would like to thank my wife, Kathleen, and my children, Shane, Meghan, and Rosemary, for putting up with me during the editing of this work and for sharing my enthusiasm for baseball and politics. I would also like to acknowledge Headmaster Richard Heath and Sandia Preparatory School for encouraging my academic pursuits. I hope the book contributes to a civil discourse on the role baseball plays in American and global political questions of power and influence.

Part One

Baseball and Domestic Politics

CHAPTER 1

Baseball and Ballots: Players and Politicians

John A. Tures

You've heard of the three branches of government, right? But three bases? Given the number of ball players that have sought political office, such a notion may not be so far off. After all, hasn't baseball had two "Washington Senators" and one "Washington Nationals" teams?

With a few exceptions, baseball players are seen as local, even national heroes. But how effectively have they been able to convert their success into political careers? This chapter documents all types of baseball politicians: Hall of Fame players, major leaguers and minor leaguers, managers and owners, and even a few umpires and commissioners who pursued elected office. It examines whether having ties to baseball provides a "boost" over the average politician who pursues elected office. Finally, the chapter speculates upon reasons for the recent decline in ballplayers seeking politics, as well as a few contemporary stars who may reverse the trend in the coming years.

Baseball Politicians: Players, Owners and Others

THE PRE-WAR YEARS

It may surprise you that three of the first several players elected to the Baseball Hall of Fame also sought election to political office. Adrian Constantine "Cap" Anson was one of them. He hit over .300 in 19 of 22 seasons as a big leaguer. Not only did he amass a number of early career records in hitting (ranging from at-bats and hits to runs and runs batted in), but he compiled a distinguished record as a manager. Most of his successes as a player and coach came with the Chicago White Stockings. Later, he served a term as the City Clerk for Chicago from 1905 to 1907.[1]

Like Cap Anson, Honus Wagner was an early Hall of Fame inductee. Such a distinction came from this shortstop's impressive batting career. Like Anson, he spent the majority of his career hitting over .300, picking up batting titles in eight of those seasons on his way to racking up more than 3,000 hits. The speedy player nicknamed "The Flying Dutchman" also swiped more than 700 bases. His real claim to fame was the incredible value of his tobacco baseball card. According to legend, Wagner was a non-smoker and did not want to set a bad example for kids, so the printing of his card was rare indeed. It may shock you that the Pittsburgh Pirates star lost his only bid for office, when he was defeated in the race for Allegheny County Sheriff in 1925. Yet he stayed with the Pirates afterwards, serving as a hitting instructor. Later he became a Sergeant-at-Arms for the Pennsylvania state legislature.[2]

Most baseball fans regard Walter "Big Train" Johnson as one of the greatest pitchers ever. Some cite his 417 wins (second only to "Cy" Young), while others point to his 3,508 strikeouts, a career record which remained the best until broken by Nolan Ryan in the 1980s. Yet no pitcher is ever likely to break his career feat of 113 shutouts. He parlayed that success into victory as a Montgomery County Commissioner (in Maryland, where he had retired) in 1938. Given his amazing career, it may shock readers to learn that this early Hall of Famer couldn't win a Congressional race. In 1940, Johnson aligned himself with the Wendell Willkie Republicans and tried to defeat a Maryland Democrat incumbent. The popular Washington Senators hurler was perhaps doomed when a reporter asked him a question about policy, and Johnson responded, "When I get to Washington, I am to study up on them issues."[3]

But not all associated with baseball had it rough in the early years. The first National Baseball League President, Morgan Bulkeley, went on to serve a term as Connecticut's Governor (1889–1893) and as a United States Senator (1905–1911). Another National Baseball League President, John K. Tener, fared well. But then again, the latter had some playing experience on the field as well.[4]

In fact, Tener played for Cap Anson's Chicago White Stockings, where he pitched his team to twenty-five wins. It was in baseball that he received an early lesson in politics, as his teammates voted him their treasurer. The experience led him to become a founding member of what became the "Players' League." After his playing days were over, Tener won a term in 1908 to the United States House of Representatives from the 24th Congressional District of Pennsylvania. Two years later, he became the state's governor. Years later, Tener came back to baseball as the league's president.[5]

As Tener showed, you didn't need to have a long baseball career to win statewide office. Fred Brown pitched for two seasons with the Boston Beaneaters (later the Boston Braves ... now playing in Atlanta). He became New Hampshire's Governor (1923–1925) and later a U.S. Senator from that state (1933–1939). It is worth noting that Brown was defeated after a single term in each case.[6]

Likewise, Pius Schwert had only a brief stint in the majors, compiling eleven games with the New York Yankees between 1914 and 1915. Yet he was able to win a U.S. congressional seat from the Empire State in 1938 and 1940, dying in office a year after winning his last election.[7]

Not all "baseball politicians" chose to run for the United States Senate, the House of Representatives, or Governor. One was Victor Aldredge, a Pittsburgh Pirates pitcher. His claim to fame came in the 1925 World Series, where he won two games against Walter Johnson's Washington Senators, helping his team prevail in the Fall Classic. After hurling days were done, he served a decade in the Indiana State Senate from 1937 to 1948.[8]

Some early ballplayers never reached the major leagues, but managed to craft respectable political careers. Former United States Senate Majority Leader Scott W. Lucas got his start in the Independent League. Years later, after the army and a law career, he won the Illinois 20th Congressional District in 1934 as a Democrat. Four years later, he became a United States Senator from the "Land of Lincoln," a position he held for twelve years until his defeat. From 1949 through 1950, he was the most powerful United States Senator. Yet even after his stunning defeat, he continued to remain active in Democratic Party politics until he died in 1968.[9]

Ohio political fixture Frank Lausche also got a start in baseball. The former Cleveland Mayor, Ohio Governor, and United States Senator from the Buckeye State played minor league ball in the 1910s before joining the army, then went to law school. In each office, the Democrat served multiple terms before losing in a 1968 primary.[10]

Other minor leaguers found greater success in politics. Edward Austin Kelly was a ballplayer between 1912 and 1916, but lasted much longer as an Illinois Congressman from the Third District (1931–1943, 1945–1947) for the Democratic Party.[11] Another Democrat was Raymond J. Cannon, who played baseball between 1908 and 1922, before opting for a career in judicial politics. He even became a U.S. Congressman from Wisconsin's Fourth Congressional District (1933–1939). Yet his record was marred by losses in 1938 and two unsuccessful gubernatorial bids.[12] There's also minor leaguer Cecil "Runt" Bishop. An Illinois Republican, Bishop served in the House of Representatives from 1941 until his defeat in 1954.[13]

But few can top the fascinating career of George S. Hurley. A former farmhand for the New York Giants and New York Yankees, Hurley was elected to the state of Washington's House of Representatives. Yet the Democrat was bounced from the legislature in the McCarthy years for opposing HUAC (the House Un-American Activities Committee). Opponents accused him of attending Communist Party meetings, charges which were never proven. Throughout the 1950s and 1960s, he tried unsuccessfully to win back his seat, but finally had his comeback during the Watergate election of 1974.[14]

The early years of baseball saw major leaguers and some who didn't quite get there, as well as a baseball commissioner or two, so why not an umpire? Usually, they stay behind the catcher, gathering little attention, but that was hardly the case with Frank "Silk" O'Loughlin.[15] On one occasion, he had a police officer escort an irate ballplayer from the field. Yet his fiery personality may have been too much for the voters, who rejected his 1904 bid for the New York State Assembly. Then he want back to arguing balls and strikes with the players in subsequent years.[16]

Not all elected officials from the early years of baseball were so visible on the field.[17] Like Bulkeley, several served as owners, commissioners, or movers and shakers behind the scenes. One such politician was Martin Sennett "Mike" Conner. The former Southeastern Conference Baseball Commissioner was also the Speaker of the Mississippi State House of Representatives from 1916 to 1924, and the state's governor from 1932 to 1936.[18]

Another owner with political connections was Charles Phelps Taft. The name is, of course, a political legacy in Ohio, and Taft was no different than his family members, which include a governor, a senator, and a president. Charles Phelps Taft served in both the state house of representatives (1871–1873) and the United States House of Representatives (first district) from 1895–1897. But none of his famous family members could ever claim that they owned a baseball team. No, it wasn't from Cleveland or Cincinnati, but the beloved Chicago Cubs.[19]

Unlike Taft, Joseph M. Weiss was more than just an owner. By helping form the Cass Baseball Club, he actually helped kick start professional baseball in the city of Detroit. It shouldn't shock readers that Weiss's political connections were with the state of Michigan, where he served for a few years in the state senate (1891–1893) and the state house of representatives (1907–1908).[20]

Postwar Baseball

Some feel that World War II represented a turning point for baseball. While the game had become the national pastime before the war, major changes took place that would affect the game forever. First and foremost was the desegregation of the sport two years after the end of World War II. Second was the growing internationalization of the sport and its players, who came from around the world to play the game. Third, the sport broadened its impact from north of the Mason-Dixon Line and east of the Mississippi River to encompass the entire country ... even the continent. And finally, while still popular, the country's sport had to compete with rising interest in other games like football and basketball. Yet, with the advent of television, Americans have been able to watch the game as never before. So it makes sense to use World War II as a dividing point for baseball, as well as baseball politicians.

Since the beginning of postwar baseball, no player has achieved the success on the field or in politics than Hall of Fame pitcher Jim Bunning. While hurling for the Philadelphia Phillies and Detroit Tigers, Bunning won 224 games. At least 100 wins came in each league, along with a no-hitter in both (his perfect game came with Philadelphia in 1964). He also struck out more than a thousand hitters in both leagues, leaving him second to "Big Train" Johnson at his retirement.[21]

Bunning served in the Kentucky state senate from 1980 to 1983, when he ran for governor of the state. After a stinging defeat at the hands of Martha Layne Collins, the star pitcher made a comeback four years later by winning Kentucky's Fourth Congressional District, a position he held for six terms. In 1998, he defeated Congressman Scott Baesler (a former University of Kentucky basketball player) for Wendell Ford's open seat.[22] He won a tough reelection bid in 2004.

While Bunning may be one of the best players in the league since the end of World War II, few World Series contests could ever top the 1960 classic between the New York Yankees and the Pittsburgh Pirates. And it just so happens that three participants in those games sought political office after their playing days were done.

No member of the 1960s World Series teams was perhaps as clutch as second baseman Bobby Richardson. In the match with the Pirates, Richardson knocked in twelve runs, earning a rare World Series MVP award for a losing team member. Only Bill Mazeroski's game-ending home run helped the Pirates prevail. But Richardson and the Yankees had their redemption the next year, as they romped over the Cincinnati Reds. That October, Richardson hit .391, leading all hitters in that baseball contest. The following year, Richardson won the series against San Francisco, but this time with the glove. He snagged Giants slugger Willie McCovey line-drive to seal the win with the game on the line. Two years later, Richardson cracked thirteen hits in seven games (batting .406) with his team narrowly losing to the St. Louis Cardinals.[23]

Even after he left his playing days behind, Richardson was a baseball success, taking the South Carolina Gamecocks to the College World Series finals in 1975, losing eventually to the Texas Longhorns. But for some reason, he couldn't translate all of that success into a winning political career. He couldn't defeat an incumbent congressman while running on the Republican ticket in 1976. After his loss, he took up preaching the Bible, staying in his native South Carolina.[24]

Richardson's 1960 series rival, Pittsburgh pitcher Bob Friend also had a brush with politics in his career. Though Friend was torched by Richardson and other Yankees in those games, he had a decent career in the National League where he won 197 games (36 of them as shutouts) and struck out 1,734 batters. He also notched two wins in the All-Star Game. As for politics, he knocked off Allegheny County Controller James W. Knox, a Democrat who had held the office for almost twenty years. Friend held that post until 1975.[25]

Friend's teammate Wilmer "Vinegar Bend" Mizell (named for his hometown in Alabama) was also a pitcher. Though he lacked the career credentials of Bunning or Friend, he did pitch in both 1959 All-Star Games as a member of the St. Louis Cardinals. In addition to Pittsburgh and St. Louis, Mizell also threw for the Chicago White Sox. After his playing days were over, Mizell won a race for the United States fifth. Congressional District from North Carolina in 1968. But Mizell, like so many Republicans, found himself bounced from Congress in the post–Watergate election of 1974. Two years later, a comeback bid failed, and he retired from his second sport of politics.[26]

It seems no professional baseball team has fielded more politicians than the Pittsburgh Pirates. Not only did Jim Rooker pitch for the Bucs (and earlier with the Kansas City Royals), but he also served as their broadcaster. His "defining moment" came in the famous 1979 World Series. With his team facing elimination, behind three games to one in a best-of-seven series, Rooker took the mound in game five. He shut down the Baltimore Orioles, paving the way for an amazing team comeback in the "We Are Family" days of Willie Stargell, Dave Parker, and Bert Blyleven. During his broadcasting days, Rooker threatened to walk home if Pittsburgh blew a 10–0 first inning lead to the in-state rivals, the Philadelphia Phillies. Sure enough, the Phillies came back to win 15–11, leaving a long walk for charity for Rooker. Yet such fame didn't help Rooker in his political career. He lost a race for the 1998 Pennsylvania State House to Susan Laughlin, then failed to defeat Terry Van Horne in a 2000 Congressional Primary. Maybe the Democrats should have nominated Rooker, since they went on to lose the district for the next six years, after Melissa Hart won that year.[27]

Major Leaguers sometimes struggle in the "big leagues" in politics, but minor leaguers have made their mark in their hunt for elected office. One such player was Homer "Pete" Abele. In 1938, he played a season for Nashville, a minor league team in the Cincinnati Reds system. The Republican later went into the military, then got some experience on Senator Robert Taft's campaigns for public office. Abele won a congressional seat himself in Ohio's tenth district, but only lasted a term. But he did serve on the Fourth District Court of Appeals for twenty-five years before retiring in 1991.[28]

Most New York Yankees fans have never heard of Harry Roe Hughes, but Marylanders certainly know his name. Hughes spent time with New York's farm team in Easton, as well as at Federalsburg in the Eastern Shore League. Eventually, Hughes quit baseball to serve in the Navy, and go to law school. Yet the former minor leaguer went on to notch an impressive political career in Maryland politics, starting with the House of Delegates and the State Senate, moving on to the state's Transportation Secretary. In 1978, Hughes crushed his opposition for the governor's race (winning 71 percent), nearly duplicating the victory margin four years later (garnering 62 percent), taking almost every county for the Democrats. His administration was distinguished by environmental policies and assistance to the elderly.[29]

Another Eastern Shore Leaguer was Sherman Tribbitt. Not only did he grow up on the same street as Hughes, but he also went on to win his state's governor's office (Delaware) in the 1970s for the Democratic Party. Like Hughes, Tribbitt also had an extensive career in state politics, serving in the state legislature and a term as Delaware's Lieutenant Governor. But unlike Hughes, Tribbitt had a rocky administration, thanks to banking and energy crises. Though bounced by Republican Pete du Pont in 1976, Tribbitt was able to get a state lottery and a series of environmental and gender equality reforms passed during his four year tenure in office.[30]

Fewer baseball teams are more adored than the Chicago Cubs. It seems they even like their minor leaguers, like Jesse White. Though White did not become a fixture on the team like Ernie Banks, Billy Williams, Ron Santo, or Ferguson Jenkins, he did get a jump on his political career while serving in the 101st Airborne as a paratrooper. After the war, he found time to get kids from the Chicago Public Housing System in a "tumbling team." When he sought the Secretary of State position in Illinois, he won his race overwhelmingly, taking every county in the process in 1998. Four years later, he won reelection overwhelmingly. Not only is White a political star, but he also is also part of several city and state halls-of-fame.[31]

White isn't the only minor leaguer to achieve success in the state of Illinois. Charles M. Campbell was able to translate his limited success on the diamond into electoral victory. After a single season in the minors, in 1946 (after serving in the U.S. Navy during World War II), Campbell ran for the Illinois State House of Representatives in 1962. Not only did Campbell win that race, but served at that post for the next eighteen years![32]

As with the early days of baseball, others associated with the sport (who never took the field) became enmeshed in politics.[33] Like "Silk" O'Loughlin,

Umpire Robert Pafford sought to make the leap from calling balls and strikes (from 1954 to 1955) to calling for votes. Unlike O'Loughlin, Pafford actually prevailed, serving in Georgia's House of Representatives from 1963 to 1970, and later in the state's public service commission.[34]

In the early postwar years, the New York Yankees formed a dynasty, winning the World Series in 1947, 1949, 1950, and 1951. During that time, Joseph E. Marine was their ticket manager. So Marine figured he could later sell his ideas to New York voters. He was right, given that he served in the state's senate from 1961 to 1965. It is also noteworthy that the Yankees also won or made the World Series nearly every year Marine was in the state senate.[35]

During the early years of baseball, commissioners found success in politics. The same was generally true in the postwar years, as two league leaders sought statewide office. The best known is Albert "Happy" Chandler, a baseball commissioner who also served as Kentucky's Governor (1935–1939, 1955–1959) and U.S. Senator (1939–1945). Along the way, Chandler had stints as a state senator and a lieutenant governor. His career was noteworthy in that he had political success before and after he served as the league's commissioner. Only in office for a few years (1946–1951), Chandler will always be remembered as the commissioner who helped integrate baseball.[36]

Former 1984 Los Angeles Olympics organizer Peter Ueberroth (*Time Magazine's* "Man of the Year" for 1984) seemed like a man with unlimited potential. He served a term as baseball's commissioner from 1984 to 1989, achieving numerous successes in popularity and profitability. He turned down other opportunities to run for office, before finally deciding to take the plunge to seek California's gubernatorial post. Yet in the crowded field of 2003, interest in Ueberroth was dwarfed by the Gray Davis recall and the candidacy of movie star Arnold Schwarzenegger. He failed to win his lone bid for elected office.[37]

Even owners got into the act in the postwar era. Thomas "Tom" Bolack was not only the owner of the successful minor league franchise "the Albuquerque Dukes," but also the Governor of the state of New Mexico from 1962 to 1963.[38] And, of course, there's George W. Bush. The former managing partner of a group that owned the Texas Rangers from 1989 through 1994, the son of President George H. W. Bush[39] parlayed that name recognition into two elections as Texas Governor (1994 and reelection in 1998).[40] He also served two terms as United States President (2001–2008).[41]

Electoral Success for Baseball Politicians: Is It Better Than Average?

The successes of candidates with ties to baseball, like President Bush, Senator Bunning, Congressman Mizell, and Governor Chandler are offset by poor electoral showings of Honus Wagner, Walter "Big Train" Johnson, Bobby Richardson, and Peter Ueberroth. The question remains whether having one's name attached to baseball improves one's chances in the ballot box.

To determine how having one's name associated with the national pastime helps a politician succeed in politics, I compare the thirty-four "baseball politicians" to thirty-four candidates with no ties to the sport. I compare the two lists in terms of offices sought, and success in electoral races to determine baseball's impact upon the political arena. Furthermore, I compare the baseball politicians to each other, seeing whether players or non-players were more successful, and whether stars on the field did better than stars off the field.

Research Design

In order to compare the lists, I take all of the baseball politicians, and note each race for a separate category of office. For example, when minor leaguer Scott W. Lucas sought congressional office in 1934, and served two terms, I count Lucas' congressional race career as one case. When Lucas won two terms in the United States Senate, I count both terms together as his U.S. Senate record (one case). I am looking at Lucas's ability to run and win a race, as opposed to his ability to win multiple terms. I am therefore examining whether baseball helps a politician get his "foot in the door." How long he or she stays there is more of a matter of one's political career, rather than the baseball career. Such a measure shows that the thirty-four baseball politicians pursued sixty-one different electoral positions.

In addition to gathering data on office sought and victory, I look at a politician's state (where the political race was held, not what state they played in), how many years were served in office (losses lead to a zero count here), and for the baseball politicians, whether or not the individual was a player or non-player (commissioner, owner, umpire, etc.). Finally, for players, I look at whether the player made it to the major leagues, and what type of career the player had, as well as whether one's electoral race occurred near where the political figure was attached to one's baseball's diamond. For example, Bob Friend won his county controller seat where the Pittsburgh Pirates play, but fellow Pirates pitcher Victor Aldredge ran for state legislative races in Indiana, not in Pennsylvania.

I also assemble a list of thirty-four randomly selected politicians with no ties to baseball. These were compiled from the "Political Graveyard" website, which holds data on nearly 150,000 politicians who pursued political office from the 1800s through the present. Each politician was selected via a random number generator. Politicians elected before 1889 (when the first baseball politician was elected to office), or did not hold political office (officials listed only as convention delegates, ambassadors, or campaign managers) were also removed from the list. Each of the thirty-four politicians with no ties to baseball had the same statistics gathered, except for player/owner, player success, league position, same state success, for obvious reasons.[42] Using the same formula, I found the thirty-four non-baseball politicians had pursued forty-four offices. Rather than pick sixty-one cases, I standardized the "box scores" to compare electoral success averages.

Results

Using such a research design shows that the baseball politicians had an impressive record in their quest for political office. Baseball politicians won 83.33 percent of their races for local office, and 88.2 percent of their runs for the state legislature. In seeking United States congressional races, the record dipped to a 71.4 percent showing (still highly respectable), but in elections for statewide offices, baseball politicians prevailed in nineteen of twenty-two contests. Though they were successful in only half of their presidential pursuits, baseball politicians prevailed in a whopping 82 percent of all races for office (not counting successful reelection bids to the same office).

Though I do not directly measure reelection bids,[43] I do calculate years in office. Baseball politicians managed an average of 5.5 years in office. When removing the unsuccessful cases (lost elections which result in scores of zero), that figure climbs to nearly six years per baseball politician per office, showing a high degree of success in maintaining office, as well as winning it.

But how did the baseball politicians compare to their non-baseball counterparts? Certainly, it would be easy to assume that other politicians had a 50 percent record of success. But I inadvertently made it tougher on the baseball politicians by happening to select a group with a better-than-average success rate in many races.[44] The non-baseball politicians won 80 percent of their local races, which was the same record as those linked to baseball. While amassing an impressive 75 percent victory rate in state legislature cases, the "team" did not top the success of the baseball politicians in this category. Records for higher office were not so good for the non-baseball politicians. They won only half of all statewide contests, and less than 50 percent of their congressional races for an overall success rate of 59 percent.[45] While better than a coin flip, the non-baseball politicians did not fare as well as those associated with America's national sport.[46]

So which types of baseball players do better? Do players or people associated with baseball do better in their pursuit of local and national office? The results may be surprising.

Players and non-playing baseball politicians have similar records of success,[47] with the former winning 82.4 percent of elections sought, while the latter notched an 82.6 percent success rate in ballot box triumphs.[48] But the biggest gap may well be between the players. Those with Hall of Fame experience only won five of seven contests; only a 62.5 percent success rate. Those with solid major league careers only won a little more than half of their races. But players with less experience at the major league level, or only making it as far as the minor leagues won 96 percent of the races (with players making at least one major league game winning all five contests pursued). That means that the semi-professional players won 1.6 times as many races as more experienced Major League Baseball players.[49]

What may account for the discrepancy? Perhaps it is where the success has been achieved. After all, Bobby Richardson starred for the New York Yankees, but sought office far away in South Carolina, while "Cap" Anson did much better in Chicago (as did Pirates Pitcher Bob Friend in Allegheny County, where he played much of his career). Yet the statistics do not support this argument. Bunning played in Philadelphia and Detroit, but experienced success in electoral Kentucky. Ditto Pirates pitcher Mizell in North Carolina. And starring for the home team did little to help Wagner in Allegheny County, or Walter Johnson in nearby Maryland (outside of his local race).

Perhaps Johnson's answer concerning ignorance of the issues may play a role. Someone with some baseball experience may use that to boost a political career. But spending so much of your time in the sport may work against you in the electoral arena, where the diamond may be seen as "all you know."[50]

Why Are There So Few Recent Cases of Baseball Politicians?

Despite the success achieved in electoral politics in the past, there are few cases of contemporary baseball politicians. Aside from President Bush, Senator Bunning, and Illinois Secretary of State Jesse White, no other baseball politician exists at the writing of this article. Given the number of baseball players, commissioners, owners, and others associated with baseball, as well as the astounding electoral success rate of those who have pursued electoral office, one might expect a lot more baseball folks to have taken the political plunge.

There are several reasons for this dwindling number of baseball politician cases. With the recent advent of free agency, players (and commissioners and umpires, for that matter) are paid better than in the past, where elected office might be needed to sustain one's income. There are also perhaps greater opportunities for baseball players and others associated with the sport once the glory days are done, such as sales, public relations, and other business opportunities that are better available than in the past.

Several other reasons exist apart from money and opportunities. The recent taint of steroids and labor disputes may have diminished the sport's staying power with the public. Many believe that football or even basketball will eclipse baseball as America's favorite sport, due to the pace of the game. Furthermore, with greater numbers of international players (and stars) than ever before, there may be fewer baseball politicians to seek elected office in America. Of course, we might well see more baseball politicians spring up in the Dominican Republic, Japan, Mexico, Nicaragua, Canada, and even Cuba some day.

Yet the future of baseball politicians is not so bleak, as players and others have found other ways to become involved in the sport. In the 2006 Georgia Gubernatorial Primary contest, home run king Hank Aaron's endorsement was critical for the Democratic Party candidates. He even made a high profile endorsement of Senator Hillary Clinton in the 2008 Democratic Party Presidential Primary.[51] Not to be outdone was the role played by Atlanta Braves hurler John Smoltz (a future candidate for baseball's Hall of Fame), who made many "campaign pitches" for Republican candidates (like Georgia Secretary of State Karen Handel and Lieutenant Governor candidate Ralph Reed) on telephone answering machines.[52] Might one of the two Atlanta Braves seek elected office in the future? There's also career strikeout leader Nolan Ryan; the star pitcher served as Dr. Ron Paul's "honorary campaign chair and ad spokesman" for the Republican's 1996 congressional race.[53]

Aaron, Smoltz, and Ryan are hardly the only baseball players with potential ties to politics. Might new Hall of Famers like Cal Ripken, Jr. and Tony Gwynn seek a future in politics in Maryland and San Diego, respectively? Don't count it out. Ripken was named a Special Envoy to the State Department by President Bush in 2007, to boost America's image overseas.[54] And Gwynn has made a public issue of attacking amphetamines in baseball.[55]

Others have lent their names to campaigns on state ballot initiatives. The most noteworthy in recent years came in 2006 when several ballplayers sought to target a measure legalizing stem cell research in Missouri. Countering commercials from supporters that featured Michael J. Fox, opponents enlisted St. Louis Cardinals starting hurler (now hurling for the Milwaukee Brewers) Jeff Suppan. In fact, Suppan made his "pitch" against the measure during the World Series, while he started games for the eventual champs. Others joining him for "Missourians Against Human Cloning" included St. Louis teammate David Eckstein (the World Series MVP that year, now playing for the Toronto Blue Jays) and Kansas City Royals slugger Mike Sweeney.[56]

In a 2008 ESPN's *Page 2* article, Texas Rangers relief pitcher C. J. Wilson (a fan of Barrack Obama and grassroots politics) lamented having no one to talk politics with.[57] He cited a lack of education and an immense amount of wealth as contributing factors to baseball players caring little about politics. Maybe after his playing days are done, he'll find some voters in Texas or his home state of California who will be happy to do so.

Post Game Report

In conclusion, it has been discovered that baseball players do much better on Election Day than a random sample of politicians with no connection to the sport. While players and owners have similar success rates at the ballot box, players with greater careers actually win less frequently than those with only minor league experience or some playing time at the major league level, possibly due to ignorance of the issues or a perception that the player is more interested in the sport than politics.

While baseball once helped boost many a political career, the number of baseball politicians seems to be on the decline, despite the recent successes of Jesse White, Jim Bunning, and George W. Bush. This may be attributable to problems within the sport, better post-game financial opportunities for players, a lack of education among the athletes of today, a greater international perspective, and the rising influence of competing sports like football and basketball. Regardless, as Hank Aaron, John Smoltz, Cal Ripken, Tony Gwynn, Jeff Suppan, and C. J. Wilson have demonstrated, there is still an interest among some who throw the ball or swing the bat to jump into the political fray. The question is whether or not they are willing to join the ranks of historic baseball politicians.

Notes

1. John A. Tures, "Baseball 'Diamonds in the Rough' Seas of Politics," *Political Collector*, Summer 2003.
2. *Ibid.*
3. Ken Rudin, "On Politics: Play Ball!" *Washington Post*, March 2, 2001, and John A. Tures, "Baseball 'Diamonds in the Rough' Seas of Politics," *Political Collector*, Summer 2003.
4. Ken Rudin, "The Vice President's Health," *Washington Post*, March 9, 2001, and John A. Tures, "Baseball 'Diamonds in the Rough' Seas of Politics," *Political Collector*, Summer 2003.
5. John A. Tures, "Baseball 'Diamonds in the Rough' Seas of Politics," *Political Collector*, Summer 2003.
6. *Ibid.*
7. *Ibid.*
8. *Ibid.*
9. The Political Graveyard, http://politicalgraveyard.com/index.html (last accessed June 15, 2008), and John A. Tures, "Baseball 'Diamonds in the Rough' Seas of Politics," *Political Collector*, Summer 2003.
10. Wolfgang Saxon, "Obituary: Frank Lausche, Ex-Ohio Senator and Governor for Five Terms, 94," *New York Times*, April 22, 1990.
11. The Political Graveyard, http://politicalgraveyard.com/index.html (last accessed June 15, 2008), and John A. Tures, "Baseball 'Diamonds in the Rough' Seas of Politics," *Political Collector*, Summer 2003.

12. John A. Tures, "Baseball 'Diamonds in the Rough' Seas of Politics," *Political Collector*, Summer 2003.
13. *Ibid.*
14. *Ibid.*
15. Responding to a controversial strikeout call, the umpire was reported to say, "I have never missed one [a call] in my life and it's too late to start now. The Pope for religion, O'Loughlin for baseball. Both are infallible."
16. Political Graveyard, http://politicalgraveyard.com/index.html (last accessed June 15, 2008), and John A. Tures, "Baseball 'Diamonds in the Rough' Seas of Politics," *Political Collector*, Summer 2003.
17. Of course, there were several individuals associated with both baseball and politics who did not hold elected office. Albert D. Lasker, part owner of the Chicago Cubs team, developed "the Lasker Plan" which reorganized baseball in 1920. He was also a Republican National Convention delegate in 1936 and 1940. Political Graveyard, http://politicalgraveyard.com/index.html (last accessed June 15, 2008).
18. Political Graveyard, http://politicalgraveyard.com/index.html (last accessed June 15, 2008), and John A. Tures, "Baseball 'Diamonds in the Rough' Seas of Politics," *Political Collector*, Summer 2003.
19. John A. Tures, "Baseball 'Diamonds in the Rough' Seas of Politics," *Political Collector*, Summer 2003.
20. *Ibid.*
21. Tom Farrey, "Politicians Who Can Run," *ESPN.com*, November 1, 2000; Ken Rudin, "On Politics: Play Ball!" *Washington Post*, March 2, 2001; and John A. Tures, "Baseball 'Diamonds in the Rough' Seas of Politics," *Political Collector*, Summer 2003.
22. John A. Tures, "Baseball 'Diamonds in the Rough' Seas of Politics," *Political Collector*, Summer 2003.
23. Ken Rudin, "Political Junkie: The Hurricane and The President (Hoover, That Is)," *National Public Radio*, October 5, 2005, and John A. Tures, "Baseball 'Diamonds in the Rough' Seas of Politics," *Political Collector*, Summer 2003.
24. John A. Tures, "Baseball 'Diamonds in the Rough' Seas of Politics," *Political Collector*, Summer 2003.
25. Bill Syken, "Bob Friend, Pitcher," *Sports Illustrated*, August 9, 2004, and John A. Tures, "Baseball 'Diamonds in the Rough' Seas of Politics," *Political Collector*, Summer 2003.
26. Tom Farrey, "Politicians Who Can Run," *ESPN.com*, November 1, 2000; Ken Rudin, "On Politics: Play Ball!" *Washington Post*, March 2, 2001; and John A. Tures, "Baseball 'Diamonds in the Rough' Seas of Politics," *Political Collector*, Summer 2003.
27. John A. Tures, "Baseball 'Diamonds in the Rough' Seas of Politics," *Political Collector*, Summer 2003.
28. The Political Graveyard, http://politicalgraveyard.com/index.html (last accessed June 15, 2008); and John A. Tures, "Baseball 'Diamonds in the Rough' Seas of Politics," *Political Collector*, Summer, 2003.
29. John A. Tures, "Baseball 'Diamonds in the Rough' Seas of Politics," *Political Collector*, Summer 2003.
30. *Ibid.*
31. Jesse White, Biography of the Secretary of State, Illinois Department of State, http://www.cyberdriveillinois.com/biography/biography.html (accessed June 15, 2008), and John A. Tures, "Baseball 'Diamonds in the Rough' Seas of Politics," *Political Collector*, Summer 2003.
32. The Political Graveyard, http://politicalgraveyard.com/index.html (last accessed June 15, 2008), and John A. Tures, "Baseball 'Diamonds in the Rough' Seas of Politics," *Political Collector*, Summer 2003.
33. Others in the postwar baseball era did not get elected to office, but became involved in convention politics. James B. McCahey, Jr., also of Illinois, was born the year of the Lasker Plan. After serving as an army officer in World War II, he became a campaign manager for John F. Kennedy in his presidential primaries of Wisconsin and West Virginia. After becoming an alternate delegate to the 1960 Democratic National Convention, McCahey became a part owner of the Chicago White Sox and Milwaukee Braves in the 1960s, later becoming part of the CSX railroad company. There's also Frank E. McKenney, another Democrat. Like McCahey, he was an army officer in World War II, a Democratic National Convention delegate (in 1948 and 1956), and a co-owner of a baseball team, though it was the Pittsburgh Pirates (from 1946–1950). Though none of these three individuals were elected to their office, their ties to baseball and politics should be noted Political Graveyard, http://politicalgraveyard.com/index.html (last accessed June 15, 2008).
34. The Political Graveyard, http://political-

graveyard.com/index.html (last accessed June 15, 2008), and John A. Tures, "Baseball 'Diamonds in the Rough' Seas of Politics," *Political Collector*, Summer 2003.

35. John A. Tures, "Baseball 'Diamonds in the Rough' Seas of Politics," *Political Collector*, Summer 2003.

36. Ken Rudin, "The Vice President's Health," *Washington Post*, March 9, 2001, and John A. Tures, "Baseball 'Diamonds in the Rough' Seas of Politics," *Political Collector*, Summer 2003.

37. The Political Graveyard, http://politicalgraveyard.com/index.html (last accessed June 15, 2008), and John A. Tures, "Baseball 'Diamonds in the Rough' Seas of Politics," *Political Collector*, Summer 2003.

38. John A. Tures, "Baseball 'Diamonds in the Rough' Seas of Politics," *Political Collector*, Summer 2003.

39. It should also be noted that George W. Bush's father, George H. W. Bush, was the captain of the Yale baseball team after World War II. He went on to serve in the U.S. House of Representatives and to become U.S. Vice President and U.S. President for a term. Tom Farrey, "Politicians Who Can Run," *ESPN.com*, November 1, 2000.

40. Lois Romano and George Lardner Jr., "Bush's Move Up to the Majors," *Washington Post*, July 31, 1999, A1.

41. "Happy" Chandler, George H. W. Bush, and George W. Bush were not the only two presidential candidates who had ties to baseball. There was also the curious case of Wilbur Huckle, a little used player for the New York Mets in the 1960s and 1970s. Adoring and fun-loving pranksters created the "Metropolitan Party" and nominated Huckle to run for president in 1964. They even teased presidential candidate Barry Goldwater, ripping from his slogan to create their own: "Extremism, in defense of the Mets, is no vice." Yet Huckle was destined for future prominence when he became one of the game's first ever designated hitters. John A. Tures, "Baseball 'Diamonds in the Rough' Seas of Politics," *Political Collector*, Summer 2003.

42. These non-baseball politicians include the following: Fred G. Aandahl, Anna Afton, Robert J. Aragon, Rod R. Blagojevich, Vernon Q. "Coach" Callaway, S. H. "Bud" Dryden, T. Lawrence Eyre, P. Douglas Farr, Jacob F. Gmelich, John C. Hackett, Robert T. Hodge, Michael J. Howlett, C. Leslie Hudson, John B. Isbell, Rashied Jibri, Norman A. Knudson, Bob Kustra, Owen Middleton, J. Benson Newell, Thomas D. Nicholls, Hugh O'Malley, Eugene J. O'Mara, Alan Lee Parks, James P. Pinkham, John A. Quackenbush, William H. Sproul, Francis Frederick Tapp, Lewis D. Thill, Peter Uerling, Alexander Vineberg, M. H. Wall, Arnout Yeager, and Ig Zwarycz.

43. My sources do not always indicate the result of all reelection bids and whether it was sought. So when statistics show Charles M. Campbell serving in the Illinois state legislature, I do not know how many years he ran, ran unopposed, or lost trying to regain his seat.

44. I feel fortunate to select such a strong group, given that the results of the comparison might have seemed more suspect had a group with a success rate of 40 percent been chosen.

45. Some of this lack of success could be that the Political Graveyard of candidates also included politicians who were not in the Democratic or Republican Party. Of course, some baseball politicians do not have their political affiliation listed as well, meaning that some could have run from outside the party.

46. Results from a chi-square test reveal that the different rates of success between baseball politicians and non-baseball politicians are statistically significant (at the .05 level).

47. John K. Tener, who served as a commissioner and played baseball, is listed in both categories.

48. A chi-square test reveals no signi-ficant differences between the performance of players and non-players.

49. A chi-square test reveals that the difference between the more successful and less successful players is statistically signi-ficant (at the .05 level), with minor leaguers and those with little playing experience much more likely to win office than expected.

50. See Wilson's comments in the conclusion.

51. Georgia Politics Unfiltered, "Hank Aaron Endorses Hillary for President," January 4, 2008, http://georgiaunfiltered.blogspot.com/2008/01/hank-aaron-endorses-hillary-for.html (accessed June 15, 2008).

52. Georgia Politics Unfiltered, "John Smoltz Endorses Karen Handel," October 13, 2005, http://georgiaunfiltered.blogspot.com/2005/10/john-smoltz-endorses-karen-handel.html (accessed June 15, 2008).

53. Christopher Caldwell, "The Antiwar,

Anti-Abortion, Anti-Drug-Enforcement-Administration, Anti-Medicare Candidacy of Dr. Ron Paul," *New York Times Magazine*, July 22, 2007.

54. Jeff Barker, "U.S. Drafts Ripken as Envoy Of Good Will," *Baltimore Sun*, August 14, 2007.

55. John Shea, "Gwynn Targets Amphetamines: Estimates Half of Position Players Use 'Greenies,'" *San Francisco Chronicle*, April 23, 2003.

56. "Mike Sweeney, David Eckstein Join Jeff Suppan in Stem-Cell Battle," *St. Louis Dispatch*, November 3, 2006; and *CBS/AP*, "Stem Cell Opponents To Air Celebrity Ad," *CBS/AP*, October 25, 2006.

57. Jeff Pearlman, "Major League Ballplayers Should Care About This Election," *ESPN Page 2*, February 22, 2008.

CHAPTER 2

The Baseball Evangelist Throws Out John Barleycorn: Billy Sunday and Prohibition

Wendy Knickerbocker

Billy Sunday (1862–1935), who was this country's most successful evangelist before Billy Graham, found the Lord while playing professional baseball in the 1880s. In the days before radio, Sunday used newspaper coverage and baseball to become the most famous preacher America had ever known. Baseball was a major ingredient in his sermons and his appeal, and he was known as "the Baseball Evangelist" for several years before a best-selling author used that term in 1913 in a national magazine.[1]

Sunday's sermons reached hundreds of thousands of people, and he was widely quoted and admired. He became an influential social leader who supported and popularized conservative causes, and he was an ardent champion of Prohibition. One modern historian of American temperance has summarized Billy Sunday's role in the Prohibition movement with this statement: "While his precise impact is hard to judge, many [of his] contemporaries were convinced that the popular evangelist was of crucial importance in establishing public support for the passing of the Eighteenth Amendment."[2]

William Ashley Sunday was born in Ames, Iowa, in 1862. His father died in the Civil War a month after his third son was born, and Sunday grew up in rural poverty. His mother remarried, but her second husband was a drunkard who provided little support and abandoned the family a few years later. At that time Sunday's mother placed him and his older brother in a home for soldiers' orphans until the older boy turned sixteen. Then both boys were sent to work on their grandfather's farm. Sunday loved his grandfather, but life on the farm was difficult. Several years later he told his future wife, "My poor dear old Grand-father used to drink oh so much and abuse me and when sober he would feel so sad about it."[3] After one such altercation, Sunday left the farm and went out on his own.

In 1882 Sunday was playing baseball for the Marshalltown, Iowa, local team, when he was "discovered" by Adrian "Cap" Anson. Anson, manager of the National League's Chicago White Stockings, was a Marshalltown native, and he signed Sunday to a professional baseball contract for the 1883 season. Sunday then played in the National League for the Chicago, Pittsburgh, and Philadelphia teams from 1883 to 1890. Sunday's career statistics represent a solid though not outstanding performance: batting average .248 over 499 games, near the middle of the league's hitters for the decade; 236 stolen bases in 368 games, an excellent number; and a low fielding percentage of .883. He was an average hitter, an exceptionally fast runner who didn't get on base very often, and a frequently spectacular fielder with a high number of errors. He was good-looking and personable, as well as a flashy fielder and a speedy runner. He was also sober at a time when temperance was gaining popularity in the Midwest, and he was an avowed Christian. Professional baseball in the 1880s was a rowdy arena filled with plenty of rough characters, but Billy Sunday was polite and well behaved. Many fans loved him for that, as did his teams' management.

In its early years, professional baseball suffered some serious growing pains. Gambling on games was a recurring problem that the National League worked hard to correct. The games themselves were often barely controlled contests, with both players and fans engaging in verbal abuse and fights with each other and the umpires. Alcohol use was a problem both on and off the field, and many players were regularly drunk in public. Several team owners passed rules governing their players' behavior, with only moderate success.

The National League pledged itself to the task of making baseball respectable, in hopes of attracting more middle-class patrons. In a conscious effort to improve baseball's image and to offer wholesome entertainment, the owners of the National League teams banned liquor from their ballparks, did not schedule games on Sundays, and charged fifty cents for admission (the same price as public lectures and theater tickets).

The most influential of the National League team owners was Albert G. Spalding of Chicago. Spalding had been a star baseball player himself, and he was sincerely committed to gaining respectability for baseball and broadening its appeal. It was he who convinced the other owners not to play on Sundays and to ban the sale of liquor at games. He also expected his own team to act as good examples for other players, and he tried to impose his standards of good behavior on his players, using fines and curfews as punishment.

Spalding's interests were well represented on the field by Cap Anson, the team's manager and captain. Spalding and Anson had been teammates, and Spalding had brought Anson to Chicago because he admired Anson's playing and managerial skills. Anson was keen on discipline, and he was a nondrinker. He was also an excellent judge of baseball talent, and he and Spalding put together championship teams in 1880, 1885, and 1886. Along with Spalding and Anson, two other members of those teams are enshrined in the Hall of Fame: Mike "King" Kelly and John Clarkson.

Anson, temperate off the field and notably successful on it, was a solid and often brilliant manager. He sought strong batters and fast runners for his teams, and he encouraged base-stealing and all-out fielding attempts. Teams under Anson's direction played exciting baseball, and it was the speed that Billy Sunday displayed on the field in Marshalltown that earned him the chance to be part of the show. Anson took Sunday under his wing in Chicago, and with such able mentoring the youngster from Iowa became a dependable teammate and a popular ballplayer.

In 1883, Sunday's first season with the team, Chicago finished in second place. Spalding, who wanted a team of talented players who were also sober and well behaved, was disappointed in their performance. In the off-season he wrote, "One of the prominent evils of the season of 1883 which may be justly ranked among the abuses of professional ball playing, was the drunkenness which prevailed in the ranks of many of the club teams."[4] Spalding instructed Anson to watch the players' off-field behavior carefully and to institute a stricter training regimen. Apparently many of the players, although not Sunday, ignored Anson's rules and played by their own. The team finished fourth in 1884, and one Chicago newspaper scolded "the habits and behavior of the players whose irregularities were this year the source of much trouble and the cause of much poor play."[5]

For the 1885 season, Spalding imposed a total abstinence policy on the team, and any player caught drinking between May and October would have his salary reduced. Whether because of or in spite of the no-drinking rule, the Chicago team won the 1885 National League pennant handily, although at least one of the players had ignored the rule. George Gore, the star center fielder, was suspended after the first playoff game for generally poor play and reported bouts of drinking. Billy Sunday played center field in Gore's place for the rest of the playoffs, earning a .214 batting average while turning in a respectable, though not notable, performance. The team as a whole did not do well in the 1885 playoffs: they won two games, lost three, and had one forfeited.

Following his team's relatively poor showing, not only did Spalding repeat the abstinence policy for the 1886 season, he also secretly hired detectives to follow the players and report on their activities. In late July the detectives gave their report to Spalding. Anson and his adopted protégé Sunday were cleared right away. Some other players were quickly passed as well, but seven players were disciplined and fined for staying out late and drinking.

Adhering to a temperance pledge does not seem to have been a problem for Sunday. Although he did socialize with his teammates, he was apparently only a moderate drinker and was relatively well behaved — more like his mentor Anson than his more boisterous teammates. In his autobiography he wrote, "I never drank much. I was never drunk but four times in my life. I never drank whisky or beer; I never liked either. I drank wine.... I used to go to the saloons with the baseball players, and while they would drink highballs and gin fizzes and beer, I would take lemonade or sarsaparilla."[6]

Regardless of their off-field behavior, the Chicago team won the National League pennant again in 1886. However, once again they lost the playoffs, and Anson blamed the loss on the players' drinking and partying. That was the last straw for Spalding, and he refused to pay the bonuses that the players had been promised for winning the pennant. He also decided to remake the team, and he did not renew the contracts of three of the seven players who had been fined in July. Then Spalding did the unthinkable: he sold the superstar Mike "King" Kelly to Boston for the unheard-of sum of $10,000.

Mike Kelly was one of the most colorful players in baseball's long history and a greatly talented nineteenth-century star. He was also a famous carouser, and unfortunately his drinking shortened both his career and his life. In 1886 Kelly led the National League with his .388 batting average and with 155 runs scored, but Spalding decided that Kelly was expendable. His decision had nothing to do with winning; it had everything to do with principle. As his right fielder for the 1887 season, Spalding chose to replace the highly skilled, often brilliant, and rowdy Mike Kelly with the speedy, earnest, and sober Billy Sunday.

Although he appeared in only fifty games, Sunday had his best year for Chicago in 1887, batting .291 and stealing thirty-four bases. In 1888 he was sold to the Pittsburgh team, where he was the starting center fielder until he was traded to Philadelphia in August of 1890. During those three seasons as a full-time player Sunday placed third in the league in stolen bases each year, among the top ten fielders twice, and about the middle of the league in hitting.

During the 1886 and 1887 seasons Billy Sunday became more than a dependable and temperate ballplayer: he became an avowed Christian as well. In the summer of 1886 he joined a local church in Chicago and began teaching Sunday school and attending religious meetings when the team was on the road. Sometime after that, he publicly accepted Christ at the Pacific Garden Mission in Chicago, and he began speaking at YMCAs whenever and wherever he could.[7] His enhanced reputation led Chicago fans and one well-known reporter to regret losing him in 1888: "Chicago has lost, and Pittsburg [sic] has gained, one of the cleverest young ball players in the country."[8]

Pittsburgh baseball fans welcomed their new outfielder. "Sunday is a consistent Christian and a young man of most exemplary habits, whether on or off the ball field."[9] In the fall of 1888 Sunday married Helen "Nell" Thompson, daughter of a Chicago businessman, whom he had met two years earlier at church. For the next three years Sunday spent his winters working at the Chicago YMCA.

In the spring of 1891, Billy Sunday opted out of his contract with the Philadelphia Phillies. He quit professional baseball to accept a full-time job at the Chicago YMCA, with little experience in ministry. His title at the YMCA was Assistant Secretary of the Religious Department, but he was primarily a street minister. He worked from 8:00 A.M. to 10:00 P.M. six days a week, for $84 a month, substantially less than his ballplayer's salary. In 1893 he was offered the job of assistant to J. Wilbur Chapman, a widely known evangelist who had studied with Dwight Moody. Sunday's new mentor preached temperance, personal salvation, and middle-class values in revivals throughout the small cities of the Midwest, and Sunday accompanied him for the next three years. In January of 1896 Sunday went out on his own, holding his first solo revival in Garner, Iowa.

Advertising was an immediate concern for Sunday. Chapman had a wide reputation, and bringing attention to his revivals had not been a problem. Sunday, however, was a relative unknown as a preacher. Baseball was quite popular everywhere in the Midwest, so Sunday utilized his reputation as a baseball player to spark interest in his revivals. One newspaper reporting on the upcoming Garner revival "to be conducted by W.A. Sunday" noted that "this must be 'Billy' Sunday who used to play ball for Anson with the Chicago White Stockings. 'Billy' is as true a Christian gentleman as he was a rattling ball player, and that is saying a good deal."[10]

Sunday spent the next several years holding revivals in the small towns of the rural Midwest. He later referred to those years as his time on the "kerosene circuit." Sunday spent that time honing his skills as a showman. The most popular, and often only, forms of entertainment in those small towns were revivals, traveling variety shows, and baseball games. Sunday learned to be a one-man combination of all three.

He knew how to please a crowd from his days as a baseball player. The fans had loved Sunday's speed and recklessness, and he knew it. He ran for stolen or extra bases at every possible opportunity, as much to hear the applause as to gain the base. His authorized biographer described his appeal to fans. "Sunday was the sort of figure the bleachers like. He was always eager — sometimes too eager — to 'take a chance.' What was a one-base hit for another man was usually good for two bases for him. His slides and stolen bases were adventures beloved of the 'fans'— the spice of the game. He also was apt in retort to the comments from the bleachers, but always good-natured. The crowds liked him, even as did his team mates."[11] He never lost that ability to connect with an audience.

Sunday had a natural gift for rhetoric, and he made masterful use of everyday language and themes. In the words of one admirer, "Other preachers have said the same things before, but never in the same way — the way that the highbrow, lowbrow, or middlebrow all can understand.... He has gone out to the people, found them where they are, and delivered his message in terms they could grasp.... And throughout the message he appealed to his hearers' reason, to the reason of every man and woman in the vast audience. He made religion seem as sane as eating or sleeping or going to a ball game."[12]

Sunday was in constant motion when he preached, never still for more than a few seconds, and his sermons were physically demanding and acrobatic performances. He used his athleticism and energy to express his muscular version of Christianity. He spoke directly to men, and men understood him. He was a former baseball player, and Christian or not, there was nothing sissy about him, and he preached a man's religion. In fact, he told his audiences, Jesus had been a man's man. "Jesus was no dough-faced, lick-spittle proposition. Jesus was the greatest scrapper that ever lived."[13]

In his sermons, Sunday told stories about the things he knew, particularly baseball and temperance. Baseball supplied him with accessible banter and commentary as well as authentic anecdotes. Temperance was a natural theme for Sunday. Alcohol had been partly responsible for much of the hardship and pain of his childhood. As a young man he had seen the effects of drinking on his baseball teammates and others among his contemporaries. If those experiences were not enough, as a street minister in Chicago he would have been exposed daily to dissipation and the negative aspects of alcohol.

Although he became a loud defender of fundamentalism, Sunday had little interest in, or knowledge of, theology. He preached a two-fold message: temperance and personal salvation through Christ. Sunday's theology was the simple evangelical message of the Gospel. "I am an old-fashioned preacher of the old-time religion, that has warmed this cold world's heart for two thousand years."[14] His ministry, like baseball, was populist and democratic. He used the common vernacular and stayed away from complicated theology. He preached a simple, accessible Christianity in the language of America's heartland, and it worked. People rallied to hear his sermons in ever-increasing numbers.

As Sunday continued holding revivals throughout the Midwest he made steady gains in popularity and stature, especially as a temperance preacher. By 1905 he had developed a special sermon on Prohibition, called "Booze, or, Get on the Water Wagon." This sermon expressed the crux of Sunday's message in a detailed excoriation of the liquor industry and an exhortation on the destructiveness of alcohol. The cure for an individual's problems was acceptance of Jesus Christ; the cure for society's problems was Prohibition. "Jesus Christ was God's revenue officer."[15] For Sunday, all of America's problems, such as crime, poverty, and violence, were rooted in alcohol. "The saloon is the sum of all villainies. It is worse than war or pestilence. It is the crime of all crimes. It is the parent of crimes and the mother of sins. It is the appalling source of misery and crime in the land."[16]

The "Booze" sermon was aimed at men, for two reasons: first, men were the protectors of their families, and liquor was a threat to families; and second, only men could vote, and therefore only men could get rid of liquor. Yet Prohibition was not merely a political issue; rather, it was a moral issue, and it was what God wanted. "You men have a chance to show your manhood. ... [I]n the name of all that is good and noble, fight the curse. Shall you men, who hold in your hands the ballot ... refuse to rally in the name of the defenseless men and women and native land? No. I want every man to say, 'God, you can count on me to protect my wife, my home, my mother and my children and the manhood of America.'"[17]

Sunday tried out his "Booze" sermon in December of 1905, at the end of a revival in Burlington, Iowa. Burlington had a local ordinance on saloon hours that was not being enforced, and local Prohibition supporters had been part of the group that brought Sunday to town. During the revival Sunday called for the enforcement of anti-liquor laws. After preaching his "Booze" sermon, Sunday asked, "How many of you men would stand by Mayor Caster if he would put the lid on and close up the salons tight on Sunday and put the gamblers out of business?" All 4000 men in attendance shouted that they would.[18] Within days the mayor of Burlington issued a proclamation that greatly limited saloon hours. From then on Sunday preached his "Booze" sermon during each of his revivals.

In 1907 Sunday's revival in Fairfield, Iowa, had generated so little interest that Sunday found himself speaking to a half-empty hall. To wake up the town, he organized the local businesses into two baseball teams and scheduled a game between them. Sunday arrived for the game wearing a uniform from his days as a professional, and he proceeded to play for both teams. Iowa newspapers spread the story, and the town of Muscatine was ready for Sunday's revival in November and December. There Sunday started a petition drive for a referendum on local-option Prohibition, and Muscatine went "dry" shortly thereafter. Ottumwa, Iowa, also went "dry" after Sunday's revival in late 1908. Although Iowa did not approve statewide Prohibition until 1915, Sunday's efforts in the preceding years were credited with creating public interest in and influencing legislative action on the issue.

After his success with local-option legislation, the Baseball Evangelist began advocating statewide Prohibition in his revivals. By then Sunday was widely recognized both as an evangelist and as a force in the Prohibition movement, and he began being invited to preach his message in larger cities as well as smaller ones. In early 1908 he held his first large-scale revival, in Bloomington, Illinois. In December of that year Sunday made his first trip to a city of over 100,000 people when local Prohibition forces invited him to Spokane, Washington. In 1912 he held his first campaign east of the Alleghenies, and from then on he was in constant demand all over the country.

Sunday was never a member of the Anti-Saloon League, nor was he ever on their payroll, but whenever he held a revival the League provided assistance for his efforts. When Sunday held a revival in Wheeling, West Virginia, in February and March of 1912, the League provided transportation for Sunday to give his "Booze" sermon in other parts of the state during the day and to return to Wheeling at night. In November of that year West Virginia voted to add an amendment prohibiting alcohol to the state's constitution.

Sunday was known for attracting a large number of men to his revivals, partly due to his down-to-earth language and straightforward approach, and converting men was considered to be one of Sunday's particular strengths. In 1913 Bruce Barton, author of the best-selling *The Greatest Man Who Ever Lived*, noted that "no other evangelist owes so little of his success to emotionalism: none other can number a larger proportion of men than women on his convert rolls."[19] Sunday's baseball past was an integral part of his ministry: it was a prominent ingredient in his sermons and a large part of his appeal to men.

As his revivals grew larger, Sunday began holding special meetings for specific groups. Notable among these meetings were those "For Women Only" and "For Men Only." In his sermon "Chickens Come Home to Roost," Sunday denounced impure living and licentiousness. In "A Plain Talk to Men," he stressed Christian manliness. "Many think a Christian has to be a sort of dish-rag proposition, a wishy-washy, sissified sort of a galoot that lets everybody make a doormat out of him. Let me tell you the manliest man is the man who will acknowledge Jesus Christ."[20]

One of Sunday's most popular sermons for men was "The Devil's Boomerangs, or, Hot Cakes Off The Griddle." In it he implored men to choose temperance and a decent life, and the sermon contained several baseball anecdotes. It ended with Sunday telling about three of his teammates, Mike Kelly, Ed Williamson, and Frank Flint, who drank themselves into dissipation and early death. At the end of the story Sunday asked, "Did they win the game of life or did I?"[21]

By 1913 Billy Sunday was a prominent national figure, as an evangelist, a Prohibition advocate, and a former professional baseball player. That year the national weekly magazine *Collier's* asked him to choose an all-star baseball team. In the article he wrote, "I still love the game.... I don't want to sit in the grand stand. The spiked shoes I wore are at home. My old suit hangs there, too. It is dusty and moth eaten, but it is my old baseball suit. Boys, I wouldn't trade it for the best diamond in Tiffany's shop."[22]

In March of 1914 Sunday spoke at Carnegie Hall, and later that year *American Magazine* took a poll asking "Who Is the Greatest Man in the U.S.?" Billy Sunday placed eighth, tied with Andrew Carnegie. In the same year a compilation of Sunday's sayings and excerpts from his sermons was published under the title, *Burning Truths from Billy's Bat*.

A version of Sunday's "Booze" sermon that was published in 1914 began, "I am the sworn, eternal, uncompromising enemy of the Liquor traffic. I ask no quarter and I give none. I have drawn the sword in defense of God, home, wife, children, and native land."[23] In June and July of 1914 the Anti-Saloon League invited Sunday to Colorado to hold a revival in Colorado Springs, to support Prohibition before an upcoming statewide election in November.[24]

A month or so later, in September, Sunday returned to Colorado for a two-month revival in Denver. Denver was the proud home of a champion minor league baseball team, and on Sunday's arrival the *Denver Post* carried the headline, "Billy Sunday Leads Lord's League Stars." Sunday was referred to as a "revivalist, athlete and former baseball star of big league magnitude." Revival participants were noted as "fans."[25] Sunday capitalized on the local baseball interest by umpiring a game between the Denver Bears and the Sioux City Indians. Local newspapers gave the umpire as much coverage as the game. In an interview for the *Rocky Mountain News*, Sunday compared baseball to the game of life. "The men are trying to make the bases and get to home but the devil's always trying to get in the way and kill the run. The people in the grandstand are there to see you make a run or an out, and the umpire represents the Lord a-watching and a-hoping that you'll get there with the goods!"[26]

Prohibition soon shared Denver's attention with baseball. On October 3 there was a huge Prohibition parade, as 10,000 people marched through Denver to Billy Sunday's tabernacle. The next day Sunday delivered his "Booze" sermon. He ended his Denver campaign three weeks later with this admonition: "My last word to you, is don't forget November third. Watch out for the whiskey bunch."[27] After Colorado voted in favor of statewide Prohibition on November 3, one pastor gave much of the credit to "the work of Billy Sunday in Colorado Springs and Denver. His mighty philippics against 'the whiskey bunch' created a new conscience in those cities and changed the votes of many thousands."[28]

By this time Sunday had become a dominant figure in the Prohibition movement. According to one modern biographer, "Sunday reached more people individually with his Booze Sermon than [William Jennings] Bryan, Frances Willard, Carry Nation, and William E. 'Pussyfoot' Johnson talked to in their combined lifetimes. By 1915 Sunday had spoken to nearly forty million people, and more came to see him every day. For weeks at a time, as many as 50,000 people a day heard him preach on the evil of liquor. No one else commanded numbers like that — not even entertainers, not even presidents."[29]

On January 18, 1915, President Woodrow Wilson received Sunday at the White House. Sunday had lunch with William Jennings Bryan, and then he spoke at Convention Hall. In March of that year he held his largest revival to date in Philadelphia, claiming to have brought 42,000 people to Christ. During that revival, at the age of fifty-three, he played in an old-timers' baseball game in Philadelphia and hit a home run.

In the spring of 1916, Sunday held a revival in Baltimore. One night five players from the New York Yankees, including star player and future Hall of Famer Frank "Home Run" Baker, walked down the tabernacle aisle to take Sunday's hand and accept Christ. Baker wrote admiringly, "As Billy Sunday spoke I looked around that vast tabernacle. It appeared to me as a miracle of our country's democracy. The people met to see and hear a man born in a log cabin, trained in professional baseball, converted in a rescue mission, and the most potent single personality in our land to-day."[30]

In September and October of 1916, Sunday went to Detroit for a revival prior to Michigan's Prohibition referendum. He had been invited by the Detroit Pastors' Union, with the strong support of local Prohibition forces. According to the *Detroit News*, when Sunday pulled into the train station on September 9 he was met by a huge crowd. Among the greeters were many baseball fans who remembered Sunday when he played against the Detroit National League team. Several people remarked that in appearance he hadn't changed much, even all those years later.[31]

The revival was successful from the beginning. A men's-only meeting in late September brought 29,000 men into the tabernacle, which had been built for 16,000. The crowd, with a large proportion of working men, heard the "Booze" sermon. At the end Sunday implored, "Come on manhood of Detroit, stand up, stand up for Jesus. Come up here and say, 'Bill, by the grace of God, I'll live a different life.'"[32]

In October Sunday traveled to Ann Arbor, where he instructed the crowd to vote for Prohibition. On November 5, Sunday's last night in Detroit, he asked how many men planned to vote for Prohibition, and a reported 10,000 stood up. Prominent among those who streamed forward to take Sunday's hand were two former Detroit ballplayers from Sunday's era, Charlie Bennett and future Hall of Famer Sam Thompson.

The next day, which was the day before the referendum, Sunday finished his Michigan trip with a stop in Grand Rapids. After his sermon he waved an American flag and coaxed some 7,000 men to shout their affirmation for Prohibition.[33] On November 7, a significant majority of Michigan voters cast their ballots in favor of Prohibition.

On April 8, 1917, Billy Sunday opened the largest revival of his career, in New York City, with these words: "I notice you're the same warm-hearted, enthusiastic bunch you used to be when you sat in the grandstand and bleachers when I played at the old Polo Grounds. It didn't matter if a fellow was on the other side or not. If he made a good play he got the glad hand rather than the marble heart."[34] The New York revival was the pinnacle of Sunday's career. By the end of the revival in June, over 98,000 people had taken Sunday's hand and accepted Christ. During that revival Sunday began calling for national Prohibition. He told New Yorkers, "This whiskey business is a question for the government, not the states to battle, and you know it."[35]

Later that summer Sunday addressed the question of whether baseball should be suspended during World War I. "I notice with a good deal of mistrust a lot of agitation to minimize athletic sport on account of the perilous war which this nation has entered. No greater mistake could be made. Baseball is needed now more than ever before. What are soldiers if they are not good athletes?"[36] Just as Sunday's status as a former player had always enhanced his reputation, his influence as a national social leader enabled him to be an ambassador for baseball.

That fall, during a revival in Los Angeles, Douglas Fairbanks, Sr., put together a team of movie stars and challenged Sunday and his staff to a baseball game. Mary Pickford and Charlie Chaplin served as umpires, and the movie stars won, 1–0. The game was a benefit to raise money for American soldiers, and it garnered much national attention. Some months later Sunday sought to carry his ambassadorship overseas and planned a trip to France, but at the request of President Wilson he stayed home and sold millions of dollars worth of Liberty Bonds instead.

In December of 1917 the U.S. Congress submitted the Eighteenth Amendment to the states for ratification. The amendment was ratified in January of 1919, with national Prohibition to take effect on January 17, 1920.

Billy Sunday was holding a revival in Norfolk, Virginia, when Prohibition officially became law. The day before, on January 16, 1920, he presided over an elaborate funeral for John Barleycorn. A long black coffin was paraded through Norfolk, coming to rest in Sunday's tabernacle. Sunday led the congregation in singing "John Barleycorn's Body Lies a-Mouldering in the Grave" before belting out an ebullient new version of the "Booze" sermon. He ended by saying, "The reign of tears is over. The slums will soon be only a memory. We will turn our prisons into factories and our jails into storehouses and corncribs. Men will walk upright now, women will smile, and the children will laugh. Hell will be forever for rent."[37] Billy Sunday had won a hard-fought victory over his lifelong enemy.

After the enactment of Prohibition, Sunday altered his "Booze" sermon somewhat, emphasizing the blessings of Prohibition for the country instead of the evils of the liquor industry. He continued to preach temperance and to advocate for full enforcement of Prohibition even as the movement for repeal gathered strength. He blamed interest in repeal on anti–American forces and groups. He campaigned vigorously for Republican political candidates and against candidates whom he thought were against Prohibition, notably Al Smith.

While Sunday's stature as a national leader was undiminished through the years of World War I, his influence waned in the 1920s. His later revivals were held in smaller cities, with smaller crowds. He remained very popular, however, and his sermons on salvation, temperance, and personal decency still commanded attention. He continued preaching right up until his death of a heart attack in November of 1935. A few weeks earlier he had attended one game of the 1935 World Series.

Temperance had been Billy Sunday's road to personal success. During his time as a part-time player for the National League's mighty Chicago White Stockings, it was probably his demeanor and behavior, as much or more than his playing skills, that kept him on the roster. The combination of being sober and a Christian as well as a speedy runner and a daring fielder made him attractive to other teams, where he performed well as a full-time outfielder. Being well known and well liked as a baseball player earned him increasing recognition as an evangelist. Soon his message of personal salvation through Christ and personal success through temperance and Christian morality resounded through the country.

During Billy Sunday's forty years as an evangelist, he was always identified as a baseball player, and as such he was seen as an exemplary model of Christian manliness and American decency. Sunday's magnetic revival presence and his powerful sermons were a driving force in the American public's acceptance of Prohibition and ratification of the Eighteenth Amendment. The Baseball Evangelist's temperance crusade is a notable example of the intersection of baseball with American politics.

Notes

1. Bruce Barton, "Billy Sunday—Baseball Evangelist," *Collier's*, July 26, 1913, 7+.
2. Mark Edward Lender, *Dictionary of American Temperance Biography: From Temperance Reform to Alcohol Research, the 1600s to the 1800s* (Westport, CT: Greenwood Press, 1984), 476.
3. Letter to Helen Thompson, May 15, 1888. Quoted in Robert F. Martin, *Hero of the Heartland: Billy Sunday and the Transformation of American Society, 1862–1935* (Bloomington: University of Indiana Press, 2002), 19.
4. *Spalding's Official Base Ball Guide and Official League Book* (Chicago: A.G. Spalding, 1884), 44.
5. *Chicago Tribune*, Oct. 26, 1884, 8.
6. Billy Sunday, "Mr. Sunday's Autobiography," in *Billy Sunday, the Man and His Message*, by William T. Ellis (Philadelphia: John C. Winston, 1936), 499.
7. The events surrounding Sunday's conversion are discussed at length in chapter nine of my book, *Sunday at the Ballpark: Billy Sunday's Professional Baseball Career, 1883–1890*,

ed. David B. Biesel, American Sports History Series (Lanham, MD: Scarecrow Press, 2000).

8. Harry Palmer, *Sporting Life*, Jan. 25, 1888, 4.

9. *Pittsburg Dispatch*, Apr. 25, 1888, 6.

10. Quoted in William G. McLoughlin, Jr., *Billy Sunday Was His Real Name* (Chicago: University of Chicago Press, 1955), 11.

11. William T. Ellis, *Billy Sunday, the Man and His Message: With His Own Words Which Have Won Thousands for Christ*, authorized ed. (Philadelphia: John C. Winston, 1914), 34.

12. "How a Baseball Idol 'Hit the Trail,'" *Literary Digest*, July 8, 1916, 94.

13. Quoted in McLoughlin, *Billy Sunday Was His Real Name*, 179.

14. Quoted in Ellis, *Billy Sunday, the Man and His Message: With His Own Words Which Have Won Thousands for Christ*, 146.

15. Billy Sunday, "The Famous 'Booze' Sermon," in *Billy Sunday, the Man and His Message: With His Own Words Which Have Won Thousands for Christ*, by William T. Ellis (Philadelphia: John C. Winston, 1914), 86.

16. *Ibid.*, 89.

17. *Ibid.*, 114–115.

18. McLoughlin, *Billy Sunday Was His Real Name*, 31.

19. Barton, "Billy Sunday — Baseball Evangelist," 8.

20. Billy Sunday, "A Plain Talk to Men," in *Billy Sunday, the Man and His Message: With His Own Words Which Have Won Thousands for Christ*, by William T. Ellis (Philadelphia: John C. Winston, 1914), 204.

21. Billy Sunday, "The Devil's Boomerangs, or, Hot Cakes Off the Griddle," in *Billy Sunday*, by D. Bruce Lockerbie (Waco: Waco Books, 1965), 31.

22. Billy Sunday, "My All-Star Nine," *Collier's*, Oct. 18, 1913, 30.

23. Quoted in W.A. Firstenberger, *In Rare Form: A Pictorial History of Baseball Evangelist Billy Sunday* (Iowa City: University of Iowa Press, 2005), 69.

24. Some historians and several of Sunday's contemporaries, notably Carl Sandburg, thought that Sunday was employed by business interests as a strikebreaker, especially during his Colorado revivals. This essay is not the place to consider that argument, but perhaps it would be well here to quote John Reed: "Is Billy Sunday sincere? I think he is.... He is generous, even reckless with his money — he seems to have no idea of its value. Everyone who talks with him loves him.... I think he is just ignorant, that's all." Quoted in McLoughlin, *Billy Sunday Was His Real Name*, 252.

25. James Warnock, "'Playing Centerfield in the Lord's Ball Club': Billy Sunday's 1914 Denver Campaign," *Nine* 4, no. 1 (1995): 67.

26. *Ibid.*, 72–73.

27. McLoughlin, *Billy Sunday Was His Real Name*, 248.

28. *Ibid.*, 243.

29. Firstenberger, *In Rare Form: A Pictorial History of Baseball Evangelist Billy Sunday*, 72.

30. "How a Baseball Idol 'Hit the Trail,'" 94.

31. Larry D. Engelmann, "Billy Sunday: God You've Got a Job on Your Hands in Detroit," *Michigan History* 55, no. 1 (1971): 11.

32. *Ibid.*, 15–16.

33. *Ibid.*, 23.

34. Quoted in McLoughlin, *Billy Sunday Was His Real Name*, xix.

35. *Ibid.*, 232.

36. Billy Sunday, "A Defense of the Grand Old Game," *Baseball Magazine*, July 1917, 361.

37. Jeff Hill, *Defining Moments: Prohibition* (Detroit: Omnigraphics, 2004), 32.

CHAPTER 3

Red Press Nation: The Baseball Rhetoric of Lester Rodney
Scott D. Peterson

"There were empty patches in the upper stands again — and while it's silly to say that interest is waning in the World's Series — the danger flag is up.... There was one famous sports columnist missing from the press box at Yankee Stadium yesterday." — Lester Rodney, *Daily Worker*, October 8, 1937

"As the Yankees were galloping around the basepath in the sad sixth, the Yankees fans were chanting: 'Close the door, they're coming through the window, close the window, they're coming through the floor! ...' Fire burst out in the wooden seats of the left field bleachers after the game and Nip McManus, superintendent of the Stadium, hinted that it was rank sabotage by Giant rooters. 'But if they want to protect the Giants,' said Mr. McManus with considerable heat, 'they set fire to the wrong park. There'll be no more ball games here this year.'" — John Kieran, *New York Times*, October 8, 1937

Lester Rodney and John Kieran were both at Yankee Stadium for Game Two of the 1937 World Series, but it's not clear that they saw the same game. Rodney paid attention to who wasn't there: a Brooklyn *Eagle* columnist who was recovering from a beating at the hand of thugs — ostensibly for his role in the strike by writers for the paper. He also noted the empty seats and used them as the basis for the long-term drawbacks of what he called the Yankee "monopoly." As Kieran reveals, the seats might have emptied due to the fire that broke out or was set, but that's not his main concern. Instead, Kieran stresses the romping Yankees and the reactions of their fans. While the above quotes would point toward a contrary conclusion, it is indeed likely that both sportswriters saw the same game. The key difference is that Rodney was less constrained by a party line, despite writing for a Communist newspaper. It was the alternative nature of the *Daily Worker* that allowed him to call the game as he saw it without resorting to the "hokum" found in the mainstream press. An analysis of his rhetorical strategies reveals that although he often used the same techniques employed by John Kieran of the *New York Times*, they used those strategies in strikingly different ways.

Lester Rodney grew up in Brooklyn in the early part of the last century. According to him, it was a typical American boyhood filled with various sports—baseball, basketball, and track.[1] While he wasn't especially politically minded, he became attracted to the ideals of the Communist Party while he was attending college at Columbia in the early 1930s.[2] After changes in party ideology made it possible for the *Daily Worker* to have a Sunday sports section, Rodney wrote a letter to the editor suggesting some improvements and made the "mistake" of putting his return address on the envelope, leading to a job writing for the paper.[3] In the fall of 1936, sports became a daily feature that occupied one of the paper's eight pages. As the editor, Rodney championed social and political issues right away, addressing labor and segregation practices of major league baseball and supporting youth sports. Breaking the color line was a favorite cause, one that Rodney took up in 1937 and stayed with until he was drafted into the army during World War Two. His efforts, however, were not widely known—or appreciated—until *Press Box Red*, Irwin Silber's biography of Rodney, came out in 2003. During that time, Rodney's outsider status allowed him to cover the uncoverable story, ask the unaskable questions, and take the unthinkable actions—like writing an open letter to baseball commissioner/czar K. M. Landis and deluging his office with letter campaigns and signatures from petition drives.

Like Rodney, John Kieran was a baseball player as well as a baseball writer.[4] He was born in 1892 and died in 1981. He started his career in 1916 and served in the army in France during World War One. In 1927, he became the first writer to have a byline under in the "Sports of the Times" column of the *New York Times*.[5] After writing that column for fifteen years, he joined the *New York Sun* in 1942 as a general columnist. He was also a panelist on the radio program, "Information Please."[6] Richard Orodenker categorizes Kieran as a "Matty" writing in the "Gee Whiz" school. Modeled after Christy Mathewson, the "Christian Gentleman," Matties are "graceful, polished writers" and "baseball's elegant phrasemakers."[7] The "Gee Whiz" school tended to be optimists, mythmakers, and sentimentalists.[8] According to Orodenker, Kieran "believed in the myth of the best game" and "mandarin that he was, saw in baseball the possibilities of a wonderful education."[9]

By the 1930s, baseball sportswriting was ready to enter its fourth generation. Henry Chadwick, the father of baseball writing and English immigrant, is the best known writer from the first generation. Chadwick's love for baseball is evident in his enthusiasm for the game—which is the enthusiasm of the convert since he grew up playing cricket in his native land. At the same time, however, his Victorian upbringing is obvious as well.[10] His dominance in the field slowed/prevented the development of an American voice, partially due to the fact that his accounts of games were objective by virtue of being largely impartial. He was more interested in the moral subtext of the game — including the propensity of the players for swearing — than rooting for one side or the other.

Charles Dryden and Leonard Dana Washburn represent the second generation of baseball writers — and the first to take on a unique American idiom. These writers grew up playing the game, a key difference from Chadwick and the first generation. This distinction allowed them to infuse a native spirit, as well as the spirit of youth into their writing. If Virginia Woolf had access to the writing of this second generation, she would have said the same things that are so oft quoted about Ring Lardner. These writers invented words — just as Lardner and the Elizabethans did. And they used baseball as an organizing structure.[11] The sportspage was still being invented during this phase of baseball writing, and to a certain extent, these baseball writers were still inventing sportswriting as well. According to Orodenker, these writers "went well beyond the quaint lists of baseball terms Chadwick had often composed.[12] What's more, even though the concept of objectivity was being developed in other areas of journalism,[13] baseball writers often favored the narrative over the facts:

> There was also a conscious effort on the part of some newspapers, mostly in Chicago, to make baseball and other news more appealing. Often a reporter's "bug" knowledge was not even necessary if he had a keen sense of what might make an interesting story about a particular game or player.[14]

As the American idiom began to emerge, story was valued over substance and objectivity was not part of the equation.

By the early twentieth century, sportswriting had come to take on the shape we know today. Writers like Ring Lardner traveled with the players and were thus "imbedded" within the fabric of the teams. What's more, the owners of the teams recognized the power of good press and courted their favor. The flip-side of this, however, is that the writers focused on and wrote about only what the owners wanted publicized, making them a part of the public relations machinery that developed during and after World War One.[15] When they weren't hiding behind objectivity or the unwritten code, the writers were actively building/creating myths of the players, building their images. These practices came at the time when Progressive leaders recognized the social value of sports and thus actively promoted them — which is a far cry from fifty to sixty years earlier when the Puritan attitudes toward play still held sway about leisure activities and the idea of play for pay. Thus sportswriters helped make Babe Ruth one of the first true baseball celebrities — but they did so without reporting the other elements of his character which are so well known now. Just as major league baseball needed Sosa and McGwire to bring the fans back after the debacle of the 1994 strike, the game needed Ruth to take the edge off the Black Sox scandal, making it easier to stay with the program and report on the things that would boost ticket sales and promote the Progressive and imperialist agendas of the owners and the politicians.

The 1930s represent an inter-regnum of sorts. The post World War One bubble of prosperity had burst nationally and world wide. Ruth passed the torch to Gehrig and DiMaggio, and the Yankees machine continued to win championships without missing a beat. Baseball was not forced to cut back on the number of teams and by the end of the decade the ultra-conservative owners were convinced to give night baseball a try — only to find the increase in ticket sales, which Negro League barnstormers had discovered ten years earlier. Sportswriters were still imbedded — or in bed with — the teams and were company men/women — reporting the company line and ignoring anything that was unpleasant or untoward. Matties of the "Gee Whiz" school, like John Kieran, were still writing, while Rubes of the "Aw Nuts" school, like Ring Lardner, were lost, but a new type of sportswriter — one with a social conscience, as well as the optimism of a Gee Whiz writer and the skepticism of an Aw Nuts devotee — was appearing on the scene. The first sportswriter with a social — or political conscience — was Lester Rodney, and writing for *The Daily Worker*, a newspaper of the American Communist Party, allowed him to write what he saw without worrying about the prescribed lines of the times.

Methodology

Borrowing from Kathleen Turner's notion that rhetorical history "offers us the opportunity to see rhetoric as a perpetuated and dynamic process of social construction, maintenance, and change rather than as an isolated, static product,"[16] it is the goal of this paper to understand how myths are made — or unmade — in the process of baseball writing by studying a specific set of writings for their value as indicators of political and social tensions around the dynamic of baseball. Toward that end, this paper will analyze columns and spot reporting from an alternative and a mainstream newspaper. Since he did both kinds of sportswriting for the *Daily Worker*, Rodney's work will serve as examples of the alternative press. The columns of John Kieran and the spot reporting of Roscoe McGowen, both of the *New York Times*, will serve as the examples of the mainstream press. The examples will be drawn from the 1937 baseball season because it is the first full season covered by

Rodney. This body of writing will be evaluated with regard to the following questions:

1. To what degree does the piece show evidence of narrative?
2. To what degree does the piece show evidence of identification?
3. To what degree does the piece show evidence of myth creation/unmaking?

The answers to these questions will serve as the basis for my overall argument that Lester Rodney's status as an outsider allowed him to unmask the myths created in the mainstream press and call for social change.

While promoting his paradigm of *homo narrans*, or storytelling as the fundamental quality of human nature, William Fisher points to the culture-generating qualities of narrative when he views the world as a set of stories that we must choose from on a daily basis.[17] John Lucaites and Celeste M. Condit discuss the role of narrative in the formation of social consciousness.[18] Condit further discusses how rhetorical critics have been urged to examine "the rhetorical coins of mass consciousness, especially ideographs, myths, and narratives"[19] to provide a more complete view on the rhetorical efforts of humans. Following these definitions, baseball writing becomes a culture-generating piece of rhetoric when it tells the story or narrative of a game.

The narrative aspects of baseball have been noted by numerous writers. The form of the game, as well as its function, both lend to storytelling in early accounts of baseball games.[20] In addition to spot reporting, narrative can be translated into baseball columns as well. These columns often tell the "story" of a conversation with a manager or player or a fan, supplying setting, actions, and other narrative details to put the reader into the same room as the writer and the interviewee. The language used to carry out these narratives — the phrasing, word choice, slang, and metaphor/simile — will play a large role in my analysis, along with the underlying functions of the stories.

Baseball writing also takes on a rhetorical function when the author persuades the reader to identify with him/her, which falls in line with Kenneth Burke's notion of how identification and division work together to create a sense of identity, as well as the revisions of that notion that pushed the idea of "persuasion" toward identification, according to Condit.[21] In his analysis of Burke, Bryan Crable suggests that identity "is based upon our identification with (and internalization of) shared material, our 'I' simply a particular cluster of adopted 'corporate we's.'"[22] This quality of mind is present in baseball writing when the narratives or stories serve as a prime source of the shared material the reader identifies with and internalizes in conjunction with the writer or columnist. Further, the corporate quality of our "I's" as being a conglomeration of accepted "we's" is important from a narrative perspective since stories told from the first person plural take on the quality of greater authority, as exemplified by the concept of the royal or editorial we — or the wise/worldly columnist. Further still, the partisan quality to strong identification gives rise to a greater sense of personal and social identity, which in turn creates the conditions required to bring about a unique or original voice.

A third function of baseball writing is the creation of a mythology to meet some personal, local, or national need. According to Glanville, modern sport was invented by the British for the British, which "might explain the slightly fractious Establishment need to present a robust anachronism as the national sport: a kind of imperial glue."[23] Often that glue takes the form of myth, or a "compensatory function which all professional sport fulfills in our tame, urbanized world."[24] As noted above, that mythical function was exploited by journalists, major league baseball owners, and social reformers in a conscious effort to shape the image of players, teams, the game as a whole, and the nation.

Analysis: The Pre-Season

Holdouts and other labor issues were prominent features in Rodney's columns in the spring of 1937. Spring training camps were almost a month away, but Rodney was right there with the inside scoop on who was holding out for what. He named names and told how much. What's more, he quoted the players, letting them speak for themselves: "I expect to find a figure of $20,000 on my contract," says Van Lingle Mungo.[25] Jake Powell, an outfielder for the Yankees, was just as candid: "I'm twenty-eight and I've got to collect while the collecting is good." Although these players are making several times more than the average worker of 1937, Rodney casts them as fellow workers of his audience, asserting that the players "have just grievances against the owners, these men who are thrown on the ash heap when they hit 35 years of age. They can't get what they are worth to the big business of baseball, and they can't fight back." Rodney uses key terms, such as "grievance," to win over his audience and encourage them to identify with the players. Narrative-wise, he plays into the exploitative management vs. exploited workers story that was a large part of communist rhetoric. He uses metaphorical language when he urges further identification by making use of the unionization narrative: "It's a great racket — for the owners. A ball player's union would make them howl plenty — and the ball players are beginning to talk...." "Racket" and "howl" are the loaded, evocative terms here for making Rodney's audience — who are up against rackets in their own lives and would like to make their bosses cry out in pain — identify further with the players. In addition, the ellipses indicate that the story is to be continued — or that this is only the beginning of the story.

The "story" continues when Rodney reports how five Yankees are participating in the "first mass holdout in modern baseball history."[26] Rodney's use of narrative is present again when he reports that one of the players was signed for a raise: "Tony Lazzeri was signed yesterday at an increase and thereby lies the tale of five contracts, an Associated Press reporter, and mass pressure from a bunch of ball players beginning to learn the secret of organization." Note how the phrase "beginning to learn" hints at the ongoing nature of the story, along with the identification factor created by the reference to the power of unionizing.

The next part of the story is also well known to Rodney's readers as he goes on to write, "Like all good employers, [Jacob Ruppert] ran weeping to the Associated Press and spilled a bucket of tears which were spread all over the town's papers the next day. You — know all about 'the wicked,' ungrateful ball players. The reaction, as you might expect, was a merry ha-ha and a 'Come, across, Colonel.'"[27] The narrative here is both the usual business of baseball, as well as the capitalist narrative on the larger scale, and the dialogue could be from the players, the alternative press, or the fans— or the collective voice of all three. Once again, Rodney is calling for his readers to identify with the workers and against the owners. To do this, he uses the second person address to bring them right into the story. What's more, the language and tone he uses while speaking of "beer magnate" Colonel Ruppert shows that he is openly critical of the owners and the way baseball is operated.

Rodney uses the holdout situation as the springboard for a larger campaign to improve baseball. He starts his column on February 25 with a scenario of an imagined future: "Lou Gehrig, Joe DiMaggio, and Tony Lazzeri sit down on the bases in the ninth inning of a 0-0 ball game with the Detroit Tigers and demand that the ball player's union be given the right to collective bargaining with owner Jake (Beer Baron) Ruppert."[28] In this fantasy, the timing of the sit-down strike is important since it would frustrate the fan's desire to see how the story/game turns out. Referring to Ruppert as a "Beer Baron" places him in the same company of the robber barons of the previous century. Rodney goes on to outline the option to strike, the ability to unionize, and the ending of the Jim Crow laws as the three actions required to make things "less rotten" in major league baseball and improve the "captivity" of the players. Rodney also voices a vote of confidence for his readers: "John Q Public is getting to be more and more the class conscious member of a trade union."

As spring training continues, Rodney reports on "the growing viciousness of the baseball magnates against the demands of holdouts."[29] He builds metaphors around the situation: "I'll have my ham and eggs without the ham" to comment on how the Yankees would be incomplete if they started without Gehrig in the lineup.[30] Rodney is openly critical in later column when he claims, "Baseball isn't the game it might be, but a long shot."[31] He goes on to outline the "lopsided" labor conditions and the "UnAmerican discrimination against the Negro Stars." He adds a third point, comparing the situation to Nazi Germany: "Hold-out players still have as much chance with the owners and their stooge Judge Landis as a German worker has with Hitler and Goebbels." Here is more identification as the reader is urged to side with the ball player/German worker against the owners/Hitler and Landis/Goebbels in this particular metaphor. At the same time he's currying favor with his reading public, Rodney is seeking to earn sympathy for the players by suggesting players like Gehrig are not so savvy in the ways of business: "He's now the greatest day-in-and-day-out ball player in the world, and any estimation of the amount of money he's coined for the dough dizzy magnates like Ruppert, Yawkey, and Briggs would amaze even Columbia Lou, a fairly innocent soul as such things go."

Two weeks later, Rodney extends the metaphor: "Don't be surprised if on opening day, the baseball players raise their arms in a fascist salute before the umpire calls Play Ball."[32] Here is another scenario and it goes equally against the baseball tradition as players refusing to finish a game. The impetus is a ban by Phillies manager on movies and newspapers—except the comics—and the banning of player's wives from training camp by the Detroit manager. Rodney sees this as being "directly in line" with "the dictatorial attitude toward ballplayers" created by the "take it or leave it" salary arrangements. By the end of the column, Landis has become synonymous with Hitler (supplanting the owners): "Over the whole setup rules Judge Landis, whose vicious anti-labor verdicts some years back stamped him for what he is. Heil!" Thus, over the course of the pre-season, Rodney made use of narrative and identification to draw his reader into the story and demystify the image of the game of baseball and the owners. What's more, he drew the players as fellow workers to further encourage his readers to identify with them, even though they earned several times the average wage.

In his column in the *New York Times*, John Kieran makes only a handful of mentions of the holdouts during the spring of 1937. The first mention is to downplay them: "Discount the holdouts. They will all be in when the band strikes up."[33] Most likely, he uses "discount" in the sense that we are not to put much stock in them. At the same time, however, the phrase could also be taken in the sense that the value of the holdouts should be lowered— either salary-wise or in the estimation of the readers. In the same column, he makes a specific reference to the holdout by Dizzy Dean: "The Cardinals still have Dizzy Dean though Branch Rickey, with a salary debate impending, never overlooks an occasion to say that Dizzy would be traded if the Cardinals could get a reasonable return." A salary "debate" implies a contest where the two sides abide by the same rules and speak from a position of equal power — a situation not enjoyed by major league players in 1937 as Rodney pointed out repeatedly in his columns and reports. The full phrase indicated by the ellipses in the quote attributed to Rickey is "reasonable return on investment," a phrase from the capitalist narrative that refers to goods bought and sold. A month later, Kieran touches on the holdouts again, first in a Grantland Rice-esque poem: "That holdouts in baseball are strictly a gag;/ That bouts in the ring are first put in the bag...."[34] Kieran goes on to treat Dizzy Dean with the same light, satirical tone: "And what in the world is the Dizzy Dean diet? There's a real subject for scientific investigation. There must be a list of items on his grocery list that are not good for the brain." Kieran makes reference to the "debates" between Dean and the St. Louis owner over salary: "It seems that Owner Breadon mentioned that he was offering Dizzy more money than Carl Hubbell was getting from the Giants. To which Dizzy retorted in effect: 'Pooh for Hubbell! Who's he? Just a pitcher. He can't bring 'em through the turnstiles like Old Dizz.'" Kieran goes on to say, "In a dieting way, that's 'the berries' with whipped cream." A bad diet was the source of the disputes in the poem that started the column, so Kieran continues his theme with the metaphor likening Hubbell to a full-fledged dessert. After taking Dean to task for being brash enough to suggest that he had "various offers in other lines for his unique services," Kieran concludes by saying of Dean, "He is right when he says he is a gate attraction. He is an amusing talker and he keeps at it incessantly. He has a strong voice and he uses rollicking gestures. But there is no variety to his orations. He ought to say something sensible once in awhile, just for a change." It is hard to tell here whether Kieran is pro-owner or anti–Dean. Either way, it is clear he has little sympathy for the holdout.

Roscoe McGowen was a spot reporter for the *New York Times* and serves as another comparison to Lester Rodney in the study. Gehrig's "salary controversy" comes up during a "party to the press," but the bulk of what Gehrig and McGowen had to say dealt with the records he had and was chasing.[35] All talk of the impending holdout is over by the end of the first section and only gets four words at the end of the teasers: "No word on salary." Gehrig said he had no plans for "further discussion and did not know when the argument would be resumed." Once again, "discussion" and "argument" imply equal footing. McGowen does mention that Gehrig was asked if he thought things would grow serious and quoted the player indirectly: "Gehrig only grinned in an embarrassed manner and remarked that he had no way of knowing about that." Note the subjective assessment of Gehrig's grin; it could have been an "aw shucks" gesture, but it could have been a grimace of anger that McGowen willfully misread.

Three weeks later, McGowen touches on the holdout situation again, this time devoting a whole column to it. In it, he's keeping score (what else to do in the spring before the games start?), noting how the Dodgers had signed four players, while there was "no action for the Yankees," causing them to fall behind in the "contract-signing league" with thirteen holdouts to eight of the Dodgers.[36] The Yankees players are described as "still being a bit stubborn," which makes them sound a bit childish, although McGowen tempers this in the next sentence by saying, "As usual, of course, the most important men are those still on the outside." Like Kieran, he downplays the seriousness of the dispute by saying the four key Dodger holdouts have "writer's cramp or have lost their fountain pens" — again downplaying the seriousness of the dispute and making the players sound weak or careless. McGowen quotes Yankee owner Ruppert directly with regard to Gehrig and Lefty Gomez:

> "I haven't seen Gehrig or heard a word from him since he was in my office with his proposition," said the colonel crisply. "Neither have I heard from Gomez. Somebody told me he was going to Boston — I don't know!" And his tone sounded as if he were saying: 'I don't care.'"

McGowen could have just as easily read the petulance of a child that wasn't getting his way into Ruppert's words, but seems to support the Colonel's right to be crisp and curt about his puerile ball players, which might explain why the owner was quoted directly on the matter, while the player wasn't.

On the day the Dodger camp was set to open, the two top pitchers remained unsigned, but there was no mention of the term holdout, and McGowen hinted that the reason was due to a late arrival: "Van Lingle Mungo and Fred Frankhouse cannot be signed before their initial exercising because Business Manager John Gorman has delayed his arrival here for one reason or another."[37] While the players are taken to task for failing to communicate with the owner, the management, however, can hold things up for "one reason or another" without having their feet held to the fire. There is no further mention of holdouts or labor disputes in McGowen's spot reporting for that spring. As with Kieran, narrative, myth, and identification are all absent from McGowen's writing as he touches on the labor situation. In addition, he adopts a similar pro-owner or anti-player tone, making the players out to be the unreasonable parties in the issue.

Analysis: The Early Regular Season

As March turns to April, Rodney continues the "wage slave" metaphor from earlier in the pre-season and adds a Brothers Grimm element when he reports on U.S. Representative Raymond Cannon, who spoke to Congress about the labor practices of major league baseball: "It was about high time that the lovely fairy tale mask was ripped off the face of this big business—

and don't ever forget that it is a big business—and the amazing and un–American set-up shown for what it is."[38] Rodney goes on to quote Cannon and point out the "Black List" that "binds the player for life—but the magnate can discharge him on 10 days notice." He finishes the column by quoting National League President Ford Frick, who gave the standard line about how the Supreme Court had granted that baseball was a "peculiar business" which required the ten-day firing clause to be successful. Rodney points out how Frick used to write for Hearst's *New York Journal*—a paper noted for its anti-labor stance.

When Kieran treats the same issue, he begins with the world and American political scene—the civil war in Spain, Germany's drive to build the largest warships in the world, and strikes by coal miners and auto workers, topics Rodney touched on several times in his column that same spring. Kieran uses this backdrop to belittle Cannon's "throbbing letter" to Attorney General Cummings, and went on to refer to Congress as "Heartbreak House" after it was read there.[39] The sarcasm piles up from there as Kieran refers to the "wicked capitalists" and "merciless magnates" (both terms Rodney is fond of using for the owners) who are mistreating the "oppressed peons of the ivory trade":

> Admittedly it is tough to take a fellow off the farm and make him submit to the hardships of life in big hotels and traveling on limited trains and a bare existence on anything from $3,500 to $36,000 (Mr. Gehrig's figure) a year with hard labor in the way of baseball games thrown in, provided it isn't raining on any particular day.

Clearly, Kieran is on the attack here as hinted at by the title of his column: "Bringing up the Cannon," using sarcasm as his cudgel as he hints that the congressman needs to be "brought up" like a child. By contrast, Rodney used quotes and straight-ahead reporting, an interesting reversal in tactics. While Rodney is deadly serious about his references to conflicts like the Spanish Civil War, Kieran uses the war reference to belittle and downplay Cannon's efforts to bring about fair labor practices.

Once the season begins, Rodney returns to narrative, metaphor, and identification. On the last day of the pre-season, he relates the story of a conversation—real or imagined—he shares with an "old park attendant" who was "putting the finishing touches on the grounds."[40] The fellow pulls a "long manuscript" from his pocket and began to read about seeing Christy Mathewson taking the mound on opening day. Besides hinting at the possibility that there are more baseball writers than we could ever imagine, Rodney shows his allegiances with the working man as well as the political struggles of the world and America—the same tactic employed by Kieran in his sarcastic attack on Cannon.

When the first pitch was finally made, Rodney takes his readers into the stadium: "As you wander through the crowd you become amazed all over again at the hold this professional game has on such a large section of the American people. There are milkmen, butchers, truck drivers, and salesman with their tell-tale brief cases hidden beneath their seats."[41] In contrast with these working folk, Rodney refers to the reserved seats "where the mayors, borough presidents and Tammany ward-heelers hog the spotlight. The camera men have a name for them — they call them 'lens louses.'" After this sharp juxtaposition, Rodney returns to identification again when he writes,

> You remember the mild horror expressed by a friend of yours when he read of 40,000 murdered in Spain — blown to bits by fascist shells and bombs. You look around at the teeming mass of talking, reading, shifting humanity and picture them all blown suddenly to bits by a concentrated fire of shells and bombs.

Rodney's story starts with that realization and he keeps the second person address as he shows his press card and solicits comments on the Spanish Civil War, thus combining narrative and identification by putting his reader in the story with him. He gets one "no comment" from a "plain-looking man" and an answer of "amazing conscience" from a "tow-headed be-sweatered high school kid": "You can put in your newspaper — whatever it is — that we young Americans **would** care to express an opinion — and that there's nothing far away about people fighting fascists for the right to eat and run their own country."[42] Once again, Rodney closes his column with a hint of the larger story that is so often absent from mainstream sports pages: "There was a baseball game played, and it was a good one. Close, well played and exciting. And the opening game." Rodney picks up the story a week later when he reports how the Cuban All-Stars, a barnstorming team of African Americans is fighting — and dying — in Spain, leading in with "this is about a baseball team that isn't playing baseball right now. A team that figured there were more important things to be done."[43] He goes on to narrate the death of the Cuban All-Star shortstop, ending with a direct challenge: "The game was over for Johnny, but he had thrown the batter out and won. Put that in a scenario, Hollywood." He also provides direct criticism: "Their skin is too dark in color for the magnates and their stooge officials who run our national pastime." As before, there can be no doubt where Rodney's sentiments lie on this issue.

Rodney's championing of the common man, as well as his narrative and identification strategies, continue as he devotes his dramatizations to a class parable illustrating the inequities of an empty, gated park in a wealthy neighborhood while poor children play ball in the streets. The idea for this column comes from "Lil Lefty," a comic strip character from the pages of the *Daily*

Worker.[44] Another column portrays a vignette of a conversation with a barber — another working class personage, and the archetype of a local baseball expert — and provides a look at why so much of sports writing is drivel. In the last two cases, Rodney asked for feedback from his audience, honestly wanting their opinion and to know what interests them. What more could he do to get his readers to identify with his cause than to invite them into the conversation by inquiring about their perspective.

By contrast, Kieran's early season columns and spot reports are filled with scattershot pieces about Patriot's Day games (then the purview of the Boston Braves) and definitions of "a Mathewson": "a fellow who has a great head and an arm to match."[45] He also has a series of "interviews" with various managers — Joe Cronin of the Red Sox (whom Kieran calls "the Fenway Millionaires"), Rogers Hornsby of the St. Louis Browns, and Pie Traynor of the Pittsburgh Pirates. These "interviews" are sprinkled with player dialogue and player dialect, banter, and even a few bits of inside stuff among the usual hokum. In the case of Traynor, Kieran got a two-for-one deal in that coach Jewel Ens joins in, and the two of them tell stories on themselves and their rivals. In fact, letting the players or managers do the talking seems to be Kieran's number one strategy in his columns. Occasionally, a manager will say something that has echoes of Ring Lardner's busher. But there is no hint of labor unrest or the whole segment of the American population that was being kept off the major league diamonds. McGowen's spot reporting is also devoid of labor for racial controversy. His reporting is mostly straight-up with only a few instances of narrative and metaphoric language. In short, it is business as usual in the mainstream press. There are some engaging stories and glimpses at the inner game to be had, especially in Kiernan's "interviews," but their significance stops at the turnstile.

Analysis: The Late Season

Moving ahead past the All-Star Game to the last dog days of August, there was only one real pennant race that season. After a turn on page seven to fill in for a political columnist (which Rodney used as a platform to critique ex-sportswriters turned columnists), he proves he isn't immune to the "crooshul" series between the Cubs and the Giants, who are battling for the National League crown. Before he can get to that series, however, he devotes a column to answering a question about why there is such interest in the upcoming Joe Louis fight. He encourages identification with his audience by claiming there

> can be no doubt in the minds of any thinking people that the terrific barrage of heavily laid on sports ballyhoo, even discounting the normal amount

demanded by those fundamentally interested, is part and parcel of the whole pattern of deadening, diverting entertainment consciously fostered by American capitalism.[46]

This capitalist "lullaby" acts to "tap" and "divert" what Rodney identifies as "the whole American restless, energetic, mostly unsatisfied love of sports competition." Rodney goes on to argue that "[t]he overlords of America didn't want Joe Louis to become champion" since the capitalist machinery — the "paid lackeys" that make up "85 per cent of the newspapers" will create a boomerang effect by highlighting the achievements and superiority of an African American. By extension, this could also explain why the powers that be kept the Negro League stars out of the spotlight in the mainstream press.

After that straight ahead cultural analysis, it was back to baseball: Rodney donned his spot reporting hat to identify what he felt might well be the turning point of the Giants' season: down 7–2 in the bottom of the ninth, the Giants rally for a win to pull within three games of the front-running Cubs, instead of falling five games back. Rodney narrates the key events in a staccato, shorthand style:

> First thing anybody knew there were two runs in, the score was 7–4, two were on. Jim Ripple at bat, and 40,000 of the usually staid New York fan type were yelling their heads off. Some customer from the Bronx, who sat in the upper right-field tier, has that baseball proudly displayed at the supper table tonight.[47]

The jump-cut technique used here forces the reader to supply the missing event: the three-run home run that tied the game (which also prefigures a game fourteen years later when an equally dramatic shot will be hit and heard around the world).

Subsequent columns defend the exploited worker — Van Lingle Mungo — from "the pin-headed Dodger magnates" and "Captain Bligh" Burleigh after the Dodgers suspended an over-worked Mungo without pay for not being able to perform.[48] Two days later, we can see Rodney's idiom begin to take shape in his spot reporting as he turns to alliteration ("Master Mel Ott," "demonic Dick Bartell"), active verbs ("drubbing," "shellacked"), and more literary references ("Prince Hal" Schumacher) and dialect that is reminiscent of Lardner's rube: "It was a nice gesture, but Ryba didn't seem to appreciate it, from the way he kicked the resin bag around. He probably wasn't brung up right."[49]

Late August into September also marks the first player interviews in Rodney's writing, which is likely a reflection of the one-year waiting period before he could get his credentials from the Baseball Writer's Association.[50] After a fairly standard interview with Paul Waner that revealed Rodney's knowledge of hitting mechanics, an interview with "Joltin' Joe" leads to the banner headline of "DiMaggio Calls Negro Greatest Pitcher; Says Satchel Paige Is Tops— Statement a Whack at Jim Crow."[51] Although the story appears in the part of the sports page usually reserved for spot reporting, Rodney uses it as a podium to remind his readers of DiMaggio's immigrant status and argue that "the average big league ball player would welcome the Negro Star into the game." He also reminds his readers how the "clique of wealthy magnates" have made desegregation and unionization taboo topics. Claiming another victory by getting National League president Ford Frick "to admit there is nothing in the rules that prohibits Negroes from playing," Rodney calls on "Johnny Fan" to apply "[j]ust a little more pressure" to create the scenario where Joe DiMaggio would step in against Paige.

Rodney goes on to interview Paige, printing his request for "American sportsmanship" in the form of a game between his Negro League All-Stars and the winners of the World Series.[52] The interview gives Paige the chance to share his shrewd assessment of the situation: "There must be something wrong somewhere. Must be just a few men who don't want us to play big league ball. The players are O.K. and the crowds are with us." The interview also allows Paige to issue a counterargument to the "phony bugaboo" that Negro pitchers are wild and might "skull" a white player. The efforts of the *Daily Worker* on behalf of the Negro Stars are summarized the next day and on the following Monday, the top spot reporting story is about the 25,000 fans who came out to the Polo Grounds to see a young pitching prospect no-hit Paige's Santo Domingo All-Stars. The pennant-chasing Giants are relegated to a tiny square between the banner and the cartoon. A week later, the Negro League game is back in the top spot — this time Paige prevailed — and on September 30, the *Daily Worker* printed a letter from a fan in support of the Negro League players.

As if this isn't enough, Rodney uses his column on September 21 to call for a new kind of fan: one with a social conscience. As support, he offers that six of the eight boxers on the upcoming fight as evidence of a "new trend in sports."[53] He also cites sporting events to benefit the "Scottsboro boys" (who were jailed in the South after being falsely accused of rape) and Loyalist Spain, as well as the rise of labor sports and the Young Communist League as further evidence of the trend. What's more, he claims that people are hearing "the onrushing colossus of college football overtaking and breaking into the monopoly of big league baseball."[54] Besides the competition from football, Rodney isn't sold on this year's October classic either: "1937's super-super extravaganza may not be all that. It looks like New York's two teams again and the fans may be just a wee bit this side of hysterical on the encore." What's more, three days later, he asks his readers to forget the World Series and college football for one day to focus on The Third Workers Olympiad, which featured the first competition between athletes from the U.S. and the U.S.S.R.

He held up the event in contrast to the "loud-mouthed Nazi hippodrome"[55] of the year before.

By contrast, Kieran spent his August into September "interviewing" players, managers, and traveling secretaries. On occasion, the dialect is reminiscent of Jack Keefe, Ring Lardner's busher, as in the case of this dialogue from Charlie Grimm, the manager of the Cubs: "Stainback's got a lotta stuff — should be a great player — can do everything — but we put him in there the other day and first thing he comes up with is a stomach ache or something. Another time he'll bend an ankle or his teeth have to be fixed."[56] The interviews contain inside information as well, as revealed by Cardinals manager "Onkel Franz" Frisch who's dishing on Paul Dean: "He can't pitch up here, but he can pitch down in Texas, where it's so hot that your shoes catch fire if you walk fast."[57] The only time politics enters Kieran's columns that fall is to avoid discussing them: "Keep politics out of baseball. That's what Joseph Edward Cronin says, with tears in his eyes."[58] Cronin is the manager of the "platinum-plated Fenway Millionaires," which is Kieran's nickname for the Boston Red Sox, who spent a lot of money on players that year — to no avail. According to Kieran, Cronin is a Yankee victim, who has "taken that Soak-the-Rich chorus of the hustings as their theme song on the diamond." This is as close as Kieran comes to discussing politics, but it's clearly in the service of being clever, just as the closest he comes to addressing segregation is to refer to the owner of the Red Sox as "Uncle Tom Yawkey" in the same column. When a meeting with American League President Will Harridge affords him the opportunity to discuss labor or Jim Crow issues, Kieran prefers to talk old times with former umpire Tommy Connolly. Red Sox Catcher Moe Berg wants to talk politics, but that is only because "[a] ball player doesn't like to talk of his own team unless it's winning."[59] But Berg's credibility is also called into question in the same column: "So that's what happens when the Yanks grab a ball game from outraged visitors by scoring eight runs in the ninth inning. The catcher for the losing side goes out and buys *An Enquiry Concerning Human Understanding* by David Hume."

Each of these interviews is a narrative in that it is a sketch of a conversation, complete with setting and descriptions of actions. By way of identification, Kieran couches what he might have to say in such a way that it reflects what the reader is thinking — or ought to be thinking to be as witty and urbane and baseball savvy as Kieran. Taken together, these two strategies often portray the interviewees as colorful figures and all around good fellows — especially if they are members of management.

It's also business as usual for McGowen in his columns from that fall. He describes the "explosive" offense of the Dodgers and the "dynamiting" done by the regulars in a game won by the Dodgers over the Phillies.[60] On the road with the Dodgers in Pittsburgh, he makes reference to a literary metaphor: "But the Dodgers wasted two golden opportunities and as they rolled away to Chicago manager Burleigh Grimes was sourly reviewing a tragedy in one act that might be called 'Ruined by a Rookie,'"[61] but this clever title is as close as he comes to using narrative and encouraging identification beyond routine scoring recaps. When Paul Waner collects his 200th hit and becomes the first National League player to collect that many hits in eight seasons, McGowen reports this fact without fanfare or myth-building description. If he doesn't touch on the no-hitter pitched at the Polo Grounds against Satchel Paige's team, we can give him a pass because he was out of town. Unfortunately, we can't offer the same excuse to Kieran.

Conclusion

While the 1937 baseball season is not remembered for the heroics of a Bobby Thompson or the dramatics of a Reggie Jackson, it is significant in that it was the first full year of Lester Rodney's tenure as the sports editor of the *Daily Worker*. Like his mainstream colleagues, John Kieran and Roscoe McGowen, he used narrative and identification in his baseball writing to entertain and engage his readers. While McGowen was a spot reporter, Rodney and Kieran were featured as columnists, and with that regular platform, they were more able to use their baseball writing to engage in the cultural work of mythmaking. The key difference between the mainstream and alternative writers, however, was their use of politics.

When Kieran and McGowen made use of narrative, they seemed to see baseball players as a source of colorful stories, but little more. By contrast, when Rodney employed narrative, it was often to point to a social injustice within the world of baseball or the wider world — or both at the same time. When McGowen used identification, it was to encourage their readers to side with the owners instead of the players. As a columnist, Kieran created a breezy, aloof persona to encourage his readers to identify with his faintly bemused take on the game and its players. The only times that persona shifted was when people like Representative Cannon tried to bring politics into the baseball world. Rodney, on the other hand, encouraged his readers to see the players as exploited — and excluded — fellow laborers. What's more, he asked his readers to become involved politically through letter campaigns and protest marches.

Perhaps the greatest difference between the two was in the area of mythmaking. When Kieran refers to the St. Louis manager as "Onkel" Franz or McGowen coins a clever title like "Ruined by a Rookie," it is to reinforce the positive images of baseball and its players. When they discuss the holdouts, it is to show how a few ungrateful players are acting like spoiled children, but that they should be discounted because most of the players are good fellows. The writing of Kieran and McGowen illustrates how labor issues were avoided in the mainstream myth of baseball — except to make examples of the disloyal — and shows that segregation does not appear at all in that myth because African American players were part of a entirely separate world. By contrast, Rodney actively works to problematize that mainstream myth, showing that labor issues and the injustices of segregation were present on any given day of the baseball calendar from pre-season to post-season, as well as running deep within the fabric of American culture.

Thus, while the 1937 baseball season was unremarkable in many ways — Who could be surprised that the Chicago Cubs faded down the stretch and gave way to the New York Giants in the race for the pennant?— it does mark the year that baseball writing became political through the efforts of Lester Rodney. This is not to say that baseball became "politicized" right away. Even when the game became desegregated ten years after Rodney first interviewed Satchel Paige, Jackie Robinson was chosen as someone who would keep the politics of race out of the equation. And another twenty years would pass before Curt Flood reintroduced labor politics to the game by challenging the Reserve Clause and taking his case to the Supreme Court. When the optimism of the "Gee Whiz" style was crossed with the "Aw Nuts" skepticism in the writing of Lester Rodney, the sentimentality and cynicism of both styles was left out, perhaps leaving room for a social conscience.

Notes

1. Irwin Silber, *Press Box Red* (Philadelphia: Temple University Press), 22.
2. *Ibid.*, 6.
3. *Ibid.*, 8.
4. Richard Orodenker, *The Writer's Game: Baseball Writing in America* (New York: Twayne), 55.
5. *Ibid.*, 54.
6. *Ibid.*
7. *Ibid.*, 9.
8. *Ibid.*, 11.
9. *Ibid.*, 55.
10. *Ibid.*, 29.
11. *Ibid.*, 36.
12. *Ibid.*, 32.
13. Brent Cunningham, "Rethinking Objectivity," *Columbia Journalism Review* 41 (2003): 26.
14. Orodenker, 32.
15. Cunningham, 26.
16. Kathleen Turner, *Doing Rhetorical History: Concepts and Cases* (Tuscaloosa: University of Alabama Press, 1998), 4.
17. William R. Fisher, "Narration as a Human Communication Paradigm: The Case of Public Moral Argument," *Communication Monographs* 51 (1984): 8.
18. John L. Lucaites and Celeste M. Condit, "Re-constructing Narrative Theory: A Functional Perspective," *Journal of Communication* 35 (1985): 90.
19. Celeste M. Condit, "The Critic as Empath: Moving Away from Totalizing Theory," *Western Journal of Communication* 57 (1993): 178.
20. Scott D. Peterson, "Of Ourselves We Sing: Finding an American Voice Through Early Baseball Journalism," in *Baseball/Literature/Culture Essays 2006–2007*, ed. Ronald E. Kates and Warren Tormey, 11–21 (Jefferson, NC: McFarland, 2008).
21. Condit, 178.

22. Bryan Crable, "Rhetoric, Anxiety, and Character Armor: Burke's Interactional Rhetoric Identity," *Western Journal of Communication* 70 (2006): 8.
23. Brian Glanville, *People in Sport* (London: Secker & Warburg, 1967), 38.
24. Ibid., 33.
25. Lester Rodney, *Daily Worker*, January 25, 1937, 8.
26. Lester Rodney, *Daily Worker*, February 6, 1937, 8.
27. Ibid.
28. Lester Rodney, *Daily Worker*, February 25, 1937, 8.
29. Lester Rodney, *Daily Worker*, March 2, 1937, 8.
30. Lester Rodney, *Daily Worker*, March 10, 1937, 8.
31. Lester Rodney, *Daily Worker*, March 15, 1937, 8.
32. Lester Rodney, *Daily Worker*, March 31, 1937, 8.
33. John Kieran, *New York Times*, February 14, 1937, 74.
34. John Kieran, *New York Times*, March 14, 1937, 82.
35. Roscoe McGowen, *New York Times*, January 31, 1937, 77.
36. Roscoe McGowen, *New York Times*, February 21, 1937, 65.
37. Roscoe McGowen, *New York Times*, March 1, 1937, 23.
38. Lester Rodney, *Daily Worker*, April 8, 1937, 8.
39. John Kieran, *New York Times*, April 4, 1937, 76.
40. Lester Rodney, *Daily Worker*, April 20, 1937, 8.
41. Lester Rodney, *Daily Worker*, April 22, 1937, 8.
42. Lester Rodney, *Daily Worker*, April 22, 1937, 8, (bold in the original).
43. Lester Rodney, *Daily Worker*, April 29, 1937, 8.
44. Lester Rodney, *Daily Worker*, May 6, 1937, 8.
45. John Kieran, *New York Times*, April 18, 1937, 74.
46. Lester Rodney, *Daily Worker*, August 26, 1937, 8.
47. Lester Rodney, *Daily Worker*, August 27, 1937, 8.
48. Lester Rodney, *Daily Worker*, August 30, 1937, 8.
49. Lester Rodney, *Daily Worker*, September 2, 1937, 8.
50. Silber, 34.
51. Lester Rodney, *Daily Worker*, September 13, 1937, 8.
52. Lester Rodney, *Daily Worker*, September 16, 1937, 8.
53. Lester Rodney, *Daily Worker*, September 21, 1937, 6.
54. Lester Rodney, *Daily Worker*, September 27, 1937, 8.
55. Lester Rodney, *Daily Worker*, September 30, 1937, 10.
56. John Kieran, *New York Times*, September 2, 1937, 26.
57. John Kieran, *New York Times*, September 3, 1937, 22.
58. John Kieran, *New York Times*, September 10, 1937, 32.
59. John Kieran, *New York Times*, September 13, 1937, 28.
60. Roscoe McGowen, *New York Times*, September 12, 1937, 57.
61. Roscoe McGowen, *New York Times*, September 19, 1937, 77.

CHAPTER 4

Bob Dole and the Brooklyn Dodgers

Raymond I. Schuck

On September 17, 1996, starting pitcher Hideo Nomo of the Los Angeles Dodgers pitched a no-hitter while defeating the Colorado Rockies 9–0. Two days later, Republican presidential candidate Bob Dole opened a speech in the West Hills section of Los Angeles with reference to Nomo's no-hitter. In the reference, Dole said, "I'm going to be like Nomo. I am going to pitch a no-hitter from now until November 5." Dole then added, "The Brooklyn Dodgers had a no-hitter last night, and I'm going to follow what Nomo did. And we are going to wipe them out, between now and November 5."[1] In using this statement to compare his campaign to Nomo's performance, Dole misrepresented a significant aspect of the no-hitter by referencing the Brooklyn Dodgers. Nomo played for the Los Angeles Dodgers, not the Brooklyn Dodgers, who had ceased to exist nearly forty years earlier, when the franchise moved to Los Angeles between the 1957 and 1958 seasons. In the days that followed, Dole's reference provided fodder for humor at his expense, while the statement was also used as a means through which to critique Dole, particularly on the grounds that his reference to the Brooklyn Dodgers illustrated that he was lost in the past and out of touch with American society in the mid–1990s. Meanwhile, some accounts defended Dole's reference, suggesting that Dole's use of the Brooklyn Dodgers associated him with some positively-valued aspects of American culture that the Brooklyn Dodgers signified, the most prominent of which was an idyllic version of the American past that was seen as simpler and, thus, better than the present. In reaction to the discourse surrounding Dole's reference, Dole's campaign attempted to justify his reference by suggesting that it was deliberate, stating that Dole had been joking in saying the Dodgers were in Brooklyn and that the reference constituted "a little mirth."[2]

This instance does not appear to have been particularly significant to the outcome of Dole's campaign, as Dole trailed Democrat incumbent Bill Clinton by a large margin throughout the election. Indeed, some have argued that the re-election of Bill Clinton was never in doubt from the time that Dole became the Republican candidate.[3] However, the reference was not easily and quickly forgotten. A couple weeks after the election, syndicated columnist Art Buchwald, while describing fictional scenarios for what principal players from the election were doing post-election, wrote, "Bob Dole is now commander of the Topeka, Kan., American Legion Post No. 6. He's working to get a tax cut for members and also to bring the Brooklyn Dodgers to Kansas."[4] The following spring, while reporting on Bill Clinton speaking to a classroom about Jackie Robinson integrating baseball with the Brooklyn Dodgers, an article in *The Pacific Stars and Stripes* began with the line "Finally, the answer 'Brooklyn Dodgers' was the correct one" and followed that line with mention of Dole's reference to the Brooklyn Dodgers and the "ribbing" that Dole took.[5] Even nearly twelve years after Dole made the reference, some accounts continued to mention it. For example, in a piece from June 9, 2008, reporting on the lack of enthusiastic campaign slogans by 2008 presidential contestants, *San Francisco Chronicle* political writer Carla Marinucci noted that Bill Clinton's 1996 slogan "Building a Bridge to the 21st Century" worked because it was "a dramatic forward-looking contrast to the far-older GOP candidate Bob Dole, who slipped and once talked about the 'Brooklyn Dodgers' on the campaign trail."[6]

Dole isn't the only politician to have made an incorrect reference involving baseball. Pat Brown, while running for governor of California and not wanting to offend fans of either the Los Angeles Dodgers or the San Francisco Giants, once said that he wanted the two teams to meet in the World Series, which cannot happen, since both play in the National League.[7] On a more national stage, in 2004 Democrat John Kerry would also face criticism while running for president for being out of touch with American culture after erring in a baseball reference. When asked which Red Sox player was his favorite, the Massachusetts senator and self-proclaimed Red Sox fan replied "Manny Ortez"—a name that both combined the names of the 2004 Red Sox's two most prominent hitters, Manny Ramirez and David Ortiz, and misspoke one of their names.[8] Yet, among these examples, Dole's reference to the Brooklyn Dodgers is particularly significant for what it can illuminate about the intersection of politics and baseball. Because Dole referenced the Brooklyn Dodgers, his statement, either mistakenly or jokingly, drew upon a prominent signifier from American culture that carries with it both its own specific connections to American identity and connections that draw upon the more generalized associations of baseball to American identity. As such, Dole's reference engaged with a significant source of meaning in American culture that had the potential to serve as a form of cultural capital that could connect Dole with the American public that he wished to serve. At the same time, though, because of the context of his reference, the meaning of the Brooklyn Dodgers also provided a means of portraying Dole as out of touch with the American public. While the reference may not have done much in this instance to change perceptions of Dole, it did serve to reinforce such perceptions, whether they were positive or negative in their assessment of his ability to lead on a national level. As such, Bob Dole's reference to the Brooklyn Dodgers during his 1996 presidential campaign illustrates a significant aspect of the relationship between baseball and politics. The reference shows how baseball serves as a significant means through which the political identities of national politicians are advanced and maintained, both through connection to cultural associations with the game of baseball itself and through connection with cultural meanings that are associated with specific entities from American baseball to which politicians refer. In the process, the practices of making the references and then using the references as significant means of characterizing the identities and qualities of candidates reinforce the status of baseball as a significant part of American identity, while also reinforcing the ideological connections upon which that connection of baseball to American identity rests.

Dole's Reference as Cultural Capital

On the one hand, Dole's reference contained the potential to serve as a form of cultural capital, or "a form of knowledge, an internalized code or a cognitive acquisition which equips the social agent with social empathy towards, appreciation for or competence in deciphering cultural relations and cultural artifacts."[9] Both on the national level and on more localized levels, references to baseball have historically served as instances through which American political candidates assert their identification with the communities that they hope to represent. On a more localized level, for instance, much discourse surrounded Hillary Clinton's use of references to rooting for the New York Yankees as she campaigned in 2000 to represent the state of New York in the United States Senate, including concerns that the expressions were a transparent ruse to show communality with New Yorkers.[10] Nationally, endorsements by major league baseball players have been utilized by presidential candidates ranging from Babe Ruth's public support of Democratic presidential candidate Al Smith in 1928 through Curt Schilling's 2007 public endorsement of Republican presidential candidate John McCain.[11] Additionally, many presidential candidates have made use of references to American baseball or to specific baseball teams, both as a way to characterize themselves and as a way to characterize opponents.[12] These references potentially illustrate both a form of knowledge and a type of empathy toward deciphering social relations. The references can convey that the candidate knows the workings and significance of American baseball, while they can also convey empathy in the form of communality with the individuals whom the candidate hopes to represent. On localized levels, these references are meant to reflect communality with states, cities, or local governments in distinction from others; on the national level, the references are meant to reflect communality with the United States in distinction from other nations.

To some degree, such baseball references are representative of the prominent practice of referencing any sport. Beyond just baseball, many sports can serve as rhetorical resources through which individuals attempt to make connections to groups, causes, etc. For politicians, this means that sport can serve to illustrate connectedness and communality with their constituencies.[13] However, baseball offers specific attachment to American identity because of the cultural associations that have historically been identified with the game. This attachment is conveyed in the film *Field of Dreams*, when renowned but reclusive writer Terence Mann says to the story's protagonist, Ray Kinsella, "The one constant through all the years, Ray, has been baseball. America has rolled by like an army of steamrollers. It's been erased like a blackboard, rebuilt, and erased again. But baseball has marked the time. This field, this game — it's a part of our past, Ray. It reminds us of all that once was good and could be again."[14] The statement summarizes much of the film's main argument that through everything that has happened since the mid–1800s in the United States of America, baseball has provided a stable, reliable framework for American identity and American culture. Notable within this connection is the reference to the past. Baseball is considered representative of a past that is seen as good and, often, better than the present. What constitutes the society of the past that is celebrated is left rather nebulous (and, thus, also polysemous) in a kind of nostalgic haze that appears in many other works that preach the significance of baseball in American culture. Still, this idealized image of the American past, like the connection of baseball to American identity, often rests on beliefs that, as Nick Trujillo and Leah R. Ekdom have suggested in an analysis of American sports writing, are based in schemas that make sense of the interplay of oppositions such as winning and losing, tradition and change, teamwork and individualism, work and play, experience and youth, and logic and luck.[15] Often, this nostalgic rhetoric implies that the "good old days" of the past of both baseball and the United States maintained schemas that much more effectively balanced these oppositions. Jeremiads about losses of such things as work ethic, tradition, and teamwork often prominently accompany these connections of baseball with an idyllic American past. Mann's statement itself offers such a jeremiad, asserting the need for Americans to be reminded of what in the past was once good and, thus, by implication is lacking in the present, but is still available to be reclaimed.[16]

References to baseball thus provide cultural capital as they offer the possibility of drawing upon these connections to American identity and an idyllic American past. When the Brooklyn Dodgers are the object of reference, these connections are heightened by the specific meanings that have become prominently associated with the Brooklyn Dodgers in American culture. Many of these meanings are featured in a passage by Dan Riley in the introduction to the book *The Dodgers Reader*, which contains a collection of excerpts and manuscripts from various sources to represent the Dodgers, both in Brooklyn and Los Angeles, and their cultural meaning. According to Riley, "Being of both East Coast and West Coast, being of both the old, homogeneous America and the new, multicultural one, being of both noble experimentation and self-aggrandizing opportunism, the Dodger character in many ways symbolizes the national character. Up, first, from the white working class neighborhoods of urban America, struggling for identity and respectability, then emerging strong at mid-century and turning a rich, multicolored face to the World, then following the inevitable American move west, El Dorado pursued more eagerly then any pennant, and finally settling into a haze of hyped-up happiness."[17] While Riley is also discussing the Los Angeles Dodgers, many of the cultural associations with the Brooklyn Dodgers are mentioned in this passage. The Brooklyn Dodgers represent the East Coast of the United States, a homogeneous society of the United States' past, "noble experimentation" toward multiculturalism, white working-class neighborhoods in the United States, urban populations in the United States, the Western geographical movement of the United States, and, ultimately, in large part because of these other associations, the national character of the United States itself. That sense that the Brooklyn Dodgers represent American national character has also been expressed elsewhere, within numerous accounts that associate the team explicitly with American identity, most directly when the Brooklyn Dodgers have been called "the original America's team."[18] Among other things, then, the Brooklyn Dodgers signify both American identity and the American past.[19]

Memories of the Brooklyn Dodgers along these lines were at a particularly high level around the time of Dole's reference, perhaps even contributing to a cultural environment that fostered the belief that the American public might identify with the "good old days" rhetoric that Dole used. The early to mid–1990s witnessed a series of prominent accounts of public memorializing of the team and the borough of Brooklyn that included a series of memoirs and histories of the team, perhaps most prominently represented by the

1997 publication of Doris Kearns Goodwin's *Wait Till Next Year: A Memoir*, which recalled her childhood growing up a Brooklyn Dodger fan, as well as a series of videos remembering the Brooklyn Dodgers that were produced and aired on ESPN in 1996.[20] Even more culturally prominent was the way in which the Brooklyn Dodgers were featured in Ken Burns's widely-acclaimed *Baseball* miniseries, which aired on Public Broadcasting in 1994. *Baseball* opened with a three-paragraph account of the history of the Brooklyn Dodgers that reflected many of the cultural significations prominently attributed to the team. The placement of the story of the Brooklyn Dodgers at the beginning of the miniseries implied that the story of the Brooklyn Dodgers to a significant degree represented the most important aspects through which the game of baseball was intertwined with the history of the United States—an intertwining that was a fundamental premise that the miniseries sought to demonstrate. Such an implication was representative of the kinds of connections that dominated this surge in public memory of the team. When Bob Dole referenced the Brooklyn Dodgers, the cultural knowledge upon which his reference drew appeared within the context of this surge in memory of the team and drew upon the prominent associations that undergirded both that surge and the more lasting cultural prominence of the team. In this way, Dole's reference potentially served as a form of cultural capital that could endear him to the American public by showing that he understands significant aspects of American culture and identity.

The occurrence of this kind of cultural capital in connection with Dole's reference to the Brooklyn Dodgers is illustrated by a piece by Calvin Trillin from the October 4, 1996, issue of *Time* magazine. As Trillin wrote,

> I was not among those who jumped on Bob Dole for referring to the National League team that plays in Los Angeles as the Brooklyn Dodgers. I know what it's like to mention Carl DeRose, the sore-armed right-hander who pitched a perfect game for the Blues in 1947, and draw nothing but puzzled looks from people who call themselves baseball fans.
>
> In fact, when Dole spoke at the convention about the glories of a simpler America, I allowed myself to think, just for a moment, that maybe if he got in he'd issue some sort of Executive Order forcing all professional baseball teams to return to their cities of origin forthwith.[21]

Here, Dole's reference to the Brooklyn Dodgers was celebrated because it connects Dole with a sentiment of wanting to bring back an idealized version of American society from the past that the author saw as "simpler" and, for all intents and purposes, better. The association of Dole with an idyllic past is also reflected in a column for *The New York Times* from September 20, 1996, titled "Subtle Ploy: Dole Cites Beloved Bums." In the column, Clyde Haberman, in at least somewhat tongue-in-cheek fashion, offered an argument for why Dole's reference was not a mistake at all, but a ploy to woo voters, especially in New York. As Haberman explained the ploy, "By conjuring up the Brooklyn Dodgers, who last took the field in 1957, Mr. Dole offers himself as a bridge — that word should be ready for retirement soon — to an era lost in nostalgic mist. He will bring us back to a dreamy Age of Pericles on the Hudson, recalled by many as a time when the city reigned supreme in noble spheres of human endeavor, baseball included, with at least one New York team making it to the World Series every year. Who wouldn't want those days back?"[22] Haberman added that the reference builds off a comment from Dole from earlier in the year in which Dole described his time in Brooklyn in 1943–1944 in an Army study program as "heaven." Haberman also adds that, since the Brooklyn Dodgers were the team that integrated major league baseball, the reference potentially draws the votes of African Americans, who otherwise tend to vote for Democrats. Even given the tongue-in-cheek aspects of Haberman's account, it does illustrate, along with Trillin's fantasy, how Dole's reference might reflect a sentiment about returning to the past with which some people agreed. In the process, Dole's reference served as a form of cultural capital that identified Dole as part of a community with these individuals by conveying that he had the knowledge and empathies that demonstrated inclusion in that community.

Disciplining Dole

For as much as Dole's reference might have served to draw upon a form of cultural capital, numerous responses to the reference, including those that ridiculed the reference, suggest that the reference reinforced the sense that Dole was out of touch with American society in the 1990s. Commonly, individuals poked fun at Dole's reference. Shortly after the reference, a sign in Chico, California, greeted Dole with the statement "Welcome to Brooklyn, Bob."[23] Members of the press also joined in the fun. For instance, the September 30, 1996, issue of *Sports Illustrated* ran a short sidebar featuring pencils of defunct National Football League and National Hockey League teams. The caption alongside the photograph read, "Bob Dole may have put the Dodgers back in Brooklyn last week, but as these pencils (still in stores) show, he's not the only one with a skewed sports compass."[24] Even some contemporary Dodgers got in on the act. Eric Karros, then the Dodgers' starting first baseman, said, "Wow, it's just outstanding to be playing for the Brooklyn Dodgers. My dad was a big fan of the Brooklyn Dodgers, and now that I'm playing for Brooklyn, I'm just sure I've made his day."[25]

Beyond simply poking fun at Dole, numerous accounts characterized Dole's reference to the "Brooklyn Dodgers" as emblematic of some aspect of

Dole's identity. While the *Sports Illustrated* caption focused just on Dole's sports knowledge, which it characterized as "skewed," other accounts connected the reference beyond sports. In a quotation that was carried by newspapers around the country, *The Columbia (S.C.) State* suggested that "while it was a mirthful reference, some voters might view this as a too-serious attempt by Dole to fulfill his pledge to be a bridge to the past."[26] This comment implies concern that Dole being too connected to the past might negatively affect his ability to lead the country. Other accounts offer similar sentiments, including an Associated Press report that suggested that Dole's reference to the Brooklyn Dodgers "calls attention to his age of 73," as well as a column by Chuck Raasch in the *North Hills News-Record* that asserted that through this reference Dole "dates himself," and a short in the *Seattle Times* claimed the reference as evidence that Dole is "out of touch."[27] Combining poking fun at Dole with a greater critique of the Republican candidate, humorist Mark Russell suggested that in the October 6, 1996, presidential debate, Bob Dole "will either dazzle the nation with an articulate and comprehensive grasp of the issues presented in a compelling manner — or he will be himself."[28] While indicating other things that would constitute Dole being himself, Russell noted that Dole should not mention the Brooklyn Dodgers or a number of other things that signify the 1940s–1950s, like "the Andrews Sisters, his old Studebaker, [and] recommend[ing] statehood for Hawaii."[29] Here, the commentary expands upon the idea that Dole is too connected to the past, offering explanation for the concern by characterizing Dole as the opposite of having "an articulate and comprehensive grasp of the issues."

A more detailed explanation of the significance of Dole's reference was provided by *New York Times* columnist Maureen Dowd. In a piece titled "The Artless Dodger," Dowd offered recognition of both the potential cultural capital of a reference to the Brooklyn Dodgers and the reasons to be concerned about Dole's reference. As Dowd wrote,

> His gaffe was an expression of a deep truth, of a reflexive idealism. It was the same spirit that caused Russia to change the name of Leningrad back to St. Petersburg.
>
> Such a slip can be forgiven, even celebrated, if Mr. Dole was saying that he would prefer to live in a world where people honor their roots and don't betray fans for crassly commercial reasons.
>
> If he were really revealing his desire for a better world, a world in which the Dodgers are always in Brooklyn, in which the Avenue of the Americas is always Sixth Avenue, and the differently abled are just people with disabilities, that would be attractive.
>
> But I fear that it's just another measure of Bob Dole's disassociation, more evidence that this is a man who goes home and sits in a dark room, flipping back and forth between C-Span 1 and C-Span 2, failing to absorb any sensation or experience that isn't parliamentary.[30]

Here, Dowd acknowledged the potential usefulness of harkening on the kind of past that the Brooklyn Dodgers often signify in American culture, yet Dowd suggested that given the context and manner of its usage, Dole's reference to the Brooklyn Dodgers is the mark of an individual who is not just wanting to bring back aspects of a society from the past, but who is, as Dowd later states, "stuck in" the past. Dowd implies that Dole draws so much on the past that he is unable to comprehend fully and adequately the issues of the present and, thus, he would be unable to lead effectively in the present or, to use one of the most prominent metaphors of the 1996 presidential race, Dole would be ineffective at building a bridge to the reclaimed past that he hopes to achieve.

These associations of Bob Dole with being lost in the past and, thus, disconnected with American society in the mid–1990s reflect themes that dominated representations of Bob Dole during the 1996 presidential campaign. Voters voiced concern about Dole's age and the potential ramifications of his age.[31] Age and the implications of age constituted a consistent theme in media coverage of the election as well, as accounts discussed its relevance to Dole's ability to lead and as accounts much more often referred to Dole's age than they did with the other candidates.[32] These themes were reinforced by the Clinton campaign's more effective use of the "bridge" metaphor, as Clinton invoked the metaphor "to contrast his move toward the future with Dole's retreat to the past," while "Dole's discourse, while at times discussing the future, focused primarily on the past and explicitly rejected a foundation of monetary gain and concern for the economy."[33]

As Dole's reference was used as a means of suggesting that Dole was out of touch with American society, the responses to Dole's statement served as a form of disciplining both Dole in particular and national politicians in general. As Michael L. Butterworth has suggested, "Baseball may be used ideologically to discipline the notion of what is 'American' and, consequently, what is not."[34] Butterworth focuses on how "ballpark rituals participated in a discursive formation that defined Americans not only by who they are, but by who they are not. Understood as a constitutive force of American identity, baseball helped reproduce the boundaries that define what it means to be 'American' and justified further the need for a foreign policy motivated by (real or imaginary) external dangers."[35] Such recognition of the rhetorical and ideological roles of baseball might be extended to the discourse of presidential candidates. While a presidential candidate may not be expected to know minute details of American baseball, clearly he or she is expected to know some of the grander narratives and more significant aspects of American baseball and its history. Certainly, in other kinds of situations lack of such knowledge has been used as a litmus test for being American. As interviewees in Studs Terkel's *The Good War* have attested, American soldiers in the European front during World War II would identify German spies by their lack of knowledge of baseball in general and the Brooklyn Dodgers in particular.[36] While the application of such a litmus test for American identity might or might not apply to national politicians (with this perhaps depending on context as well), at the very least lack of baseball knowledge certainly appears to be cause to call into question the degree to which one understands and connects with American society. While Dole incorrectly referenced the Brooklyn Dodgers, this actually provided the basis for connecting to American identity, as it asserted connection with an entity that has been prominently linked with American character and American history; however, reference to the entity as if it existed in the present, when it ceased to exist nearly forty years earlier, provided a means through which to call into question Dole's ability to lead in the present, thereby disciplining Dole and, at the very least, forcing an explanation of the reference that attempted to convey that he did recognize the reality of the present. In this case, such explanation appeared in the form of asserting that Dole was in the know the whole time and that the reference was a joke that was meant to convey that. As a disciplinary measure, discourse that critiqued Dole on the basis of his reference reflected how cultural capital could work to exclude on the basis of what is or is not shown to be known, reflecting the process by which, as Pierre Bourdieu has suggested, "Art and cultural consumption are predisposed, consciously and deliberately or not, to fulfill a social function of legitimating social differences."[37] In this case, Dole was identified through his reference as different from what many individuals expected in a presidential candidate and a representative of an American national community. For those who critiqued Dole, that difference consisted of being out of touch with contemporary American society and, thus, unfit to lead it.

The Implied Significance of Baseball

While Dole's reference served, depending on one's disposition, as capital or as a means for discipline, both the capitalizing and disciplinary aspects of the event maintain a similar base that illuminates an important aspect of the convergence of baseball and politics: that knowledge of significant aspects of American baseball constitutes one of the expectations to hold national political office. In the process, Dole's reference and other baseball references by presidential candidates reinforce two other important aspects of the role of baseball in American society. First, they reinforce the prominence of baseball in the United States. By implying that knowledge of the significant aspects of American baseball is a necessary requirement to lead the country, continuing practices of referencing baseball by presidential candidates and continuing practices of scrutinizing these references reinforce the status of baseball as a significant and important part of American identity and American society. Second, and in part by virtue of the first aspect, these same practices reinforce the ideological components of baseball's attachment to American identity. They suggest that values that are associated with baseball are fundamental to the United States itself, whether these values involve beliefs about work, beliefs about competition, beliefs about the social order, or other sets of beliefs. In the specific case of the Brooklyn Dodgers, references to the team and scrutiny over the use of such references reinforce the ideological affirmations that are embedded in the prominence that is given to the Brooklyn Dodgers as cultural signifiers, especially as the team is portrayed as emblematic of the United States, of American baseball, and of idealized visions of the history of the United States.

Ultimately, Bob Dole's reference to the Brooklyn Dodgers provided a means for mocking Dole, a means for identifying with Dole, and a means for critiquing Dole. Dole himself seemed to take all of this in stride, even joking about the incident after the election. In a form letter to reporters who had covered his campaign, Dole included the line, "In any event, please let me know if I can ever be of assistance — maybe get you tickets to a Brooklyn Dodgers game."[38] This line is representative of a sense of humor that Dole has shown throughout his political career, in which he has very readily made fun of himself.[39] The line also reinforces once again the significance of the reference, since it works off the premise that his reference had not been forgotten. Additionally, the line further illustrates the significance of baseball as a form of knowledge that is expected of national politicians. This line was, perhaps, Dole's way of responding to the disciplining that his reference received by reasserting his cultural capital. With the line, not only did Dole articulate his knowledge of the Brooklyn Dodgers, by humorously alluding to his previous reference he articulated his recognition of the requirement that presidential candidates exhibit knowledge of prominent aspects of American baseball. Whether Dole's initial reference was intentional or made in error, the line in his letter was clearly in the know and, as such, further cemented the expectation that national politicians in the United States know baseball.

Dole's reference, his subsequent allusion to his reference, and the discourse that surrounded Dole's reference might, then, illustrate, in part, why national politicians have gotten involved in American baseball issues from antitrust legislation to labor negotiations to performance-enhancing substances. To get involved, even amid criticism for interfering and grandstanding, demonstrates knowledge and concern for a realm of activity that has time and again been affiliated with American identity; not to get involved potentially indicates a lack of connection with the American public. Getting involved protects an investment: the cultural capital provided by American baseball. Yet, as the case of Bob Dole illustrates, the use of that capital carries with it the potential for discipline as well.

Notes

1. Adam Nagourney, "Dole Delivers a No-No to the Glory Days of Brooklyn," http://query.nytimes.com/gst/fullpage.html?res=9404E3D61F3AF93AA2575AC0A960958260 (accessed 30 June 2008), ¶ 4.
2. "Dole Loses Grip on Campaign Pitch," *Syracuse Herald-Journal*, 20 September 1996, A2.
3. Paul S. Herrnson and Clyde Wilcox, "The 1996 Presidential Election: A Tale of a Campaign That Didn't Seem to Matter," in *Toward the Millennium: The Elections of 1996*, ed. Larry J. Sabato (Boston: Allyn and Bacon, 1997), 121.
4. Art Buchwald, "Where are the Pols of Yesterday?" *Annapolis Capital*, 20 November 1996, A14.
5. "Clinton Plays to the Home Crowd," *Pacific (Tokyo) Stars and Stripes*, 17 April 1997, 31.
6. Carla Marinucci, "Candidates' Pitches Lack Punch, Experts Say," http://www.sfgate.com/cgi-bin/article.cgi?f=/c/a/2008/06/08/MN5I114OH2.DTL (accessed 30 June 2008), ¶ 35.
7. Lou Cannon, "Sense of Humor is Candidates' Best Friend," *Chicago Daily Herald*, 24 September 1996, sec. 1, p. B.
8. This reference was followed later in the campaign season with a well-publicized error in making a prominent football reference as well, as Kerry mistakenly called the stadium of the Green Bay Packers "Lambert Field" instead of "Lambeau Field."
9. Pierre Bourdieu, *The Field of Cultural Production*, ed. Randal Johnson (New York: Columbia University Press, 1993), 7.
10. "Repeating Clinton Yankees Myth, Matthews Asked: '[D]oesn't She Know She Looks Like a Fraud,'" http://mediamatters.org/items/200710260010 (accessed 30 June 2008).
11. For more on Babe Ruth's public endorsements of Al Smith, see Robert W. Creamer, *Babe: The Legend Comes to Life* (New York: Simon & Schuster, 1974); and Marshall Smelser, *The Life that Ruth Built* (Lincoln: University of Nebraska Press, 1975). For more on Curt Schilling's endorsement of John McCain, see "Dec. 5 — Curt Schilling Campaigns with John McCain," http://www.johnmccain.com/ste/EventDetail.aspx?guid=e0726c98-10b5-4eb7-ac10-14cd388a72a9 (accessed 30 June 2008).

12. For numerous examples of presidential references to baseball, see "U.S. Presidents & Major League Baseball," http://www.baseball-almanac.com/prz_menu.shtml (accessed 30 June 2008).

13. Raymond I. Schuck, "Off the Field: The Integration of Major League Baseball as a Rhetorical Resource," *Journal of Communication Studies*, forthcoming.

14. *Field of Dreams*, dir. Phil Alden Robinson, 107 min., Universal, 1989, motion picture.

15. Nick Trujillo and Leah R. Ekdom, "Sportswriting and American Cultural Values: The 1984 Chicago Cubs," *Critical Studies in Mass Communication*, 2 (1985): 262–281.

16. It should be noted that these versions of the past are idealized in ways that often fail to recognize the politics that they embody. The idyllic American past that is being recalled perpetuates racism, sexism, and homophobia by positing the value of a society in which white, male, and heterosexual identities remained much less challenged in their assertions of authority than they have been since. This idyllic past both implicitly and, at times, explicitly delegitimizes gains toward equality that have developed since the 1940s and 1950s, in large part as a result of the Civil Rights Movement, the feminist movement, the gay rights movement, and other social movements.

17. Dan Riley, introduction to *The Dodgers Reader* (Boston: Houghton Mifflin, 1992), xi.

18. Riley, for instance, writes, "With apologies to the PR depts. of Dallas Cowboys and Atlanta Braves, the Dodgers come closer than either or any other to truly being America's Team" (Riley, xi). Also, the phrase is connected to the team in *The Brooklyn Dodgers: The Original America's Team*, 300 min., Hart Sharp

video, in conjunction with the ESPN television network, 2005, 2-disc DVD set.

19. Notable in Riley's passage is that the past is not explicitly characterized as idyllic by calling it "good" or "better than the present"; however, the exclusions and marginalizations of the past are indicated implicitly by recognizing that the past that the Brooklyn Dodgers signify is "homogeneous" and, thus, filled with a large degree of similarity among people. Riley's passage alludes to a major similarity later when Riley notes that it is the *white* working-class neighborhoods that the Brooklyn Dodgers represented. In other words, the image of the past that the Brooklyn Dodgers represent is one built on white identity, white culture, and affirmation of all people subverting themselves to a homogeneous society based in white cultural authority.

20. See Doris Kearns Goodwin, *Wait Till Next Year: A Memoir* (New York: Simon & Schuster, 1997); and *The Last Trolley: A Tale of Two Cities*, 60 min., Capital Cities/ABC Video Publishing, Inc., 1996, videorecording. Other memoirs, histories, and celebrations of the team from the time period include Richard Goldstein, *Superstars and Screwballs: 100 Years of Brooklyn Baseball* (New York: Plume, 1991); Peter C. Bjarkman, *The Brooklyn Dodgers* (Secaucus, NJ: Chartwell, 1992); Larry King, with Marty Appel, *When You're From Brooklyn, Everything Else is Tokyo* (Boston: Little, Brown, 1992); Bruce Chadwick and David M. Spindel, *The Dodgers: Memories and Memorabilia From Brooklyn to L.A.* (New York: Abbeville Press, 1993); Wilfrid Sheed, *My Life as a Fan* (New York: Simon and Schuster, 1993); Myrna Katz Frommer and Harvey Frommer, *It Happened in Brooklyn: An Oral History of Growing up in the Borough in the 1940s, 1950s, and 1960s* (New York: Harcourt Brace, 1993); *The 1955 Brooklyn Dodgers: Yesterday's Heroes Come Alive in a Tribute to an Unforgettable Team*, (New York: New York Daily News, 1995); Stewart Wolpin, *Bums No More! The Championship Season of the 1955 Brooklyn Dodgers* (New York: Harkavy Press, 1995); and Ellen M. Snyder-Grenier, *Brooklyn! An Illustrated History* (Philadelphia: Temple University Press, 1996). In addition to these works, a more academic treatment of the history and meaning of the Brooklyn Dodgers appeared at this time in Carl E. Prince, *Brooklyn's Dodgers: The Bums, the Borough, and the Best of Baseball 1947–1957* (New York: Oxford University Press, 1996).

21. Calvin Trillin, "Playing Catch-Up Ball," *Time*, 4 November 1996, 21.

22. Clyde Haberman, "Subtle Ploy: Dole Cites Beloved Bums," *New York Times*, 20 September 1996, sec. B, p. 1(L).

23. Cannon, sec. 1, p. B; "Dole Loses Grip on Campaign Pitch," A2.

24. Jack McCallum and Richard O'Brien, eds., "Scorecard," *Sports Illustrated*, 30 September 1996, 16.

25. Tom Friend, "Dodgers Now Look South for Their Biggest Rivals," *New York Times*, 22 September 1996, sec. 8, p. 13(L).

26. "What Other Papers are Saying," *Syracuse Herald-Journal*, 28 September 1996, A5.

27. Sunnyside Dole: Dole Still Optimistic Despite Lack of Luck," *Valley* (Monessen, Penn.) *Independent*, 21 September 1996, 4A; Chuck Raasch, "Dole's Campaign Still Stuck in Low Gear," *North Hills* (Warrendale, Penn.) *News Record*, 24 September 1996, A9; "Dole Retreads Anti-Drug Slogan From Reagan Era," http://community.seattletimes.nwsource.com/archive/?date=19960919&slug=2350040 (accessed 30 June 2008), ¶ 7.

28. Mark Russell, "Candidates' Escapades Better than Sunday Funnies," *Chicago Daily Herald*, 6 October 1996, sec. 1, p. 2.

29. Ibid.

30. Maureen Dowd, "The Artless Dodger," *New York Times*, 19 September 1996, A27.

31. Herrnson and Wilcox, 132.

32. Herbert L. Abrams and Richard Brody, "Bob Dole's Age and Health in the 1996 Election: Did the Media Let Us Down?" *Political Science Quarterly*, 113 (1998): 471–491.

33. William L. Benoit, "Framing Through Temporal Metaphor: The 'Bridges' of Bob Dole and Bill Clinton in their 1996 Acceptance Addresses," *Communication Studies*, 52 (2001): 78.

34. Michael L. Butterworth, "Ritual in the 'Church of Baseball': Suppressing the Discourse of Democracy after 9/11," *Communication and Critical/Cultural Studies*, 2 (2005): 108.

35. Ibid., 109.

36. Studs Terkel, *The Good War* (New York: Pantheon, 1984), 354–355.

37. Pierre Bourdieu, *Distinction: A Social Critique of the Judgment of Taste*, trans. Richard Nice (Cambridge, MA: Harvard University Press, 1984), 7.

38. Bill Tammeus, "They Talked and Talked in '96, and This is What They Said," *Moun-*

tain (Placerville, Calif.) *Democrat*, 2 January 1997, A-6.

39. For more on Dole's use of humor, including the self-deprecating aspects of it, see Charles R. Gruner, "A Rejoinder to Levasseur and Dean on 'The Dole Humor Myth,'" *Southern Communication Journal*, 62 (1997): 153–157.

CHAPTER 5

Are We There Yet? Major League Baseball and Sexual Orientation

Lisa Doris Alexander

The greatest and most memorable moments in sport involve the breaking of barriers—those times when the political sphere intersects with the sporting world. John Carlos and Tommie Smith brought international attention to racism in the United States with their Black Power salute during the 1968 Olympics. Billie Jean King struck a blow for the feminist movement by beating Bobby Riggs in the "Battle of the Sexes" tennis match. Before *Brown v. the Board of Education* which rendered segregated public spaces unconstitutional or Executive Order 9981 which desegregated the armed forces, Jackie Robinson and Larry Doby helped prove that racial integration could work. Throughout the 1990s and 2000s, while the political realm argued over issues involving sexual orientation, same-sex marriage, domestic partner benefits, etc., the sports world seemed largely uninvolved. As of the 2008 season, no U.S. professional male team-sport athlete has come out during his career though Gerry Callahan makes the argument that "baseball, because of the individual nature of the game, would give a gay player the BEST shot at success. The NFL would sooner accept a member of al-Qaeda than an openly gay player."[1] Despite a lack of out active players, Major League Baseball (MLB) has not *completely* ignored the issue, and the League's response to several incidents revolving around sexual orientation may provide clues as to how MLB, which includes players, managers, coaches, and sportswriters, would react to the presence of an out active ballplayer.

The panic concerning gay players in MLB began in earnest in 1999 when former major leaguer Billy Bean's sexual orientation was revealed in a newspaper article. Having been a member of the Tigers, Dodgers, and Padres organizations from 1987 to 1995, Bean wrote in his 1999 autobiography *Going the Other Way* painted a picture of professional baseball which included gay "jokes," slurs, and other symptoms of rampant homophobia. Bean made the argument that, during his playing years, "baseball wasn't ready for a guy like me, no matter how well I played. The game wasn't mature enough to deal with a gay ballplayer."[2] Reaction to Bean's story was mixed. Some players seemed to shrug their shoulders at the thought of a gay teammate, much like Bean's former teammate Brad Ausmus, who was quoted as saying, "It wouldn't have made any difference to me when we played together and it doesn't matter to me now."[3] Others took the opportunity to express their discomfort with the idea, such as Yankees pitcher Andy Pettitte who said, "There would be the question of being comfortable."[4] Bean responded to the reactions within MLB by writing,

> The bonds of teammates, I was learning, were far stronger than prejudice.... The silence from other quarters was deafening. The baseball powers-that-be could not be bothered to call or issue a statement. Bud Selig ... didn't seem to give a damn about the questions my stories raised.[5]

The silence from both the commissioner's office and the Major League Baseball Player's Association (MLBPA) was hardly surprising since the prevailing ideology is that all male athletes in general, and professional baseball players more specifically, are heterosexual which, by consequence, obscures both the presence of gay and bisexual athletes and the underlying homophobic environment within sport/MLB culture.

The possibility of out gay ballplayers and anti-gay sentiments within the clubhouse are interconnected and speculation regarding gay ballplayers did not end with Bean's admission. In the same year Bean began openly discussing his sexual orientation, *Sports Illustrated* ran an interview with former Atlanta closer John Rocker in which he expressed his feelings about a wide variety of topics. When asked about New York City, Rocker stated, "It's the most hectic, nerve-wracking city. Imagine having to take the [Number] 7 train to the ballpark, looking like you're [riding through] Beirut next to some kid with purple hair next to some queer with AIDS right next to some dude who just got out of jail for the fourth time right next to some 20-year-old mom with four kids. It's depressing."[6] The pitcher went on to disparage anyone who was not an English-speaking, heterosexual, white male. Rocker's comments fit the definition of fighting words: "those [words] 'which by their very utterance inflict injury or tend to incite to an immediate breach of peace,' and which are commonly understood to convey direct and visceral hatred or contempt for human beings on the basis of their sex, race, color, handicap, religion, sexual orientation, or national and ethnic origin."[7] In response to Rocker's fighting words, Commissioner Bud Selig suspended the closer for seventy-three days with pay, fined him $20,000, and ordered psychological counseling. There were some who found the punishment too lenient and others who thought it was too harsh. In either case, though Selig was remarkably silent about Bean's account of anti-gay sentiments in the clubhouse; the punishment handed down indicated that Selig would not tolerate fighting words outside the clubhouse. However, when an arbitrator later reduced the suspension to fourteen days and the fine to $500, some believed that MLB was excusing Rocker's racist and homophobic remarks.[8] In responding to Rocker's outburst, Bean wrote that the closer "simply got caught saying what some people think but are afraid to say. It's easier for baseball to blame the outburst on the player than look in the mirror. They need to make it clear that harassment won't be allowed on the field or in the locker room."[9] Granted, Selig's original ruling could be interpreted as cracking down on fighting words and other forms of harassment. If that was the case, then Selig would hand out similar punishments to other players who made racist and/or homophobic remarks. Unfortunately, that did not happen.

Having learned absolutely nothing from John Rocker's public outburst and the resulting condemnation, during the 2001 season, pitcher Julian Tavárez, who was with the Chicago Cubs at the time, called San Francisco Giants fans "a bunch of faggots" after they booed him during a game.[10] Instead of making yet another example out of Tavárez, and living up to Bean's hope that MLB would not tolerate such behavior, the Commissioner went in a different direction. According to *Chicago Sun-Times* columnist Jay Mariotti, Selig "whose heavy-handed stance in the Rocker saga represented some of his finest work, went mushy on Tavarez. He didn't issue a suspension and deferred to the Cubs, who criticized Tavarez, slapped him with a fine and pointed him toward the mound, where he kept his place in the rotation."[11] What makes the punishment, or lack thereof, so ironic is the fact that the Cubs have one of the longest track records of any major league franchise of embracing their gay, lesbian, and bisexual base (GLB) base.[12]

Rocker and Tavárez were not the only people within the baseball establishment to utter fighting words. In 2007 the ongoing feud between White Sox manager Ozzie Guillén and *Sun-Times* columnist Jay Mariotti devolved in a very public fashion. While Mariotti had a habit of calling Frank Thomas "the big skirt" and referring to former Cubs pitcher LaTroy Hawkins as LaToya,[13] Guillén upped the ante by calling Mariotti a "f--king fag."[14] Guillén was quick to apologize to the GLB community, but not to Mariotti and the manager was fined an undisclosed amount and ordered to attend sensitivity training.[15] While one tirade could be characterized as the ignorance of that individual, three outbursts—that the press reported—signal a larger problem. The Rocker, Tavárez, and Guillén comments, as well as the accompanying minimal penalties, were not simply isolated and unconnected incidents, they reflect a more overarching heterosexist and homophobic environment present in MLB. The utterance, publication, and acceptance of fighting words sends the message that gay players are not wanted in MLB and if they are already present, they should stay in the closet.

Two years after the Bean and Rocker stories broke, MLB once again found itself entangled with sexual politics. In 2001, *Out* magazine editor-in-chief Brendan Lemon wrote in an editorial that "for the past year and a half, I have been having an affair with a pro baseball player from a major-league East Coast franchise, not his team's biggest star but a very recognizable media figure all the same."[16] After Lemon's admission, sportswriters again seized the opportunity to discuss how an openly gay athlete would be received by teammates and fans. Sports talk radio host Jim Rome posed the question about teammate reaction to baseball veteran Eric Davis, who replied,

> I think it would go real bad. I think people would jump to form an opinion because everybody already has an opinion about gays already. But I think it would be a very difficult situation because with us showering with each other ... being around each other as men. Now you're in the shower with a guy who's gay ... looking at you ... maybe making a pass. That's an uncomfortable situation.[17]

Davis's remarks echoed comments made earlier by Andy Pettite and others in response to Bean's book. Concerns expressed by players had little to do with on-field production or fan reaction and had more to do with the prospect of being hit-on by a teammate. Attempting to debunk the notion that baseball players are somehow irresistible to both males and females, Bean responded by writing,

> It infuriates me to think that players would actually believe that a gay teammate would be any less serious about his job than they are. It takes a huge amount of work to reach the majors, and I wonder if they really believe a player would sacrifice his career for a cheap thrill. Being gay doesn't mean you lack self-control.[18]

In the months following Lemon's editorial, the discussion surrounding the possibility of an out ballplayer remained fairly abstract since no active player had come out in response to the editorial. The discussion moved from abstract to specific following a 2002 interview with Mets manager Bobby Valentine in *Details* magazine. When asked whether or not baseball was ready for an openly gay player, Valentine replied, "The players are a diverse enough group now that I think they could handle it."[19] Shortly after Valentine's interview was published, *New York Post* gossip columnist Neal Travis framed Valentine's statement as a "pre-emptory strike" due to "a persistent rumor around town that one Mets star who spends a lot of time with pretty models in clubs is actually gay and has started to think about declaring his sexual orientation."[20] Though Travis's column did not name names, it was clear to many that Travis was referring to Mike Piazza. According to *Pittsburg Post-Gazette* sports columnist Ron Cook, Travis "didn't have to [mention Piazza]. He's the only Mets star who fits that description"[21] since it was common knowledge that the catcher had a weakness for club-hopping with supermodels and Playboy Playmates. There was no question in sportswriters' or fans' minds that Travis's article was referring to Piazza.

It took less than twenty-four hours for Piazza to respond. The catcher held an impromptu press conference prior to a game in Philadelphia where he declared, "First off, I'm not gay. I'm heterosexual. That's pretty much it. That's pretty much all I can say. I don't see the need to address the issue further."[22] Piazza went on to state, "In this day and age, it would be irrelevant. If the guy is doing his job on the field ... I don't think there would be any problem at all."[23] On some level Piazza's comments seem disingenuous because if a player's sexual orientation would be irrelevant as he claims, why go to the trouble of holding a press conference to publicly proclaim his heterosexuality? Though the catcher did not feel the need to address the issue further following the press conference, other baseball players, managers, and journalists continued to ponder whether MLB was ready for an openly gay player. Former Phillies manager Larry Bowa remarked, "I'd probably wait until my career was over. If he hits .340, it probably would be easier than if he hits .220."[24] This sentiment underscored the notion that production on the field is far more important than life off the field. When asked whether or not he would accept a gay teammate, Yankees pitcher Mike Mussina replied, "I'm going to make the assumption that I already have, that there already is a player like that out there. I don't have any problems with it. It's part of society."[25] Mussina's comments underscored an important point that was missing from the discussion thus far: there have always been gay athletes in professional baseball, even, possibly, on the vaunted New York Yankees.

In the wake of Piazza's actions, sport journalists shifted the focus of their writing from hypothesizing about gay player's identities to asking whether or not a player's sexual orientation was cause for a press conference. Most columnists agreed that the *Post* column, which could not be substantiated, did not deserve this much attention; however, the lack of evidence did not stop anyone from writing about it. Some, like *San Francisco Chronicle* columnist Bruce Jenkins questioned Piazza's tactics: "You'd think he would just shrug it off, and that the Mets would have no reaction whatsoever."[26] *New York Times* columnist Harvey Araton agreed with Jenkins's puzzlement:

> Irresponsible and unfair as the item in *The New York Post* was, I'm wondering what the Mets accomplished or were even thinking with their unfortunate overreaction. The better response, for the sake of discouraging such future

musings, would have been: You don't have the right to ask unless I want you to know. Instead, we had Piazza, a gentleman, calmly stating, "I'm not gay," in addition to a variety of Mets voicing anger and disgust, including [catcher] Vance Wilson, who chimed in with the gem, "He lives his life morally right." [This] leads me to think, contrary to Valentine's interpretations of baseball's diversity, that the standard antigay expressions so prevalent in our macho sports culture are now merely spoken in a variety of languages.[27]

While some journalists like Araton may have questioned their right to know, many sportswriters continued to comment on the story. At the same time, some sportswriters expressed discomfort with player's homophobic remarks as Araton facetiously referred to Vance Wilson's comment as a gem. Despite the seeming disapproval of homophobic and heterosexist comments, it could be argued that one of the largest obstacles keeping gay ballplayers in the proverbial closet is not teammate reaction but the almost inevitable media frenzy. Due to the public nature of their professions, celebrities (actors, athletes, politicians, etc.), are under constant surveillance by news organizations. Because of this, some celebrities are inclined to regulate their behavior, especially if they believe that their career will be jeopardized if they are outed (whether or not they are actually gay). Gerry Callahan of *The Boston Globe* discussed the ramifications faced by an out athlete, saying, "It would affect his relationship with his teammates, his fans, the media, the advertisers. To think otherwise is to be as naive or as disingenuous as those who ask, 'Who cares?'"[28] In this case the media has the dual purpose of reporting on and regulating celebrity behavior. The constant discussion surrounding "comfort" helps to reproduce the notion that the default sexuality of professional athletes is heterosexual and helps to keep gay and bisexual players in the closet during their careers. The media scrutiny might also help explain why players are more willing to come out after they have left professional sports—if an athlete is no longer in the spotlight, the need to discipline/control their behavior diminishes.

Though the discussion surrounding openly gay players in MLB was tabled after Piazza's press conference, the issue would return less than one year later due to a controversy with Kazuhiro Tadano. According to *Baseball America*'s Chris Kline, "With a 93–94 mph fastball and three quality secondary pitches, [Tadano] was one of the most talented amateur pitchers in Japan [in 2002]."[29] Despite the talent, the right-hander, whom scouts expected to be chosen in the first round of Japan's amateur draft, was not chosen at all. If Tadano was as talented as scouts observed, the pitcher should have been picked up by a major league team; however, despite being close to securing a deal on more than one occasion, that did not happen. Quietly, word circulated that "Tadano (along with several of his college teammates at Rikkyo University) was paid to take part in a pornographic video that contained acts of homosexuality."[30] Coming so soon after the Piazza media circus and Bobby Valentine's declaration that baseball players could handle an openly gay player, multiple clubs passed on signing Tadano, arguably because scouts assumed he was gay.

The discrimination Tadano faced because of his participation in the pornography video is indicative of how scared MLB was of having an out gay player. In this case, the mere hint of homosexuality was enough to keep Tadano out of both the Japanese professional leagues and MLB. After some time, Cleveland signed Tadano to a minor league contract, and the team made it clear that "they would support Tadano when the video became public knowledge."[31] When word of the video finally reached the U. S. sport media, Tadano quickly stated through an interpreter, "I'm not gay. I'd like to clear that fact up right now"[32] and added that he participated in the video as a way to support himself while in school.[33] The fact that several major league clubs initially passed on signing Tadano is not that surprising; neither is the fact that at least one team put winning above other concerns though Tadano's stint in the majors lasted only two seasons. What is interesting is the relative lack of attention Tadano's situation garnered.

The question surrounding Mike Piazza's sexual orientation made national headlines while Tadano's taped homosexual encounter did not illicit the same level of media response. It is possible that sportswriters learned from the Piazza debacle and decided that a player's personal life was off-limits, but there is no evidence to suggest that is the case. The feeding frenzy which ensued in 2007 when former NBA player John Amaechi came out highlights sportswriters' continued interest in players' sexual orientation. There were definite differences between Piazza and Tadano: the former was an already established player in the nation's largest media market, which helps to explain the increased media attention. However, Tadano's struggle paralleled existing controversies which were gaining national attention at the time. Three months after Cleveland signed Tadano, the U.S. Supreme Court ruled that sodomy laws were unconstitutional,[34] and later that same year the Massachusetts Supreme Court ruled that the state's ban on same-sex marriages was unconstitutional.[35] Both decisions were interpreted as steps forward for GLB rights in the United States. Though Tadano quickly affirmed his heterosexuality, the difficulties he faced making it to the majors based on the mere perception of homosexuality coincided with discussions surrounding GLB rights in much the same way the integration of MLB coincided with the civil rights movements during the 1950s and, therefore, could have been framed as a much larger and more influential story than it was.

One of the reasons why Tadano's story was downplayed by sport journalists may have to do with unconscious stereotypes regarding Asian masculinity. Charles R. Lawrence III's notion of unconscious racism hypothesizes that, since racism played a large part in America's shared past, all Americans unconsciously harbor negative opinions about nonwhites. Because society no longer tolerates overt racism the way it once did, the negative attitudes created by the shared racist history will find another outlet.[36] Some of those lingering attitudes concern sexuality and the construction of different masculinities. As Chong-Suk Han points out, "For decades, the mainstream media have usually portrayed Asian men as meek, asexual houseboy types or as sexual deviants of some kind."[37] In the article "Representing and Reconstructing Asian Masculinities," Allen Luke goes further when he writes, "We have all the characteristics of something Other, something more feminine in the normative eye of Western sexuality: slender and relatively hairless bodies, differently textured and colored skin and straight hair. In Western public representations of masculinity we are defined in terms of absence, lack or silence."[38] As Luke points out, Asian men broadly and, by extension, Tadano are the opposite of the masculine ideal. At one point, *Details*, the same magazine that asked Bobby Valentine whether MLB was ready for an out player, "featured an item entitled 'Gay or Asian,' and challenged its readers to ascertain whether a given man was, in fact, gay or Asian"; a situation which highlights how popular media frames Asian masculinity as congruent with homosexuality.[39] These lingering stereotypes meant that not only did it seem as though Tadano's heterosexuality was *not* assumed but questions surrounding the pitcher's sexual orientation were framed as un-newsworthy.

One year after Cleveland signed Tadano to a minor league contract, the Boston Red Sox won their first World Series in over eighty years. Framing themselves as "idiots," the Red Sox often resembled an unkempt Little League team instead of the World Champions. Partly because of the team's increased notoriety following the win and partially due to their scruffy-looking image, several members of the Red Sox agreed to appear on the television series *Queer Eye for the Straight Guy* to raise money for charity. Airing on Bravo beginning in 2003, *Queer Eye*

> is predicated on the basic assumption that straight men are unrefined, ungroomed, and simply need a gay man's help to attain a higher fluency of culture, charm, and sophistication. In each episode, the "fab five"— Carson (fashion), Kyan (grooming), Jai (culture), Thom (interior design), and Ted (food and wine)— inflict their areas of expertise on a hapless straight man, who, more often than not, is depicted as a clueless slob with a good heart and a woman who loves him the way he is but would like to see him improved.[40]

To that end, *Queer Eye* opened its third season by making over five Red Sox players: center fielder Johnny Damon, first baseman Kevin Millar, catchers Doug Mirabelli and Jason Varitek, and pitcher Tim Wakefield. The five were treated to manicures, pedicures, hair treatments, waxing, and fashion makeovers at the team's spring training facility. It is interesting to note that all of the players chosen to participate in the *Queer Eye* episode were white, married, and in addition all but one of the wives were in attendance during the makeovers. Though Mirabelli began the episode with the comment "Who said it was bad to be gay? I am now gay"[41] as he enjoyed a rose petal pedicure, *San Francisco Chronicle* reporter Gwen Knapp noticed that "in a few scenes, a couple of the Red Sox seem uncomfortable, and they're all incredulous that gay celebrities have visited their clubhouse. But the entertainment value of the show hinges on the culture clash between grungy jocks and style gurus."[42] The discomfort Knapp noticed was more amplified in the deleted scenes included on the DVD, which showed Wakefield visibly uncomfortable and agitated at having Carson in his personal space during a fitting.[43] And just prior to the episode being aired, Mirabelli admitted, "We had a lot of fun. But if I had thought about it some more, I'm not sure I would have done it."[44] In interviews after the episode aired, Mirabelli and Millar quickly reminded reporters that the primary rationale behind taping the episode was to raise money to repair a Little League field which was devastated by Hurricane Charley the year before.

Outfielder Johnny Damon, who seemed the least fazed and the most comfortable throughout the episode, discussed the matter with journalists and said, "If there's a gay guy in baseball, we have to help him out, I'd smack him on the butt, just like I do everybody else."[45] Damon's comments appeared less than two months after *Sports Illustrated* released a poll which gauged fan attitudes about homosexuality in sport. According to Jon Werthem,

> Of 979 people interviewed, 86 percent agreed that it is O.K. for male athletes to participate in sports, even if they are openly gay, yet nearly a quarter of the respondents agreed that having an openly gay player hurts the entire team. "It was like, I'm O.K. with this, but if you press me, I have some doubts," says Doug Schoen, whose firm, Penn, Schoen & Berland Associates, conducted the poll.[46]

Though the *Sports Illustrated* poll did not ask players how they felt about openly gay athletes, and readers have no way of knowing how representative the sample is, the overwhelming number of respondents who agreed that openly gay male athletes could participate in sports is encouraging. When asked whether he would accept a gay teammate, the one baseball player Wertheim quoted in the piece, Ken Griffey, Jr., "laughed and said, 'Wouldn't bother me at all. If you can play, you can play.'"[47] This prompted Wertheim to conclude, "Who knows? With attitudes like Griffey's, there will come a day when locker rooms and clubhouses cease to double as walk-in closets."[48]

Though Gerry Callahan suggests that MLB would offer an openly gay athlete the best chance of success due to the individual nature of the game, the fact remains that no gay MLB player has come out during his career.[49] When WNBA star and Olympic Gold Medalist Sheryl Swoopes came out in

2005, *Pardon The Interruption*'s Tony Kornheiser remarked that gay male athletes "are scared to death to come out and say if they are homosexual that they are, scared to death.... In fact, Mike Piazza went out of his way to run to a press conference to say I am not gay."[50] The brouhaha surrounding Brendan Lemon's editorial and Mike Piazza's alleged "outing" illustrate how media representatives regulate celebrity behavior which, in turn, effectively keeps gay athletes from coming out during the careers and sends heterosexual athletes running to press conferences to reaffirm their sexual orientation. As the California Supreme Court struck down the state's ban on same-sex marriage and New York State moved to recognize those unions, MLB has yet to find ways to discourage homophobic tirades from its members.[51] Is baseball out of touch with the changing political realities or is baseball signaling the fact that the nation is not quite as ready as it seems to embrace equality based on sexual orientation? There is no way to know for sure until an active player comes out. When all is said and done, as Jim Buzinski, creator of outsports.com, points out, "Everybody will say, 'We aren't ready.' Society was not ready for Jackie Robinson. If you are going to wait for everybody to be ready, nobody will do it."[52]

Notes

1. Gerry Callahan, "Issue Too Big to Come Out," *The Boston Herald*, 24 May 2002, 119.
2. Billy Bean, *Going the Other Way: Lessons from a Life in and out of Major League Baseball* (New York: Marlowe, 2003), xvi.
3. Ibid., 217.
4. Ibid., 218.
5. Ibid., 217–8.
6. Jeff Pearlman, "At Full Blast," *Sports Illustrated*, 27 December 1999, 61.
7. Charles R. Lawrence III, "If He Hollers Let Him Go: Regulating Racist Speech on Campus," in *Words That Wound: Critical Race Theory, Assaultive Speech, and the First Amendment*, ed. Mari J. Matsuda, Charles Lawrence III, Richard Delgado, and Kimberlé Crenshaw (Boulder: Westview Press, 1992), 451.
8. S.L. Price, "Cat & Mouth Game," *Sports Illustrated*, 13 March 2000, 42.
9. Bean, *Going the Other Way*, 238.
10. Jay Mariotti, "Hearing an Ugly Side to Athletes," *The Sporting News*, 14 May 2001, 7.
11. Ibid.
12. "Baseball and Gay Fans Come Together," *Outsports*, http://www.outsports.com/baseball/2004/0803gaydays.htm.
13. Rick Telander, "In Big Picture, Mariotti's Huge Part of Story," *Chicago Sun-Times*, 26 June 2007, 94.
14. Joe Cowley, "Selig Sends Guillen to School: Sox Manager Ordered to Attend Sensitivity Training, Pay Fine," *Chicago Sun-Times*, 23 June 2007, 126.
15. Ibid.
16. Brendan Lemon, "Letter From the Editor," *Out*, May 2001, 15.
17. David Nylund, "When in Rome: Heterosexism, Homophobia, and Sports Talk Radio," *Journal of Sport & Social Issues* 28:2 (2004): 153.
18. Bean, *Going the Other Way*, 153.
19. Dave Kindred, "Everything Evolves, Even the Word 'Babe,'" *The Sporting News*, 3 June 2002, 64.
20. Neal Travis, "In and Out with the Mets," *The New York Post*, 20 May 2002, 011.
21. Ron Cook, "Sports Can't Get Out of the Closet," *Pittsburgh Post-Gazette*, 24 May 2002, C-1.
22. Rafael Hermoso, "Piazza Responds to Gossip Column," *New York Times*, 22 May 2002, D5.
23. Kindred, "Everything Evolves," 64.
24. Tom D'Angelo, "Gay Issue Remains in Closet," *Palm Beach Post*, 26 May 2002, 7B.

25. *Ibid.*, 7B.
26. Bruce Jenkins, "Baseball Isn't Ready to Open the Closet Door," *San Francisco Chronicle*, 25 May 2002, C2.
27. Harvey Araton, "Baseball Focuses on the Trivial," *The New York Times*, 23 May 2002, 1.
28. Gerry Callahan, "Issue Too Big to Come Out," *The Boston Herald*, 24 May 2002, 119.
29. Chris Kline, "Tribe Ignores Past, Reaps Rewards," *Baseball America*, http://baseballamerica.com/today/news/030904tadano.html.
30. *Ibid.*
31. *Ibid.*
32. "Indians Pitcher Asks Forgiveness for Role in Gay Porn Video," CBS Sportsline, http://cbs.sportsline.com/mlb/story/7041300.
33. Kline, "Tribe Ignores Past."
34. *Lawrence et. al. vs. Texas 02-102* (2003).
35. *Hillary Goodridge & Others vs. Department of Public Health & Another, SJC-08860* (2003).
36. Charles Lawrence III, "The Id, the Ego, and Equal Protection: Reckoning with Unconscious Racism," in *Critical Race Theory: The Key Writings That Formed the Movement*, ed. Kimberlé Crenshaw, Neil Gotanda, Gary Peller, and Kendall Thomas (New York: The New Press, 1995), 237.
37. Chong-suk Han, "Gay Asian-American Male Seeks Home," *Gay & Lesbian Review Worldwide* 12:5 (2005): 35.
38. Allen Luke, "Representing and Reconstructing Asian Masculinities: This is Not a Movie Review," *Social Alternatives* 16: 3 (1997): 32.
39. Han, "Gay Asian-American Male Seeks Home," 35.
40. Jay Clarkson, "Contesting Masculinity's Makeover: *Queer Eye*, Consumer Masculinity, and 'Straight-Acting' Gays," *Journal of Communication Inquiry* 29:3 (2005): 236.
41. Bradley Holms, "Queer Eye for the Red Sox," *Queer Eye for the Straight Guy*, Scout Productions, 2005.
42. Gwen Knapp, "Is It Time to End the Hostility Toward Gays in the Pros?" *San Francisco Chronicle*, 5 June 2005, D1.
43. Holms, "Queer Eye for the Red Sox."
44. Knapp, "Is It Time to End the Hostility Toward Gays in the Pros?" D1.
45. *Ibid.*
46. L. Jon Wertheim, "Gays in Sport: A Poll," *Sports Illustrated*, 18 April 2005, 64.
47. *Ibid.*, 65.
48. *Ibid.*
49. Callahan, "Issue Too Big to Come Out," 119.
50. Michael Wilbon and Tony Kornheiser, "Significance of Coming Out," *Pardon the Interruption*, ESPN, 26 October 2005.
51. "California Ban on Same-Sex Marriage Struck Down," CNN.COM, http://www.cnn.com/2008/US/05/15/same.sex.marriage/index.html?iref=newssearch; and "New York to Recognize Gay Marriages," CNN.COM, http://www.cnn.com/2008/US/05/29/nygay.marriage/index.html?iref=newssearch.
52. D'Angelo, "Gay Issue Remains in Closet," 7B.

CHAPTER 6

Professional Baseball Wages in the Era of Integration

Michael J. Haupert

Beginning in 1885, African American baseball players were banned from playing in the same league as white players. This unwritten segregation of professional baseball persisted for more than half a century. The only sources of employment for professional baseball players of African American descent were leagues organized exclusively for black ballplayers. Such leagues first emerged in the late nineteenth century and lasted until 1961, though they dwindled considerably during the decade after the integration of Major League Baseball (MLB). This is all well known to students of baseball history. What is not as well known is how those players fared in the way they were paid.

This article serves as a preliminary study of how black and white players were paid in their segregated leagues, how those salaries compared to blue collar workers and how the salaries changed when MLB reintegrated beginning in 1947. The data available cover the years 1917–59.[1]

Literature Review

Gary Becker in *The Economics of Discrimination* identified three primary types of discrimination: employer, coworker and customer. Studies of all three of these types of discrimination have been undertaken using the professional baseball market as a laboratory for study. While baseball is a trivial sector of our economy when measured by total employment, scholars argue that it is a good place to look at discrimination because of its very public nature. Most recently, Paul Holmes in "New Evidence of Salary Discrimination in Major League Baseball" notes that the importance in studying discrimination in baseball is that if it could exist in such a highly publicized and scrutinized industry, the lessons we learn from it may be useful in understanding it in a wider context. He also claims that the clearest example of discrimination in MLB would be violations of the "equal pay for equal work" principle as set forth in the Equal Pay Act of 1963 and the Civil Rights Act of 1964.

In "Tasting Standard Theories of Economic Discrimination" Jonathan A. Lanning tests for these three types of discrimination and finds that only employer discrimination can be supported by evidence in the first decade of integrated baseball. Other researchers have considered various forms of customer and coworker discrimination.

Lawrence Kahn further segments the types of discrimination into salary discrimination (unequal pay for equal work), hiring discrimination (in the form of quotas), retention discrimination, and positional segregation in "The Sports Business as a Labor market Laboratory." Salary discrimination is the most studied type in sports. The typical research design is to regress the log of salary on performance variables, team characteristics, market characteristics, and a race dummy. These studies have found little evidence of salary discrimination in the sports industry. In fact, Keven J. Christiano ("Salary Discrimination" and "Salaries and Race") and Anthony H. Pascal and L. A. Rapping ("The Economics of Racial Discrimination in Organized Baseball") show the opposite: a significant white shortfall in salary. This seems unlikely to be the result of reverse discrimination, but rather omitted variables. In the case of Pascal and Rapping, they find a white shortfall in salary for pitchers, but during their sample period there were so few black pitchers that those who did pitch were decidedly above average pitchers.

But there is evidence of other sorts of discrimination, including customer, hiring, retention, and stacking of minority players at certain positions. For example, Christiano ("Salaries and Race") found that in baseball blacks are overly represented at the outfield position and underrepresented at infield and catcher. Pascal and Rapping (1972) find that white rookies during the 1950s received higher signing bonuses than equally qualified blacks. Lipman states in "Sports Marketers See Evidence of Racism" that there was some endorsement discrimination, whereby whites got more endorsement income. In "Racial and Ethnic Employment Discrimination" Bellemore found that blacks and Hispanics were less likely to be promoted to the majors than whites in the 1960s and 1970s. Robert Jiobu reported in "Racial Inequality in a Public Arena" that blacks in the 1970s and 1980s had shorter careers than whites.

Before investigating the question of discrimination in MLB, however, the opportunity cost of black ballplayers needs to be addressed in order to put their participation in segregated baseball leagues into perspective.

What Were Ballplayers Paid Before Integration?

We already know that major league players were handsomely paid during the period of segregation. Research into the financial structure of the New York Yankees has provided us with copious and detailed information on player wages.[2] We know that the average player earned a wage several times higher than the average annual wage of manufacturing workers. What is less certain is how well the Negro League players fared. There are several sources of financial data for Negro League teams, though the quality and quantity of these data varies. The financial records of the Hilldale club, often referred to as the Daisies, are quite extensive. We have fairly detailed accounts from 1915 to 1927. Other teams, such as the Newark Giants and the Kansas City Monarchs, also provide us with detailed financial information, but for shorter periods of time in the 1940s and post-integration 1950s respectively. Finally, there is a small amount of payroll information for the Birmingham Barons during the latter half of the 1920s.[3] There are likely other sources available, but to date they have either not been discovered or they have not been publicized.

Table 1 summarizes the average wages of New York Yankee players and an assortment of average wages from various Negro League teams for available years. No salary data are available for Negro League teams for the years 1933–39, so those years have been omitted from the table. For all salaries the amount listed is contracted pay, not including bonuses, fines, or other deductions.

It is certainly no surprise that before integration MLB salaries were significantly higher than those paid to Negro Leaguers. The American and National Leagues were larger, more established, much more financially successful, and drew far more fans than the Negro Leagues did. The resulting revenue streams were significantly higher for MLB, therefore the salaries earned by the players were much higher.

The Yankees averaged $564,000 in total revenue each year from 1915–21 as compared to $25,500 for Hilldale. While the salaries the Yankees paid their players were higher than their Negro League counterparts, the Yankees were relatively stingier. During that time period the Yankees paid their players between 13 percent and 45 percent of their total revenues, averaging 30.9 percent. Hilldale, on the other hand, paid out an average of 37.3 percent of their revenues to their players. In part this was due to the difference in labor markets between the two leagues. MLB players were restricted by the reserve clause, thus reducing their bargaining power. Team owners knew the players had no other options for playing baseball professionally and exploited that advantage. Black ballplayers, on the other hand, were not subject to the reserve clause and therefore had more bargaining leverage with their teams. This is reflected by the greater percentage of the total revenues the teams devoted to paying their players.

While it is insightful, it is not necessarily relevant to compare the wages of white to black players since neither could play in the other league. Of greater interest is the opportunity cost of the players. In other words, if they were not ballplayers, what would they be doing, and how much money would they earn?

We know from previous research that the majority of professional baseball players during this era were not highly educated workers.[4] While there are examples of players who moved from baseball to other professional careers, such as John Montgomery Ward, who entered the legal field after baseball, or Bobby Brown, who became a doctor after his playing career ended, most players pursued jobs that would be described as blue collar. They entered manufacturing, agriculture or basic service industries, jobs which did not require specialized skills or advanced training. In fact, many of these players did not even wait until they retired to begin plying such trades. Many players supplemented their MLB income by working during the off season. Only a few players were famous enough to parlay their on-field skills into off season income opportunities from endorsements or the lecture circuit. It was much more common for a player to work in a factory. This was not unusual before the inflated salaries brought about in the post–free agency era. As a result, the manufacturing wage is a reasonable wage to consider as an opportunity cost for professional baseball players.

Despite the fact that Negro Leaguers were making only a fraction of what the average Yankee player was earning, they were doing quite well when compared to the average worker. Figure 1 shows the relative wage of Negro League players to the average manufacturing wage in the U.S., which I have labeled white workers, and their wage relative to the average salary of African American blue collar workers.

The wage labeled white workers is the U.S. average wage for manufacturing workers. The series labeled black workers is computed from research done by economic historians on relative race-based wages in the first half of the twentieth century.[5] While economy wide series of specific race-based wages for this period are not available, there are some samples available that have allowed economists to estimate relative wages for workers based on race. Using this research, a blue collar wage index for black workers based on the wages of Southern textile workers has been constructed. This is used as the representative opportunity cost for black workers.

The length of the baseball season must also be dealt with. For the most part, the season is six months long. Spring training and post season play may extend the length of the season by a few weeks on either end. However, players were not paid for these extended parts of the season, though they might get a share of the gate during barnstorming trips taken at the end of spring training, and they received a share of the gate for post season championship play. As mentioned, most players worked in the off season. For this reason, the proper idea of an opportunity cost for the players is not the annual wage of manufacturing workers, but the six month wage — that is, the salary they could have earned during the six months they spent playing baseball. During the other six months of the year the average player was working at another job, therefore only during the baseball season did he forego the opportunity to earn a manufacturing wage.

Negro League players did quite well when compared to the alternative choice for black workers (Figure 1). During the baseball season they earned between 128 percent and 275 percent of the six month wage of black laborers. Even relative to white workers they held their own, surpassing the average manufacturing wage of white workers by 1931, and certainly better than the average black worker did relative to the average white worker (Figure 2). The average white worker earned between two and nearly four times what the average black worker earned through 1930 and 1.5 times as much in the 1940s. A black ballplayer earned roughly half as much as the average white worker earned in six months between 1917 and 1930 and 20 percent to 80 percent more during the next two decades.

After Integration

The disrupted labor market during World War II helped improve wages for African Americans. While wages improved for average workers the American labor market certainly could not be described as color blind. Nor, of course, could baseball. Beginning in 1947, though, MLB did begin to hire talented black players out of the Negro Leagues and integrate them into the majors. Along with the integration of the sport came a tremendous boost in salaries for black players — at least for those who made it to MLB.

After integration the salaries of black players who made it to the majors increased dramatically while those players left behind in the Negro Leagues saw their salaries stagnate. These results need to be tempered by a couple of observations. First, the samples are small. For the Negro League data, the salaries are averages of players for only one team each season. In the first years of an integrated MLB, there were only a few black players — and it should be noted that those blacks who did make it in the early years were anything but average. They were among the best the Negro Leagues had to offer. This helps explain the rather startling results seen in Figure 3, which shows the significantly higher average wages of black relative to white major leaguers in the first years after integration.

The players who were left behind in the Negro Leagues were not only less talented on average, but they were left in a lower quality league that had been decimated by the signing of the best players by MLB. This lower quality league drew fewer fans, thus the falling salaries of Negro League players after integration (Table 4).

As Figure 4 illustrates, blacks in the majors earned four to twelve times as much as the six month salary of white workers, and white ballplayers earned between four and six times as much as the six month salary of white workers. By 1952 black MLB salaries had fallen below that of white players, but were still comfortably ahead of the white manufacturing wage.

The fall in black ballplayer salaries is due to an increasing number of black players coming into the league, with the younger and less experienced new players pulling the average salary down. After the initial wave of the most accomplished black players into the league, less certain prospects began to arrive. The first crop of former Negro Leaguers to make it to MLB included Hall of Famers Jackie Robinson, Larry Doby, Roy Campanella, and Willie Mays, along with Don Newcombe, Monte Irvin and Luke Easter. While the latter crop included luminaries such as Hank Aaron and Ernie Banks, it also featured the likes of Bob Boyd, Quincy Trouppe, and George Crowe. The declining quality of black players was reflected in their falling wages. As the number of black MLB players increased, a race wage-gap emerged and remained for the duration of the sample period. Black and white wages both increased at a slow but steady pace with a persistent gap of about $2000. The first black major leaguers were paid more than their white brethren, but as the number of black players increased and their average quality decreased, their average salary fell and a wage gap emerged.

Satchel Paige is the embodiment of the change in fortune for black players. Table 2 shows an example of his salaries before and after integration. He made as much as $1,422 with the Birmingham Barons in 1929 while in the prime of his career. In 1953, he earned $25,000 (worth $16,009 in 1929 dollars) from the St. Louis Browns—at the age of 47 no less.

Testing for Discrimination

This study focuses on employer discrimination. While Lanning looked at the rate of integration and claimed it was too slow, thus suggesting that discrimination of opportunity for blacks occurred, this study uses a unique database of ballplayer wages in both black and white leagues to look at how ballplayers were paid to determine if wage discrimination took place. For those blacks who were able to make it to the majors, were they treated like whites in regard to their contracts? To answer that question salaries and other contract details, including bonus clauses, contract length and type (annual vs. monthly) are examined.

A test for the presence of employer discrimination is conducted using a simple regression. Salary is regressed on performance indicators and a race dummy to test for salary differences due to race. The model used is the standard semilog form employed most frequently in the literature. There are enough observations to run separate regressions on pitchers and hitters (Table 5). For each position salary was regressed on a series of variables. The basic form of the model in each case is ln real salary = $ß_1$race + $ß_2$experience + $ß_3$performance +e. A dummy variable is used for black players.

Experience is measured separately for MLB and Negro Leagues. Playing in at least one game constituted a season for the experience measure. Player age at midseason is also included. The correlation of these two variables is discussed below.

The performance variables for hitters include lagged values of at bats, home runs, batting average, and slugging average. During this pre–free agency era of contracting, multi-year contracts were almost unheard of. Indeed, of the 800 plus player contracts in the sample, only three were multi year contracts, and all three of those were two year contracts given to first year players in the late 1950s. For pitchers, the performance data include games, ERA, wins, innings pitched, and strike outs, all lagged one year.

The rationale for one year lags is the system of contracting that existed at the time. With the reserve clause firmly in place, contracts were routinely of the one year variety, therefore they were able to be adjusted easily from one year to the next, with little fear of being turned down by the players. As I have already established, the opportunity cost of being a ballplayer was substantial, so there was little danger that a player would refuse his contract, as there were no really good alternatives, so he had a weak threat point. As a result, the contracts were able to be adjusted easily and therefore should naturally be related to recent performance. As the R^2 of .72 for hitter regressions suggests, most of the variation is indeed picked up by the variables in the model. The R^2 for pitchers is not as high, though 57 percent is still a strong result.

Of interest is the race dummy, which takes on the value of 1 for black players, 0 otherwise. Note that for both pitchers and hitters it is significant and positive, suggesting that being black was worth a 22.4 percent salary boost for hitters and nearly 12 percent for pitchers. This is likely a result of the higher than average quality of the early black entrants into MLB.

For both hitters and pitchers, NL experience is insignificant, supporting the claims of Lanning in "Testing Standard Theories of Economic Discrimination" that MLB owners did not value Negro League experience. MLB experience is highly significant and worth nearly 8 percent per year in additional salary for hitters and 5.5 percent for pitchers. Hitter salaries are positively affected by increases in at bats, home runs, and batting average. For pitchers the only significant performance variable is lagged wins, which is worth a 5 percent salary increase per win.

A Closer Look at Contracts

While the early crop of Negro Leaguers did well with regard to salaries, there are other, non-monetary means by which they could have been discriminated against. For example, there were both monthly and annual contracts. Annual contracts were not guaranteed, as they are today. They featured a clause allowing the team to void a contract with only ten days notice. Despite their one-sided nature, they were better than the greater uncertainty and lower pay of a monthly contract. So, it was possible that while average salaries for blacks were competitive, monthly contracts could have been imposed on them in disproportionate numbers. Secondly, bonus clauses, while not as common as they are today, were added to some contracts. Next, while rare, perhaps multiyear contracts were disproportionately awarded to whites?

The answers to these questions can be found in Table 3, which lists summary data for contracts. Black players were slightly less likely than whites to get monthly contracts, received bonus clauses twice as often, and while only one black player had a multiyear contract (Billy Harrell, 1955, Cleveland — his first MLB contract) this compares favorably to the paltry two white players (James Hook in 1957 and Ron Jackson in 1954, in both cases their first contract) who got multiyear pacts. In sum, there does not appear to be any evidence that black ballplayers were discriminated against on these margins.

Age, Experience and Salary

In the pre–free agency era the most important determinant of a player's salary was his experience in the major leagues. The tendency was for teams to increase player salaries annually, or at least renew them at the status quo. There are, of course, exceptions to these tendencies. Player salaries, if they were to decrease, usually did so when a player changed teams.

In this section the relationship between experience, age, and salary for a sample of black and white players who were active between 1947 and 1959 (the period during which every team integrated) is examined. The sample includes 95 black players, 60 of whom played in the Negro Leagues, and 69 white players.[6]

Such a wide range of time presents problems when looking at salaries. This problem is addressed by calculating real wages instead of using actual (nominal) annual salaries. For this calculation the year-end consumer price index was used.

Care must be taken when interpreting the data. At the higher end of the age and experience range there are very few observations. Thus the range has been truncated at 20 years of experience and age 39 because beyond those limits there are fewer than five observations for each year. As a result, caution should be observed in any attempt to glean insights from the last couple of observation points. They are more for illustrative purposes. The same can be said of young ages as well. There are a few players in the sample who debuted in the league as teenagers, but the numbers were small enough that the series begins at age 20.

Given the impact of experience on salary, the logical place to begin is by looking at salary as a function of years of experience (Figure 5). When viewed in this way, black players fare very well. The average black player earned more per year of experience than the average white player from the rookie year through twelve years of experience, the maximum for any black player in the sample.

Another way of viewing the data is by age (Figure 6). While age and experience are closely correlated, the relationship is not perfect. We know that not every rookie is a young man. This is especially true when we look at black players entering the league in the first years following integration. Some of the first entrants were veteran Negro Leaguers. Jackie Robinson was 28, Roy Campanella 26, Monte Irvin 29, and Satchel Paige 41 when they debuted.

Black players earn more per year of experience than white players, but white players earn more at each age than black players. How can we explain this apparent contradiction? The average white player debuted in the majors at the age of 22.2, while the average black did not reach the majors until the ripe old age of 26.3 — a full four years age difference. Thus, by the age of 26, the average white player had four years experience and was earning at that experience level, while the average 26 year old black player was earning a rookie wage.

A rookie black player was 26 years old and most had already spent time in the Negro Leagues, thus they tended to have more overall experience than a white rookie. While the NL experience was not directly rewarded, it was indirectly rewarded in the sense that they were better players who could earn a higher salary. This means that a player with a year of experience was paid more than a rookie, but a black rookie with a year in the NL was not paid more than a black rookie with no time in the NL.

The pattern of pay for black and white players over the course of their careers was similar — salaries were positively correlated with experience over the first several years of a player's career. Salaries do not decrease until the end of the run, and then the number of observations is small, so little weight can be put on this observation.

Black players differed from whites in that they tended to be older when they arrived in the league and older at every level of experience. This is exemplified in the average career length of players. The average black player in the sample had a major league career lasting just under four years, while the average white player had a career lasting nearly eleven years. The financial impact of this outcome was that the average white ballplayer earned a real salary of $658,000 over his career while the average black player earned only $211,000.

Conclusion

On the surface, it appears that black players held their own in terms of salary with whites. When looking more closely at the details however, it is not quite so clear. Despite earning more on average in the first few years after integration and being compensated at a higher rate based on their experience, the average black player started his career at a later age and thus had a shorter career. It remains to be seen through further research and a more comprehensive data set how these trends fared over time.

When segregation was the rule, black players earned only a fraction of what their white counterparts earned, in part because they could not generate as much revenue for their teams as could major leaguers. Once integration began, the lot of the black player improved remarkably — for those players who escaped the Negro Leagues and made it to MLB. As we have seen, the black ballplayer was always ahead of the game as far as his opportunity cost was concerned. More work remains to be completed to form a more robust analysis of the labor market during the period of reintegration of major league baseball. However, it seems clear already that being a ballplayer was a good profession, no matter the color of one's skin.

Table 1.
Average Salaries in Segregated Leagues Selected Years 1917–46

Year	Yankees	Negro Leagues	Source of Negro League salary data
1917	$ 3,306	$ 217	Hilldale
1918	$ 3,171	$ 304	Hilldale
1919	$ 3,213		
1920	$ 5,110		

Year	Yankees	Negro Leagues	Source of Negro League salary data
1921	$ 5,016	$ 331	Hilldale
1922	$ 7,944		
1923	$ 9,838		
1924	$ 7,332		
1925	$ 8,942		
1926	$ 8,284	$ 307	Birmingham
1927	$ 8,465	$ 498	Birmingham
1928	$ 9,182	$ 329	Birmingham
1929	$ 9,171	$ 356	Birmingham
1930	$10,878	$ 317	Birmingham
1931	$ 9,263	$ 827	Hilldale
1932	$ 9,416	$ 960	Hilldale
1940	$11,759	$ 803	Newark
1941	$10,769	$ 927	Newark
1942	$11,060	$1,350	Newark
1943	$ 9,646	$1,159	Newark
1944	$11,944	$1,470	Newark
1945	$ 7,203		
1946	$ 7,742	$1,933	Newark

SOURCES: Cash Thompson archives, Birmingham Barons archives, Thomas Y. Baird Collection, Haupert-Winter Yankee Financial Records.

Table 2. Satchel Paige Salaries Selected Years

Birmingham Barons		Cleveland Indians and St. Louis Browns	
year	salary	year	salary
1927	$ 688	1948	$15,000
1928	$ 600	1949	$15,000
1929	$1422	1951	$25,000
1930	$ 658	1952	$25,000
		1953	$25,000

SOURCES: Birmingham Barons archives, Haupert salary database.

Table 3. Summary Contract Data

	Sample size	Percent monthly	Percent with bonus clauses	Number multiyear
Black players	314	13.4%	3.2%	1
White players	492	14.2%	1.6%	2

SOURCE: Haupert salary database.

Table 4. Average Salaries of Black Players in Negro League and MLB after Integration

Year	Negro Leagues	MLB	MLB/NL
1948	$1353	$10,250	7.6
1950	$ 300	$12,000	40.0
1952	$ 733	$ 6,000	8.2
1953	$ 720	$ 6,000	8.3
1954	$ 300	$ 6,000	20.0
1955	$ 298	$ 7,000	23.5

SOURCE: Haupert salary database.

Table 5. Regression Results

Variable	Dependant variable ln real salary	
	hitters	pitchers
Intercept	9.3422	9.8796
Standard error	0.1587	0.2389
Black	0.2242*	0.1188*
Standard error	0.0388	0.0612
Age	0.0064	-0.0004
Standard error	0.0050	0.0085
Negro League experience	0.0033	0.0153
Standard error	0.0083	0.0111
MLB experience	0.0789*	0.0551*
Standard error	0.0053	0.0087
Lag AB	0.0010*	
Standard error	0.0001	
Lag HR	0.0207*	
Standard error	0.0025	
Lag BA	1.3791*	
Standard error	0.5491	
Lag SLG	-0.4037	
Standard error	0.2990	
Lag G		
Standard error	0.0027	0.0025
Lag ERA		
Standard error	-0.0046	0.0158

Variable	Dependant variable ln real salary	
	hitters	pitchers
Lag W		
Standard error	0.0510*	0.0098
Lag IP		
Standard error	0.0003	0.0009
Lap SO		
Standard error	-0.0005	0.0011
Adjusted R Square	0.7274	0.5742
Standard Error	0.3471	0.3685
Observations	588	229

*significant at .01

Figure 1.

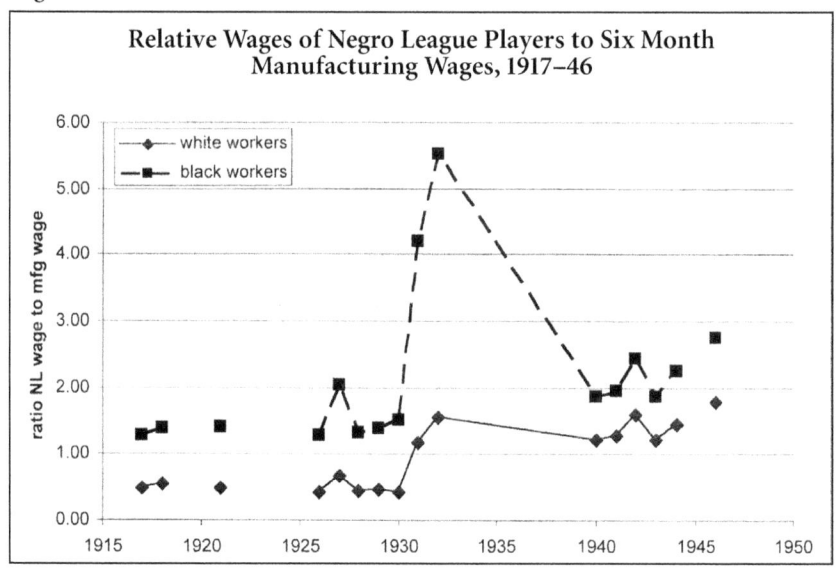

Relative Wages of Negro League Players to Six Month Manufacturing Wages, 1917–46

Figure 2.

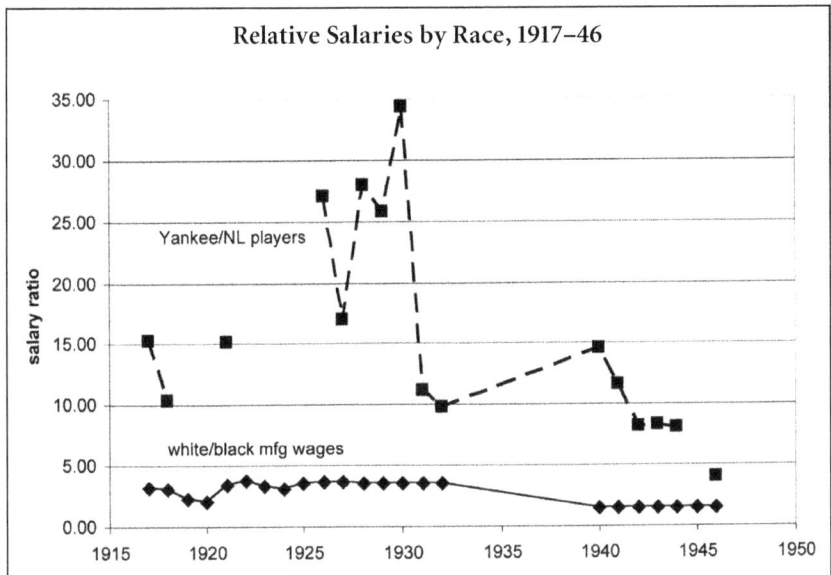

Figure 3.

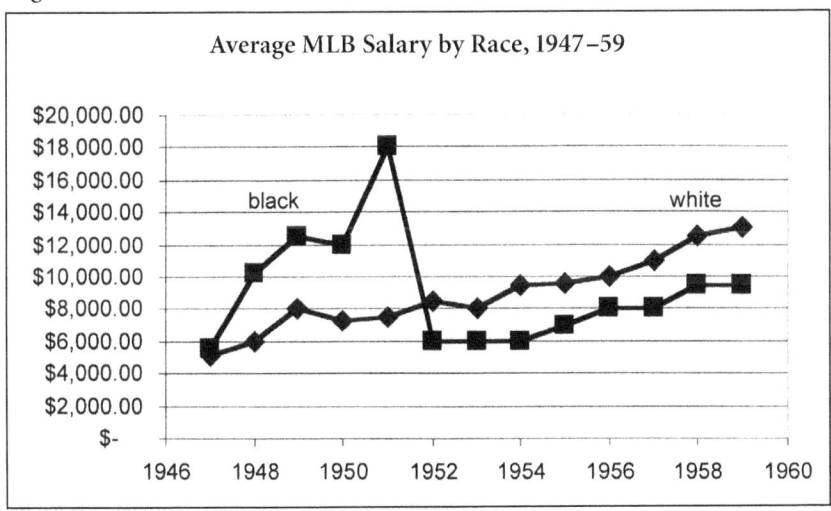

Figure 4.

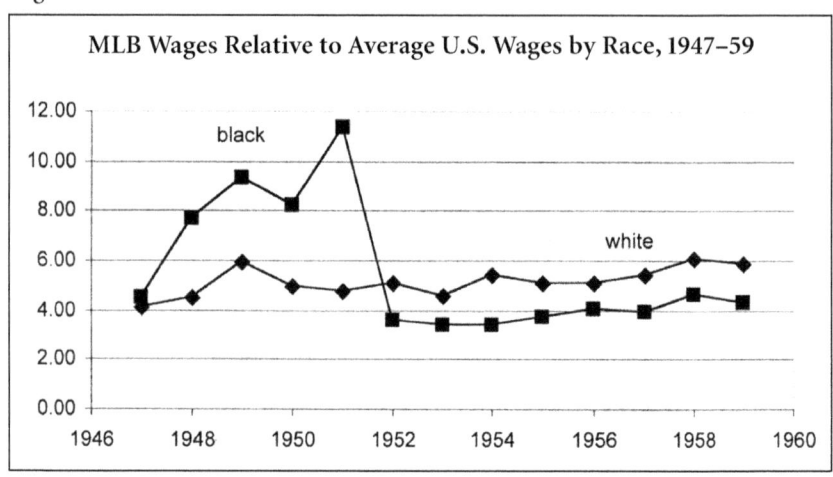

Figure 5.

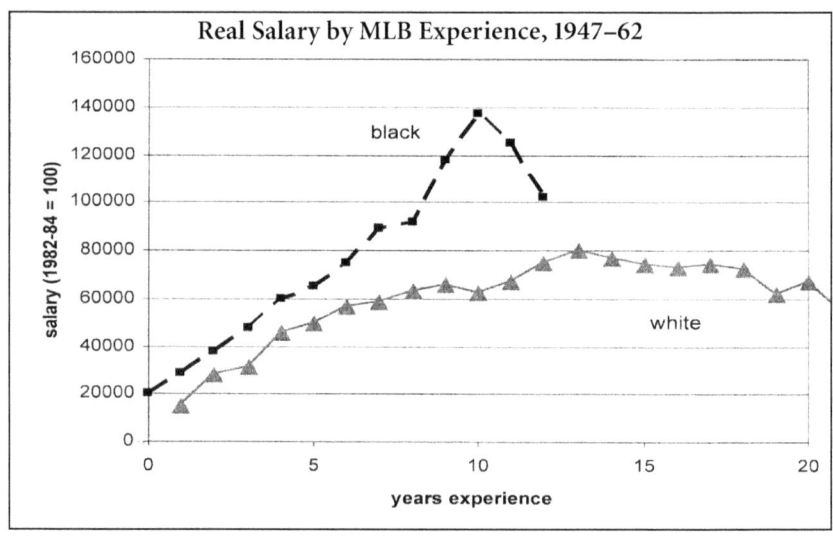

Figure 6.

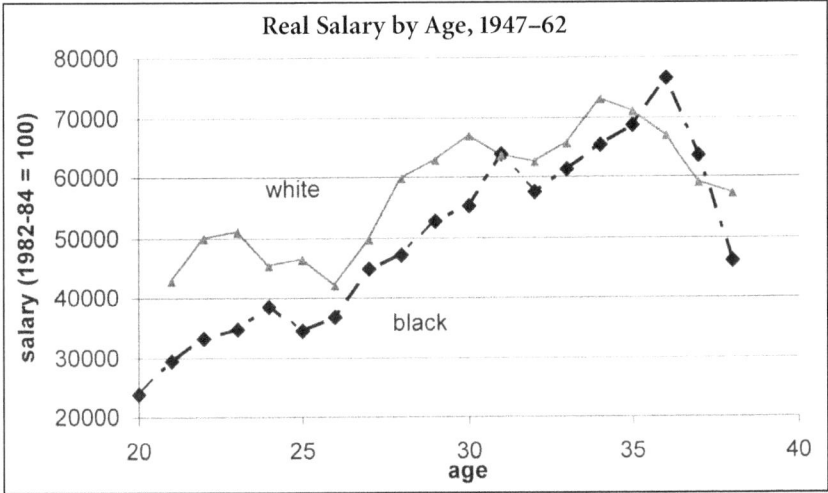

Notes

1. For a more general look at the comparison of baseball player wages to those of average American workers see Haupert, "Worth Their Weight in Gold?"
2. See Haupert and Winter, "Yankee Profits and Promise," and Haupert and Winter, "Pay Ball."
3. Unfortunately, these archives are scattered across the country in various libraries and are not available in one place. The Hilldale records are located in the Cash-Thompson Archives at the African American Museum in Philadelphia, the Newark records are located in the Newark Public Library, the Birmingham records are part of the Joyce Collection of Sports History at the University of Notre Dame, and the Kansas City records are located in the Thomas Y. Baird Archives at the University of Kansas.
4. For an overview of the relationship between college and professional baseball players see Gagnon. For a discussion of ballplayers and their post-career employment see both Topp and Lee.
5. For research on race-based wages in the early part of the 20th century see Wright, *Old South, New South;* Maloney, "Wage Compression"; and Margo, "Explaining Black-White Wage Convergence."
6. The salary data were gathered from the transaction card collection at the National Baseball Hall of Fame Library. The collection consists of approximately 30,000 cards detailing the salary and transaction history for MLB players from 1911 to 1983, with a few observations outside of those boundaries. The collection is more comprehensive for American League players than National Leaguers. In fact, there are no observations for National League players before 1940, and the coverage is somewhat spotty for the next few years. Post–World War II coverage of senior circuit players is strong, and by the 1950s it is comprehensive.

References

Becker, Gary. *The Economics of Discrimination.* Chicago: University of Chicago Press, 1957.

Bellemore, Fred A. "Racial and Ethnic Employment Discrimination: Promotion in Major League Baseball." *Journal of Sports Economics* 2:4 (November 2001), 356–68.

Christiano, Keven J. "Salaries and Race in Professional Baseball: Discrimination 10 Years Later." *Sociology of Sport Journal* 5:2 (1988), 136–49.

_____. "Salary Discrimination in Major League Baseball: The Effect of Race." *Sociology of Sport Journal* 3:2 (1986), 144–53.

Gwartney, James, and Charles Haworth. "Employer Costs and Discrimination: The Case of Baseball." *Journal of Political Economy* 82:4 (1974), 873–81.

Haupert, Michael J. "Worth Their Weight in Gold? A Brief History of Major League Baseball Salaries Compared to the Average Worker." *GameDay*, 4:2, May 2005.

_____, and Kenneth Winter. "Pay Ball: Estimating the Profitability of the New York Yankees, 1915–1937." *Essays in Economic and Business History* XXI (Spring 2003), 89–102.

_____, and _____. "Yankee Profits and Promise: The Purchase of Babe Ruth and the Building of Yankee Stadium," in William Simons, ed., *The Cooperstown Symposium on Baseball and American Culture*. Jefferson, NC: McFarland, 2003.

Holmes, Paul. "New Evidence of Salary Discrimination in Major League Baseball." Working paper, University of Illinois, 2007.

Jiobu, Robert. "Racial Inequality in a Public Arena: The Case of Professional Baseball." *Social Forces*, 67:2 (December 1988), 524–534.

Kahn, Lawrence. "Discrimination in professional sports: a survey of the literature." *Industrial and Labor Relations Review*, 44:3 (April 1991), 395–418.

_____. "The Sports Business as a Labor Market Laboratory." *Journal of Economic Perspectives*, 14:3, (Summer 2000), 75–94.

Knowles, Glenn. "Alternative Compensation Schemes as Motivator for Performance in Major League Baseball." Paper presented at the Midwest Economics Association Meetings, March 2004.

Lanning, Jonathan A. "Testing Standard Theories of Economic Discrimination: Productivity, Prejudice, and Lost profits During Baseball's Integration." Working paper, Albion College, spring 2007.

Lee, Bill. *The Baseball Necrology*. Jefferson, NC: McFarland, 2003.

Lipman, Joanne. "Sports Marketers See Evidence of Racism." *Wall Street Journal*, October 15, 1988, B1.

Maloney, Thomas N. "Wage Compression and Wage Inequality Between Black and White Males in the United States, 1940–1960." *Journal of Economic History*, 54:2 (June 1994), 358–81.

Margo, Robert. "Explaining Black-White Wage Convergence, 1940–1950." *Industrial and Labor Relations Review*, 48:3 (April 1995), 470–81.

Pascal, Anthony H., and Rapping, L.A. "The Economics of Racial Discrimination in Organized Baseball," in A. Pascal, ed., *Racial Discrimination in Economic Life*. Lexington, MA: Lexington Books, 1972.

Scully, Gerald. "Economic Discrimination in Professional Sports." *Law and Contemporary Problems*, 38:1 (1973), 67–84.

_____. "Pay and Performance in Major League Baseball," *The American Economic Review*, 64:6 (December 1974), 915–930.

Sundstrom, William. "The Color Line: Racial Norms and Discrimination in Urban Labor Markets, 1910–1950." *The Journal of Economic History* 54:2 (1994), 382–396.

Topp, Richard. "Demographics," in John Thorn and Pete Palmer, eds., *Total Baseball*. New York: Warner Books, 1989.

Whatley, Warren, and Gavin Wright. "Race, Human Capital, and Labor Markets in U.S. History," in George Grantham and Mary MacKinnon, eds., *Labour Market Evolution*. London: Routledge, 1994.

Wright, Gavin. *Old South, New South: Revolutions in the Southern Economy Since the Civil War*. New York: Basic Books, 1986.

CHAPTER 7

Sam Jethroe's Last Hit
N. Jeremi Duru

"I gave baseball a lot more than it gave me."[1]

In 1950, at the end of a triumphant season with the Boston Braves, outfielder Sam Jethroe earned Major League Baseball's National League Rookie of the Year award.[2] Forty years later, Jethroe found himself destitute with no home and without his Rookie of the Year trophy, which he sold in desperation for money.[3] A variety of factors conspired to pull Jethroe into poverty, and one such factor was racially motivated employment discrimination. As an African American, Jethroe was barred from playing Major League Baseball (MLB) for the majority of what would otherwise have been his most productive playing years.[4] Limited, as a consequence of his race, to three full seasons and one partial season in the big leagues, Jethroe fell narrowly shy of the then-four-year eligibility requirement for an MLB pension.[5] With no money and no other recourse, Jethroe sued Major League Baseball and related entities in March of 1995 for the pension he felt he was wrongly denied,[6] but gained no redress, as the United States District Court for the Eastern District of Pennsylvania dismissed the suit as untimely.[7] With the dismissal, the case lost the little media attention it had initially attracted, and Jethroe receded into the obscurity in which he had lived for years. He died several years later,[8] and his suit has received scarce attention since.

The obscurity of Jethroe's suit is unfortunate. While on first blush Jethroe's claim may seem a minor matter of one retired ball-player's fight for supplemental income in his golden years, the basic characteristics of Jethroe's suit — a claim for pension funds denied as a consequence of past racial discrimination — present a uniquely powerful claim for delayed racial justice. And as America continues to debate, with increasing intensity, the merits of compensating people for decades- and centuries-old racial injustice through reparations and other means, the characteristics of Jethroe's claim deserve a closer look. Jethroe's complaint presents a model for claims potentially open to scores of people of color formerly employed in any number of industries who, by virtue of racial discrimination suffered during their working years, are deprived pension benefits in their later years. Although Jethroe's particular claim failed, claims brought under the same model, hereinafter "Jethroe claims," have the potential to provide many former employees with restorative racial justice.

Discriminatory Denial

Sam Jethroe was the son of a farmer and a domestic worker, and was raised in East St. Louis, Illinois.[9] From his earliest days, Jethroe exhibited tremendous athletic prowess. Known for his speed, he excelled playing semi-pro baseball in East St. Louis, Illinois and St. Louis, Missouri.[10] Despite his unquestionable talent, however, Jethroe was initially unable to play Major League Baseball because of his skin color.[11]

Major League Baseball consists of two separate leagues, the National League and the American League, which, since 1903, have operated in tandem under a joint organizational structure.[12] Although teams in both Leagues employed black players during the late 1880's, members of some of the Leagues' fully segregated teams refused to play against integrated teams, and eventually the Leagues' blacks were expurgated.[13] Indeed, consequent to a "gentlemen's agreement" among major league owners, blacks would be barred from major league play until 1947.[14]

Without access to the major leagues, blacks organized among themselves and created baseball leagues for black players, which would come to be known as the Negro Leagues.[15] Like scores of other black baseball players discriminatorily denied the opportunity to play major league ball, Jethroe played for years in the Negro Leagues. In 1942, Jethroe joined the Cincinnati Buckeyes, and during his first year with the team, his on-field success was unrivaled.[16] He led the Negro American League in batting average, runs scored, doubles, triples, stolen bases, and base hits.[17] In 1944, Jethroe again led the League in batting average and did so again in 1945, during which year he led the Buckeyes to the Negro League World Series.[18] On the heels of his triumphant 1945 season, the Boston Red Sox invited Jethroe—as well as Marvin Williams, who was then starring for one of the Negro Leagues' most storied franchises, the Philadelphia Stars, and future MLB great Jackie Robinson, who would eventually be the first black player in the Majors—to their stadium, Fenway

Park, for what the club described as a tryout.[19] It was preordained, however, that none of the three would make the team. As then–Red Sox manager Joe Cronin has since said of the sham tryout, "I was in no position to offer them a job. The general manager did the hiring and there was an unwritten rule at the time against hiring black players."[20]

The empty tryout only came about, in fact, as the result of a political compromise between the Red Sox and Boston councilman Isadore Muchnick.[21] Muchnick, whose constituency consisted of many blacks, threatened the Red Sox that he would seek to ban Sunday baseball games if they did not integrate.[22] At the time, professional baseball could only be played on Sundays in Boston by permit, and permit issuance required a unanimous city council vote.[23] Muchnick indicated his intention to vote against issuance if the team did not offer black players a tryout.[24] The Red Sox were undaunted in their segregationist view, but agreed to hold a tryout if it would placate Muchnick.[25] For this reason, and no other, Jethroe had his first major league tryout. During the following years, Jethroe continued to excel with the Buckeyes as well as in Cuba's winter baseball league, where he led the league in stolen bases in two consecutive years.[26]

In 1947, the Brooklyn Dodgers promoted Jackie Robinson from their Montreal-based minor league team, which competed in the International League, and officially desegregated the major leagues.[27] Robinson's promotion did not "smash the color barrier" as is often suggested. Rather, it created a crack in the barrier wide enough for a fortunate few black players to squeeze through, but far too narrow to allow in all those who were deserving. In 1947, five black players competed on three of MLB's sixteen teams—the Brooklyn Dodgers, the Cleveland Indians, and the St. Louis Browns.[28] In the following year, 1948, the Browns re-segregated and did not hire another black player for three years, leaving the Dodgers and the Indians as the only MLB teams to employ black players.[29] In 1949, the New York Giants employed two black players, bringing the number of desegregated teams back to three and the total number of black players in the major leagues to nine.[30]

Making the Majors

In 1950, the number of blacks in Major League Baseball remained nine, a mere two percent of a League employing 400 players,[31] and despite the long odds of being one of the few blacks permitted to play, Jethroe finally broke in. Two years earlier, the Dodgers bought Jethroe's rights from the Buckeyes, and sent him to play minor league ball in Montreal, where Robinson previously played.[32] Jethroe met with great success in his first season playing with primarily white teammates. During the 1948 season, Jethroe batted an impressive .322 and stole 18 bases in 76 games.[33] His next season, however, was even more remarkable. He raised his batting average to .326, hit 17 home runs, led the League with 154 runs scored, and set an all-time International League record by stealing 89 bases.[34]

Although Jethroe starred in the Negro Leagues and in the Dodgers' minor league organization in 1948 and 1949, during which time he was arguably their best minor league player, the Dodgers had no room for him.[35] They had reached their limit for black players. Indeed, even the few teams deciding to employ black players were careful to limit the number of black players on their rosters.[36] So, rather than promote Jethroe to the Dodgers' major league club and add a fourth black face to the team photograph, the Dodgers sold him to the Boston Braves in the spring of 1950.[37] Unable to look past his talent, the Braves, an organization that had never previously employed a black player, took a chance, bucking major league tradition, and became only the fourth of the sixteen MLB clubs to employ a black player.[38]

The Braves benefited mightily from their decision. Jethroe quickly became the Braves' starting centerfield, proceeded to have an excellent year, and won the National League's Rookie of the Year award.[39] Jethroe repeated his success in 1951, but his production in 1952 did not match that of his previous two years. This was certainly due, in part, to Jethroe's age. As a consequence of the discrimination that barred him from entering the Majors earlier, as a third-year player in 1952, Jethroe was 35 years old, an advanced age for an elite athlete.[40] As an additional matter, the Braves changed managers during the season and the new manager, Charlie Grimm, apparently hostile to African Americans, alienated and marginalized Jethroe by calling him "Sambo,"[41] a racially derogatory term dating to the days of chattel slavery.[42] In the following year, 1953, the Braves traded Jethroe to the Pittsburgh Pirates, where he played sparingly, before being demoted to the Pirates' minor league team in Toronto, where he played until his retirement from baseball in 1958.[43] At the time of Jethroe's demotion, half of the major leagues' teams remained segregated, and the Leagues' final segregated team—the same Boston Red Sox that staged the sham 1945 tryout for Jethroe, Sam Williams, and Jackie Robinson—did not accept its first black player until halfway through the 1959 season.[44]

Life After Baseball

Jethroe's life in retirement was quiet. After leaving the game, he opened a mildly successful Erie, Pennsylvania, dining establishment called Jethroe's Bar and Restaurant, which, although not particularly profitable, served to help support a modest lifestyle for Jethroe and his family for over thirty years.[45] In the early 1990s, Jethroe was pressured to sell his restaurant to allow for construction of a municipal development project.[46] Intent on resurrecting Jethroe's Bar and Restaurant, but fiscally constrained from purchasing in many locations around Erie, Jethroe had little choice but to buy in one of Erie's rougher areas.[47] Not long after re-launching his business, a man was shot and mortally wounded in the restaurant.[48] The incident frightened Jethroe's customers and potential customers, and business suffered badly.[49] With his business unable to generate income, Jethroe fell into poverty, and, desperate for cash, sold the Rookie of the Year Trophy he earned some forty years earlier for a mere $3,500.[50]

Coincidentally, and tragically, as Jethroe's finances unraveled, his home burned to the ground.[51] Homeless and impoverished, Jethroe turned to living in his defunct restaurant.[52] Aged, with no money, and no job prospects, Jethroe found himself in the situation against which employee retirement benefits are designed to protect. Because, however, Jethroe was denied an MLB pension, he gained no such protection. Believing the denial to be the consequence of race-based discrimination in employment, Jethroe, in March of 1995, filed a federal suit against Major League Baseball and related entities.[53] Alleging several violations of law, Jethroe sought, among other remedies, compensation for the denied pension payments.[54]

Jethroe was correct in asserting that he was denied a pension many other former MLB players received. In 1947, MLB initiated a pension program for all retired players who logged four years in the League.[55] Jethroe, by his own admission, only played Major League Baseball for three full years and part of a fourth.[56] Jethroe did not, however, challenge the four-year requirement. Rather, he proceeded under several theories, arguing that although he did not play in the major leagues for the requisite four years, his tenure was unlawfully restricted on the basis of race, and that he was, therefore, entitled to the pension he would have received absent the discrimination.[57] On September 30, 1996, after significant motions practice, Judge Sean McLaughlin of the United States District Court for the Western District of Pennsylvania dismissed Jethroe's suit with prejudice, effectively ending Jethroe's fight for racial justice in the courts. Sam Jethroe died five years later, in June of 2001.[58]

Although Jethroe was unable to prevail with his suit, he left behind the skeletal model of a unique delayed racial justice claim deserving of attention.

Anatomy of a "Jethroe" Claim

One of the statutes central to Jethroe's suit, 42 USC §1981, known simply as "Section 1981," provides the most likely and obvious avenue for retirees bringing Jethroe claims. Indeed, as much as any statute in our body of laws, Section 1981 exists to protect people of color from discrimination. About this, there can be no doubt. Section 1981 reads, in relevant part, as follows:

> All persons within the jurisdiction of the United States shall have the same right in every State and Territory to make and enforce contracts, to sue, be parties, give evidence, and to the full and equal benefit of all laws and proceedings for the security of persons and property as is enjoyed by white citizens....[59]

Section 1981 finds its origins in the Civil Rights Act of 1866 (the "1866 Act"), enacted in the year following the Civil War's conclusion to shield non-whites from race-based oppression.[60] As Senator Lyman Trumball, then chairman of the Senate Judiciary Committee, explained in introducing the legislation that would become the 1866 Act, it was designed to strengthen the impact of the Thirteenth Amendment to the United States Constitution.[61] That Amendment, which prohibits slavery and involuntary servitude except as punishment for a crime,[62] was at the time under assault throughout America's Southern states by way of legislatively enacted "Black Codes."[63] The Black Codes served essentially to re-institutionalize slavery on a state-by-state basis, restricting blacks in seemingly innumerable ways.[64] For instance, Black Codes typically prevented blacks from owning land, traveling without passes, gathering together in even small numbers, living in certain areas, owning firearms, speaking to whites without prescribed deference, and engaging in certain professions and occupations.[65]

While Congress was certainly concerned with all of these Black Code-created deprivations in passing the 1866 Act, it was primarily concerned with guaranteeing to blacks non-abridgment of their *economic* rights.[66] Specifically, the Act was aimed at actions taken to promote black economic subservience following emancipation, and in particular, the discriminatory abridgement of employment opportunities.[67] Indeed, "Congress clearly believed that freedom would be empty for black men and women if they were not also assured an equal opportunity to engage in business, to work, and to bargain for sale of their labor."[68] Congressional debate and testimony presaging the legislation's passage reveal as much. In advocating for what would become Section I of the 1866 Act, legislators made clear that the section was squarely about protecting economic rights, and, specifically, the right to work. For instance, Representative William Windom of Minnesota stated the legislation's "object is to secure to a poor weak class of laborers the right to make contracts for their labor, the power to enforce the payment of their wages, and the means of holding and enjoying the proceeds of their toil."[69] During further discussion on the same legislation, Representative William Lawrence of Ohio also advocated for its passage stating, "It is idle to say that a citizen should have the right to life, yet to deny him the right to labor, whereby he alone can live."[70]

It seems clear, then, that Section 1981 is a statute potentially capable of securing remedies for Jethroe claimants. In that Jethroe claimants' claims were born decades earlier, however, Jethroe claimants would surely meet resistance in the form of arguments that their claims were too old to be actionable — that they should be time-barred from bringing their claims under the applicable statutes of limitation. Indeed, such arguments derailed Jethroe's federal suit. It is not necessarily the case, however, that Jethroe claims must suffer the same fate.

Indeed, because statutes of limitations apply equally to meritorious claims and merit-less claims, and thus potentially serve to deny justice on the merits, many legal scholars and lawyers express significant reservations about statutes of limitations application.[71] In fact, one of the most renown jurists in American history, Judge Oliver Wendell Holmes, opposed statutes of limitations application altogether, famously asking, "What is the justification for depriving a man of his rights, a pure evil as far as it goes, in consequence of lapse of time?"[72] Further, as Law Professor Suzette Malveaux explains, statues of limitations are especially concerning when applied in circumstances such as the Jethroe claim context, because "access to the courts is particularly important for minorities, the poor, lower socioeconomic classes, and other disenfranchised groups who must rely on the legal system for protection of basic human and civil rights."[73]

As such, courts, recognizing the injustice Jethroe claimants have endured, may be willing to turn to various statute of limitations exceptions to permit Jethroe claims to proceed despite the passage of time. Before statutes of limitations issues even reach the courts, however, lawyers defending employers from Jethroe claims have the power, and perhaps the moral obligation, to prevent these issues from impacting Jethroe claimants' suits. Although their clients may desire to press statutes of limitations defenses under circumstances in which statutes of limitations application would serve to extinguish otherwise meritorious civil rights claims, they may be morally required to resist serving as the client's "hired gun" and instead counsel their clients against such tactics.

Indeed, legal ethics rules certainly suggest such moral counseling is appropriate. For instance, Model Rule of Professional Conduct 2.1 reads: "In representing a client, a lawyer shall exercise independent professional judgment and render candid advice. In rendering advice, a lawyer may refer not only to law but to other considerations such as moral, economic, social, and political factors, which may be relevant to the client's situation."[74] Similarly, the ABA's Lawyers' Manual on Professional Conduct states, "A lawyer's recommendations arguably should go beyond advising the client about that which is merely legally permissible and ought to incorporate moral and ethical considerations as well."[75] The American Law Institute's Restatement of the Law Governing Lawyers speaks to the same effect.[76]

The most thorough scholarly explorations of legal ethics in the past thirty years sound a similar refrain. In particular, David Luban's seminal work, *Lawyers and Justice: An Ethical Study*, rejects the idea that lawyers must, or should, be bound by their client's preferred litigation strategies. Indeed, Luban seeks to defend the law "against a professional vision based only on client service and the bottom line" through "urging a professional ethic" that might guide lawyers in their decision making.[77] Luban does so by considering the interaction between role morality, which he describes as "the special obligations attached to certain social roles," and "universalistic common morality," a morality that binds all persons.[78] Luban recognizes the importance of role morality, but insists lawyers view it within the context of, and generally not allow it to supersede, the greater common morality.[79] The moral lawyer, as Luban sees it, therefore, "will challenge her client if the representation seems to her morally unworthy; she may cajole or negotiate with the client to change the ends or the means; she may find herself compelled to initiate action the client will view as betrayal; and she will not fear to quit."[80]

Another premier legal ethicist, William Simon, in his work *The Practice of Justice*, indicates general agreement with Luban. While Simon does not explicitly appeal to morality, he demands from attorneys contextual judgment, insisting that they scrutinize the purposes of any law before seeking its application.[81] Ultimately, both Luban and Simon reject "hired-gun" lawyering and recognize the potential impropriety of pleading the statutes of limitations defense — even under circumstances where it would be legally acceptable.

Law Professor Peter Margulies rejects the hired gun approach with even greater vigor, arguing that ethics rules should, indeed, *require* lawyers to engage in non-legal and moral counseling of the sort that would suggest a client forgo the statutes of limitations defense.[82] Margulies proposes a regime of ethics rules demanding that a lawyer advise his or her client to alter the client's decision or proposed action if, among other reasons:

- The action or decision will harm others;
- The action or decision violates the norm of equality of all persons;
- The action or decision is one that the client would not wish for anyone in society;
- The action or decision is one that may engender guilt;
- The action or decision will harm others in a way that ultimately will require a remedy from society at large;

- The action will result in a net cost to society if all individuals behave in a like manner.[83]

Perhaps then, considering long-standing concerns as to the ethical propriety of the statutes of limitations defense and the continued resonance of those concerns, a defense lawyer—faced with an impoverished elderly African American who brings suit because he or she was decades ago discriminated against by the lawyer's client such that he or she was ultimately denied the pension his or her Caucasian former co-workers ultimately received—might reasonably counsel his or her client to not mount a statutes of limitations defense against the claim. Such counsel does not violate the legal profession's ethical standards; indeed, the standards may reasonably be viewed as encouraging it.

A Legislative Remedy?

To the extent defense lawyers prove unwilling to take the stand that Luban, Simon, and Margulies encourage and that American legal ethics rules seem to permit, Jethroe claimants may still taste justice. Indeed, occasionally, if sufficiently grievous and renowned, a wrong enjoys a remedy outside of the judicial system, in the form of legislative action. For instance, in 1994, seventy-one years after a mob of white policemen and others torched the small black community of Rosewood, Florida and killed six of its residents in a race riot, the Florida legislature voted to compensate the riot's living survivors as well as its decedents' descendants.[84] The United States Congress took similar steps to compensate Japanese Americans interned during World War II.[85] Such legislative action is, however, rare, and in that legislatures disperse public funds, such action, when taken, generally works to remedy publicly, as opposed to privately, inflicted wrongs. Such action, therefore, is unlikely to remedy the wrongs Jethroe claimants have endured.

Legislative action, however, need not be compensatory to preserve the possibly of a remedy for Jethroe claimants. "The shelter of statutes of limitations [of course] ... has come into law by legislative grace, not as a natural right."[86] And just as statutes of limitations exist by virtue of legislative enactment, legislative enactment can prevent their application. So, while legislative action to compensate Jethroe claimants is unlikely, legislative action to free their claims from statutes of limitations application seems more feasible. The latter action would not require appropriation of public funds to individuals claiming pension deprivation as a consequence of decades old race-based employment discrimination. Rather, it would extricate such claims from the statutes of limitations yoke. Jethroe claimants' former employers would not be ordered to compensate the plaintiffs, but would simply be required to respond to the claims on the merits. The legislature would essentially be saying, "[a]s strongly as we desire finality, we desire justice even more,"[87] and denial of justice for Jethroe claimants is an unacceptable sacrifice in the name of finality.

If Congress enacted such legislation, it would be doing so with strong historical precedent. Indeed, Congress has previously done for Native Americans with delayed justice claims what this article proposes it could do for African Americans with Jethroe claims. In passing the Indian Claims Commission Act of 1946 (ICCA), Congress provided a mechanism for Native Americans to assert "claims in law or equity arising under the Constitution, laws [or] treaties of the United States" to which statute of limitations defenses were impermissible so long as the claims were filed with the Commission within five years of the ICCA's enactment.[88] Recognizing the injustices to which Native Americans have been subjected in this nation and the difficulty of bringing timely claims to remedy those injustices, Congress legislated a statute of limitations exception, which provided disenfranchised plaintiffs a taste of justice.[89] Congress could certainly do the same in the Jethroe claim context, and thus ensure a day in court for so many who have been denied such a day for so long.

Conclusion

Sam Jethroe left an enduring mark on the baseball landscape through his love for the game, the skill with which he played it, and the determination to succeed despite the racial prejudice that hounded him throughout his career. And although he died before enjoying a remedy for the discrimination he experienced, through his quest for justice, he presented a model that could conceivably result in remedies for many others of his generation. Jethroe claims carry with them the potential to provide some semblance of justice to scores of African American retirees and, in doing so, to, by whatever increment, heal this nation's racial wound.

Even in light of Jethroe's substantial success at the plate during his career, Jethroe's last hit — his justice-seeking lawsuit — may turn out to be his greatest. Way to go, Jethroe.

Notes

1. Eric Enders, "So Long, Sam: Jethroe's Death Ends One of the Most Interesting Lives in Baseball History," EricEnders.com, http:// www.ericenders.com/jethroe.htm (accessed August 8, 2007), 3 (quoting Sam Jethroe).

2. Brad Snyder, "Jethroe Seeks Legal Vic-

tory in Bid for Baseball Pension," *Baltimore Sun*, Apr. 22, 1995.
   3. Enders, "So Long, Sam."
   4. Snyder, "Jethroe Seeks Legal Victory," 1C.
   5. "Lawsuit Dismissed," *New York Times*, Oct. 6, 1996; *Jethroe v. Major League Baseball Props., Inc.*, Civ. Act. No. 95–72 (Erie 1996) at 6.
   6. Snyder, "Jethroe Seeks Legal Victory," 1C.
   7. "Lawsuit Dismissed," 13; and Enders, "So Long, Sam," 3.
   8. Richard Goldstein, "Sam Jethroe is Dead at 83; Was Oldest Rookie of the Year," *New York Times*, June 19, 2001.
   9. David L. Porter, ed., *Biographical Dictionary of American Sport: Baseball* (Westport, CT: Greenwood, 1987), 282.
   10. *Ibid.*
   11. Rich Marazzi, "Batting the Breeze," *Sports Collectors Digest*, Nov. 11, 1994, 110.
   12. Jeanine Bucek, ed., *The Baseball Encyclopedia: The Complete and Definitive Record of Major League Baseball* (New York: MacMillan, 1996), 6.
   13. Patrick Clark, *Sports Firsts* (New York: Facts on File, 1981), 12.
   14. Robert Peterson, *Only the Ball Was White* (New York: Oxford University Press, 1970), v; Howard Bryant, *Shut Out: A Story of Race and Baseball in Boston* (New York: Routledge, 2002), 24.
   15. Peterson, *Only the Ball*, v.
   16. Porter, *Biographical Dictionary*, 282.
   17. *Ibid.*
   18. *Ibid.*
   19. Bryant, *Shut Out*, 31.
   20. *Ibid.*, 32.
   21. *Ibid.*, 24–29.
   22. *Ibid.*
   23. *Ibid.*, 24.
   24. *Ibid.*
   25. *Ibid.*, 29.
   26. Porter, *Biographical Dictionary*, 282.
   27. Larry Moffi and Jonathan Kronstadt, *Crossing the Line: Black Major Leaguers, 1947–1959* (Jefferson, NC: McFarland, 1994), 1–2.
   28. *Ibid.*, 11–25.
   29. *Ibid.*, 13–14, 23–36.
   30. *Ibid.*, 15–47.
   31. *Ibid.*, 47.
   32. Porter, *Biographical Dictionary*, 282.
   33. *Ibid.*
   34. *Ibid.*, 282–83.
   35. Moffi and Kronstadt, *Crossing the Line*, 50.
   36. *Ibid.*, 11–47.
   37. Porter, *Biographical Dictionary*, 283.
   38. Moffi and Kronstadt, *Crossing the Line*, 50–52.
   39. Porter, *Biographical Dictionary*, 283.
   40. Marazzi, "Batting the Breeze," 111.
   41. *Ibid.*
   42. *Oxford English Dictionary*, 2d ed., s.v. "Sambo."
   43. Porter, *Biographical Dictionary*, 283.
   44. Moffi and Kronstadt, *Crossing the Line*, 212.
   45. Enders, "So Long, Sam," 1.
   46. *Ibid.*
   47. *Ibid.*
   48. *Ibid.*
   49. *Ibid.*
   50. *Ibid.*
   51. *Ibid.*
   52. *Ibid.*
   53. *Jethroe*, No. 95–72, at 3.
   54. *Ibid.*, 1–5.
   55. Robert A. McCormick, "Baseball's Third Strike: The Triumph of Collective Bargaining in Professional Baseball," *Vanderbilt Law Review* 35 (1982): 1131, 1147; and MLB History, http://mlb.mlb.com/mlb/history/mlb_history_people.jsp?story=com_bio_2.
   56. *Jethroe*, No. 95–72 at 6.
   57. *Jethroe*, No. 95–72 at 6–7.
   58. Goldstein, "Sam Jethroe is Dead at 83," A21.
   59. 42 U.S.C. § 1981(a) (2000).
   60. Angela M. Ford, "Private Alienage Discrimination and the Reconstruction Amendments: The Constitutionality of 42 U.S.C. § 1981," 49 *University of Kansas Law Review* 457 (2001): 460–62.
   61. B. Schwartz, *From Confederation to Nation: The American Constitution 1835–1877* (Baltimore: Johns Hopkins University Press, 1973), 191.
   62. U.S. Const. Amend. XIII.
   63. *Goodman v. Lukens Steel Co.*, 482 U.S. 656, 672 (1987).
   64. *Ibid.*
   65. Harold Hyman and William B. Wiecek, *Equal Justice Under Law: Constitutional Development, 1835–1875* (New York: Harper and Row, 1982), 319.
   66. *Goodman*, 482 U.S. at 674.
   67. *Ibid.*
   68. *Ibid.* (J. Brennan, concurring in part and dissenting in part).

69. *Cong. Globe*, 39th Cong., 1st Sess. 1159 (1866).
70. *Ibid.*, 1833.
71. Suzette M. Malveaux, "Statutes of Limitations: A Policy Analysis in the Context of Reparations Litigation," *George Washington Law Review* 74 (2005): 468; and Tyler T. Ochoa and Andrew J. Wistrich, "The Puzzling Purposes of Statutes of Limitation," *Pacific Law Journal* 28 (1997): 501.
72. Oliver Wendell Holmes, "The Path of the Law," *Harvard Law Review* 10 (1897): 476.
73. Malveaux, "Statutes of Limitations," 84.
74. Larry O. Natt Gantt, II, "Integration as Integrity: Postmodernism, Psychology, and Religion on the Role of Moral Counseling in the Attorney-Client Relationship," *Regent University Law Review* 16 (2003–2004): 235 (quoting Model Rules of Prof'l Conduct R. 2.1 [2003]).
75. *Ibid.*, 235 (quoting ABA/BNA Lawyers' Manual on Professional Conduct § 31:701 [1998] [emphasis added]).
76. *Ibid.*, 236.
77. David Luban, *Lawyers and Justice: An Ethical Study*, xvii–xviii (Princeton: Princeton University Press, 1988).
78. *Ibid.*, 105.
79. *Ibid.*, 104–47.
80. *Ibid.*, xxii.
81. William Simon, *The Practice of Justice: A Theory of Lawyers' Ethics* (Cambridge, MA: Harvard University Press, 1998), 31–33.
82. Peter Margulies, "Who Are You to Tell Me That?": Attorney-Client Deliberation Regarding Nonlegal Issues and the Interests of Nonclients," *North Carolina Law Review* 68 (1990): 215–21.
83. *Ibid.*, 221.
84. Charles J. Ogletree, "Repairing the Past: New Efforts in the Reparations Debate in America," *Harvard Civil Rights-Civil Liberties Law Review* 38 (2003): 279.
85. Jack Greenberg, "Reparations: Politically Inconceivable," *Thomas Jefferson Law Review* 29 (2007): 157 (2007); see also 50 U.S.C. app. § 1989b-4 (2000).
86. Malveaux, "Statutes of Limitations," 91.
87. Michael E. Chaplin, "Reviving Contract Claims Barred By The Statute of Limitations: An Examination of the Legal and Ethical Foundation For Revival," *Notre Dame Law Review* 75 (2000): 1588.
88. 25 U.S.C. § 70(a) (1) (repealed in 1978).
89. See *U.S. v. Dann*, 470 U.S. 39, 45 (1985).

CHAPTER 8

The Church of Detroit Baseball: American Civil Religion and Willie Horton at Comerica Park

Joshua Fleer

At Detroit's Comerica Park, Tiger legends are celebrated with their action poses emblazoned in statues overlooking centerfield. The likenesses include some of the greatest players to ever grace a ball field: Hall of Famers Al Kaline, Ty Cobb, Hank Greenberg, Hal Newhouser, Charlie Gehringer — and Willie Horton.

Willie Horton is the only one of the six whose bust is not also emblazoned on a plaque in Cooperstown. Moreover, the other five amassed baseball's most prestigious accomplishments, ranging from a batting *and* a pitching Triple Crown to a half dozen MVP Awards between them.[1] By contrast, the only category Horton led the league in during his career was games played in 1979 — as he finished his playing days, not with the Tigers, but with the Seattle Mariners.[2] Horton's playing career does not match up with the other famed Tigers.

How is it, then, that Willie Horton is given equal stature beside the other Tiger immortals? That is the question I address in the paper that follows.

Comerica Park renders an overt message to explain the question, Why Willie Horton? The ballpark venerates Horton as a Detroit icon for his actions both on the field and in the community. Through this lens created at the ballpark, a specific vision of America is revealed and instilled. Horton symbolizes what sociologist Robert N. Bellah explained as the glue — the common set of values in a democracy — that holds Americans together. The First Amendment safeguards individual citizens from governmental interference into their religious beliefs and behaviors. However, a well institutionalized civil religion shapes collective memory and informs public life.

111

The civil religion can be seen manifested in presidential speeches and in phrases like "In God We Trust" on the dollar bill. America's sacred scriptures, which include the Declaration of Independence, the Constitution, the Bill of Rights, and what has been referred to as the Lincolnian "New Testament,"[3] spell out America's most basic values. The American civil religion promotes a measure of religious tolerance when it comes to individuals but is specific with respect to God's involvement in America. "And," as Will Herberg deduces, "it is a civil religion in the strictest sense of the term, for, in it, national life is apotheosized, national values are religionized, national heroes are divinized, national history is experienced as a *Heilsgeschichte*, as a redemptive history."[4]

Christopher Evans identifies baseball with American civil religion, especially during the Progressive Era. Progressive Era reformers in the social gospel movement, leaders such as Washington Gladden, envisioned a new millennium penetrating all of American culture.[5] "The emergence of baseball as the American national pastime," Evans writes, "reflected Gladden's faith that popular amusements, like baseball, served as clear signs of God's kingdom on earth."[6] However, baseball could not live up to the millennialist movement's specific ideal. Evans looks back on Progressive Era baseball and determines in hindsight — taking into consideration baseball's sins of greed, racism, and urban flight — that the kingdom of baseball failed those who anticipated it to usher in social progress.

Nevertheless, the ballpark in the twenty-first century continues to foster its role in an American civil religion. Even while baseball's claim, as Evans explains, "that the game can redeem America and serve as a light to the nations" never lived up to its promise, Comerica Park continues to portray the message of transcendent redemption. The ballpark communicates an understanding of national purpose, especially in wartime, and it offers an "understanding of the American experience in the light of ultimate and universal reality."[7] The ballpark in Detroit portrays a consensus myth of the game's role within the context of American civil religion, and it provides a narrative of a common set of values which are perceived to join together the diverse American democracy.

Comerica Park boasts memorials to an assortment of communal crises as well as the nation's most sacred events. For example, none of the other statues included with Horton are memorialized for their on-field talent alone. Like Horton, Charlie Gehringer is endorsed on the pedestal of his statue as a hometown hero. World War II veteran Hank Greenberg is acknowledged for putting his baseball career on hold to become, as the ballpark declares, "a national hero" for honoring both his religion[8] as well as the U.S. armed forces through, not just one, but two tours of duty against the decidedly evil Nazi threat to peace, justice, and freedom.[9] The ballpark is often home to organizing symbols and myths in the national consciousness.

The day Comerica Park opened, five statues graced the centerfield concourse with space allotted for one more. Had the objective been merely to find an additional statue to fill the void, the choices of past Tigers who achieved distinguished records and won prestigious awards are extensive.[10] However, the selection of Willie Horton fulfilled a distinct purpose.[11]

Horton symbolizes the Tigers' identification with the disenfranchised community. As the plaque affixed to the Horton statue reads, he "was instrumental in helping crush the violence that erupted during the 1967 riots in Detroit." Even more revealing, the Tiger hero's widely circulated quote, which attributes the Detroit Tigers as divine urban messengers, is inscribed on a ballpark wall: "I believe that the 1968 Tigers were put here by God to heal this city."[12] The ballpark, through the symbols and language attributed to Willie Horton, serves to inculcate and disseminate an American consensus myth.

America's Third Time of Trial

On July 23, 1967, the Tigers played a doubleheader at Tiger Stadium. By the second game, sirens blared in the distance from outside the stadium, and those seated in the upper deck on the first base side saw smoke billowing above Tiger Stadium's left field roof.[13] After the games, fans discovered that racial tensions had reached a breaking point. Rioters had set the city on fire. After the final out, Horton did not take time to shower or change into clothes. Still in full uniform, he drove deep into the riot zone. Flames leapt out of the windows of homes and businesses. Upturned cars wobbled on their rooftops like floundering pill bugs. Looters barreled down the streets with pillaged goods. Amateur snipers took aim from atop buildings. "I exited my car, climbed on the roof and started shouting at people until I got their attention," Horton remembers in his autobiography. "'Go home, Willie, don't stay down here,' someone said. 'We don't want you to get hurt.'"[14] The U.S. National Guard moved in and patrolled Detroit's streets with tanks and armored vehicles. Forty-three people were killed, 1,189 were injured. More than 7,200 were arrested.[15]

The following months resulted in mass "white flight," in which businesses and people with means fled from Detroit to the suburbs. The NFL's Lions eventually left for Pontiac. The NBA's Pistons followed, settling in Auburn Hills. The Tigers stayed. Those who remained in Detroit bought more guns in 1968 than at any other time in Detroit's prior history.[16] That was followed with the assassinations of Martin Luther King, Jr., and Robert F. Kennedy. Detroit was immersed in, what Robert Bellah called, American civil religion's third time of trial.[17]

Bellah identifies the American Revolution and the Civil War as America's first two times of trial.[18] While the first time of trial concerned the question of independence and the second involved the subsistence of the Union as a city upon a hill,[19] a defining component of the third time of trial at home concerned oppressed racial groups.[20]

What made America "a nation with a soul of a church," in the view of G. K. Chesterton, was "America is the only nation in the world that is founded on a creed. That creed is set forth with dogmatic and even theological lucidity in the Declaration of Independence."[21] As noted above, the sacred scriptures of the civil religion include the Declaration of Independence and the Constitution. "Both the Constitution and the Civil War amendments are thoroughly secular documents," Bellah explains, "but they embody the moral commitment of a covenant people to order its life by the highest standards of which it is capable."[22] For the American civil religion partisan, America's pattern followed that of Biblical times in which a profound conversion experience led to covenant.[23] Just as a covenant is needed for a convert, a constitution was needed for a revolutionist. The amendments following the Civil War conversion experience further cement the nation's covenant in the consciousness of many Americans.

However, America never lived up to its intuited divine calling — even before the Constitution, America had been founded on "the bondage and genocide of other races."[24] In the tumultuous decade of the 1960s, the time had come again for widespread questioning whether the pervasive self-image of America as "the golden door"— to use a phrase from the inscription on the pedestal of the Statue of Liberty — for the "huddled masses yearning to breathe free"[25] still held meaning.

Malcolm X articulated a counter narrative in his autobiography — released shortly before Detroit's violent expression of discontent. The dissident's life story hinged on an event that hit close to home for Michiganders. Malcolm X was raised and educated in and around Lansing, Michigan's capitol city. There, an interaction unfolded between Malcolm and a Mr. Ostrowski. When the trusted junior high teacher asked his bright and esteemed pupil (Malcolm combined excellent grades with popularity among his peers expressed in his election as student body president.) what career direction Malcolm might pursue, the young standout responded, "Lawyer." Mr. Ostrowski squelched his student's ambition with the rebuke, "We all here like you, you know that. But you've got to be realistic about being a nigger. A lawyer — that's no realistic goal for a nigger."[26] The white mentor pushed manual labor as an alternative and repelled Malcolm in a direction that led him to drop out of school and land in prison. Malcolm X's formative moment epitomized similar discrepancies within the national narrative throughout the state and exposed as fraudulent the Statue of Liberty's and Declaration of Independence's promises.

America's third time of trial called into question the prevalent national understanding of the country's identity and purpose. While the crisis of justice reverberated at home, it was also exposed abroad. Among the factors that spun America into its third time of trial were disreputable American involvements in identity-rattling events in the world like the Vietnam War.[27] The third time of trial forced America to decide once again "whether," in the words of Lincoln, "that nation, or any nation so conceived, and so dedicated, can long endure."

While the tradition of civil religion in national life threatened to come undone, the ballpark served to bring people of all races and creeds together. Fans continued to stand in unison for the singing of the National Anthem prior to each game. "I trust in God" and "I love my country" remained the first two lines in the Little League pledge. Detroit, as native Michigander Rebecca Stowe writes in her essay about her childhood affection for Willie Horton and the Tigers, allowed fans to maintain regional loyalty while the rest of the country degraded the city as the nation's Murder Capital.[28]

After the 1967 riots, Opening Day in Detroit, April 9, 1968, was postponed for King's funeral. Two months after the civil rights leader's death, and hours after winning California's presidential primary, Kennedy was shot and killed. The Tigers played this time. As Detroit *Free Press* columnist Joe Falls described the situation, fear gripped the city that spring.[29] Michael Novak contends that during this time of horror and despair, the American spirit needed baseball. "In the well-ordered world of baseball," Novak explained, "an assassination is a grievous, savage, and blasphemous intrusion."[30] As difficult as times were, the ballpark offered a place of tranquility to palliate many Americans' anxieties. Indeed, when President Lyndon Johnson declared June 9, 1968, a national day of mourning, the largest crowd of the season to that point—several hundred more than capacity—crammed into Tiger Stadium.[31]

Horton describes in his autobiography *The People's Champion* what he and the Tigers meant to the city disillusioned with America.

> Early in the 1968 season it started to become clear to me that our team had an assignment that was even more important than winning a pennant. It seemed to me that there was some divine inspiration at work here. It seemed to me that the Tigers' real undertaking in 1968 was to help unify the city of Detroit, to bring black and white together. Our aim was to restore harmony to an area that had been a battleground for four days the summer before. Our mission was to heal the city.[32]

The "divine inspiration" Horton perceived at work through the Tigers during the tumultuous year of 1968 nourished a national consensus narrative. Through well-placed symbols and displayed quotes, Horton's message continues to receive a hearing at the ballpark.

For those in attendance at the Detroit ballpark, Horton symbolizes citywide recommitment to a national theological creed as well as to a national responsibility as a covenant people. In keeping with American civil religion, the quote the Tigers chose to display at their new home, Comerica Park, the Deity with the generic moniker "God"—to whom people of all faiths can relate—engages in a specific activity in American history. The Tigers inscribed Horton's statement of faith: "I believe the '68 Tigers were put here by God to heal this city." Horton, now Special Assistant to the Tigers' General Manager and CEO, reflects on his myth-embodying quote: "God knew the city of Detroit needed an event to restore some harmony to our neighborhoods. The 1968 Tigers did the work for Him."[33] It is this kind of specificity with regard to God's special interest in America that, Bellah explains, saved American civil religion "from empty formalism and served as a genuine vehicle of national religious self-understanding."[34] It is also this kind of specificity that allows the ballpark to communicate its distinct message about who Americans are with respect to a set of Platonic ideals.[35]

Moral and Spiritual Meaning in Myth

At least one challenge to Horton's legacy has been raised. George Cantor acknowledges the power of Horton's claim on the city but has yet to see direct fruits of God's concurrent involvement. "The belief has passed into Detroit folklore," Cantor writes in hindsight.

> Many people swear, as Willie Horton says, that they were "put here by God to save the city." At the risk of sounding sacrilegious, it should be pointed out that the Almighty didn't have much of a follow-through. The city's racial split was too wide for the temporary euphoria of a championship to overcome.[36]

Other questions could be raised in rebuttal, advancing Willie Horton's and the Tigers' influence: How low might the city have fallen had God not used the 1968 Tigers? What if the team left for the suburbs like so many other sports teams? Without the 1968 Tigers, would the God of American civil religion have preserved Detroit at all? Would the city have reached the point of disillusionment beyond return? However, the ballpark pursues none of these lines of questioning for the same reason it does not pursue Cantor's: his analysis of the succeeding history following the riots does not fit within a grander *Heilsgeschichte*, or redemptive history.

Cantor's reservation, no matter how perceptive, remains a foreign voice in the ballpark. It remains unincorporated into the ballpark's working myths and, therefore, does not tell Detroit's story within the greater context of America's story. Instead, Horton's account remains Detroit's ballpark narrative and thus provides moral and spiritual meaning with respect to the city.[37] Horton's legacy represents restored faith in America for a city that was in the depths of the nation's third time of trial. Through Willie Horton, the Tigers do not "enslave Americans to a sanitized past,"[38] as Christopher Evans warns against in his work on baseball and American civil religion. Instead, the ballpark encourages attendees to experience the past as redemptive history. Horton's narrative gives meaning to and offers an interpretation for one of the community's deepest shared experiences.[39] At the same time it contributes to the melioristic tendency of American civil religion that the third time of trial is well on its way to being solved.

In his essay on baseball and civil religion, Evans argues that in the turn of the twentieth century, baseball — through the influx of permanent ballparks — augmented the Protestant theological vision preached by social gospelers to redeem urban areas.[40] But Evans questions the 1950s and 1960s trend in which teams departed from their early urban stadiums for suburban locations. "No greater indictment of the kingdom of baseball's failure," Evans explains, "can be found than professional baseball's mass exodus from the very centers in America that it was enshrined to redeem: the cities."[41] However, the Horton statue stands out as a blatant reminder that the Tigers did not fail Detroit in this manner during the nation's third time of trial.

In the midst of pervasive Detroiter "white flight," the Tigers further cemented Horton's version as the city's narrative. Not only did the team remain in the city, they expressed their commitment to staying in the city. "This franchise belongs to the inner city of Detroit," Tigers owner John E. Fetzer (1956–1983) said. "I'm just the caretaker."[42] After Tom Monaghan took over ownership from Fetzer, he reiterated his predecessor's vow never to leave the city. Even by 1988 when Monaghan began to namedrop other suburban cities actively courting the Tigers, the remarks were recognized as standard public relations procedure to generate public funding for a new downtown Detroit stadium rather than an indication of any genuine intent to depart.[43] It is no coincidence that a short time after Monaghan was exposed as a phony friend to the city that he opted to sell the team to a proven Detroit entrepreneur in Mike Ilitch, who immediately prophesied, "There is no way I would move this team out of the city. Never."[44]

Further cementing the myths that Horton embodies, Michigan governor Jennifer Granholm signed into state law a 2004 bill that declared October 18 as "Willie Horton Day." Using the language engraved on the plaque affixed to the statue at Comerica Park, the bill read in part, "In 1967, Willie used his ambassadorship and goodwill to help crush the violence that erupted during the riots in Detroit."[45] The statewide bill moved Horton's narrative beyond baseball fans in Detroit to Michigan citizens in general.

Even though Horton spent his Detroit career at Tiger Stadium (which ceased to be the home field for the Tigers in 1999), his sculpture and preserved quote ensure the Tigers' meaning and mission are remembered in their new home at Comerica Park. It does not matter that Horton's playing career did not match up with many other former Tigers. Horton's encounter is considered sacred because it has done precisely what Bellah credits as the purpose of myth within American civil religion — to reveal "what reality is and how we should act in relation to it."[46] The Willie Horton statue and augmenting quotes provide Michiganders with an interpretation of who they are in light of an American covenant understanding.

American Dream

Biographers Grant Eldridge and Karen Elizabeth Bush play to the myth in summing up Horton's effort to counteract dissenting voices. "He was absolutely sure," they write, "that, if young people of all races had hope — that is, if he could give them something to dream about — just knowing that the dream was possible would help them get along in the world."[47] The biographers praise Horton for enlivening a specific "dream" — the American Dream.

Horton symbolizes the American Dream for Detroit's youth — that America offers every inhabitant the opportunity to pursue happiness. Horton's first achievement listed on the statue's plaque reads, "Raised in a Detroit housing project and overcame adversity to become a Tiger hometown hero." Horton's experience gave him a unique platform to preach the American Dream to those who where otherwise least likely to subscribe to it. His credibility was enhanced with the ability to proclaim to Detroit's youth, "I had the same problems you have. I know what you do and how you think."[48] Horton provided reassurance in the face of Malcolm X's narrative and others like it during America's third time of trial. He promoted the myth that if he could make it as a baseball player, they too could be anything they wanted to be. "Maybe you want to be a doctor or lawyer or a good mechanic," Horton told an assembly of boys from Detroit. "It doesn't matter what it is — you just have to find it for yourself and make it your life."[49]

Echoing the American theology Benjamin Franklin taught — that "God helps them that help themselves" — Horton preached to Detroit youths during his playing days, "If you have a dream, you need to work hard to achieve it."[50] His message to Detroit is a modern day version of the American ethic that people "are endowed by their Creator with certain inalienable Rights" and in America they are born with life and liberty, so happiness is within grasp. The message is that so long as they are willing to put forth the effort,

America offers everyone an equal opportunity to fulfill their dreams, just as the Creator intended. Horton's statue provides a constant reminder to Detroiters of a hometown dream fulfilled.

That Horton grew up and remained in Detroit provides the myth genuine usefulness. Failure to ground a value system within the soul of the people leaves those principles isolated from meaning.[51] As a distinctive Detroiter, Horton's statue is capable of stimulating idealism genuinely Detroit's own.

Conclusion

Willie Horton did not compile Hall of Fame statistics. Yet his inclusion amidst the Tiger's statues confers upon him an honor far rarer than enshrinement in Cooperstown.[52] Horton's message exhibited at the ballpark should not be interpreted as "enslaving Americans to a sanitized past," as Evans warns against in his work on baseball and American civil religion. Detroit's ballpark does not evade or conceal the city's riots and racial tensions during America's third time of trial. Indeed, the 1967 riots prove central to the Willie Horton statue's meaning. Instead, the ballpark interprets the trial in light of an ultimate and universal reality. The Horton myth reinserts Detroit within the larger context of the national story, highlighting American civil religion in all of its dynamism.

The danger in the ballpark's interpretation is that it downplays diversity and ignores contemporary tensions while it promotes American exceptionalism. Scholars such as Amanda Porterfield express concern that American civil religion's "tendency to chauvinism" often allows Americans with the most power to define the values for all.[53] Indeed, the ballpark communicates an overarching set of American virtues and commitments that disregard dissenting voices such as William Lloyd Garrison who viewed the Constitution as a "pact with the devil." At the ballpark, Cantor's observation that "the Almighty didn't have much of a follow-through" is one such alienated voice.

Willie Horton's statue at Comerica Park demonstrates that ballparks are like other places of worship because they reach beyond the material universe to inform a specific people's history — specifically, they inform the transcendent meaning of the nation for partisans of American civil religion. The ballpark's surrounding symbols, as we have seen in the Horton monument, are a clue to the ballpark's religious tone. The prominently positioned statue serves as a statement of faith as well as representative of a specific moment of, to use Will Herberg's term, *Heilsgeschichte*. Horton's sculpture overlooks every game from centerfield as a reminder of the Tigers' sacred meaning and divine mission within American civil religion. The Willie Horton myth continues to communicate to a city that was in the depths of the nation's third time of trial — and continues to travail — that the great experiment is worth continuing.

Notes

1. Ty Cobb won the batting Triple Crown in 1909 with the most home runs, RBIs, and highest batting average, while Hal Newhouser won the pitching Triple Crown in 1945 with the most wins, strikeouts, and lowest earned run average. Among the six MVPs were Hank Greenberg in 1935 and 1940; Charlie Gehringer in 1937; Hal Newhouser in 1944 and 1945. The Baseball Writers Association of America (BBWAA) began awarding the Most Valuable Player Award in 1931. While Cobb retired in 1928, three years before the BBWAA began awarding their MVP, he won the first ever MVP in 1911 when the Chalmers Award made the distinction between "player of the year" (determined by batting average) and Most Valuable. Cobb won co-player of the year the previous season in 1910 before Chalmers changed its designation. Al Kaline finished second twice in 1955 and 1963 and in the top ten nine times. In addition, Cobb, Gehringer, Greenberg, Newhouser, and Kaline combined for fourteen batting titles, five home run titles, eight RBI titles, two earned run average titles, and four strike-out titles.

2. On a smaller scale, Horton did set a single game record for putouts in a game with twelve.

3. Among Lincoln's orations included in the Lincolnian New Testament are his Second Inaugural and Gettysburg Addresses. Robert N. Bellah, "Civil Religion in America," *Dædalus* 96 (Winter 1967): 10.

4. Will Herberg, "America's Civil Religion: What Is It Whence It Comes," in Russell E. Richey and Donald G. Jones, eds., *American Civil Religion* (New York: Harper and Row, 1974), 78.

5. Gladden wrote, "Every department of human life — the families, the schools, amusements, art, business, politics, industry, national politics, international relations — will be governed by the Christian law and controlled by Christian influences.... The complete Christianization of all life is what we pray for and work for, when we work and pray for the coming of the kingdom of heaven." Washington Gladden, *The Church and the Kingdom* (New York: Fleming H. Revell, 1894), 8, quoted in Christopher H. Evans, "The Kingdom of Baseball in America: The Chronicle of an American Theology," in Christopher H. Evans and William R. Herzog II, eds., *Faith of 50 Million: Baseball, Religion, and American Culture* (Louisville: Westminster John Knox Press, 2002), 37.

6. Evans, "The Kingdom of Baseball in America," 37.

7. Bellah, "Civil Religion in America," 18.

8. On the Comerica Park concourse, Greenberg is described: "A national hero to millions of American Jews, he sat out Yom Kippur during the heat of the 1934 pennant race." See also Hank Greenberg, edited and with an introduction by Ira Berkow, *Hank Greenberg: The Story of My Life* (New York: Times Books, 1989), 267.

9. Greenberg's statue itself reads in part, "Entered the Army in 1941, interrupting his career." Elsewhere in the ballpark concourse, the Tigers give more specific details. "Greenberg was the first Tiger inducted into the military during World War II, interrupting his outstanding baseball career for four full seasons. He finished his tour in 1941, two days before the attack on Pearl Harbor, and immediately re-enlisted. After his Army discharge, he hit a home run his first game back on July 1, 1945, and helped the Tigers return to the World Series." In addition, former Tigers Al Benton, Jimmy Bloodworth, Tommy Bridges, Hoot Evers, Billy Hitchcock, Fred Hutchinson, Johnny Lipon, Barnie McCosky, Les Mueller, Pat Mullin, Birdie Tebbetts, Virgil Trucks, Dick Wakefield, and Hal White are honored for their service to the country.

10. In the long history of the Detroit Tiger franchise, many players have had stellar baseball careers complete with plenty of records. The very season Willie Horton's Tigers won the 1968 World Series, his teammate and two-time Cy Young Award winner, Denny McLain, was unanimously voted American League MVP. That season, McLain became Detroit's only, and the major league's last, pitcher to date to win thirty games or more in a season.

In addition to McLain, two other Tigers without statues at Comerica Park have won the MVP: Willie Hernandez (1984) and Tiger Hall of Famer Mickey Cochrane (1934). Tigers Hall of Famers not emblazoned in statue (nor their numbers retired) at Comerica Park, who went into the Hall with a Tigers cap, include Cochrane, Sam Crawford (who set the career record for triples), Harry Heilmann (who won four batting titles in 1921, '23, '25, and '27, hitting .403 in 1923), George Kell (who won a batting title in 1949 and became a longtime Tigers announcer following his baseball career), Heinie Manush (who won a batting title in 1926), and player/manager Hughie Jennings.

11. See Mike Ilitch, "A Special Tribute," in Kevin M. Allen and Willie Horton, *The People's Champion: Willie Horton* (Wayne, MI: Immortal Investments, 2004), 195–196.

12. Horton's assertion is often reiterated in Detroit's media. I most recently heard the quote on "Tigers Weekly," Fox Sports Net, June 22, 2006.

13. George Cantor, *The Tigers of '68: Baseball's Last Real Champions* (Dallas: Taylor, 1997), 1.

14. Kevin M. Allen and Willie Horton, *The People's Champion: Willie Horton* (Wayne, MI: Immortal Investments, 2004), 65. The book is given prominent visibility at the ballpark. One of the Tigers' promotions for the past several seasons has Horton signing copies of his autobiography during batting practice prior to each Saturday home game at Comerica Park.

15. *Ibid.*, 66.

16. Joe Falls, *The Detroit Tigers: An Illustrated History* (New York: Walker, 1989), 127.

17. Bellah, "Civil Religion in America," 16–19. See also Robert N. Bellah, *The Broken Covenant: American Civil Religion in Time of Trial*, 2d ed. (Chicago: University of Chicago Press, 1992), 87–111.

18. Bellah, "Civil Religion in America," 9–11.

19. For the role of the Civil War in the American civil religion, see also Harry S. Stout, *Upon the Altar of the Nation: A Moral History of the Civil War* (New York: Viking, 2006).

20. Bellah, *The Broken Covenant*, 88.

21. Quoted in Sidney E. Mead, *The Nation With the Soul of a Church* (New York: Harper and Row, 1975), 20. From Raymond T. Bond, ed., *The Man Who Was Chesterton* (Garden City, NY: Doubleday Image, 1960).

22. Bellah, *The Broken Covenant*, 62. Pierard and Linder echo Bellah as they write that "the colonial evangelicals who believed that their own church covenants were vehicles of God's action in history came to see the founding documents as new covenants which bound together the people of the nation and secured for them God's blessing and call to historic mission." Richard V. Pierard and Robert D. Linder, *Civil Religion and the Presidency* (Grand Rapids: Academie, 1988), 55.

23. Even more definite, Bellah writes, "But without a new order, without a new system of control, liberation cannot become liberty and quickly becomes despotism." *The Broken Covenant*, 85.

24. *Ibid.*, 62.

25. For Bellah's interpretation of this most archetypal of American symbols see *The Broken Covenant*, 89.

26. Malcolm X, as told to Alex Haley, *The Autobiography of Malcolm X* (New York: Ballantine, 1992), 41.

27. For a dissenting view, see R. Laurence Moore, *Religious Outsiders and the Making of Americans* (New York and Oxford: Oxford University Press, 1986). Moore writes, "Our failures in Vietnam have properly had to answer for many things, but the disruption of 'normal' religious behavior is not one of them" (x).

28. Rebecca Stowe, "Sentimental Willie," in Tom Stanton, ed., *The Detroit Tigers Reader* (Ann Arbor: The University of Michigan Press, 2005), 167.

29. Joe Falls, *The Detroit Tigers* (New York: Walker, 1989), 127.

30. Michael Novak, *The Joy of Sports: Endzones, Bases, Baskets, Balls, and the Consecration of the American Spirit*, rev. ed. (Lanham, MD: Madison, 1994), 286.

31. Cantor, *The Tigers of '68*, 73. Attendance was listed at 52,938, while capacity was 52,220.

32. Allen and Horton, *The People's Champion*, 68–69.

33. *Ibid.*, 92.

34. Bellah, "Civil Religion in America," 8.

35. R. Laurence Moore perceptively argues that what makes American civil religion bankrupt is that it tends to define national culture "by reference to a set of Platonic ideals." *Religious Outsiders*, xiii.

36. Cantor, *The Tigers of '68*, 217–218.

37. Voices, such as Hal Butler's, that affirm the narrative cite sociologists who confirm Horton's version. Hal Butler, *The Willie Horton Story* (New York: Julian Messner, 1970), 174.

In addition, voices like catcher Bill Freehan, also with local roots, corroborate Horton's testimony. "A baseball team and a world championship can't cure such social ills," Freehan said. "But I honestly think that pride in our team helped the healing process and gave everyone a focal point to look at and feel like it belonged to everyone who lived there." Quoted in Richard Bak, *A Place for Summer: A Narrative History of Tiger Stadium* (Detroit: Wayne State University Press, 1998), 304.

38. Evans, "The Kingdom of Baseball in America," 48.

39. Bellah, *The Broken Covenant*, 153.

40. Evans, "The Kingdom of Baseball in America," 38.

41. *Ibid.*, 42.

42. Michael Betzold and Ethan Casey, *Queen of Diamonds: The Tiger Stadium Story*, 2d ed. (West Bloomfield, MI: Northmont, 1997), 101.

43. *Ibid.*, 223–235. Betzold and Casey title their chapter detailing the chronology of PR maneuvering for a new publicly funded stadium during Monaghan's latter years as owner, "The Empty Threat." See also Bak, *A Place for Summer*, 332–364.

44. Betzold and Casey, *Queen of Diamonds*, 328.

45. State of Michigan House Bill No. 5200, 92nd Legislature (April 8, 2004), http://www.legislature.mi.gov/(S(i3v4jorbtsu0bdeu0dds45))/mileg.aspx?page=getObjectName=mcl-435-321. Horton joined a limited and elite group (seven total) to be honored with a day designated in their honor: President John F. Kennedy (1966), eighteenth-century freedom fighter Casimir Pulaski (1972), civil rights activist and Michigan resident Rosa Parks (1997), human rights leader Cesar Chavez (2003), president and Michigan native Gerald R. Ford (2003), and Michigan resident Henry Ford, who "made an automobile that was affordable for his workers" (2003), http://www.legislature.mi.gov/(S(5hpyku452xjcog45nxqmdyvt))/mileg.aspx?page=GetMCLDocument&objectname=mcl-435-303.

46. Bellah, *The Broken Covenant*, 153.

47. Grant Eldridge and Karen Elizabeth Bush, *Willie Horton: Detroit's Own Willie the Wonder* (Detroit: Wayne State University Press, 2001), 93–4.

48. Butler, *The Willie Horton Story*, 8.

49. *Ibid.*, 9.

50. Eldridge and Bush, *Detroit's Own Willie the Wonder*, 94.

51. Bellah, *The Broken Covenant*, 112–138.

52. While eleven Tigers are enshrined in the Baseball Hall of Fame, the club honors only six players in statue at the ballpark.

53. Amanda Porterfield, "American Civil Religion Revisited," *Religion and American Culture: A Journal of Interpretation* 4 (Winter 1994).

Part Two

The Diplomacy of Baseball and the International Game

CHAPTER 9

The Nationalist Pastime: The Use of Baseball to Promote Nationalism Globally

Russ Crawford

"Base Ball has been known in the Northern States as far back as the memory of the oldest inhabitant reacheth, and must be regarded as the national pastime, the same as cricket is by the English."[1]

Since William T. Porter wrote that passage in the *Spirit of the Times*, a weekly sporting newspaper published in New York City in 1857, baseball has been the nominal National Pastime of the United States. As the country was well advanced in the process of dissolution that would lead to the American Civil War (1861–1865), the need for anything that would provide unification was urgent.

Porter's call also began the career of using baseball to promote ends beyond pleasant physical exercise. Throughout the late nineteenth century and beyond, baseball has been used to promote nationalistic agendas, not only in the U.S., but also in other nations where the sport had become popular. This essay will consider that use of baseball to promote nationalism, beginning with the U.S. and then considering the ways in which the game was employed by Japanese modernizers and Cuban revolutionaries to build their own sense of national identity in the face of "interesting times."

The National Pastime

In the 1850s, the U.S. faced several challenges that led to the need for a unifying force. The most visible historically was the precipitous slide towards civil war over the question of state's rights to allow the ownership of slaves that would lead to the secession of Southern states and the Civil War in 1861. Neither baseball, nor for that matter, mom, apple pie, or political compromise, could do anything to reverse this process that was as old as the nation.

However, in the long run, baseball was able to offer solutions to other problems that also beset the struggling nation. In the 1840s and 1850s, large numbers of German and Irish immigrants began entering the U.S., which caused many old-line Anglo-Saxon Protestants to react with alarm over the effect that these "popish" (Catholic) elements might have on the culture. Nativist fears led to the creation of the American Party, also known as the Know Nothings in the 1850s, and even those who did not harbor dark fears of plots emanating from Rome felt that something must be done to promote national unity and patriotism.

Before the "melting pot" narrative offered a solution for mass immigration, which brought teeming masses to American shores, baseball served as a means of assimilating diverse nationalities into American culture. The New York baseball fraternity, where the game as we know it began, actively promoted the sport for this purpose, and many of the original teams, often featuring immigrant players, used patriotic imagery, such as Union, Washington, Liberty, and the like in their team names.[2]

Baseball and the Melting Pot

While baseball was unable to provide the unifying force that would hold the nation together, the Civil War was instrumental in spreading the popularity of the sport to men from all sections of the nation. Many of the soldiers who were introduced to the game were the same German and Irish immigrants that had been such a source of concern before larger issues had come to the fore. After the war, the once fraternal game of middle-class Protestant clerks expanded to include legions of new Americans. Ethnic tensions had by no means gone away, and some of the games between old stock and immigrant nines often took on an overtone of ethnic animosity that threatened the play on the field, as one team fought for their right to be considered American and the other fought to deny them that right.

Even before the war spread the popularity of the sport, the celebrated match between the old-stock Protestant middle-class Excelsiors and the Irish Catholic working- class Atlantics demonstrated the tensions that could arise when class, ethnicity, and nationalism formed the milieu in which the game was played. After splitting the first two games of the scheduled three game series, a series of questionable calls by the umpire caused a near riot by the

Atlantics' fans, leading the Excelsiors' captain to pull his team from the field. The team's retreat was met by the Atlantics' fans pelting the Excelsiors' omnibus with stones, and commentators in the *New York Clipper* darkly stated, "The cause of the disorder was the spirit of faction ... in which the foreign element of our immense metropolitan population and their ... offspring especially, delights to indulge."[3]

Despite the early tensions that existed within the game, when professionals began taking over the sport, ethnic heroes such as King Kelly became heralded not only by Irish fans, but by supporters of whatever team he happened to be playing for at the time. Kelly's popularity was such that his exploits were made into the popular song *Slide Kelly Slide* that became a national hit.[4] The utility of the National Pastime as a tool in the melting pot would continue, helping Native Americans (Louis Sockalexis, Jim Thorpe), Jewish Americans (Hank Greenberg), Italian Americans (Joe DiMaggio), and finally African Americans (Jackie Robinson and Lary Doby in 1947) claim their right to be part of American culture.[5]

This process was not one of the old guard bringing in new blood to the game, but rather it was the act of immigrants pushing their way in, claiming their place in the game and in American life. This may have been hotly contested at the time, but it also provided a nationalistic narrative for baseball that helped swell national pride, and expand the pool of those sharing that pride.

Baseball and American Exceptionality

Baseball also aided the nation in its early years when English sportsmen dominated popular sports such as horse racing, prize fighting, and cricket, which would rival baseball in popularity until the late nineteenth century. Porter's call for the enshrinement of baseball as the American national game was indeed an effort to find a game that Americans could play better than all others. Once baseball was anointed as the chosen National Pastime, considerable effort was put into creating evidence that baseball was indeed an American game, and that it was superior to the British national sport of cricket. A. Sedgwick, writing in *The Nation* in 1869, argued for baseball being the national sport by contrasting the supposed national characteristics of Americans and Britons, claiming that Americans were "less brutal ... and more fond of novelty,"[6] which led to the former embracing baseball, a, presumably, more humane and contemporary sport.

Albert G. Spalding also concluded that the two sports were good fits for their respective cultures, and in *America's National Game* (1911), he argued,

"Cricket is a splendid game; for Britons. It is a genteel game, a conventional game — and our cousins across the Atlantic are nothing if not conventional. They play cricket because it accords with the traditions of their country so to do; because it is easy and does not overtax their energy or their thought." He further argued: "I claim that Base Ball owes its prestige as our National Game to the fact that as no other form of sport it is the exponent of American Courage, Confidence, Combativeness; American Dash, Discipline, Determination; American Energy, Eagerness, Enthusiasm; American Pluck, Persistence, Performance, American Spirit, Sagacity, Success; American Vim, Vigor, Virility."[7] In short, baseball was truly American because it matched the superiority of the Americans who played and enjoyed it.

The Spalding World Tour 1888

Spalding felt that the American game had such value that he undertook a proselytizing mission to bring baseball to the rest of the world. In 1888, he organized and led a tour that included stops in Hawaii, New Zealand, Australia, Egypt, England, France, and parts in between.[8] The players, which included Spalding's Chicago White Stockings and an opposition team made up of all-stars from the other National League teams played exhibition matches between themselves as well as playing local teams. Although declining to play in Hawaii (then a sovereign nation) because the only day available was Sunday, they did play a game in the shadow of the Pyramids and performed one exhibition under the eyes of the Prince of Wales.[9]

In England, Spalding had agreed to play cricket against an English team, a move that might have proved disastrous for the Americans. However, Spalding negotiated to instead make the game Rounders, a British children's game that many Britons, and some Americans, felt was the game from which baseball evolved. The Americans acquitted themselves well, losing 16–14, winning a moral victory after falling far behind in the first at-bat. Then the visitors handed the English a drubbing in baseball, defeating the home team 18–0 before the game was called.[10]

The controversy surrounding the evolution of baseball from the English game of Rounders threatened the nationalistic narrative that baseball was uniquely American and led to the formation of the Mills Commission to investigate the matter in 1905. Colonel A.G. Mills, who headed the commission, issued the final report in 1907, concluding, "First: Base Ball had its origin in the United States, and Second: That the first scheme for playing it, according to the best evidence obtainable to date, was devised by Abner Doubleday at Cooperstown, New York, in 1839."[11] Spalding would write the same story line into his *America's National Game*, and the legend of Abner Doubleday, Civil War hero and baseball pioneer, would pass into nationalistic mythology. Later historians would join box score inventor and critic of the Doubleday legend Henry Chadwick in linking Rounders and baseball, but for a nation seeking to carve out its distinct place in the world, the American origins of baseball were set.

Japan: Baseball as Modernity

While Spalding's World Tour failed to greatly popularize baseball in the rest of the world, it did expand the marketing potential for his sporting goods company. His and other's push for the internationalization of baseball was matched by a pull coming from people in other lands who enjoyed the sport, but who also had other reasons for embracing the game. One of those nations was Japan, which was in the process of embracing modernization and Westernization after two centuries of isolation.

In 1635, the Tokugawa Shogunate passed the *sakoku* (exclusion policy), which forbade most Japanese contact with the rest of the world. This was done to deny the *daimyos* (Great Lords) access to Western weaponry and to keep out Christianity, which was seen as a destabilizing religion.[12] For the next two-hundred years the island nation existed, save for brief annual visits from Dutch traders, in near total isolation. This isolation was aided by the peripheral location of the Japanese islands; far from established trade routes. While this allowed the Japanese to develop their culture free from outside influences, it also made them vulnerable when the outside world finally demanded entrance. With the expansion of the whaling industry in the mid nineteenth century, the islands came into play, and the treatment of shipwrecked sailors, who were beheaded, caused Westerners to take alarmed notice of the islands. This concern, along with a general mood of Western aggressiveness that followed the easy British victory in the first Opium War (1839–42), led the West to turn its gaze onto Japan and to take steps to open the nation to Western trade.[13]

First contact occurred in 1853, when Commodore Matthew Perry of the U.S. Navy arrived in Edo Bay (modern Tokyo) with four capital ships and demanded the Japanese accede to several demands contained in a letter from American President Millard Fillmore. The outdated Japanese naval defenses could not match the modern firepower of the American fleet, and the government capitulated with the signing of the Convention of Kanagawa in 1854. Like sharks drawn to blood in the water, other Western powers including Britain, France, and Russia soon negotiated their own treaties, all of which contained extraterritoriality provisions, which allowed Westerners accused of a crime in Japan to be tried under their native law, rather than under the Japanese legal code.[14]

Dissatisfaction with the unequal treaties added to the discontent of those *daimyo* that had been successfully excluded from any role in governance after the battle of Sekigahara in 1603, and in coalition they overthrew the Tokagawa Shogunate under the banner of restoring imperial power. The Meiji Restoration lodged effective power with the oligarchs, made up of *daimyo* primarily of the Choshu and Satsuma domains, who were anxious to undertake a radical program of modernization and Westernization. They wasted little time, and almost immediately sent delegations across the U.S. and Western Europe to recruit technicians and also began sending students to the West for study. The Iwakura Mission visited foreign lands between 1871 and 1872, with an eye for recruiting experts to help Japan modernize.

Despite Tom Cruise's role in *The Last Samurai*, the Japanese were particularly impressed with American expertise in "education, agriculture, and animal husbandry."[15] They preferred the French, and after 1871, the Prussians for their military help, but perhaps Cruise as a dashing agricultural agent would not have been so compelling.

The Apostles of Baseball

In addition to being a source for experts, the West also served as a dumping ground for "family black sheep and ne'er-do-wells."[16] One of those ne'er-do-well students was Hiraoka Hiroshi, who was shipped off to the U.S. to study and hopefully make something of himself. Upon arrival in 1871, Hiraoka became enamored with becoming a railroad engineer, and he also became an ardent fan of the Boston Red Stockings of the National Association of Base Ball Players. Hiraoka also became friends with Albert Spalding, a pitcher for the Red Stockings at that time, and when Hiraoka returned home he would use that friendship to receive baseball equipment for the team he would start. Using the connections that he had made as a translator and guide for the Iwakura Mission that visited Boston in 1872, Hiraoka was able to land a prominent job with the Shinbashi Railroad Bureau, and after introducing his managerial colleagues to the American game, in 1878, he founded the Shinbashi Athletic Club (SAC), the first private baseball club in Japan. The SAC built the first baseball field in Japan, designed and kept up to the standards that Hiraoka had observed in Boston, and the game was presented to the local spectators as a "pleasurable, but structured, group enterprise that entailed the discipline of work."[17]

Hiraoka moved in the upper echelons of Japanese society and introduced many of his class to the sport. One of the Tokugawa was also taken with the game and established a rival team named the Hercules club, and as more clubs formed, the possibility of a regular schedule of games became a possibility. As popularity for the game spread, baseball became modernity incarnate,[18] and a visible symbol that the Japanese were joining the West, becoming strong enough in the late nineteenth century, after defeating China in the Sino-Japanese War (1894–1895), to negotiate away the unequal treaties they had been forced to sign.

The groundwork for the first Japanese baseball clubs had already been sown by the *oyatoi* (living machines) or foreign technicians and consultants recruited by the Iwakura Mission and others to help jump start Japanese industry. One of these experts was Horace Wilson, who arrived in 1872, to become an instructor in Tokyo's Daigaku Minamiko, which later became Keiseiko University. Wilson arrived in Japan with baseball equipment in his luggage and began almost immediately to teach the game to his students. By 1876, he had taught his charges well enough for them to begin competing against teams of Americans assembled from the residents of the foreign settlement in Yokohama.[19]

Wilson was not alone in his passion for baseball, and many Americans from fellow *oyatoi* to missionaries fired with zeal for Muscular Christianity also arrived with baseball equipment among their personal effects. Baseball soon became a favorite sport for many Japanese alongside sumo wrestling and samurai martial arts. Spalding, now a sporting goods seller and baseball executive, helped this trend by sending equipment to Hiraoka and by attempting to establish a presence in the new Asian market. However, the Japanese, demonstrating the business acumen that would fuel the economic miracle of the 1970s, soon began making their own equipment. Mizuno, still an important name in sporting equipment, was one of the early *zaibatsu* (large business conglomerates) that challenged Spalding's penetration into the Asian market.[20]

In the early twentieth century, as more and more Japanese universities began fielding baseball teams, they began traveling to the U. S. to compete with American university nines, and American university teams reciprocated. These junkets brought favorable attention, not only for the skills of the Japanese athletes, but also for Japan's Westernizing efforts.

Waseda University became the class of the Japanese system, playing home and away series with a variety of American university teams. In 1910, the Chicago University team traveled to Yokohama for a series of games with Waseda and Keo Universities.[21] Those teams, including Chicago, that traveled to Japan found a warm welcome and left behind many friends when they went home. J.J. Pegues, the captain of the Chicago team, wrote an article detailing his experiences, and he reported on the "royal treatment" that he had enjoyed, not only in Japan but throughout Asia, and he concluded by stating that "it was with a feeling of regret that we had to part with the many friends we had made there."[22]

Defeating the West at Their Own Game

The Japanese experienced considerable success on the road, and in 1911, the Waseda team defeated a scratch team made up of Manhattan College and local semi-pro players 11–4. The reporter who covered the game argued that the Japanese players were at the same level as the average American college nine, and especially lauded their aggressiveness on the base paths, along with their general fundamental skills. The star of the game was the Waseda pitcher Matsuda, of whom the reporter gushed, "In pitching, batting, fielding his position, and general all around play he bore the marks of a finished performer."[23] By 1911, the Waseda team penetrated into the heart of the Midwest, with the Japanese splitting a double header with Ames College of Iowa,[24] and by July of that year had made it to the East Coast. These games demonstrated to the Americans who saw them that the Japanese were indeed now fit to be included in the West.

The Japanese had also learned the extreme fan behavior that was exhibited in early baseball matches between old stock Protestants and Irish Catholic immigrants. Pitcher Matsuda Suitiki, who would be so lavishly praised by the *Times* reporter, related a three game series played between Waseda and Keio Universities that mirrored the earlier match between the Excelsiors and the Atlantics. Before the third game of the series could be played, the president of Waseda decided to call the game off, "lest the students become even more excited and somebody be killed."[25] The sport was becoming popular enough that in 1915, 20,000 fans attended a game to watch the University of Chicago defeat Waseda 5–3.[26]

The success that Japanese university teams had against American opponents was a significant factor in promoting feelings of nationalism. In Yokohama, Japanese players were initially prohibited from playing games against Americans at the Yokohama Cricket and Athletic Club (YCAC). The reason given was that they were too diminutive to stand against the Westerners, which was part of the racist Western narrative used to describe the Japanese, of which the Japanese were well aware. Finally, in 1896, through the efforts of William B. Mason, an American teacher at Ichiko, a game was scheduled between Ichiko, a preparatory school for the Imperial University, and the YCAC. The Ichiko team won handily 29–4, which led to a rematch, and again

Ichiko won 32–9, despite the YCAC nine being reinforced by ringers from the *Charleston* and *Detroit*, two American warships visiting Yokohama. Ichiko then defeated a team made up solely from members of the *Detroit* crew, before falling to a team bolstered by the *Olympia*, George Dewey's flagship. The Japanese press mentioned the probable reason for the 14–12 loss was that the shortstop from the *Olympia* had played professional baseball before joining the Navy.[27]

These victories and the subsequent success of university teams against their American opponents were important markers for the Japanese, who realized how far behind the West they had fallen under Tokagawa rule. Each victory and the subsequent positive press they received for them in the West were visible signs that the Japanese had overcome their "backwardness" and had joined the modern Western world. Coupled with their success in conflicts such as the Sino Japanese War and in the Russo-Japanese War (1904–1905), these events helped build nationalistic pride in Japan.

The popularity of baseball in Japan and the high quality of their play even convinced American writers that the nation was indeed part of the West. Some writers, such as one who wrote an article for *The New York Observer and Chronicle*, attributed Japanese skill at the National Pastime as a case of Americanizing Orientals,[28] pointing to the way the Japanese and also the Chinese had taken to baseball as a sign of the superiority of the American race over Asians in general, but others were more laudatory and less jingoistic. According to the unnamed author of "Baseball in Japan" for *Outlook* in 1914, "That the Japanese have taken to (our National Game) with astonishing avidity may be adduced as additional evidence, if any is necessary, that there is no impassable gulf between East and West." The same article recounts the observations of New York Giants Manager John McGraw who had nothing but praise for the skill of the Japanese players, along with an amusing anecdote about the Native American Jim Thorpe, a member of the Giants, who broke the rickshaw he was trying to ride into the ball park.[29] The picture painted of a Native American playing for an American baseball team in Japan presents a picture of a world where race and ethnicity were subsumed to the meritocracy that was baseball, at least according to the narrative of the game. That this was not the case is incontrovertible, but the narrative remained, and after African Americans were finally allowed into the clubhouse, it began to attain some reality.

Baseball and International Relations

The Japanese adoption of baseball came at the same time as they were adopting other Western practices, such as imperialism. As Japan began to acquire many of the material features of the West, they also sought other markers of Westernization, such as imperial possessions. As a result of the Sino-Japanese War, Japan gained Formosa (Taiwan) and territory in China, and after the Russo-Japanese war, they obtained a free hand in Korea and annexed that country in 1910. With a growing empire of their own, Japanese baseball teams began touring their new satellites popularizing the game, both as a sport, and as a symbol of modernity.

The laudatory tone of the articles about Japan concealed an increasing tension between Japan and the West, particularly in the United States. Despite continuing close contacts between Japanese and American baseball clubs, which in the 1920s and 1930s included barnstorming tours led by immortals such as Babe Ruth and Lou Gherig, the course of the two nations continued to drift further apart. The participants in one of the last of the big league barnstorming tours of Japan in 1932 included catcher Moe Berg. Berg was an odd choice, in that the "good field, no hit" phrase was coined to describe his play; but Berg did have other skills. Among them were a facility for languages, a dozen in all, and close ties to the American intelligence community. In addition to his barnstorming play, the player/spy is also credited with taking photographs and films that allowed General Jimmie Doolittle to plan his 1942 bombing raid on Tokyo, and that also aided in the 1945 firebombing of Tokyo, a raid that caused more deaths than the atomic blast at Hiroshima.[30]

Despite the bitterness between the U.S. and the Japanese that culminated in World War II, baseball continued to be and remains popular in Japan. There are now several Japanese players playing in Major League Baseball, including marquis players such as Daisuke Matsuzaka, and MLB is now working to develop talent in China as well.

For the Japanese, baseball became an important visible symbol of modernity, and a marker along the road to achieving parity with the West, which had been the national focus since Commodore Perry sailed into Edo Bay in 1853. Success on the playing field helped demonstrate to many, both Japanese and Americans, that the Japanese were joining the West, but in other parts of the world, baseball became a symbol of resistance to European control.

The U.S. and Cuba: Baseball as Revolution

First European contact with Cuba came on October 12, 1492, when Christopher Columbus reached the island and claimed it for Spain. For the next four-hundred years, Spaniards dominated the island, bringing in the culture of their homeland, including their sport-ways, epitomized by bullfighting. The island remained loyal to Spain despite the loss of most of its

American colonies after Napoleon's conquest of Spain in 1808 spurred independence movements in Latin America, and by the end of the nineteenth century it was one of the few remaining possessions of the once vast empire.

During the first half of the nineteenth century, U.S. pro slavery forces in and out of the government viewed Cuba as a target for annexation that would strengthen their hand against Northern interests. Thomas Jefferson was the first U. S. President to consider acquiring the nation in 1808,[31] but the most serious efforts occurred in the 1840s and 1850s, when James K. Polk and James Buchanan in 1847 and 1854, respectively, made serious efforts to annex or purchase the island.

Drive for Annexation

Polk was worried that Great Britain might take the island from Spain and could thereby have the ability to strangle U.S. trade in the Caribbean. In order to acquire the territory, in 1847, Polk authorized a maximum of one-hundred million dollars, but the Spanish, who had been in decline for centuries and who had already lost Florida to the U. S., refused the offer, stating that they would rather see the island "sink into the ocean," than to see it transferred to any other power.[32]

Interest in annexation continued, however, and in 1854 the Ostend Manifesto, originally a set of secret instructions to American diplomats, including then-minister to Great Britain Buchanan, directed them to make an effort to purchase Cuba for $120,000,000. Should the Spanish decline the offer again, the manifesto continued, the U.S. would be justified in taking the island from them. When the manifesto was leaked to the press, it became a further bone of contention between pro and anti-slavery forces in Congress, and the plan languished.[33]

The Filibusters

Others, however, were not deterred by American political concerns, and in the late 1840s and early 1850s, non-governmental efforts were made to take Cuba away from Spain. Filibusters, independent adventurers who sought to take over territory for personal gain and aggrandizement or to promote American expansion, turned their eyes to Latin America and the Caribbean. William Walker, who briefly declared himself President of Nicaragua in 1856, before being executed in Honduras in 1857, was the most famous of these men,[34] but others such as Narciso Lopez had dreams of taking Cuba from Spain.

Lopez was a Venezuelan who had chosen to throw his lot in with Spain during the revolution there and became a general in the Spanish army. While serving in Cuba, Lopez fell out of political favor and decided that the island needed new leadership. After his first attempt at fomenting revolution on the island failed in 1848, Lopez moved his efforts to the United States where he organized two additional filibustering expeditions. Lopez gained the support of many American expansionists, including John L. O'Sullivan, who coined the term "Manifest Destiny." Despite that support, Lopez's expeditions never managed to create a popular uprising against the colonial administration, and following his capture during his final invasion in 1851, Lopez was executed.[35]

Cubans and the Desire for Modernity

While the public and private sectors in the U.S. cast a covetous eye on Cuba, many Cubans were also casting an envious eye on their northern neighbor. As trade contacts between the two countries increased (the island sold 94 percent of the sugar crop to the U.S. by 1880), Cubans began traveling regularly to the U.S. for business or sending their sons to university. The comparisons between the rising industrial giant and the colonial backwater were not favorable for the latter, and many Cubans came to see the U.S. as the model they should emulate moving forward. Advocating adopting the U.S. model was tantamount, however, to an act of treason against the colonial administration. While some Cubans were willing to take that step, others turned to symbolic action to show their displeasure with Spanish rule.[36]

Along with an American university degree, many young Cubans returned to the island with baseball equipment in their luggage. Much as the Japanese would during the Meiji Restoration, the Cubans saw baseball as a marker of modernity since it had become central to the culture of the quintessentially modern U.S., and as with Hiraoka Hiroshi, students led the way in introducing baseball. The same push-pull relationship that existed in Japan also existed in Cuba, with university students introducing the game in the mid 1860s, and American visitors, deck hands from American ships loading sugar in this case, helping to popularize it.[37]

The first Cuban attempt at gaining independence from Spain was in the Ten Year's War (1868–1878). Baseball became popular with many of the refugees who fled the island for the U.S., and when they returned, they helped spread the game's popularity even more. At the same time, American business interests were also becoming pervasive with more and more Americans visiting the island and taking advantage of the stop to get in a little baseball.

Baseball and Bullfighting

In addition to being a symbol of modernity, baseball was also a chance for Cubans returning from the North to show their independence from the pervasive Spanish culture. Bullfighting was the Spanish national pastime, and Cubans who embraced the modernity of baseball often saw this as a symbolic act rejecting the backwardness of sport that their colonial overlords promoted. The revolutionary leader José Martí, while in exile in the U.S., had remarked, "In every neighborhood there is a baseball game" and "children in New York like baseball and pistols more than they like books."[38] On the other hand, Martí condemned bullfighting as "a futile bloody spectacle ... intimately linked with our colonial past."[39]

Others echoed Martí's distaste for bullfighting by making comparisons between it and the more modern sport. *El Sport*, a Havana newspaper, argued, "American sport does not attract a multitude desirous of seeing blood; it attracts a public wishing to pay homage to reason and justice, which serves to teach and moralize." *El Base Ball*, also from Havana, asserted, "Baseball — allow us to affirm — has contributed much to redeem us from such degrading spectacles (as bullfighting), absorbing the attention of our excitable youth, who through such a useful pastime, experience an awakening of their intelligence and at the same time acquire a healthy physical development."[40] The hyperbole employed by the Cuban press was little different than that used by baseball enthusiasts and their supporters in the American press, but in Cuba enthusiasm for baseball often went along with enthusiasm for change in government.

Spanish authorities were not oblivious to this, and after the beginning of the final struggle against the Spanish in 1895, the colonial authorities banned the game. By this time, the problem was not that baseball was symbolically opposed to bullfighting, but that baseball teams were donating their gate receipts to the rebel cause. In charging this, the Spanish were correct. Cubans living in Key West and Tampa, outside the range of Spanish power to ban the sport, did indeed form leagues and then sent their gate receipts home to aid the independence effort.[41]

Not only did baseball provide funds for the revolution, but the sport also supplied many of the leaders of the Liberation Army. Among these were Major Eduardo Machado, Colonel Pedro Llanio, Captain Manuel Pastoriza, and Major Carlos Maciá.[42] The most famous example of a baseball official supporting the revolution is Emilio Sabourín, who was a player-manager of the Havana Baseball Club, and one of the main promoters of professional baseball before the war. The Spanish authorities arrested Sabourín, and he was sentenced to twenty years at their colonial prison in Morocco, but died after serving only two, and therefore missed independence.[43]

In the same manner as the Japanese, Cubans also served as missionaries helping spread the gospel of baseball. During the Ten Year's War, Cuban refugees not only fled to the U.S., but also to other nations around the Caribbean. One of those was the Dominican Republic, which proved to be fertile ground for the game. Americans, usually in the form of the United States Marine Corps, also spent a considerable amount of time in the Caribbean, which also helped spread the popularity of the game.[44]

Whether playing or cheering on their favorite teams, Cubans were not taking to baseball simply as a method for opposing continued Spanish rule; they also heartily enjoyed the sport and made it their own national pastime. This continued after the war, and contact between the U. S. and Cuba grew rapidly after 1898. The first professional league play began in 1878, two years after the formation of the National League in the U. S., and Esteban Bellan was among one of the early professional players in the U. S., playing for the Troy Haymakers of the National Association in 1871. In the early twentieth century, Cuba became a popular destination for professional baseball players during the winter and was an important location for interracial play before the major leagues re-integrated in 1947.[45]

Baseball continued to be the national pastime despite the takeover by Fidel Castro in 1959. Castro himself played the sport at Havana University (the only documentary evidence shows F. Castro being the losing pitcher 5–4 in 1946) and has promoted the sport since he came to power. The Cuban leader was never given a tryout by an American major league team as legend has it, but one of the photographs of him at the Museo de la Revolución shows Fidel at the bat, and he did create a tongue-in-cheek team called the Barbudos (the Bearded Ones) during the early days of the revolution.[46]

Conclusion

Baseball, at its core, is an (allegedly) fun game (I struggled). However, the sport can also support various interpretations of what the action on the field means. Clearly, one of the meanings that baseball can be used to support is nationalism. Whether searching for unity in the U. S., modernity in Japan, or revolution in Cuba, baseball lends itself well to promoting nationalistic goals, and the game continues to promote nationalism in each of these countries.

The National Anthem, the conspicuous display of the flag, the use of the sport to help train soldiers to work together, and patriotic "support the troops" programs, all support nationalistic ends in the United States.[47] For Cuba and Japan, strong play in international competition also enables nationalism to swell periodically. In the inaugural World Baseball Classic in 2006, Japan finished first and Cuba second. In the Little League World Series, Japan has finished in the top two in one-sixth of the contests, (ten of sixty),[48] while Cuba has been ineligible since the enactment of the 1962 embargo. Cuba has been eligible for the Pan American Games and for other amateur baseball competition; and they have dominated. They won the Gold in the Pan American Games in all ten competitions since 1971, and have also won three of the four Olympic Gold Medals since the sport was made official for those games.[49]

With the increasing globalization of talent in Major League Baseball, one might think that nationalism will decrease in importance, but that will not likely happen anytime soon. Arguably, this combination has been around too long and has been too useful for it to go away any time soon.

Notes

1. William T. Porter, "Our National Sports," *Spirit of the Times; A Chronicle of the Turf, Agriculture, Field Sports, Literature and the Stage*, January 31, 1857, p. 51.
2. Ben Rader, *Baseball: A History of America's Game* (Urbana: University of Illinois Press, 1992), p. 12.
3. *Ibid*, p. 18.
4. Richard O. Davies, *Sports in American Life: A History* (Malden, MA: Blackwell, 2007), p. 56.
5. See Joel Zoss and John Bowman, *Diamonds in the Rough: The Untold Story of Baseball* (Chicago: Contemporary Books, 1996), p. 115–145; and "The Ballpark as Melting Pot."
6. Zoss and Bowman, *Diamonds in the Rough*, p. 65.
7. *Ibid*, p. 66.
8. Dean A. Sullivan, ed., *Early Innings: A Documentary History of Baseball, 1825–1908* (Lincoln: University of Nebraska Press, 1995), p. 177.
9. Zoss and Bowman, *Diamonds in the Rough*, p. 393.
10. Mark Lamster, *Spalding's World Tour: The Epic Adventure that Took Baseball Around the Globe—And Made It America's Game* (New York: Public Affairs, 2003), p. 232.
11. Sullivan, *Early Innings*, p. 295.
12. Kenneth B. Pyle, *The Making of Modern Japan* (Lexington, MA: D.C. Heath, 1996), p. 16.
13. Anne Walthall, *Japan: A Social, Cultural and Political History* (New York: Houghton Mifflin, 2006), pp. 127–128.
14. Peter Duus, *Modern Japan* (New York: Houghton Mifflin, 1998), p. 69.
15. Sayuri Guthrie-Shimizu, "For the Love of the Game: Baseball in Early U.S.-Japanese Encounters and the Rise of a Transnational Sporting Fraternity," *Diplomatic History*, November 2004, p. 642.
16. *Ibid*., p. 647.
17. *Ibid*., p. 648.
18. *Ibid*., p. 649.
19. *Ibid*., p. 643.
20. *Ibid*., p. 651.
21. "College Nine Sails for Japan," *New York Times*, September 11, 1910, p. C5.
22. J. J. Pegues, "International Baseball," *The Independent*, January 19, 1911, p. 126.
23. "Japanese Batting Rally," *New York Times*, July 2, 1911, p. C7.
24. "Waseda Wins and Loses," *New York Times*, May 21, 1911, p. C6.
25. "Japs Wild Over Baseball," *New York Times*, May 7, 1911.
26. "20,000 Japs See Ball Game," *New York Times*, September 25, 1915, p. 13.
27. Guthrie-Shimizu, "For the Love of the Game," p. 656.
28. "Association Work for Young Men: Americanizing Orientals," *The New York Observer and Chronicle*, September 6, 1906, p. 306.
29. "Baseball in Japan," *Outlook*, January 17, 1914, p. 112.
30. Zoss and Bowman, *Diamonds in the Rough*, p. 112.
31. Charles Martin, *The Policy of the United States as Regards Intervention* (New York: Columbia University Press, 1921), p. 140.
32. *Ibid*., p. 142.
33. *Ibid*., p. 143.

34. Robert E. May, "Young American Males and Filibustering in the Age of Manifest Destiny: The United States Army as a Cultural Mirror," *Journal of American History*, December 1991, p. 857.

35. J. Fred Rippy, "Anglo American Filibusters and the Gadsden Treaty," *The Hispanic American Historical Review*, May 1922, p. 157. See also Tom Chaffin, *Fatal Glory: Narciso Lopez and the First Clandestine U.S. War Against Cuba* (Charlottesville: University Press of Virginia, 1996).

36. Louis A. Perez, Jr., "Between Baseball and Bullfighting: The Quest for Nationality in Cuba, 1868–1898," *The Journal of American History*, September 1994, p. 496.

37. Zoss and Bowman, *Diamonds in the Rough*, p. 406.

38. Perez, "Between Baseball and Bullfighting," p. 499.

39. *Ibid.*, p. 505.

40. *Ibid.*, p. 493.

41. Louis A. Perez, Jr., *Cuba and the United States: Ties of Singular Intimacy* (Athens: University of Georgia Press, 2003), pp. 71–72.

42. Perez, "Between Baseball and Bullfighting," p. 513.

43. Rob Ruck, The *Tropic of Baseball: Baseball in the Dominican Republic* (Lincoln: University of Nebraska Press, 1991), p. 2.

44. *Ibid.*, p. 4.

45. Bruce Brown, "Cuban Baseball," *Atlantic Monthly*, July 1984, located online at www.astonisher.com/archives/cuba_baseball.html.

46. Roberto González Echevarría, *The Pride of Havana: A History of Cuban Baseball* (New York: Oxford University Press, 1999), p. 7.

47. Stephen W. Pope, "An Army of Athletes: Playing Fields, Battlefields, and the American Military Sporting Experience, 1890–1920," Naval Postgraduate School Thesis, December 2005, p. 436.

48. www.littleleague.org.

49. Brown, "Cuban Baseball," www.astonisher.com/archives/cuba_baseball.html.

CHAPTER 10

More Than a Game: Baseball Diplomacy in World War II and the Cold War, 1941–1958

Bryan C. Price

"Only through the medium of the game of baseball could we [the people of Japan and the United States] have this kind of understanding."[1]—Nobusuke Kishi, Japanese prime minister, 1958

When President George W. Bush threw out the ceremonial first pitch at Yankee Stadium during the 2001 World Series, a little over a month after the terrorist attacks of September 11, the city of New York and the nation shared a cathartic moment. It was an emotional and patriotic scene — the traditional bunting ringing the field, a heartfelt American anthem performed by the son of the city's fire commissioner and accompanied by over 55,000 patriotic fans, a majestic bald eagle swooping towards home plate from centerfield, thunderous chants of "U-S-A" reverberating around the stadium, and an oversized banner hanging from the mezzanine that read: "USA Fears Nobody. Play Ball."[2] Although other professional sports like football and hockey returned to their regular schedules around the same time, the return of baseball was special, creating a moment only the National Pastime could provide and restoring a desperately needed sense of normalcy during a chaotic time with the country at war. For anyone taking in the scene, baseball and the patriotic fervor oozing out of the stadium seemed to fit perfectly. However, there was a time when baseball was not perceived in this patriotic light. The game was not always the unmistakable symbol of Americana that it is today.

The experience of organized baseball during World War II redefined how baseball was viewed by its fans, the citizens of this country, and even the

United States government. During World War I, the government threatened to suspend the regular season in order to provide more manpower for the war effort, and the national media vilified many of the game's best players for dodging the draft and avoiding their wartime duties. When the Japanese bombed Pearl Harbor on December 7, 1941, organized baseball was determined to avoid repeating the mistakes it made during World War I and set out on an ambitious public relations campaign to promote the game as an integral cog in the U. S. war machine. The leaders of organized baseball succeeded in not only securing a guarantee from the President Franklin D. Roosevelt to continue the game throughout the war, but also in cementing the now familiar image of baseball as an indelible symbol of America and American values. In fact, baseball became such a revered symbol of America that it would later play an important role in foreign diplomacy after the war and, at one point, was even thought of as a potential weapon against the growing threat of Communism.

America's monopoly of the atomic bomb and the success of its war-time economy propelled the United States into its role as the world's most powerful nation. With this newfound status came new responsibilities and a fresh outlook on foreign relations. The United States would never again crawl back into an isolationist shell, the way it did following World War I. Instead, America assumed responsibility for stabilizing the economic and political institutions of Europe, set out to stem the growing tide of Communism, and embarked on a campaign to promote democracy and American values throughout the world.[3]

Baseball played a unique and important role in America during World War II and in the years that immediately followed. Promoted as the national game as early as the mid-1860s, baseball was by far the most popular sport in the United States in the first half of the twentieth century and was deeply imbedded into the American psyche well before the attack on Pearl Harbor.[4] However, it was not until World War II and America's patriotic response that baseball achieved religion-like status. At no other time did the game of baseball figure so prominently in the lives of everyday Americans as it did during World War II and in the early Cold War years. Because of World War II, the National Pastime emerged not only as America's most beloved sport, but as a definitive symbol of democracy.[5]

As a result of baseball's "pedestalization,"[6] a term that describes the process by which baseball was transformed into something more than a game during World War II, America felt justified in exporting baseball all over the world, and in the early stages of the Cold War, in using the game as an instrument of foreign diplomacy. The leaders of organized baseball and a cooperative press, not the United States government, were responsible for this pedestalization of baseball. Organized baseball and newspapers like *The Sport-*

ing News needed baseball to continue for their own economic survival. At the outset, the government cooperated only half-heartedly with these promoters, but it wasted no time in capitalizing on baseball's elevated status, using the game, now a full-fledged symbol of America, to promote democracy and American values in the post-war period.

While the pedestalization of baseball was well under way on the homefront, American servicemen were already unintentionally spreading the game all over the world during World War II and in the years of occupation afterward. The game was popular in the military for several reasons. Soldiers loved the game because it was what they did for fun growing up and simply playing the game reminded them of home. American military commanders loved baseball for the same reasons, but the game also provided their troops with a healthy, recreational outlet and kept them out of trouble.[7]

However, it was this grass roots form of baseball that opened new doors for the National Pastime. Wherever the United States military traveled, soldiers played baseball. Few Europeans were familiar with the game, and baseball had been completely abandoned in Japan by the time American GIs started playing after the occupation. However, wherever American soldiers played, they often drew a crowd of curious fans. The American GI has generally been known to be a benevolent and generous soldier, so it was natural for them to teach and share one of their most beloved and cherished gifts, the game of baseball.

Many Europeans in Allied occupied territory immediately took a liking to the game.[8] In many instances, baseball was the only medium in which the Americans and the vanquished could communicate effectively. Americans had brought baseball with them during the First World War, but the Americans were not overseas long enough for the game to establish a significant foothold. However, in the years after World War II, Americans found the game a cheap and easy way to break down some of the cultural barriers between them and the peoples of the occupied nations.

Japan was a completely different environment because baseball was not new to the Japanese. Baseball boomed in Japan after World War I, and the game became one of Japan's cultural links to Western societies. A total of six American major-league teams toured Japan during the 1920s and 1930s. However, after serious diplomatic strains developed between Americans and the Japanese in the mid-1930s, after 1935, no professional American team would see Japanese soil for the next fifteen years.[9] After World War II, two questions remained about the reintroduction of baseball in Japan. First, would the Japanese embrace an American game like they did earlier in the twentieth century, after four years of war in the Pacific and two atomic bombs dropped by the Americans? Second, and more importantly, were the Japanese deemed worthy, according to American standards, to play baseball after the

Japanese government banned it in 1940 and after the sneak attack on Pearl Harbor? As early as 1942, *The Sporting News* called for the "civilized democratic peoples of the world" to deny the game to the "Jap agents of Hell" in the future.[10]

By the conclusion of the war, baseball had become such a natural extension of American culture that even in the absence of a unified government policy, the game began to play a role in foreign relations, both in Europe and Japan. With the emergence of the Soviet Union and the shadow of Communism hanging over all of the politically unstable nations of Europe and the Far East, the United States was eager to promote democracy and American influence throughout the world. The U. S. wanted to exert its democratic influence in Europe, stabilize the political and economic institutions in Germany, and revamp the same institutions in Japan.[11] After six years of war and millions of casualties on both sides, there was a natural tension between the Axis powers and the Allied nations. The United States government sought ways to bridge this psychological and emotional gap.

Baseball was a perfect fit for American foreign policy. The game could facilitate improved relations with the defeated nations. At the same time, baseball could inject American values in a lasting way, better than almost any other form of cultural exchange. According to sports historian William Miller, the introduction of American baseball in Western Europe would help "assist the U.S. image there ... as a symbol of social and political freedom to workers and mercantile interests."[12] It was difficult to identify any disadvantages with America planting the seeds of baseball overseas. The United Sates would be sharing the best American culture had to offer. The possibilities were endless. An editorial comment in *Baseball Magazine* agreed:

> The seed of baseball has been planted in every country American troops have been. The seed will be planted wherever they go. So eventually we shall have practically world coverage. The armies of occupation will play baseball. It will be part of the program to keep them out of possible mischief, their minds centered on healthful recreation. The natives if not permitted to fraternize with the Americans will observe the fun and benefits the boys derive from the sport. They may become interested and try it on their own. The seed of baseball may sprout and bud all over the world.... The American influence will be in all.[13]

A free-lance writer in Tunisia echoed similar sentiments in October 1945, in regards to the power and influence of baseball. Baseball had "the considerable merit of grouping under a single banner, individuals belonging to different milieu, and subject to different customs." The game could unite different peoples "better than any other tie." The author continued, "When you see, under the sign of sport, men who were fierce enemies yesterday, extend the hand, and unite in fervent hurrahs, every hope is permitted."[14]

Similar to the way Europeans had planned to civilize the untamed savages of the New World with Christianity, Americans attempted to democratize any willing client state with the game of baseball. When the People's Republic of China sent their famous table tennis team to the United States in a sign of good will between the two nations in the 1970s, it was a continuation of the "Ping-Pong Diplomacy" they used with their Far East neighbors.[15] One could argue that the United States practiced "Baseball Diplomacy" after 1945. Because of baseball's pedestalization in World War II, at home and abroad, the game was used as a definitive symbol of America and helped the United States establish stronger foreign relations with the nations of Europe and Japan.

Like it did with many European nations, American servicemen brought the game of baseball to Germany during World War II. Germany, in particular, embraced the game and became one of the leaders in organizing an official European baseball league.[16] American servicemen held several clinics for the German people, particularly the German youth, and helped Germans establish several leagues of their own.[17] In 1953, Germany established the German Amateur Baseball Federation, which would become the model for future European amateur baseball leagues and ultimately for the European Baseball Federation. The game flourished in Germany's biggest industrial cities, including Mannheim, Frankfurt, Munich, and Marburg.[18]

Although sharing the National Pastime was a motivating factor for the United States in exporting baseball to Germany, it was not the only one, nor was it the most important. In the eyes of many Americans, Germans had a reputation for being a militant people after World War I and World War II. Americans often unfairly equated every German citizen with the Nazi party and assumed all Germans were militant, anti-Semitic, and godless people.[19] One way to cure Germany's ills and incorporate democracy and American values into the German people was through a healthy dose of baseball.

As early as September 1945, Americans began formally teaching baseball to the German people. The 331st Infantry Regiment of the 83rd Division held a baseball clinic for German children in early September. An article appearing in *The Sporting News* illustrates how Americans at home interpreted what was most likely an act of kindness by a few baseball-crazy American GIs. The title, "Combat Men Using Baseball to De-Nazify German Youth," suggests that the Americans were doing more than simply teaching baseball. The article's author reports that two American soldiers in the unit "adopted a plan of Americanization which incorporates our good old American sport of baseball.... . The kids like the Americans and they're not as war-minded as some would think. Many of them have never participated in any sports and take this opportunity as a means of becoming acquainted."[20]

Another American unit, the 71st Division, held a similar clinic for German youth outside Augsburg in October 1945. The clinic included baseball instruction over a period of four days and attracted over 350 German children, ranging from eight to fifteen years of age, and their parents. According to an article appearing in *The Sporting News*, the clinic's organizers took "an interesting step toward re-educating German youth in democracy and sportsmanship though the medium of baseball ... with highly successful results."[21]

The United States government also thought that baseball could be an important element in Germany's future, especially among Germany's youth. The pamphlet "Democratic Group Leadership of German Youth Groups," printed by the American European Command (EUCOM) Division for German Youth Activities, stressed the importance of baseball in the democratization process of Germany's younger population.[22] In addition, in the State Department's *Occupation of Germany: Policies and Progress*, Control Council Directive No. 23 of December 17, 1945, addresses the limitation and demilitarization of German sports. The directive gave a laundry list of several sports prohibited by the occupation forces. However, baseball fit nicely with the directive's goal of promoting physical education that would "concentrate on elements of health, hygiene and recreation which will exclude ... sport elements of assimilated military character."[23] Boxing and parachuting were deemed militant activities, whereas the game of baseball was considered to be a civilized, democratic sport.

Italy enjoyed a similar introduction to American baseball. Immediately following World War II, American military personnel first taught the game to the Italians at Nettuno and Anzio before the game blossomed in the larger city of Milan.[24] Clinics similar to those held in Germany were offered to the Italian people as early as 1948, and Americans built the first permanent baseball field, one of the best in Europe at the time, in Trieste in 1951.[25] In a span of six years after baseball's introduction in Italy, sixty-three teams, all with factory sponsorship and donated American equipment, sprouted up across Italy. The number would climb to eighty-two teams by the mid-1950s. The sport became Italy's second largest spectator sport, "just a rung below the traditional and beloved soccer."[26]

After the Italians' overwhelmingly positive response to the game of baseball, the American government took measures to further promote the game in Italy as a sign of goodwill and as an institution that positively reflected the United States. In 1952, the United States Information Service printed and distributed thousands of free copies of the official baseball rule book of the major leagues, the "Regolamento Tecnico del Gioco del Baseball."[27] In addition, the Information Service imported films of famous American baseball stars for training purposes. According to an article appearing in the *New York Sunday Herald-Tribune Magazine* in September 1953, the United States, "mindful of the propaganda benefits of this cultural exchange," was looking to enhance their position in Italy through the game of baseball:

> On a good, sound sand-lot level, baseball is a great builder of good will toward America. If you want to play ball well, you've got to play it *all Americana*. Baseball teaches individual initiative keyed to team responsibility, a lesson Italy greatly needs. It is an outlet for youthful energies and enthusiasms which in Italy have been hitherto largely absorbed by political marching and rioting. It cuts across snob lines in society.... And who is the model for baseball and its attendant virtues? Uncle Sam.[28]

Baseball continued to be an important part of Italian American relations into the late 1950s, as the game gained in popularity and the other nations of Europe improved their baseball organization. The president of Italy's top baseball team sent a letter to President Dwight D. Eisenhower in 1958, asking him to keep their American coach in Italy. The team's coach, Kenneth Opstein, worked with the U.S. Information Service and had been recalled to the United States for stateside duty. The team president wrote, "We know you are busy with many grave problems of great importance in your country, ... but it seems impossible to suspend his [Opstein's] departure through regular bureaucratic ways ... so we are turning to you, Mr. President. You are our last and only hope of keeping Mr. Opstein in Italy."[29] This so-called crisis was obviously not vital to American interests, but it illustrates the passion Italians had for baseball, and their appeal to the President of the United States gives us insight into how they felt about the game and their assumption that Eisenhower felt the same way. It is unknown whether the Italian team president knew about Eisenhower's soft spot for baseball. Despite a distinguished career in the military that included service as the Supreme Allied Commander in Europe during World War II, not to mention his two terms as the 34th President of the United States, Eishenhower lamented later in life, "Not making the baseball team at West Point was one of the greatest disappointments of my life, maybe my greatest."[30]

In 1958, Prince Steno Borghese, the Commissioner of Baseball in Italy and the Commissioner of the European Baseball Federation, journeyed to the United States for a five-day visit to meet with Americans interested in supporting the growth of baseball in Italy. The Prince was a guest of Baseball For Italy, Inc., a private organization that provided equipment and funding for Italian baseball leagues. In a public statement, Joseph Jordan, the organization's vice president, spoke to the power of baseball in foreign relations. The organization was devoted to "the promotion of good will and to the strengthening of the ties between the United States and Italy through the sport of baseball." Jordan argued that "there is nothing more American than baseball and that if it can catch fire in other countries, it can serve as a bridge over which people can be brought together."[31]

In a similar vein, Duncan Hamilton, a fifteen-year-old American boy, wrote a letter to *The Sporting News* in February 1964, explaining why baseball should be exported around the world, based upon his experiences growing up in Italy from 1958 to 1962. Sharing an understanding of soft power that went beyond his years in age, Hamilton wrote, "Baseball is a wonderful game and should be shared with the other peoples of the world.... Sports tie together people from different nations.... It is little things like that which help make allies for the United States, not especially airplanes or dollars."[32]

The history of baseball in Italy and Germany illustrate attempts to promote American and democratic values through the game of baseball. Not all governments were receptive; however, and it is interesting to speculate as to the reasons why. American missionaries introduced baseball in China as early as 1881, but after the Communists took over in 1949, the game was denounced "as an example of Western decadence."[33] In addition, the Communists, particularly the Red Guards, persecuted Chinese baseball players, coaches, and officials as scheming capitalists. Some Chinese baseball players were even forced to humiliate their own coaches in public in order to avoid the wrath of Communist persecution. Not surprisingly, baseball was officially banned in Red China from 1960 to 1974.[34]

Bill Arce, an American combat veteran who served in Germany during and after World War II, personified the spirit of "Baseball Diplomacy" and also experienced similar foreign antipathy in regards to baseball. During the winter of 1944–45, Arce served as an infantryman during the war and promised "to do something good in his life" if he were to survive the war. Arce, feeling lucky to have survived the horrors of the Battle of the Bulge, wanted to leave his mark and give the people of Europe something to remember him by. Arce decided to give them the gift of baseball.[35] Arce has enjoyed an illustrious baseball career, beginning when he was a team captain at Stanford University, a perennial collegiate powerhouse. He is a member of the National Athletic Intercollegiate Association Coaches Hall of Fame and the American Baseball Coaches Association (ABCA) Hall of Fame, and served as president of the United States Olympic Baseball Committee in 1975, and president of the ABCA in 1994. Despite these impressive accomplishments, Arce's most important contributions to the game of baseball may have been overseas, in Europe as well as in the People's Republic of China. In the words of Bill Clark of the *International Baseball Rundown*, "Arce, as much as anyone in the game, is responsible for baseball's popularity and strength around Planet Earth."[36] In exporting the game of baseball around the world, Arce was not seeking profit or fame. He personally financed his own trips, generated interest in the game, and served as a worthy ambassador of baseball.

While it may not have been his principal motivation, Arce's work in exposing Europeans and others to the game of baseball served to promote

American values and the tenets of democracy. Apparently the State Department of the United States agreed. When Arce sought government funding for a trip to Holland in the early Cold War years, State Department officials politely denied his request due to a lack of available resources. However, the State Department added that they might be interested in funding a trip to Czechoslovakia or some other nation behind the Iron Curtain instead. According to Arce, the State Department "wanted to use it [baseball] as a political tool if they could."[37]

Because baseball symbolized America and political freedom, the government of the Czech Republic discouraged the game from the late 1950s into the late 1980s. As a result, organized baseball did not exist in Czechoslovakia until Communism fell in 1989. After the Czechs shed the cloak of Communism, they embraced baseball and have quickly fielded some of the most competitive teams in Europe, strengthening the argument that baseball is a democratic sport or is at least perceived as one.[38]

The most telling example of baseball's influence in foreign relations is the game's history in Japan. Baseball gained a strong following in Japan after the Reach All-Americans toured the country in 1908. Up until 1935, no fewer than seven American professional baseball teams toured Japan, the most famous of them the 1934 Major League All-Stars featuring Babe Ruth.[39] However, the souring of Japanese-American relations after 1935 can be traced through its effect on baseball. That same year, the Japanese Board of Education passed a ruling prohibiting school children from playing baseball because it interfered with the concentration on war calisthenics.[40]

In 1940, the Japanese government canceled all radio broadcasts of American professional baseball in Japan. In an effort to remove all American influence, common phrases such as *play ball, strike,* and *out* were replaced with Japanese words. Team names such as the Senators, Tigers, and Giants were replaced with Japanese team names, complete with Japanese lettering. The coup de grace, however, took place in August 1940, when the government of Japan terminated the game of baseball.[41] To many Americans in the baseball community, the death of baseball in Japan foreshadowed worsening relations between the United States and Japan. The Japanese did not simply get rid of baseball; Japan had officially rejected the game because it represented America and American values.

These factors were not forgotten nor forgiven after World War II. Considerable debate in the United States ensued concerning baseball's future in Japan. But the overwhelming enthusiasm the Japanese had for baseball's return and General Douglas MacArthur's democratization policies favored the reintroduction of the game.[42] The Japanese welcomed American participation in resurrecting baseball in their country. The Japanese not only loved to watch and play baseball, but some influential Japanese felt the game might help Japanese-American relations during the occupation. On September 16, 1945, an article appearing in *The New York Times* reported,

> Japanese newspapers clamored today for a revival of baseball, banned by the Government during the war, as a means of "promoting understanding between the Japanese and Americans." ... Letters to the newspapers have suggested games between the Japanese and American occupation teams. The different habits and customs of the two nations, one letter said, could be much more easily reconciled on the baseball field than by "Japanese Government officials, in their broken English, meeting with the American authorities."[43]

When organized baseball officially returned to Japan in 1946, the game's popularity skyrocketed. In 1947, baseball drew more fans than Sumo wrestling, Japan's proclaimed national sport.[44] The Japanese reintroduced American baseball team names and, in an attempt to copy their American contemporaries, had Japanese dignitaries throw out the ceremonial first pitch before important games. The Japanese even began the American tradition of razzing the umpire during games, something that immediately caught the eye of several American observers. In 1949, Norman Cousins wrote in *Collier's Magazine*, "The Japanese are as baseball crazy as ever, and the way they now treat umpires probably is the best proof that democratization has succeeded."[45] In the words of Sotaro Suzuki, vice president of the Nippon Professional Baseball League, the Japanese did everything they could to "follow American ball" after World War II.[46]

Many Americans agreed that reinstituting baseball in Japan was a positive sign. MacArthur, a former baseball player himself at the U. S. Military Academy at West Point, New York, supported baseball as an alternative to those sports with militaristic overtones.[47] Frederick Lieb of *The Sporting News* wrote, "It may take America a long time to forget the treachery of Pearl Harbor, the march from Bataan, the horror prison camps, but it is possible the baseball field will furnish some future mutual meeting ground with our erstwhile foe."[48] Lefty O'Doul, who led the first postwar tour of American baseball players in 1949, had his own reasons for returning to Japan. "Jesus," O'Doul remarked after the trip, "so many of my friends in Japan got killed in the war. So many. Awful. Right after the war I went back. I wanted to, because I knew if we brought a baseball team over there it would help cement friendship between them and us."[49]

Although baseball was expected to heal old wounds and forge new friendships between Japanese and Americans, the U.S. government found yet another use for the game. In the midst of the Korean Inchon landing in September 1950, Major General William F. Marquat, a key member of MacArthur's staff, was looking to calm and pacify the Japanese people while the United States prepared to go on the offensive in the Korean War. Because Marquat wore dual hats as the officer in charge of the economic and scientific rehabilitation of Japan as well as the International Baseball Commissioner for Japan, he planned a modified international World Series between the American National Baseball Congress (NBC) champions, a U. S. amateur team, and the Japanese national team. More importantly, he timed the series to specifically coincide with the timing of the Inchon landing on the Pusan Peninsula, arguably one of the most daring amphibious landings ever attempted.[50]

The historic series between the Japanese team and the NBC champions was a unique example of baseball's multi-purpose role in American foreign policy. The series differed from previous Japanese-American baseball tours in that this was the first time a non-professional team had visited Japan. Unlike the highly publicized tours of previous years which featured some of the greatest American players of all time, this series featured a team comprised of only amateur ball players from Fort Wayne, Indiana, champions of a national annual tournament sponsored by the NBC and held in Wichita, Kansas, dating back to 1934.[51]

However, the extraordinary Japanese reaction to the American team illustrates how baseball-crazy the Japanese really were. Upon arriving in Japan, the Fort Wayne Capeharts were given a tickertape parade through downtown Tokyo. Over a million people turned out to cheer the American champions in an hour-long parade down Ginza Avenue.[52] Then, following the parade, over ten thousand Japanese fans greeted the Americans at a pep rally where the American manager received the key to the city of Tokyo. Fifty thousand fans crammed into 45,000-seat Tokyo's Korakuen Stadium to see General MacArthur's wife throw out the first pitch to open the series.[53] Over 70,000 fans witnessed the only Japanese victory over the Americans in Osaka's Kosehein Stadium.[54] The five-game series' total attendance was a staggering 317,000 fans, more than the attendance of the World Series between the New York Yankees and Philadelphia Phillies in the United States that year.[55] To put the Japanese reaction in the proper perspective, Fort Wayne and Elk City, Oklahoma, home of the team the Capeharts defeated to advance to the "International World Series,"[56] never played for a crowd larger than 12,000 during the entire NBC tournament held in the U. S.[57]

The NBC and sponsors such as Coca-Cola funded the trip, so American motivation to garner profits from the trip was nonexistent.[58] Marquat had more important goals in mind. Because of the increased mobilization of forces needed for the Inchon landing, the number of American soldiers in Japan was drastically reduced, and there was fear that anti-American Japanese would cause domestic unrest. He hoped that the Japanese-American baseball series would distract the Japanese and draw attention away from the paucity of American soldiers remaining in their country. Secondly, because games three and four were scheduled during the Inchon landing, the series would hopefully give the impression that everything was business-as-usual in occupied Japan.[59]

Marquat's actions leading up to the September series illustrated his sense of urgency. The Fort Wayne team did not have passports nor the inoculations required to enter Japan, but Marquat used his military position and rank to side-step these regulations. Less than forty-eight hours after winning the NBC championship, the Fort Wayne Capeharts flew to the Shima Islands, where they fell under military jurisdiction and Marquat's orders, and were quickly routed into Tokyo.[60] Marquat even cut orders for Captain Charles W. Cookson, Executive Secretary of the NBC and Secretary of the Treasury for the International Baseball Congress (IBC), to return to active duty service and lead the American contingent during the trip.[61] To the general public, the series was simply a promotion of international baseball and a symbol of improved relations between the two nations. However, Marquat confided in Cookson that the series was of "vital importance to the interests of the United States" and that the real intention behind the series was "to keep the country as quiet and calm as possible."[62] More importantly, Marquat ordered Cookson to give this privileged information to no one, not even the NBC global commissioner and editor of *The Sporting News*, J. G. Taylor Spink.[63]

The Japanese reaction to the American amateurs was not entirely consistent with Japanese public sentiment towards the Americans occupying their country in the immediate run-up to the series. Cookson recalls an incident a week before the NBC champions arrived in which a Japanese citizen threw acid in an American Army officer's face in downtown Tokyo. Although American officials warned the NBC team to be on the alert for similar anti-American attacks, the Fort Wayne Capeharts enjoyed nothing but Japanese hospitality and undoubtedly more attention then they would have ever received at home. Cookson described the Japanese as "baseball-crazy" and fondly remembered the gifts, parties, and dances during their baseball tour.[64]

Cookson and the American baseball players did not expect such a positive response from the Japanese. A veteran of the 71st Infantry Division fighting in the European theater during World War II and later stationed in Germany where he experienced the uneasy German reaction to occupation, Cookson found the Japanese response to the American team both confusing and awe-inspiring. The Americans were visiting a city that was leveled by fire bombing less than five years before. Marquat had cut through red tape to get the American team to Japan because he felt the need to pacify a restless nation and protect American interests.[65]

Why, then, were the Japanese so enthralled with this series? And why were they so hospitable to the Americans? The Japanese-American series came and went unbeknownst to most Americans. Surely, the attraction for the Japanese was not the American players themselves, for the United States could have sent a much more impressive delegation of professional players. The attraction was not the American players, but American baseball. Marquat's official comment gave little hint of his real intentions:

> It is impossible to overestimate the significance of this tournament in terms of international goodwill and mutual understanding between the United States and Japan. During this critical period in the Free World history it is most appropriate that representative teams from these two nations should meet in keen rivalry on the baseball diamond and mutual friendship and admiration off the playing field.[66]

The NBC tour of Japan in 1950 touched off a flurry of American goodwill baseball tours to Japan in the next decade. Major league teams participated in six tours of Japan from 1951 to 1958, continuing to promote American values and American goodwill to the people of Japan.[67] New York Giants manager Leo Durocher, notorious at home for his brash personality and antipathy for authority, headed a fourteen-game trip to Japan in 1953 and received numerous accolades for being "the greatest ambassador we ever sent to the Orient."[68] According to an article in *Reader's Digest*, Major League Baseball Commissioner Ford Frick received letters from "American generals stationed in Japan and Korea, State Department officials, American businessmen working in Tokyo," and "distinguished Japanese citizens" applauding the 346,000 Japanese in attendance and giving "unstinted praise of Durocher's ambassadorial qualities."[69] The success and popularity of these American baseball goodwill tours did not go unnoticed by the Japanese government. Commenting on the St. Louis Cardinal trip in 1958, Japanese Prime Minister Nobusuke Kishi of Japan said, "It has had a tremendous impact on the good will of the people of Japan for the United States. Only through the medium of the game of baseball could we have this kind of understanding."[70]

Whether it was behind the Iron Curtain or the Great Wall, baseball symbolized American values and democratic freedom. According to a statement made by National League President Ford Frick in April 1944, "The real example of genuine democracy is on the playing fields of America. It is the one place American youth meets on common ground and the real lesson of democracy can best be preached."[71] During this time period, people inside and outside the United States commented on the universal language of baseball and how it broke through cultural, political, and even ideological barriers between the nations. Because of the pedestalization of baseball, many Americans considered the game to be a cure for the world's ailments. Some may still ponder what would have happened if someone followed up on South Dakota Representative Karl Mundt's suggestion to introduce baseball in the Soviet Union, and to organize annual Russian-American games to improve relations between the two nations.[72] Would the Cold War have been the same?

Before, during, and immediately after the war, baseball remained the National Pastime and America's most beloved sport. For all intents and purposes, the rules, traditions, and idiosyncrasies of the game remained intact. Yet baseball evolved into something much more than just a game from 1941 to 1958. For example, the playing of the National Anthem to start a baseball game seems so commonplace today, so appropriate, and for lack of a better term, so *American*, that many treat it as another one of baseball's time-honored traditions, when in fact it only became an accepted practice before every game during World War II.[73] What was once considered an enjoyable pastime before the war was transformed into a revered American institution, a symbol of all that was worth fighting for, and a working illustration of a way of life America hoped to export to other countries after the war.

When one examines the patriotic rhetoric that characterized the promotion of baseball's continuation during World War II, it is difficult to fathom how a sport acquired such an elevated status. In retrospect, some of the arguments during the war concerning the importance of baseball and its capacity to influence foreign relations are far-fetched. For example, Japanese motivation to fight Americans would not have intensified if the major league season was cancelled by the United States government.[74] The American war effort would not have collapsed if the homefront did not have baseball games to attend. The Axis and Allies would have still fought World War II even if all nations involved played organized baseball.[75] Regardless of how outrageous these arguments sound today, they were not considered outrageous in the 1940s and 1950s. The pedestalization of baseball occurred because Americans believed in the power of baseball. It is not a coincidence that the Communist nations of China and Czechoslovakia banned baseball in their countries at one point or another. Neither is it an accident that these nations quickly took up the game after the cloak of Communism was lifted from their political situation.[76] In the 1940s and 1950s, baseball symbolized America, even to its enemies.

The unique status of baseball during the 1940s and 1950s, and the roles the game played as a result of this "pedestalization," are a historic first. For the first time in the United States, and long before the advent of Ping-Pong Diplomacy, sport was used as a tool of domestic and foreign policy. On the homefront, baseball played an important part in the war effort. Overseas, the game served as a morale booster for the troops. After the war, baseball served as an ambassador of democracy and American values. No other institution can claim to have played such diverse roles at home and abroad. During this critical period in history, baseball was truly more than a game.

The author would like to thank his father, Jay Price, and advisor, Col. Gary Tocchet, as well as the research staff at the Baseball Hall of Fame Research Library in Cooperstown, New York, for their support and assistance.

Notes

1. "Value of Card Trip Apparent in Air Reports," *The Sporting News*, 7 January 1959, 16.
2. Teddy Greenstein, "Flag-Waving Fans Cheer Bush at Series," *Chicago Tribune*, 31 October 2001.
3. James M. McCormick, *America Foreign Policy and Process* (Itasca, IL: F.E. Peacock, 1998), 39–40.
4. Benjamin G. Rader, *Baseball: A History of America's Game* (Chicago: University of Illinois Press, 1992), 12.
5. Richard Goldstein, *Spartan Seasons: How Baseball Survived the Second World War* (New York: Macmillan, 1980), 34–5.
6. Luke Spencer, "The Pedestalization of Baseball by Americans," accessed 31 January 1998, http://www.middlebury.edu/~ac400b/costner.html.
7. Telephone conversation with Bill Arce, 10 February 1998, Claremont, California. Arce served in the Army in Germany during World War II, fought at the Battle of the Bulge, and has led a distinguished career in baseball, not only in the United States, but overseas as well. Arce was instrumental in baseball's development in the Netherlands and the People's Republic of China. He is a wealth of knowledge concerning the history and current state of international baseball.
8. Roger C. Panaye, *European Amateur Baseball* (Antwerp: Federation of European Baseball, 1978), 12–20.
9. Richard C. Crepeau, "Pearl Harbor: A Failure of Baseball?" *Journal of Popular Culture* 15.4 (Spring 1982), 67–74. Article is in the World War II file at the National Baseball Hall of Fame Library, Cooperstown, New York.
10. J.G. Taylor Spink, "Looping the Loops," *The Sporting News*, 1 January 1942, 1.
11. John Morton Blum, *V Was for Victory* (New York: Harcourt Brace Jovanovich, 1976), 302–323.
12. William B. Miller, "The American Sports Empire," in *Sports in Modern America*, ed. William J. Baker and John M. Carroll (St. Louis: River City, 1983), 149.
13. Clifford Bloodgood, "Editorial Comment," *Baseball Magazine*, July 1945, 253.
14. "Game Boons in Tunisia," *The Sporting News*, 4 October 1945, 19.
15. Kuang-sheng Liao, *Antiforeignism and Modernization in China, 1860–1980* (New York: St. Martin's Press, 1984), 164, 216; and Judy Hoarfrost, "Ping Pong Diplomacy 25th Anniversary Celebration," accessed 26 April 1998, http://paddle-palace.com/cgibin/cgiwrap/paddlepalace/webc.cgi/diplomacy.html.
16. Panaye, 12.
17. A.L. Marder, "350 Youths Attend Clinic Held by 71st Division Diamond Stars," *The Sporting News*, 18 October 1945, 14; and J. G. Taylor Spink, "Combat Men Using Baseball to De-Nazify German Youth," *The Sporting News*, 13 September 1945, 12.
18. Telephone conversation with Claus Helmig, 17 February 1998, Mainz, Germany. Helmig, a wealthy German industrialist, was instrumental in developing Germany's organized baseball program and is involved with the European Baseball Federation today.
19. Blum, 47–52.
20. J.G. Taylor Spink, "Combat Men Using Baseball to De-Nazify German Youth," *The Sporting News,* 13 September 1945, 12.
21. Marder, 14.
22. Franz Nitsch, "Sport, Bildung und Demokratie," *Die Deutsche Bibliothek* (Margburg: Schuren, 1996), 37–8. Article sent to author by Claus Helmig.
23. Department of State, *Occupation of Germany: Policy and Progress, 1945–46* (Washington, D.C.: Government Printing Office, 1947), 103.
24. Conversation with Bill Arce.
25. William Mahoney, "Field of Fame," *The Stars and Stripes*, 8 April 1955.
26. Blake Ehrlich, "Slide, Luigi, Slide!" *New York Sunday Herald-Tribune Magazine*, 6 September 1953, 10.
27. Ibid.
28. Ibid.
29. Associated Press, "Italian Baseball Team Asks Eisenhower to Stay Recall of Its American Manager," 11 October 1958, article appearing in the Foreign Baseball File at the National Baseball Hall of Fame Library, Cooperstown, New York.
30. Accessed at www.baseball-almanac.com on 30 November 2008.
31. "Europe Baseball Head Here to Enlist Support," *The New York Times*, 1 December 1958, article appearing in the Foreign Baseball File at the National Baseball Hall of Fame Library, Cooperstown, New York.
32. Duncan Hamilton, "Share Game with World, 15-Year-Old Fan Urges," *The Sporting News*, 15 February 1964, 14.

33. Uli Schmetzer, "Chinese Baseball Hanging in There," *Chicago Tribune*, 3 May 1991, 6.
34. *Ibid.*
35. Conversation with Bill Arce.
36. Bill Clark, quoted in John Lister, "Baseball in Europe: The Last Frontier," Undergraduate Senior Thesis, Claremont McKenna College, California, 24 April 1997, 20.
37. Conversation with Bill Arce.
38. John Lister, "Baseball in Europe: The Last Frontier," Undergraduate Senior Thesis, Claremont McKenna College, California, April 1997, 28–9.
39. Crepeau, 67–9.
40. Red Parton, "Japanese Plan to Resume Pro Ball Next Spring," *The Sporting News*, 22 November 1945, 9.
41. Crepeau, 69–70.
42. *Ibid.*, 72–3; Parton, 9; United Press, "Return of Baseball is Sought in Japan," *The New York Times*, 16 September 1945, 1; and Yoshio Akao, letter to Robert Quinn, 13 July 1949, in the Foreign Baseball file at the National Baseball Hall of Fame Library, Cooperstown, New York.
43. United Press, "Return of Baseball Sought in Japan," *The New York Times*, 16 September 1945, 11.
44. David Voigt, *America Through Baseball* (Chicago: Nelson-Hall, 1975), 103.
45. Norman Cousins, "Slide, Fujimura, Slide!" *Collier's Magazine*, 5 November 1949, 28.
46. Voigt, 103.
47. Robert Obojski, *The Rise of Japanese Baseball Power* (New York: Chilton Book Company, 1975), 42.
48. Frederick G. Lieb, "MacArthur Takes Over Where Major Stars 'Took' Japanese Eleven Years Ago," *The Sporting News*, August 1945, 14.
49. Obojski, 43.
50. Telephone conversation with Charles W. Cookson, 7 February 1998, Wichita, Kansas.
51. Bob Broeg, *Baseball's Barnum: Ray "Hap" Dumont* (Wichita: Wichita State University Press, 1989), 18.
52. National Baseball Congress, "First Official Inter-Hemisphere Playoff," *National Baseball Congress Guide 1950* (Wichita: National Baseball Congress, 1950), 3.
53. *Ibid.*, 4–5.
54. Broeg, 115.
55. *Ibid.*, 116.
56. *Ibid.*, 111.
57. *Ibid.*, 121.
58. *Ibid.*, 114.
59. Conversation with Cookson.
60. Broeg, 115.
61. Conversation with Cookson.
62. *Ibid.*
63. *Ibid.*
64. *Ibid.*; and National Baseball Congress, *National Baseball Congress Guide 1950*, 24–7.
65. *Ibid.*
66. National Baseball Congress, *National Baseball Congress Guide 1952* (Wichita: National Baseball Congress, 1952), 319.
67. Untitled pamphlet found in the Foreign Baseball file at the National Baseball Hall of Fame Library, Cooperstown, New York.
68. Quentin Reynolds, "Giant in Japan," *Reader's Digest*, May 1954, 6.
69. *Ibid.*
70. "Value of Card Trip Apparent in Air Report," *The Sporting News*, 7 January 1959, 16.
71. Ford Frick, quoted in Goldstein, *Spartan Seasons: How Baseball Survived the Second World War* (New York: Macmillan, 1980), 35.
72. United Press, "Introduction of Baseball in Russia Is Suggested," *The New York Times*, 10 September 1945, 8.
73. Rader, 156.
74. Edwin M. Rumill, "Keep 'em Playing," *Christian Science Monitor*, 17 April 1941, 7.
75. James M. Gould, "The President Says 'Play Ball,'" *Baseball Magazine*, 68 (March 1942), 475.
76. Schmetzer, 6; and Lister, 29.

CHAPTER 11

Exporting the Horsehide American Dream: The Hidden Side of Nicaraguan Baseball

Robert Elias

While visiting Cooperstown in 1986, I was struck by the statue of the "Sandlot Kid," which stands outside the Baseball Hall of Fame. It portrays a young ballplayer from an earlier era, who is holding a bat and wearing an odd, broad-brimmed hat. It seemed instantly familiar, but I couldn't place it until I finally made the surprising connection: the hat was exactly the same one worn by, of all people, Nicaraguan revolutionary Augusto César Sandino, and it was a major symbol of the Sandinista Revolution. I never expected that a year later, in 1987, I would be seeing images of that hat, in person, all over Nicaragua. I had joined a Baseball for Peace tour there, and began a fascination with baseball's role in that beleaguered nation.

Baseball has long been associated with the characteristics of the American dream, such as democracy, freedom, fair play, and equal opportunity. We have often assumed baseball could make the same contributions elsewhere. Repeatedly, U.S. foreign policy has exported the American way abroad — to extend the American dream to other lands. As far back as Albert Spalding's 1888 World Tour, baseball has been a part of that uplifting mission. While our national pastime has not always taken root, it has caught on in some nations. Among them, Nicaragua has been relatively ignored, despite the sport's long history there. Yet rarely has baseball been so intricately intertwined with a country's domestic and international politics. To understand this, it's necessary to examine Nicaraguan baseball through several eras and several significant political shifts—from the American game to the Somozan game to the Sandinista game to the Contemporary game.

The American Game, 1847–1932

In our 230 years as a nation, the U.S. has intervened militarily in other countries more than 275 times, and Nicaragua has been a favorite target. This began in 1847, but 1855 is particularly notable since that year the American, William Walker, and his militia actually took over Nicaragua and set up a slave republic. The *New York Daily News* applauded Walker, claiming, "Los yankis ... have burst their way like a fertilizing torrent through the barriers of barbarism." Rather than civilizing, however, Walker unleashed a bloody tyranny.[1]

Early on, a pattern of U.S. intervention was established, purportedly to "protect American interests," which continues to this day. The invasions were prompted largely by profit seeking, under the protection of the U.S. military or U.S.-installed puppet dictatorships. But U.S. officials also claimed they were civilizing Nicaragua and spreading the American dream. Many Nicaraguans embraced that dream, with hopes for progress, democracy, and prosperity. But in practice, they have been repeatedly disappointed, and increasingly resentful of the exploitation and broken promises. The U.S. decision in 1902 to build a canal in Panama instead of the canal that had been promised for years to Nicaragua, was the first major letdown. It would not be the last.

Meanwhile, baseball played a key role in "uplifting" the Nicaraguans. In 1887, they were "liberated" from British cricket by baseball brought to the Atlantic Coast by a U.S. businessman, and "civilized" by baseball on the Pacific Coast in 1890 by Nicaraguan students returning from the U.S.[2] In his book *Confronting the American Dream: Nicaragua Under U.S. Imperial Rule*, Michel Gobat explains that Nicaraguan elites accepted baseball to make their nation more cosmopolitan. Baseball was chosen because it promoted modern, civilized notions of self control, physical vigor, orderly competition, and a work ethic, instead of the violent, corrupt, irrational, unruly attributes associated with Spanish colonialism.[3] Baseball embodied the ingredients of the American dream,[4] which U.S. Manifest Destiny was already eagerly exporting.

But beyond being a set of values, baseball was also employed as a means of social control and distraction. For these purposes, the U.S. military strongly promoted the sport in Nicaragua, and in 1904 the U.S. Consul General started the first Nicaraguan team, the Boers. Named after the on-going Boer War, it launched a pattern of naming teams after either wars or international destinations, including clubs called Russia, Japan, Chile, and Paris.[5]

When in 1909 the Nicaraguans began asserting their independence from the U.S., the reaction was swift. U.S. troops arrived to install an American mining executive as the new president. In 1910, the Dawson Pact turned Nicaragua into a U.S. colony—making an eventual revolution inevitable.

By 1912, the U.S. Marines had begun an occupation that would continue until 1925.[6] Baseball was consciously used to quell dissent. The Nicaraguan National League was formed in 1914[7] and included a U.S. Marine team. Clifford Ham, the American running most of the Nicaraguan economy, said, "Three cheers for the American Marine who is teaching baseball and sportsmanship! It is the best step towards order, peace and stability."[8] Exploitative U.S. agribusiness firms, such as United Fruit and W.R. Grace, promoted baseball in Nicaragua "to control and civilize the locals."[9] Baseball was employed to pacify the masses, although sometimes Nicaraguans used it as resistance, trying to beat the Americans at their own game.[10]

The U.S. Marines left in 1925, but returned the next year, allegedly to crush a "Nicaraguan-Mexican-Soviet" conspiracy to launch another Bolshevik revolution. According to American officials: "[T]here is no room for any outside influence other than ours in the region." The Marines outraged the Nicaraguans by commandeering a cherished Managua ball field for a landing strip during the renewed occupation, which lasted until 1933.[11]

The U.S. created the soon-to-be-hated Nicaraguan National Guard, which joined U.S. troops to target Augusto Sandino, who was leading the guerrilla war against the U.S occupation and Nicaraguan dictators.[12] Sandino protested the "foreign exploitation of the country by the money powers of Nicaragua and Wall Street." Echoing Sandino, the decorated U.S. General Smedley Butler admitted, "I spent most of my time as a high-class muscleman for big business, for Wall Street, and the bankers ... I helped in the raping of half a dozen Central American republics."[13] Reflecting Sandino's fame in the Caribbean, the city of Santiago, Dominican Republic named its baseball team after him. But when U.S. troops installed Rafael Trujillo as Dominican president in 1930, the dictator renamed the Sandinos the Eagles, after the U.S. bird.[14] Nevertheless, many Dominican parents continued to name their newborn sons Cesar (after Sandino's middle name), including future major leaguers Cesar Cedeno and Julio Cesar Franco.

The Somozan Game, 1933–1979

In 1933, the Marines left Anastasio Somoza, Sr., in charge of the National Guard and the country, although the U.S. retained control of three-fourths of Nicaragua's economy.[15] Somoza soon assassinated Sandino, and in 1936 a U.S.-assisted coup gave him the presidency. As President Franklin Roosevelt indicated: "He may be a son of a bitch, but he's our son of a bitch." Anastasio, Sr., had studied in Philadelphia and returned to Nicaragua as a Philadelphia Athletics fan. He declared baseball the Nicaraguan national sport, built a national baseball stadium (named after himself), and subsidized the National Guard team. By the 1940s, Nicaraguans were big fans of U.S. baseball, and most rooted, ironically, for the New York Yankees. Newborn male babies in Nicaragua were routinely ushered into the world with the phrase: "Born with a glove and ball in his hand."

In 1954, Somoza, Sr., aided the CIA invasion of Guatemala, toppling its democratically elected government. But in 1956, Somoza was assassinated, only to be replaced by a new dictator, his son Luis Somoza. The Nicaraguan Professional Baseball League was also started that year, and provided winter baseball for U.S. major leaguers, such as Jim Kaat, George Scott, Ron Hansen, Jack Kralick, Phil Regan, Bert Campaneris, Zoilo Versalles, Luis Tiant, Fergie Jenkins, and Lou Pinella. Nicaraguans are still talking about the monster home run hit — of all people — by Marvelous Marv Throneberry. By 1960, the League was ailing financially, but Somoza ordered the teams to continue.[16]

In 1961, Somoza helped the U.S. launch the Bay of Pigs invasion of Cuba. In 1967, Luis's brother, Anastasio Somoza, Jr., was installed as President, the third Somoza dictator. Anastasio, Jr., cut baseball funding and ended the Nicaraguan professional league after eleven years.[17] Somoza rediscovered the political uses of baseball by 1972, however, and campaigned for the World Amateur Baseball Championship (the WABC) in Managua, featuring a Nicaraguan team led by future major leaguers, Dennis Martinez and Tony Chevez. The tournament would distract Nicaraguans from the poverty and miserable conditions the dictatorship had established.[18]

Shortly after the WABC, a massive earthquake devastated the nation. Old friend, President Richard Nixon, had recently praised Somoza at a White House dinner in his honor, for "a quarter-century of service to the cause of peace and freedom." Now Nixon pledged the help of U.S. paratroopers. Meanwhile, the dictator was confiscating millions in international aid, with U.S. complicity. Roberto Clemente had managed the Puerto Rican team in Managua only a couple of weeks before, and when he heard about Somoza's looting, he vowed to deliver aid in person.[19] He died trying, in a plane crash — a casualty of longstanding U.S. support of Somozan dictatorships.

In 1973, Nicaragua again hosted the WABC, and despite the earthquake, Somoza found $500,000 to host the event. Nicaragua won its game against the Americans, but the U.S. won the tournament. Then, in 1974, the U.S. hosted the tournament in Florida, amidst controversy. Among other things, the Nicaraguans believed they were cheated out of the championship: When the U.S. and Nicaragua ended up tied, the rules called for a one game playoff, which Nicaragua won. But the WABC President, American William Fehring, insisted on a two-out-of-three series, which the U.S. came back to win for the tournament crown.[20] Baseball was becoming central to increasing U.S.-Nicaraguan tensions.

The Sandinista Game, 1979–1990

In 1977, the FSLN (Sandinista National Liberation Front) led the growing opposition to the Somoza regime. Pittsburgh Pirates prospect Albert Williams was pitching in Charleston, but returned to his native Nicaragua to be a FSLN guerrilla for sixteen months. Exiled just before the Revolution succeeded, Williams eventually made it to the majors with the Minnesota Twins in 1980.[21]

A former Brooklyn Dodgers fan and Nicaragua's leading writer, Sergio Ramirez wrote an epic novel about the Revolution, *To Bury Our Fathers*, structured in nine innings, as well as baseball short stories. In "The Centerfielder," he described Somozan repression and a ballgame among prisoners, used to cover up the torture and execution of a former national team star ballplayer.[22] In the late 1970s, Somoza discovered an abandoned statue of Benito Mussolini sitting astride a horse. He spent one million dollars to have it sent from Italy, replaced the head with his own, and erected it in front of the National Baseball Stadium. In response, the Nicaraguan poet and Catholic priest Ernesto Cardenal wrote a poem predicting the statue's impending fall.

In 1979, President Jimmy Carter sent Somoza military aid to fight off the rebels, but the Sandinista Revolution succeeded anyway,[23] Somoza was exiled, and a mob tore down his statue. In *Under Fire*, Hollywood's version of the Revolution, a young boy was shown trying to throw a hand grenade with the motion of the hometown idol, Dennis Martinez,[24] who would lead the Baltimore Orioles on a Nicaraguan visit in 1980. On that trip, the Orioles' Elrod Hendricks observed: "Hopefully this trip will spread good will between our two countries ... despite the poverty ... they love baseball better than anything and they know all the players. They used to be Yankee fans, but with Dennis an Oriole, they root for us now."[25]

In the early 1980s, President Ronald Reagan endorsed "low-intensity warfare," and the CIA created the Contras (short for Counterrevolutionaries) from former National Guard soldiers, who launched a dirty war on the nation.[26] Trying to justify a U.S. military intervention by proving Soviet and Cuban subterfuge, U.S. Marine Colonel Oliver North excitedly revealed satellite photographs of Nicaraguan baseball fields, exclaiming: "The Nicaraguans play *soccer*, not baseball. The *Cubans* play baseball!"[27] Of course, North was ignorant about Nicaragua baseball.

But instead of associating the American game with U.S. imperialism and pushing soccer as an alternative, the Sandinistas kept supporting baseball. According to John Krich:

> [T]he ongoing loyalty to baseball found both [in Nicaragua] and in renegade Cuba makes perfect sense. The two anti–American nations treasure all aspects of American culture, including Hollywood movies and fashions and jazz....

> [T]o appreciate and nurture baseball suggests a level of cosmopolitanism and ... even a taste for the absurd, which would also encourage nationalism and political sophistication. [I]n the family of nations, the sons who most resemble the father are the most likely to challenge the father's authority.[28]

As Interior Minister Tomas Borges indicated, "Our favorite sport might be anti-imperialism, but we also love baseball."[29]

Thus, with different words, the U.S. Marine Corps Hymn — a legacy of the occupation — was played at many Nicaraguan ballgames. The *Raiders of the Lost Ark* theme song advertised Radio Sandino baseball game broadcasts, and Nicaraguans picked up major league games on Armed Forces Radio. The Sandinista newspaper *Barricada* reported extensively on the U.S. major leagues, and at one point ran a debate about whether or not Reggie Jackson should be admired. One side claimed it was natural to support the best; the other side condemned such celebrity as legitimizing the myth of upward mobility, endorsing corporate ownership and neglecting U.S. poverty. Why, it asked, did New York City renovate Yankee Stadium while its schools were deteriorating?[30]

Even though Somoza fled with most of the country's treasury, the Sandinistas insisted on putting baseball into their national budgets. Baseball was used to promote certain values, such as equality, community, and service.[31] The new Sport Institute sponsored an extensive grassroots infrastructure to promote baseball playing, with teams for young and old alike. The new Hernan Tomares Ordonez Amateur League replaced corporate teams with public, government, and regional clubs, including the first national black team, from the Atlantic Coast.

Initially, to protect their local leagues, the Sandinistas discouraged U.S. baseball scouts, using a rationale similar to that made against professionalism by the amateur leagues in the U.S. in the 1860s. Even so, several Nicaraguans played in the major leagues during this period, including the aforementioned Albert Williams (Pirates, Twins, 1980–84), David Green (Brewers, Cardinals, Giants, 1981–87) and Porfi Altamirano (Phillies, Cubs, 1982–84).

In 1984, Nicaragua beat the U.S. in the politically charged Olympic preliminaries, but then lost to Japan, 19–1, on a night when "even the Contras cried." That year, the Dantos Sports Factory (named after Sandinista hero German "Danto" Pomares) began producing baseball equipment. Operated by the Sandinista Army, making baseballs and Managua Sluggers was considered a patriotic mission and symbolic independence from the U.S. Baseball's morale-boosting value was not lost on the Contras, who ambushed hardwood trucks to block the production of baseball bats.[32] Even with a civil war raging, the Sandinistas endorsed baseball, similar to the "green light" issued by Franklin Roosevelt during World War II.[33] As in the U.S., however, when ball players were drafted, the quality of league play suffered. Reminiscent of the North and South in the U.S. Civil War, a pickup baseball game was played, under a white flag, between Sandinista soldiers and the Contras, at the Honduran border.

Nicaragua's baseball czar was Defense Minister, Humberto Ortega, who claimed, "The only way we want to compete with the United States is through baseball." Even so, in 1985 the CIA mined Nicaraguan harbors and the Reagan administration imposed a trade embargo.[34] Despite deepening hostilities and poverty, the Sandinistas rebuilt the earthquake-damaged Somoza Stadium and renamed it the Rigoberto Lopez Stadium after the man who assassinated the dictator.[35] The Masaya Stadium was renamed after Roberto Clemente, and the Chichigalpa ballpark was renamed the Heroes and Martyrs of September Stadium, as a kind of anti–Yankee Stadium. Heroic soldiers threw out the first pitch at ballgames, and four Nicaraguan Heroes of the Century were recognized: one of them was the 1950s baseball star, Eduardo Green, the father of major leaguer David Green.

In 1985, the first Baseball for Peace tour was led by the Californian Jay Feldman (and backed by Dusty Baker and others) to promote good will, supply electrical and baseball equipment (including donations from the San Francisco Giants and Oakland Athletics), repair war-damaged baseball parks, and sponsor U.S.-Nicaragua baseball games.[36] As Feldman indicated: "I look at Baseball for Peace (whose logo was a peace symbol formed by three baseball bats) as war reparations. We've done such destruction to that country.... I've wanted to atone in a small way to the Nicaraguan people."[37] Based on his visits, Feldman "began to think of baseball as a metaphor for the revolution," perhaps even changing the game on the field: "Before the revolution," observed one player, "there used to be terrible fights between the players and the umpires ... but since the triumph, we've seen that we're all brothers in the struggle, and now it's impolite to be abusive towards umpires."[38] According to Feldman, "Every conference on the mound is a regular summit meeting ... the pitcher, the catcher, the manager, all the infielders—and if it's a game situation in the late innings, even the outfielders come in. It's socialist baseball."[39]

As far back as World War I, throwing baseballs was endorsed to train U.S. soldiers learning how to hurl grenades. But in Nicaragua it was the reverse: In the 1970s, Julio Medina ran through Leon throwing bombs at Somoza's National Guard. By 1986, he was a star catcher for the Leon team, throwing out opposing runners.[40] By that year, however, baseball was hurting in Nicaragua. Some blamed politics, claiming the Sandinistas used revolutionary loyalty to staff teams and keep good players from leaving the country.[41] Others argued that the civil war and embargo made it impossible to produce more competitive teams.[42]

In 1986, a second Baseball for Peace tour arrived, which John Krich described in his book, *El Beisbol*. "If ping pong diplomacy could promote an opening to China," Krich argued, "then surely a more mutually beloved sport was worth trying here. Where governments had failed, baseball might succeed." About the Sandinistas, Krich asked: where else "could we find sworn revolutionaries who interrupt their dialectics to remind us that their favorite player is Ernie Banks?" Inspired by Nicaragua, Krich began signing his autograph as "Sandino Koufax." In the end, Krich observed: "If the bleacher bums of Leon are the enemy, then it's only more proof that the enemy is ourselves."[43]

According to Krich, given the repeated interventions, "In Nicaragua, and in all Latin America, sooner or later everyone's on the disabled list." Or worse: by 1986, at least 170 ballplayers had been killed by the Contras. As coffee farmer, Marco Gonzales noted: "If you had a war in the U.S. like ours, you would now have over a million dead." Sounding like Japanese internment camp residents in the U.S. during World War II, Gonzalez continued: "It is important that we never be caught in a war mentality.... And one of the main ways of fighting this is by playing baseball."[44]

In 1987, Nicaragua sent a team to the Pan American Games in Indianapolis. The Nicaraguan model, Bianca Jagger, had been beaten by the National Guard while a student, but now appeared to cheer her native team: "Here is a country the size of Iowa, a country of three million people, in the only arena where they can compete. Which is baseball."[45] Back in Nicaragua, a new baseball initiative from California donated baseball equipment, toys, and educational supplies as a kind of people-to-people diplomacy.[46]

That same year, I joined the third Baseball for Peace tour. We rebuilt the Geronimo Robles Stadium in Boaco, when we weren't playing the occasional ballgame. A Nicaraguan national team member insisted on trading his 1983 Pan American Games medal for my Louisville Slugger. One young soldier, swinging his rifle as if powdering a fastball, wondered how devoted baseball players could do anything but support social revolution. We found this link being made everywhere we went.[47]

By 1988, Nicaraguans were becoming exhausted by the war's destruction, but baseball helped keep them together.[48] With Dennis Martinez no longer on the Orioles, many Nicaraguans began rooting for the Yankees again, despite the suffering caused by U.S. policies. In 1989, the U.S. military invaded Panama and threatened to extend the intervention to Nicaragua. President George Bush, Sr., campaigned hard against the reelection of Sandinista President Daniel Ortega. The fourth Baseball for Peace mission arrived in Nicaragua.[49] Fearing repercussions from hostile U.S. policies, tour members were surprised that Nicaraguans were still willing to distinguish between *yanquis* (the U.S. government and military) and *norteamericanos* (the American people).[50]

In 1989, Roberto Clemente's widow, Vera, returned to Nicaragua, where she accepted the Eduardo Green Award, posthumously, for Roberto—a national hero and the first foreigner to ever receive the award.[51] The Sandinistas still championed grassroots and national baseball, but U.S. big league teams and scouts were also courted. President Ortega expressed his hope that Nicaragua could settle its differences with the U.S. on the ball fields, and revealed that he, too, had been a life-long Yankee fan.[52]

The Contemporary Game, 1990–2006

In 1990, the U.S. promised to end support for the Contras and embargo if the Sandinistas lost the elections, and a weary Nicaraguan public voted Ortega out of the presidency. In 1991, Dennis Martinez achieved godlike status, pitching a perfect game for the Montreal Expos.[53] The new conservative government tried to exploit Martinez, arranging a two-day national celebration and an audience with new President, Violeta Chamorro.[54] About his no hitter, Martinez observed: "After all they have been through, the turmoil, the earthquake, the war, I think this was the big moment to bring happiness to the Nicaraguan people." Amidst the euphoria, however, were signs that this might have been baseball's high point in Nicaragua.

In 1993, a new political party, the Third Democratic Way, was created to put Dennis Martinez on the next presidential ballot. Nicknamed El Presidente years earlier, Martinez was still consumed by his baseball career, and thus declined the bid, saying: "I cannot comment about the invitation at this moment. But I have my right to be a candidate, as the Nicaraguan I am. Nicaragua needs a change."[55] His comments reflected the deep dissatisfaction Nicaraguans already felt toward the conservatives—with Sandinista social reforms eliminated, and poverty and unemployment higher than ever. With its government and economy back under the control of international bankers and U.S. multinational corporations, Nicaragua could get some small relief only through charity.[56] Anti-Americanism was high, and might explain the rock that smashed through the baseball Team USA bus window at the Pan American Qualification Tournament in Managua.[57]

By 1998, Nicaragua had shed Cuba as an ally. When seven Cubans arrived from Havana, all were given refugee status. Four of them were baseball players.[58] In the U.S., Dennis Martinez pitched his last season, replacing Juan Marichal as the winningest Latin American pitcher in MLB history.[59] In Managua, the ballpark was renamed the Dennis Martinez National Stadium but, like the rest of Nicaragua, it was hard hit by yet another disaster, Hurricane Mitch. Martinez flew in to help with the recovery. Despite his continuing popularity, Martinez again declined a presidential run, instead setting up the

Dennis Martinez Foundation in Granada and joining the U.S. State Department Speaker Program for youth baseball.

In 2005, Nicaragua slipped below Haiti as the Western Hemisphere's poorest nation. As Dan Gordon has observed, the class divisions are also much wider. Among other things, the inequality has hurt baseball, which no longer unites the classes.[60] Ball playing is in decline. Historically, baseball has been promoted, if not exploited, by *both* the political right and the political left. But the new government has neglected baseball, and soccer has made new inroads.[61] The International Soccer Federation has arrived to promote the sport, while Major League Baseball has been largely inactive.

The Nicaraguan Baseball Dream?

What happened to the baseball American dream in Nicaragua? Baseball may have been imported from the U.S. to Nicaragua with condescension, for profit and social control, and to "civilize the heathens," but hasn't baseball also contributed something positive to Nicaraguan society? If so, it now seems fleeting. Does Nicaragua's threatened shift away from baseball suggest a rejection of America and the failure of the American dream there? The U.S. has given Nicaragua the gift of baseball; but have we given it anything else worth celebrating? In the past, Nicaraguans sometimes used baseball to resist American policies, but is the move now toward soccer a more profound protest against the ugly history of U.S. intervention? Can sports play that role in international politics?[62]

During Nicaragua's 2006 national elections, baseball showed it still sometimes competes with politics: the news was abuzz with the campaign-interrupting and season-ending, five-inning, rain-shortened no-hitter thrown by the latest Nicaraguan major leaguer; Boston Red Sox rookie Devern Hansack. But most attention focused on threats the U.S. made against Nicaragua if it reelected Sandinista Daniel Ortega; asserting that his victory would bring the risk of nuclear or biological terrorism "within walking distance of our undefended border."[63]

Even so, Ortega won the presidency,[64] and discussed what motivated his political career: "During my childhood and adolescence, I suffered the repression of the Somoza dictatorship in every way: economically, socially, as well as at the hands of the police — because if we went out on the street to play baseball, for example, the police would beat us up and put us in prison."[65] Now, Ortega once again has the power to lead Nicaragua. Will baseball affect the direction he takes?

Before Ortega's reelection, the first World Baseball Classic was held in the spring of 2006. Nicaragua was excluded because Major League Baseball wanted greater geographical representation, and Latin America was already oversubscribed. Nicaragua also had few major leaguers (besides Hansack, Vicente Padilla is the only current Nicaraguan major leaguer),[66] or even minor leaguers, with which to publicize and man the team. Nicaragua was made an alternate to Cuba, which the State Department initially banned from the Classic because of America's continuing obsession with Fidel Castro. Ultimately, Cuba played. But in the future, will the new Nicaraguan government insist on a slot for its national team?

In November 2006, a new Nicaraguan Baseball League was formed, bringing professional baseball back for the first time since 1967. The new league has already included professionals from Cuba, Panama, Mexico, and the U.S. A new baseball academy — the American College — was also launched and jointly funded by the Dennis Martinez Foundation and Major League Baseball — possibly a sign that the U.S. big leagues care about Nicaraguan baseball after all.[67]

While Nicaraguans have rejected the conservative model, Daniel Ortega might not solve the nation's woes either. But if given a chance, he might improve Nicaragua's prospects, and even help revive baseball along the way. Although it may seem strange that a sport could play a central role, baseball might actually help promote better days ahead. After all, the U.S. has sold baseball, to Nicaragua and other nations, as a vehicle of democracy and of the other positive values of the American dream. Suppose we got serious about making that a reality? For generations, baseball has gripped Nicaragua, providing a common thread in a nation otherwise divided by politics. But, to borrow an unfortunate but appropriate phrase, baseball has always been a "political football" in Nicaragua, and full advantage has never been taken of baseball's potentially unifying properties.

Perhaps Dennis Martinez will get serious about politics after all. A hero among both the left and the right, with impeccable baseball credentials and reformist sensibilities, and yet also good relations with the United States — could a Martinez presidency heal old wounds,[68] and finally help deliver to Nicaragua some semblance of the horsehide American dream?

Notes

1. Randall E. Floyd, *The Good, the Bad, and the Mad* (New York: Barnes & Noble, 1999), 155–56.

2. Peter C. Bjarkman, *Diamonds Around the Globe: The Encyclopedia of International Baseball* (Westport, CT: Greenwood Press, 2005), 322; Michael M. Oleksak and Mary Adams Oleksak, *Beisbol: Latin Americans and the Grand Old Game* (Indianapolis: Master's Press, 1996), 11.

3. Michel Gobat, *Confronting the American Dream: Nicaragua Under U.S. Imperial Rule* (Durham: Duke University Press, 2005), 64.

4. See Robert Elias, *Baseball and the American Dream: Race, Class, Gender and the Na-*

tional Pastime (Armonk, NY: M.E. Sharpe, 2001).

5. Gobat, *Confronting the American Dream*, 64.

6. Lester D. Langley and Thomas Schoonover, *The Banana Men: American Mercenaries and Entrepreneurs in Central America, 1880–1930* (Lexington: University Press of Kentucky, 1995), 41; and Gerald S. Gems, *The Athletic Crusade: Sport and American Cultural Imperialism* (Lincoln: University of Nebraska Press, 2006), 139.

7. Richard McGehee, "The King and His Court: Early Baseball and Other Sports in Nicaragua" (paper presented at the North American Society for Sport History Conference, Auburn University, May 24–27, 1996).

8. Clifford D. Ham, "Americanizing Nicaragua: How Yankee Marines, Financial Oversight and Baseball Are Stabilizing Nicaragua," *American Review of Reviews*, 53:2 (1916), 185–191.

9. Richard McGehee, "Sport in Nicaragua, 1889–1926," in *Sport in Latin America and the Caribbean*, eds. Joseph L. Arbena and David G. LaFrance (Wilmington, DE: Scholarly Resources, 2002), 175–205.

10. Gems, *The Athletic Crusade*, 141.

11. Stephen Kinzer, "It's 'Play Ball' Time in Nicaragua," *New York Times*, April 16, 1988, 5A.

12. Ivan Musicant, *The Banana Wars: A History of United States Military Intervention in Latin America from the Spanish American War to the Invasion of Panama* (New York: Macmillan, 1990), 333.

13. Gems, *The Athletic Crusade*, 162.

14. James D. Cockcroft, *Latinos in Beisbol: The Hispanic Experience in the Americas* (Danbury, CT: Franklin Watts, 1996), 126–27.

15. Lester D. Langley and Thomas Schoonover, *The Banana Men*, 41; and Gems, *The Athletic Crusade*, 139.

16. Horacio Ruiz, "Somoza May Revive Loop in Nicaragua," *Sporting News*, 150:10 (September 28, 1960), 36.

17. Horacio Ruiz, "Nicaraguan Winter League Folds; Loss of Government Aid is Cited," *Sporting News*, 164:15 (October 28, 1967), 30.

18. Jay Feldman, "Baseball in Nicaragua," *Whole Earth Review* (Fall 1987), 1–7.

19. Smithsonian Institution, "Beyond Baseball: The Life of Roberto Clemente" (www.robertoclemente.si.edu/english/virtual_introduction.htm); Elizabeth DiNovella, "An American Story," *The Progressive* (July 2006), 43–44; David Maraniss, *Clemente: The Passion and Grace of Baseball's Last Hero* (New York: Simon & Schuster, 2006), 287–307; David Zirin, "Roberto Clemente and the Value of A Number," *The Nation* (February 6, 2006), 5; Bruce Markusen, "Roberto Clemente: Activist and Pioneer," in *Baseball As America: Seeing Ourselves Through Our National Game* (Washington, D.C.: National Geographic, 2001), 101–103; Dave Zirin, *Welcome to the Terrordome: The Pain, Politics and Promise of Sports* (Chicago: Haymarket Books, 2007), 42.

20. Pat Jordan, "Dubious Triumph in Florida," *Sports Illustrated*, 41:24 (December 9, 1974), 41.

21. Patrick Reusse, "Tamer Times for Williams," *Sporting News*, 190:5 (August 2, 1980), 39; Oleksak and Oleksak, *Beisbol*, 150; and John Krich, *El Beisbol: Travels Through the Pan-American Pastime* (New York: Prentice Hall, 1989), 87.

22. Sergio Ramirez, "The Centerfielder," in *The New Baseball Reader*, ed. Charles Einstein (New York: Penguin, 1991), 333.

23. See George Black, *Triumph of the People: The Sandinista Revolution in Nicaragua* (London: Zed Books, 1982).

24. John Krich, "Journey to the End of Baseball," *Mother Jones*, 12 (August–September 1987), 30–35, 45–47.

25. Ken Nigro, "Sobering Sight in Nicaragua — Gun-Toting Kids," *Sporting News*, 189:14 (April 5, 1980), 50.

26. The Contras were terrorists who assassinated educators, farmers, women, children, and church leaders. But to the Reagan administration, they were freedom fighters, battling what Noam Chomsky called the "threat of a good example." That is, if the Sandinistas were allowed to succeed in liberating Nicaraguans, other nations might get the idea that they could and should do so, too. This could not be allowed. See Noam Chomsky, *What Uncle Sam Really Wants* (Tucson: Odonian Press, 1993); Holly Sklar, *Washington's War on Nicaragua* (Boston: South End Press, 1988); Stephen Kinzer, *Overthrow: America's Century of Regime Change from Hawaii to Iraq* (New York: Times Books, 2006); and Cockcroft, *Latinos in Beisbol*.

27. Oleksak and Oleksak, *Beisbol*, 150; Phillip Bennett, "Game Didn't Help Them Escape Long," *Boston Globe*, August 13, 1987, D2; Editors, "Garrick Throws A Curve," Media Watch, June 1, 1989 (www.mediaresearch.org/media

watch/1989/watch19890601.asp); and Cockcroft, *Latinos in Baseball*, 153.

28. Krich, *El Beisbol*, 191.

29. Rob Ruck, "The View from Left Field," *Mother Jones*, 10 (July 1985), 13; Ronnie Lovler, "Some Revolutionary Production: When They Play Hardball in Nicaragua, the Army Puts It All Together," *Boston Sunday Globe*, November 25, 1984, 55.

30. David Russell, "Baseball, Hollywood, and Nicaragua," *Monthly Review*, 34:10 (March 1983), 22–29; and David Russell, "Revolutionary Baseball," *Working Papers* (January/February 1983), 8–11.

31. Eric Wagner, "Sport in Revolutionary Societies: Cuba and Nicaragua," in *Sport and Society in Latin America*, ed. Joseph L. Arbena (New York: Greenwood Press, 1988), 113–136.

32. Krich, *El Beisbol*, 195.

33. Leslie Bornstein, "While War Rages, Baseball Remains the National Passion in Nicaragua," *Sports Illustrated*, 63:8 (August 19, 1985), 8.

34. Arguably, this only drove Nicaragua's emerging social democracy toward a more extreme, Soviet-style communism. Brad Whorton and Eric Wagner, "Nicaraguan Sport Ideology," *Journal of Sport and Social Issues*, 9:2 (Summer/Fall 1985), 26–33; and Larry Rohter, "Play Ball! Sandinistas Change Game," *New York Times*, March 16, 1985, 2.

35. Linda Adler, "Down to the Baseball Republic," *Minneapolis Review of Baseball*, 6 (January 1986), 10; and Eric Wagner, "Sport and Revolution in Nicaragua," in *Nicaragua in Revolution*, ed. Thomas Walker (New York: Praeger, 1982), 291–302.

36. Bob McCoy, "Baseball for Peace," *Sporting News*, 200:24 (December 9, 1985), 10.

37. Jay Feldman, "The Hidden-Ball Trick, Nicaragua, and Me," *The National Pastime: A Review of Baseball History*, 6:1 (1987), 2–4.

38. Feldman, "Baseball in Nicaragua," 1–7.

39. Krich, *El Beisbol*, 210.

40. John Kerr, "Nicaragua Baseball Update," *Minneapolis Review of Baseball*, 6 (February 1986), 6; and Joel Millman, "Baseball-Nica, 1986," *Minneapolis Review of Baseball*, 6:1 (1986), 13.

41. Leo Banks, "Sandinista Baseball: Revolutionary Rules," *Wall Street Journal*, 209:58 (March 25, 1987), 28. Allegedly, Brant Alyea had to sneak out of Nicaragua to sign with the Toronto Blue Jays. As it turned out, Alyea was the illegitimate child of an unknown American ballplayer, who had played, decades earlier, in the Nicaraguan winter league. As John Krich has suggested, "Baseball's conquerors, like any other kind, have left behind bastard children in their own image" (199).

42. Robert Lipsyte, "Let's Go Nics," *The Nation*, 243:15 (November 8, 1986), 477.

43. Krich, *El Beisbol*, 199, 213.

44. Feldman, "Baseball in Nicaragua," 1–7.

45. Oleksak and Oleksak, *Beisbol*, 151.

46. Margo Freistadt, "Adventures of the 'Beisbol Man,'" *Editor & Publisher* 120: 41 (October 10, 1987), 30,64.

47. Robert Elias, "Baseball: A Force for Social Change?" *Berkeley Voice*, August 18, 1988, 13–14, 22–23; and Robert Elias, "Baseball and Social Change," *Minneapolis Review of Baseball*, 8 (January 1988), 24.

48. Steven Henson, "The Common Thread: Baseball and the Social Fabric in Nicaragua," *Minneapolis Review of Baseball*, 8 (January 1988), 27.

49. James Rodewald, "A Nicaraguan Adventure: Some Kind of Baseball on a Goodwill Tour," *Sports Illustrated*, 73 (December 24, 1990), 8–10.

50. Jay Feldman, "View from Managua: Baseballs and News in Nicaragua," *Sacramento News & Review*, January 25, 1990, 16–17.

51. Rob Ruck, "Clemente, Dreams Return to Nicaragua," *Baseball America*, November 10, 1989, 8–9.

52. See Edgardo Tijerino, *Double Play* (Managua, Nicaragua: Editorial Vanguardes, 1989), 8–9.

53. Rob Rains, "Martinez Made It a Perfect Day—National Celebration Followed Achievement," *USA Today Baseball Weekly*, 1:18 (August 2, 1991), 33.

54. "Martinez Returns Home the Hero," *USA Today Baseball Weekly*, 1:21 (August 23, 1991), 14. The U.S. also sought to exploit baseball for political reasons, extending aid to youth baseball as a symbolic gesture. See Rob Ruck, "Baseball Diplomacy," *Pittsburgh*, 25 (July 1994), 38; Rob Ruck, "Coming to Terms with the Past," Politics and Baseball Collide in Nicaragua," *Dugout*, 2 (August 1994), 11–15.

55. "Sports People: Baseball: Nicaragua Boomlet: Martinez for President," *The New York Times*, October 1, 1993, C1.

56. "Baseball Equipment Among One-Million Pounds of Material Ohio Ministry Has Shipped To Nicaragua," *International Baseball Rundown*, 5:4 (May 1996), 8; and Horace Hinshaw, "Little League Coach on Humanitarian Trip," *Pacifica Tribune*, May 2, 2007, 5.

57. "Attack Against USA Team Bus Mars Tournament in Nicaragua," *International Baseball Rundown*, 2:8 (September 1993), 1.

58. "Cuban Ballplayers Flee to Nicaragua," *The New York Times*, August 16, 1998, C1.

59. Deron Snyder, "El Presidente Elects to Extend His Term," *USA Today Baseball Weekly*, April 22–28, 1998, 11.

60. Dan Gordon, "Nicaragua: In Search of Diamonds," in *Baseball Without Borders: The International Pastime*, ed. George Gmelch (Lincoln: University of Nebraska Press, 2006), 172–195; and Dan Gordon, "Baseball on Ometepe Island," *Elysian Fields Quarterly*, 17 (Summer 2000), 76–82.

61. See Stefan Szymanski and Andrew Zimbalist, *National Pastime: How Americans Play Baseball and the Rest of the World Plays Soccer* (Washington, D.C.: Brookings Institution Press, 2005); Franklin Foer, *How Soccer Explains the World* (New York: HarperCollins, 2004), 235–248; and Eduardo Galeano, *Soccer in Sun and Shadow* (New York: Verso, 1998).

62. See Robert Elias, *The Empire Strikes Out: How Baseball Has Influenced American Globalization and Foreign Policy, and Sold the American Dream Abroad* (New York: The New Press, 2008).

63. Grandlin, "Ollie North Returns to Nicaragua," *AlterNet*, November 18, 2006 (http://sage.usfca.edu/frame.html?rtPossible= true&lang=en).

64. Joe DeRaymond, "Nicaragua Redux: The Strange Return of Daniel Ortega," *Counterpunch*, www.counterpunch.org/deraymond 11132006.html (November 13, 2006); Witness for Peace, Nicaragua, "Ortega Government Shows Some Response to Civil Society Demands," *IRC Americas Program* (Silver City, NM: International Relations Center) http:// americas.irc-online/am/4117 (March 29, 2007).

65. "Interview: Daniel Ortega, Sandinista Leader," www.cnn.com/SPECIALS/cold.war/ episodes/18/interviews/ortega/ (October 1997).

66. Padilla has pitched for the Diamondbacks, Phillies, and Rangers since 1999. Outfielder Marvin Benard played for the Giants, White Sox, and Blue Jays from 1995 to 2003, and Oswaldo Mairena pitched for the Marlins from 2000 to 2002.

67. Tim Rogers, "Nicaragua Revives Proud Baseball Tradition," *Nature Landings*, www. naturelandings.com/articles.php?article=39 (January–February 2007).

68. Gems, *The Athletic Crusade*, 142.

CHAPTER 12

The Politics of American Colonialism Through the Lens of Major League Baseball Academies
Jessica Skolnikoff and *Robert Engvall*

"Whether intrinsically so or not, sport, like virtually everything else, has also become ultimately political. Even if ... policies on sport and physical culture do not absolutely link governments to specific ideological traditions, certainly such policies can provide evidence of attitudes and objectives in such areas as health, education, social integration, mass mobilization, and foreign policy."[1]

During the 2005 World Series, between the Astros and White Sox, television analyst Joe Morgan commented about the lack of African American players on the Astros roster. Morgan, once a player with the Astros, seemed both surprised and disappointed that a major league roster could be entirely devoid of African Americans. Others have commented in recent years about the increasing role in Major League Baseball played by "Latin" players, and most recently Asian players. While much has been written, and more should be written about the relatively low numbers of African American major leaguers, the focus of this chapter beyond the local and national issues of race and ethnicity are how these connect in a more global economy and environment. Morgan's comments are particularly interesting, as we approach this issue by examining the politics of cultural identity and socialization.

It is important to acknowledge the concept of globalism that recognizes the impact that technology and travel have made in shrinking the world, and thereby making all varieties of things accessible to more people. One can clearly see the expansion of baseball into international markets with the development of overseas exhibition games culminating when the 2008 season was actually begun with a regulation game between the Red Sox and Athletics in Tokyo, Japan. But long before that, baseball was at the forefront of globalization, with its expansion into international markets through the formation of and subsequent use of "baseball academies." Many major league teams now have their own "academies" in countries becoming known for the production of quality major league players. Venezuela and the Dominican Republic are but two examples of countries sending increasing numbers of players to Major League Baseball, as these countries participate in the expansion of economic markets. At the beginning of the 2006 baseball season, there were 145 players from the Dominican Republic and 45 from Venezuela, the two largest exporters of players into major league baseball.[2]

Our intention in this chapter is to further examine social and cultural variables that may be at work within baseball academies. This examination may require that we look at larger issues that have played into the creation of baseball academies in certain countries, and that perhaps shape our collective treatment of individuals within our society. Perhaps Joe Morgan's lament, with which we began, might be better understood in a context wherein the major leagues are actively working with and training young people in Latin American countries to become their "workers."

> Just as the Spaniards had cut up Dominican land centuries before to harvest sugar, the Dodgers began plowing amid the island's sugar-cane plantations, replacing its yield stock with baseball diamonds, batting cages, and pitcher's mounds — the new growth industry of Latin America.[3]

The American Dream may seem like baseball, motherhood, and apple pie — what's not to like about giving children a chance to become millionaire baseball players in the United States? There is a nagging question, however, that those interested in social justice issues are beginning to confront: are the new baseball "farms" in somewhat marginalized and periphery nations, the current manifestation of earlier sugar and banana plantations? These plantations may have brought some income to the locals, but they were founded upon the need to reap large profits for American businesses? Obviously, we're not equating baseball "workers" to the slavery that existed on plantations of old, but the concept of a disposable workforce remains very much in play.

Within the context of globalization, and the ever increasing influence of the United States and its popular culture upon the rest of the world, we need to include the issues of "identity" and "place" that shape people's perceptions. "In the late twentieth century, Latinos were represented by thoroughly negative and derogatory images in contemporary American public discourse."[4] An example of the negative portrayal of Latinos has been illustrated in the literature which has informed us that stars such as Roberto Clemente were far from lionized by both the national media and their hometown media outlets. It is clear that even players with the legacy of Clemente suffered tremendous marginality during their playing days.

Where people are "placed" (in the perceptions of others) perhaps plays a critical role in their treatment. The labels we attach to people both consciously and subconsciously, dramatically shape those who come or hope to come to the United States in order to play "America's pastime." Given today's inflammatory rhetoric surrounding immigration from Mexico, it would seem that negative and derogatory images of Latinos still exist in the minds of a significant number of Americans. While arriving baseball players certainly find themselves in a much better economic place than do most new immigrants, they still arrive in a country that is struggling with how to handle those who do not sound, dress, act, or look like "us." President George W. Bush suggested that new arrivals to this country must adopt American values and learn English.[5] How do those mindsets translate into our treatment of Latin American baseball players?

Jonathan Mahler wrote that all but two of Major League Baseball's teams have baseball academies in the Dominican Republic.[6] These academies are charged with developing youth with raw talent but who lack baseball fundamentals into players worthy of "a look" by big league clubs. Each baseball club wants its academy to become the very best and most efficient "baseball factory" on the island. But what happens to the "factory workers" who do not get promoted. (After all, even with the best training available, a tiny percentage of those who attend Dominican baseball schools will ever actually make it to the big leagues.) What becomes of the vast majority who fail in their quest for the bright lights, big cities, and big financial windfalls that await major league baseball players? Should it concern us that baseball academies spring up in economically depressed countries, in which young men may feel that baseball is not *one* way out of dire circumstances, but the *only* way out of dire circumstances? Would there be a concern in the United States, if we created any type of academy for young people in which the "failure" rate approached 100 percent? Are we creating an avenue for young people with dreams, or are we unwittingly, perhaps, creating more streets lined with sixteen to twenty-two-year-old young men, who already view their lives as less hopeful than they otherwise might have been?

It is important to note that the odds against any individual baseball player actually achieving his dream to play in the major leagues are incredibly high. Whether that player has grown up in the Dominican Republic, Venezuela, or an exclusive suburb in the United States, the odds are that he will never achieve success on the major league level. This chapter is not meant to address whether or not players outside of the United States have even higher odds against their success, as all players have such high odds against them. Thus, a quantitative debate about the numbers would seem nearly devoid of value. Instead, it is our position that taking a look at international baseball academies is worthy not so much because of how many players "make it," but because of the implications involved for the vast majority of those who do not make it. In essence, when a young man from the United States decides (or has it decided for them) that their dream of achieving the major leagues must end, they face a number of decisions about what to do with the rest of their lives. A similar decision-making process confronts foreign-born prospects, but in many cases, the range of possible choices for them is vastly inferior to the choices facing U.S. born prospects. Does baseball owe it to prospects to take this into account?

Baseball as a popular cultural institution, invested with symbolic meaning, and held out as a representative of larger ideals, values, and beliefs, has been as "American as apple pie" for well over a hundred years. As such an institution and a cultural representative, baseball has served as a principal site where issues of national identity, ethnicity, and race have long been played out. Adrian Burgos views baseball as a playing field where different ethnic groups sought to gain acceptance as fellow Americans.[7]

We are not the first to consider the ethics of "hunting" for talent amid squalor and poverty.[8] Steve Fainaru, for example, asks, "What are the responsibilities of U.S. based teams that conduct business in poor, often corrupt societies and of an industry that wields enormous power over a pool of unsophisticated teenage ballplayers?"[9] Arturo Guevara and David Fidler consider the same question in considerable depth. Why should baseball be different from any other business wanting to keep labor costs down?[10] What is more disturbing and more worthy of our attention is when a search for cheap labor ends up treating human beings as disposable.

The history of Latin Americans in baseball is contentious at best. As Breton and Villegas state, "The history of how Latins are brought into America's game — is a story of capitalism and cutthroat competition."[11] As before it was only the rich land to harvest crops, now it is also young men that are "harvested" for baseball. According to Marco Breton and Jose Luis Villegas:

> Stories and the success of Latin players in the major leagues completely obscure the true underside of this talent search, the fact that hundreds of young Latinos are routinely discarded every year. According to statistics kept by major league baseball, between 90 and 95 percent of foreign-born players are released at the minor league level.[12]

It would seem that each time the lives of players are discussed it is in terms of histories, linear progressions of their accomplishments and statistics or personal vignettes. Whether players make it or not is generally discussed only in these rather familiar terms. However, one element that seems to be missing is the cultural piece. Not only are the academies fostering economic exploitation along the lines of United Fruit and what came to be called banana republics, but the academies are also ignoring the subtext of cultural imperialism. Cultural imperialism lies in the shadows, thereby placing these players in situations where they become both heroes and targets — they cannot go home again and this "new" culture still disdains the embodiment of how they play and live. On the surface, researchers, fans, and aficionados of the game discuss Latin players and how Latino and American culture differ from one another but what does this really mean?

How people "play" and participate in sport is culturally constructed. As Noel Dyck and Eduardo Archetti state, "These identities inevitably reflect not only stylized forms of movement and purpose, but also contexts within which they are nurtured."[13] Even though the rules in baseball may be the same or similar, how people interpret the rules and act on and move their bodies accordingly can be very different. This difference comes from not only the interpretation of the rules but also how a person acts through the embodiment of their culture. A person's culture is embodied in their every action — from walking and dancing to playing a sport. While sociologists discuss a process called socialization — how one becomes socialized in their culture from elements such as etiquette, language, and style — embodiment goes further, into a total orientation of our being. The term "habitus" has been used to identify the larger construct of embodiment.[14] Through culture people learn how to use their bodies in space, from large motor skills to fine motor skills to complete specific skills. As Dyck states, "That these selves and identities are directly or indirectly anchored by embodied performances on the fields of play renders them liable to unpredictability and risk, as well as to attempts to manage these factors and the social relationships within which they are embedded."[15]

Researchers have discussed embodied performances in football (soccer) and dance.[16] In "Playing Football and Dancing Tango: Embodying Argentina in Movement, Style and Identity," Eduardo Archetti compares the body movement in football (soccer) and tango in Argentina but also assesses the styles of football cross-culturally. He sees the playing field as one venue in which "the national can be perceived and related to specific individual features, cultural creativity and public performances."[17] Through the performances — body movement and nonverbal communication — of football and dance the actors are performing their culture. He states, "The anthropological analysis of sport is not a reflection of society, but a means of reflecting on society."[18] In his comparison of the British and Argentinean styles of football, he sees the history, economic systems, and "virtues," all being reflected in the style and performance of play:

> The conceptual opposition between British and criollo physical virtues has become encrusted in common perceptions of football. The British physical

virtues are still associated with "force and physical power," while the virtues of the criollos are those of agility and virtuoso movement. The metaphor of the "machine," as opposed to individual creativity, is constant in contemporary football imagery. "British" is still associated with industrial, and the criollo with pre-industrial social system. [19]

It is through Archetti's lens of studying these activities, in this case football, in our case baseball, that we see how we can read sport and its performers as a means of "reflecting on society."[20] We begin to see these baseball players as performers of their own culture — not only socialized in their culture — but as a place to examine their physical presence and performance.

We contend that it is possible as well to read Latino baseball players in the same way as the Argentinean football players; they also have their culture and history embedded in their body movement. Because the cultural ideals and practices are inscribed in a person's movements along with their country's history, the Latino players not only have to learn skills at the baseball academies but they must also be able to perform in a way the scouts believe will "fit in" with their teams. The small percentage that do make it as major league ball players still have the embedded culture and history of their country in their every action on and off the field. For example, what was highlighted during the World Baseball Classic was not only how players from different countries approached the basic rules of play but also how they exemplified the different instruction and style of play — in other words, how they embody their culture. This is not to stereotype all players from the same country but to acknowledge that their use of body and performance reflects/embodies the norms, values, and beliefs of their culture. Consider, can we imagine any major league player other than Hideki Matsui apologizing to teammates and fans for breaking his wrist while trying to catch a ball, something he did in 2006 while playing for the New York Yankees.

The role of the academies is to find and train young talent that develops into learning the way to play "American baseball." We contend that although these young players will learn the rules of the game — strikes, outs, plays, there is more to American baseball than the rules. There is the expectation that all players will fully accept and conform to the larger myths of American baseball, and even the larger and prevailing myths of American society. After all, these Latino players are entering the country of their "exploiters."

> In the Caribbean, and particularly in the Dominican, Americans are considered invaders, the powerful ones, the people who effectively toppled a Dominican president and inserted another one more palatable to U.S interests. Americans are the ones who own many of the sugar companies in the Dominican, the ones who have controlled the country to such a degree that scholars have called it a "company state." Meanwhile, combined unemployment and underemployment in the country has run up to 80 percent.[21]

Now, however, where social scientists have previously discussed the colonization of these Latin American countries, we now discuss our relationship in terms of globalization. With globalization, periphery nations will remain periphery nations that have the raw materials that core nations exploit. In the case of many of these countries young Latino players are now both raw material and cheap labor, and one of the commodities of these countries in the capitalist market economy.

One of the goals within colonization was to help the people of colonized countries assimilate to the dominant culture, but in many cases that assimilation process never worked. It was an illusion that colonizing countries would help the people of the countries they dominate to assimilate. Are baseball academies a microcosm of a society which couches its actions in terms of helping others, rather than admitting true goals of attempting to assimilate others to conform to their standards? Like other newcomers to the United States, arriving on our shores is only half the battle, the other and sometimes more difficult journey regardless of what level of "success" one might ultimately enjoy lies in finding acceptance within mainstream American culture.

Alan Klein, in his article "Coming of Age in North America: Socialization of Dominican Baseball Players," compares baseball academies to "the type of coming of age initiations found the world over."[22] Klein draws on his ethnographic research at the Dodgers' Campo Las Palmas baseball academy to examine the "rookie" experience of young Dominicans in the academy's process as a rite of passage. Klein's analysis of the rookie experience explains pieces of the rite of passage, such as the physical environment, wearing of the uniform, instructions, and travel as the means whereby these players start to learn about American baseball. It is through the rite of passage of the academy that the players believe that, if they embrace and incorporate this experience and have talent, they have a chance to make it to the big leagues.

However, we suggest that these players rarely complete this rite of passage and become fully incorporated into American baseball. Klein points to specific problems in the process of socialization for these players and discusses "initial problems involving language, food, and customs, and go on to things more subtle such as how to read behavior and intentions."[23] He further states that these issues have direct impact on the players' ability to meet "their potential."[24] Ideally, young recruits will enter the academies as young raw baseball talent and leave the academy as players ready to enter the American baseball leagues. However, many do not make it through this "rite of passage" and do not make it through these academies.

The Dominican Republic and Venezuela represent the richest veins in efforts to mine international baseball talent for the major leagues. Behind this search for talent is basic economics. It seems that relatively affluent American children with many more opportunities and many more sports from which to choose are not necessarily gravitating toward baseball as they once did. In contrast, Latin American boys, in particular, with vastly fewer opportunities seem drawn to baseball.

> In the United States, the smartest child in the family aspires to be an investment banker, an Internet venture capitalist, a doctor. In the shantytowns of Santo Domingo and the Caribbean, the brightest and the best dream of reaching the United States to pull their family out of poverty.[25]

Guevera and Fidler's study of the life of a young Venezuelan baseball player, Alexi Quiroz explains some of the grim tales that surrounded his individual experiences in the Chicago Cubs' "academies."[26] These tales focus upon Quiroz's desire to heighten awareness on the part of Latin American players so that Latino players begin to understand their rights to be treated professionally in the minor leagues in the United States. Regardless of what degree of accuracy we may initially give Quiroz's perceptions of his treatment, his perceptions indicate that he believed the poor treatment he received was "normal," and in the usual course of Major League Baseball team dealings with young Latin American prospects. Quiroz's career was ended by injury that he claims the Cubs medically mistreated. His story parallels that of another young Venezuelan player, Eric Relucido, who similarly claims that his shoulder injury was also handled poorly at his Venezuelan baseball academy, run by the New York Yankees. These accounts certainly speak of the perceptions on the part of a growing number of Latin American players that their status is tenuous at best, and that the academies view them as entirely expendable commodities. Those on the other side of this issue might point out that *all* baseball players' status is tenuous at best.

Certainly, one of the most compelling reasons for the high salaries that Major League Baseball players enjoy centers upon the relatively short career spans that they have, and the fragile nature of their bodies upon which their livings are made. On any given day, an athlete can suffer a career ending injury, and/or over the course of time all athletes suffer from diminishing skills. When these injuries occur to nineteen- and twenty-year-olds, it is particularly sad, but not particularly surprising, and certainly within the nature of sport generally, and baseball particularly.

> Major league teams' primary focus in Latin America is getting players as young as possible, preferably under eighteen. The major leagues' target is, therefore, Latin children. Major league teams handle Latin children in ways that would be unthinkable and illegal in the United States and Canada. The major leagues' strategy is to target Latin children and discriminate against them because cheap labor enhances profits, and the major leagues' objective is to make money.[27]

Although many young players may complete the academy's rite of passage and make it to the minor leagues, they seldom complete the passage to the "big leagues" and the American Dream. There can be no doubt that the major leagues offer opportunities that many of these children would never otherwise see. The question becomes whether we must be resigned to the coexistence of opportunity and exploitation, or whether there is a better way of providing opportunity while maintaining human decency that would preclude discrimination, economic exploitation, and cultural imperialism.

Even the players who do make it to the big leagues, we argue, never fully become part of "American baseball." Anthropologist Victor Turner's work with liminality and communitas draws attention to marginal social status and, in turn, people on the margin. Turner states that "the attributes of liminality or of liminal personae (threshold people) are necessarily ambiguous, since this condition and these persons elude or slip through the network of classifications that normally locate states and positions in cultural space."[28] These liminal people are "neither here nor there; they are betwixt and between the positions assigned and arrayed by law, custom, convention, and ceremony."[29] It is this state of being "neither here nor there" that provides insight about people who do not fit into "mainstream" culture — in this case American culture.[30] These Latin American players will remain liminal because their embodied identities will never fit into the American mythology that informs American baseball. Players embody their culture — they have learned to walk, talk, and carry themselves as Dominicans, Venezuelans, Mexicans, Columbians, and Cubans. Even if they can learn the language and to enjoy different foods and act like millionaires with fancy houses and cars, they will always embody their culture through how they carry themselves, and how they interact and react to different situations.

The research of Breton and Villegas, among others, confirms the perceptions of some, that "Latin players are high maintenance"[31] or cannot understand the "team concept."[32] Enrique Soto, Miguel Tejada's first baseball coach, said, "Baseball in America ... is not the game it is in the Dominican Republic. On the island, it's a game of instincts. But in America, it's a game of instructions."[33] These perceptions are often similarly widespread within the front office as well as Klein has reported:

> My interviews with various directors in Major League baseball pointed up that they commonly fail to promote Dominicans because of what they see as an attitudinal problem or personality flaw. Individuals with these problems are termed "headcases" in baseball circles. While the condition does not pertain exclusively to Latinos, it is commonly associated with them.[34]

Jeffrey Snowbarger, in his presentation at the 2006 Cooperstown Baseball Symposium, addressed the issue of identity in his discussion of perceptions surrounding Pedro Martinez: "Pedro Martinez is thought by Americans to be a little odd."[35] Snowbarger argued that we see Pedro through an American lens and not a Caribbean lens. Even though some of Pedro's actions might seem "odd," his flair and behavior may be better understood if we consider his cultural background. In accord with our earlier discussion of embodiment, Pedro's Dominican culture is expressed in the way he plays baseball on the field and his actions and body movement off the field. It is his public embracing of his culture that makes him not fully incorporated into "American baseball," thus making him liminal on the American baseball diamond. As Breton and Villegas write:

> Thousands emigrate to the United States, both legally and illegally, and often find themselves surviving in the barrios of New York City. And even those players with real baseball talent must first overcome humble beginnings in the eyes of American scouts, who often discard Latin players for the way they look or carry themselves.[36]

The baseball diamond and the rules might be the same, but how one moves on and off the field and communicates through verbal and nonverbal communication from different baseball countries is not the same. And for these Latin players — they will learn how to play the American game if given the opportunity but it will not be their game — it will just be another set of rules they have to learn just as their relatives did when their country was ruled by outside forces.

Conclusion

Do we, in the United States, really accept the success of "others" in our national pastime?

It is perhaps of value to note the "place" of baseball within almost every discussion of important issues ... whether it is in the "religion" of baseball; the "business" or "economics" of baseball; or for our discussion here, the "culture" of baseball. There are only a few who make it — by achieving the American dream — but just enough to keep the myth of the American dream alive, even for those not born in the United States. The myth of the American dream in baseball parallels similar myths in larger American society, in which children are taught that everyone can achieve success if they simply "work hard and play by the rules."

An exploration of the long-range potential ramifications of baseball academies outside the United States does indeed provide evidence of attitudes and ideological traditions. Baseball has a vaunted status among millions of people in the United States, and increasingly millions of people worldwide. This status has sometimes been so vaunted that it has been said to be a "religion."

Buck O'Neil viewed baseball as religion to him because "if you go by the rules, it is right."[37] But just as religion is one form of social control, so is baseball. There are controls for even larger and more "global" issues: what about rules relating to the treatment of those less fortunate than ourselves, and rules relating to the "integration" of new members into the "church" of baseball. Racial and ethnic integration into baseball has been studied, but there has been a less thorough examination of "cultural" integration.

As we write this, there is on-going debate in the halls of Congress and on the streets of America about immigration and what lasting effects that immigration has upon the United States. Basic economics, of course, drives policy concerning immigration, just as basic economics drives the push for globalization of the major leagues. "Like any business, major league teams need to increase revenues and control costs in order to make profits. These needs translate into finding new consumer markets to boost revenues and cheaper sources of labor to control costs."[38] Using baseball as a lens we might bring forth new questions that will allow us to better understand issues of identity and place as they relate to immigration issues so much in the American consciousness today.

Notes

1. Joseph Arbena, "Sport and the Study of Latin American History: An Overview," *Journal of Sport History*, 13:2 (1986), 91.
2. http://www.baseball-almanac.com/players/birthplace.php?y=2007.
3. Marco Breton and Jose Luis Villegas, *Away Games: The Life and Times of a Latin Baseball Player* (Albuquerque: University of New Mexico Press, 1999), 42.
4. Otto Santa Ana, *Brown Tide Rising: Metaphors of Latinos in Contemporary American Public Discourse* (Austin: University of Texas Press, 2002), 15.
5. "Bush: New Arrivals to the U.S. Should Adopt English, Culture," *The Oneonta Daily Star*, June 7, 2006, sec. A.
6. Jonathan Mahler, "Building the Beisbol Brand," *New York Times Magazine Section*, July 31, 2005, Magazine Section.
7. Adrian Jr. Burgos, "Learning America's Other Game: Baseball, Race, and the Study of Latinos," in *Latino/a Popular Culture*, ed. Michelle Habell-Pallan and M. Romero (New York: New York University Press, 2002).
8. Breton and Villegas; Arturo J. Guevara and David Fidler, *Stealing Lives: The Globalization of Baseball and the Tragic Story of Alexis Quiroz* (Bloomington: University of Indiana Press, 2002); and Alan Klein, *Sugarball: The American Dream, The Dominican Dream* (New Haven: Yale University Press, 1991).
9. Steve Fainaru, "Baseball's Minor Infractions: In Latin America, Young Players Come at a Bargain Price," *Washington Post*, October 26, 2001, sec. D.
10. Guevara and Fidler.
11. Breton and Villegas, 35.
12. Ibid., 47.
13. Noel Dyck and Eduardo Archetti, "Embodied Identities: Reshaping Social Life Through Sport and Dance," in *Sport, Dance and Embodied Identities*, ed. Noel Dyck and Edurado Archetti (New York: Berg, 2003), 1.
14. Gordon Marshall, ed., *The Concise Oxford Dictionary of Sociology* (Oxford: Oxford University Press, 1994), 209.
15. Noel Dyck, "Embodying Success: Identity and Performance in Children's Sport," in *Sport, Dance and Embodied Identities*, ed. Noel Dyck and Edurado Archetti (New York: Berg, 2003), 63.
16. Eduardo Archetti, "Playing Football and Dancing Tango: Embodying Argentina in Movement, Style and Identity," in *Sport, Dance and Embodied Identities*, ed. Noel Dyck and Edurado Archetti (New York: Berg, 2003);

Werner Krauss, "Football, Nation and Identity: German Miracles in the Postwar Era," in *Sport, Dance and Embodied Identities*, ed. Dyck and Archetti (New York: Berg, 2003); Anne Leseth, "Michezo: Dance, Sport and Politics in Dar-es-Salaan, Tanzania," in *Sport, Dance and Embodied Identities*, ed. Dyck and Archetti (New York: Berg, 2003); and Helean Wulff, "The Irish Body in Motion: Moral Politics, National Identity and Dance," in *Sport, Dance and Embodied Identities*, ed. Dyck and Archetti (New York: Berg, 2003).

17. Archetti, 221.
18. Ibid., 217.
19. Ibid., 222.
20. Ibid., 217.
21. Breton and Villegas, 56.
22. Alan Klein, "Coming of Age in North America," in *Inside Sports*, ed. Jay J. Coakley and Peter Donnelly (New York: Routledge, 1999), 99.
23. Ibid., 101.
24. Ibid.
25. Juan Gonzalez, *Harvest of Empire: A History of Latinos in America* (New York: Viking Press, 2000), 128.
26. Guevara and Fidler.
27. Ibid., 171–172.
28. Victor Turner, *The Anthropology of Experience* (Urbana: University of Illinois Press, 1986), 95.
29. Ibid.
30. Jessica Skolnikoff, "Hidden Differences: Life Story Narratives of Adults with Learning Disabilities" (PhD. diss., American University, 1999).
31. Breton and Villegas, 47.
32. Ibid., 73.
33. Ibid., 58.
34. Alan Klein, "Coming of Age in North America," in *Inside Sports*, ed. Jay J. Coakley and Peter Donnelly (New York: Routledge, 1999), 99.
35. Jeffrey Snowbarger, "The Enigma of Pedro Martinez: Understanding the Man, Fiction and Reality with the Help of Gabriel Garcia Marquez," 2006 Cooperstown Baseball Symposium, Cooperstown, New York, May 7–9, 2006.
36. Breton and Villegas, 37.
37. Geoffrey C. Ward and Ken Burns, *Baseball: An Illustrated History* (New York: Alfred A. Knopf, 1994), 231; and David Chidester, *Authentic Fakes: Religion and American Popular Culture* (Berkeley: University of California Press, 2005), 36.
38. Guevara and Fidler, 11.

CHAPTER 13

Recognizing — Not Just Rooting for — the Home Team: Nationalism and the Taiwanese Name Dispute at the 2006 World Baseball Classic

Glen M.E. Duerr

Taiwan, an island in the South China Sea, has sought international recognition for decades. Yet, due to the setup of the United Nations, Taiwan has never been able to gain de jure independence to sit alongside the rest of the world community. Taiwan has never displayed a violent form of nationalism, but the territory has actively sought independence for many years. One way in which Taiwan has attempted to garner greater international recognition is through participation in global sporting events such as the Olympics, soccer's World Cup, and others. The Taiwanese, however, have a real passion for baseball that, in many ways, is a real part of Taiwanese identity. This chapter, therefore, examines the importance of this national assertion through baseball using the specific case of the 2006 World Baseball Classic. The findings in this chapter assert that while participation in the Classic may not produce de jure global recognition, it does keep Taiwan on the international radar and does allow them to advance their cause globally even as China grows in political clout and may begin to assert its "One China policy."[1]

The declaration of independence by Kosovo in February 2008 did much to divide world opinion. Many states recognized the independence of Kosovo; but a number, most notably Russia and China, also rejected the idea. This, in many ways, leaves Kosovo in a diplomatic no-man's land whereby some states have set up the necessary diplomatic functions of recognition but others and, most importantly, the United Nations (UN), have not.

To bring some clarity to this situation, Kosovo must be classified in some way. As the literature states, regions like Kosovo have *de facto* independence rather then *de jure* international recognition. This means that while Kosovo may control the territory and govern it with full autonomy, it is still considered to be part of Serbia in the legal eyes of the international community. The delineation between *de facto* and *de jure* independence means that territories with *de facto* independence are different from any other UN members who, by international recognition, have *de jure* independence replete with full legal recognition. Kosovo, to the surprise of some, is not alone in this situation. Indeed, there are many *de facto* independent regions throughout the world that have almost full autonomy. One region of note is Taiwan to whom *de facto* independence was granted in 1949 when Chiang Kai-shek fled from mainland China and set-up a state that would not bow to communist rule. Taiwan is important because it is, perhaps, the best known case of a *de facto* independent territory. What happens to it may well serve as a precedent for others.

Since 1949, when Taiwan claims that the Republic of China ceased to exercise control of the island, the Taiwanese have sought to gain full international recognition of their independence on the world stage. During the Cold War and in an attempt to achieve international recognition, Taiwan allied itself with the United States insuring that China would face the threat of American military action if it came across the Taiwan Strait. Détente, in the early 1970s, however, dramatically thawed relations between China and the United States with Richard Nixon and Henry Kissinger taking the lead to divide the Sino-Soviet relationship that, while tenuous and self-serving, did unite the largest Communist entities. Later, in another attempt to show moderation to the world, the Taiwanese became fully democratic in 1996 after portraying a modicum of democratic ability in spite of rampant electoral fraud and corruption.[2] It seems as if the Taiwanese have done much to secure the backing of the United States and the international community but this has not achieved their ultimate goal of international recognition. With an ascendant Chinese economic and military power, this goal is even more far-fetched.

The aim of this chapter, therefore, is to investigate how the Taiwanese have utilized sport, specifically baseball, in their quest to gain independence and, at a minimum, retain their *de facto* independence from Chinese rule. The first step is to analyze the literature on nationalism and how and why the Taiwanese have chosen to assert claims of statehood outside of China. Secondly, the link between nationalism and sport should be solidified to see how the Taiwanese have utilized baseball specifically in their attempts to gain international recognition as a separate and independent state. This then leads into a discussion of Taiwanese nationalism through the sport of baseball. Finally, the role of tournaments like the 2006 World Baseball Classic (WBC) will be discussed to illuminate the case of Taiwanese independence claims through sport.

Nationalism

Nationalism has numerous outputs. It can be soft, as seen in patriotic fervor around the world on national holidays or flag waving at sporting events. Nationalism, however, also has harder dimensions; "Deutschland über alles" is probably the most extreme form of this but infers that harder nationalism often takes on violent tones against the other. To go one step further, Walker Connor chooses to fully delineate between nationalism and patriotism arguing that nationalism belongs to one's ethnic group and, in large measure, is more heartfelt than the softer patriotism.[3] For the purposes of this chapter, I shall use Connor's differentiation of nationalism and patriotism so when Taiwan is discussed with regards to nationalism, it is done so with definitional purpose.

Nationalism can, especially in the case of Taiwan, be expanded to territory. Nationalism does not require violence, but a significant level of passion towards one's territory is paramount such that the desire to assert political goals on behalf of one's ethnic group or territory (sometimes both) is aggressively promoted.

Moreover, nationalism is an integral part of creating national unity in the modern era. A smorgasbord of works have offered intriguing and thought-provoking reasons as to how national unity occurs; including both primordial and constructivist explanations. Anthony D. Smith argues that an *ethnie* must be present; that is, the historical existence of an ethnic group on the territory in order to assert goals of independence.[4] Benedict Anderson argues that language is a pivotal factor in creating national identity which occurred through the rise of print-capitalism.[5] Ernest Gellner asserts the notion that industrialization is the most important factor in creating a cohesive national identity.[6] Finally, John Breuilly argues that the ability to wield power is most important in asserting goals of national identity.[7] The problem, however, with each of these explanations is that while they explain vast amounts of situations, they do not adequately describe the case of Taiwan. Difficult examples like the case of Taiwan cut to the heart of this. For example, no different ethnie is present in Taiwan, language has very strong similarities to that on mainland China, industrialization has not improved the political situation of the Taiwanese, and power cannot fully explain why Taiwan may have or may have not attained independence at some point over the last half century.

In a case like Taiwan, then, the definition of nationalism should be broadened to include a number of factors such as: ethnicity, religion, language, territory, a sense of shared history, and social and cultural factors. Given Taiwan's ethnic, religious, and linguistic similarities with China, upwards of 98 percent of Taiwan is Han Chinese, their nationalist assertions are based more on territory and ideology than more common notions of ethnicity, religion, and language. Nationalism in Taiwan is also a broad based definition because cultural aspects like sport play such an integral role in national identity. Since sport is such an integral part of Taiwanese identity, it is worthwhile to examine the specific literature on nationalism and sport.

Nationalism and Sport

The link between nationalism and sport has seen a dramatic increase in the literature in recent years, and this section seeks to examine this new literature. It has become apparent that sport is a major factor in promoting a sense of identity in this increasingly globalized world and is part of a package that increases the shared identity for a given state. Some scholars are discussing the broader role of sport and nationalism as this section will show, but rarely do they discuss obtaining international recognition for a territory. An exception to this is the work of Allen Sack and Zeljan Suster who investigate the role of soccer in Croatia's recognition in 1992.[8] The link, therefore, between sport and increasing identity in a *de facto* independent territory is plausible. Sport can be used as a platform for political change given existing grievances which may include economic, social, ethnic, and religious differences.

Jeremy MacClancy describes sport as a vehicle of identity that provides people with a sense of difference and a way of classifying themselves or others into a group.[9] Sports like soccer and baseball are some of the most notable examples of this since this vehicle of identity can be multi-generational and is able to rally the most people towards a cause. Put simply, a parent may pass down his/her love for a sport to a child along with other examples of identity. MacClancy is correct in his discussion of sport as a vehicle because it can be co-opted for any given movement. The WBC, for example, in itself is a classification of one person into a national grouping as opposed to other national groupings. This may be part of an identity passed from one generation to the next. While competition amongst different countries brings people together, it also highlights differences and can often have a politically charged atmosphere.

Gerry Finn and Richard Giulianotti discuss the role of sport and globalization.[10] While many people assume that globalization leads to increased homogeneity, the authors argue that this is not entirely correct. They discuss the "Creolization" of sport because it is adapted to suit the local circumstance.[11] It also remains pivotal for national identity to use sport as a measure for distinction against other peoples.[12] This discussion is certainly apt given that globalization has not led to a widespread erosion of culture. Certainly parts of the world play baseball, and it is done so with different styles and tactics leading to increased claims of differences between disparate groups. It may, for example, distinguish Taiwanese baseball from Chinese or other Asian styles of baseball, showcasing an increased sense of the "Taiwanese way" vis-à-vis others.

Alan Bairner also discusses the role of globalization in an overview of sport and nationalism.[13] The combination of sport and nationalism are two of the most emotive issues in the world. Both involve intense devotion to a cause. Despite the increase in globalization, Bairner argues that the forces of nationalism have not been decreased as of yet and will continue in the foreseeable future through the vehicle of sport.[14] Bairner is correct in this respect given that mass migration has been most visible through sports. Consider, for example, the virtual United Nations of any lineup in Major League Baseball (MLB). Globalization and the familiarity with others, however, has not dampened the overt nationalism displayed through sport and nor is it likely to in the future. More often than not, a player is described initially based on his national origin.

Eric Hobsbawm argues that the link between sport and politics is easy because "even the least political or public individuals can identify with the nation."[15] Moreover, virtually every man (and an increasing number of women) wants or wanted to be good at the sport which they now watch. This is a prime venue for political socialization and a great venue with which to build a belief in a *de facto* independent territory or the state. Surrounded by thousands of supporters, individuals can identify themselves with primary indicators of the nation and project a collective voice through sport. This is where the link between baseball and nationalism is most easily found. It is not farfetched, therefore, to establish links between sport and demands for *de jure* independence. After all, if a *de facto* independent territory has a "national team," then it is projecting an identity onto the world through sport. The mere existence of the team suggests support from people who desire independence. While the sport itself is a motivating factor, the symbolism surrounding the game is pivotal in the desire for independence.

Following the link between nationalism and sport and the desire for international recognition, the retentive claims of the existing state (in this case China) must also be examined in order to validate the possibility for statehood on the part of the *de facto* independent territory. China, however, is a unique case because of its economic and military strength. It asserts the right for future control over Taiwan in its "One China policy" which means that the emphasis for gaining *de jure* international recognition is placed solely on the Taiwanese. Obtaining *de jure* independence may be virtually impossible given China's position in the United Nations Security Council with full veto privileges, but Taiwan still has to do something unless it merely capitulates to Chinese demands. The best option, then, may be to retain the status quo which, while it may sound easy, still requires an assertion of nationalism especially through cultural modes like baseball. Asserting nationalism through baseball may also keep Taiwan on the international radar because of its participation in various competitions which may help to stave off the realization of the "One China policy."

A (Brief) Examination of Taiwanese Nationalism through Baseball

Nationalism in Taiwan, like many other examples, has arisen through fear of the other (in this case China). With China asserting claims over the territory, Taiwanese nationalism has asserted itself in numerous ways so as to differentiate it from China. A major part of Taiwanese culture is through the sport of baseball and, unlike the Chinese, Taiwan can claim a significant history of the game and deep rooted cultural aspects associated with the sport.

In much the same way as the United States feared a communist takeover during the Cold War[16] which might have harmed baseball and the American way of life, similar fears have persisted in Taiwan. Now imagine that the United States was dwarfed by the Soviet Union and was threatened consistently. The Taiwanese, after all, are in this situation in which they fear limitations on their identity. This identity, as argued earlier, is cultural and a significant part of their culture is baseball, yet another mechanism through which Americans can relate to their situation.

Baseball, in many ways, serves as a distinctive Taiwanese cultural expression that differentiates it from mainland China.[17] Taiwan, in many senses, is a baseball-loving territory given the historical influence of American and Japanese culture.[18] The game remains a major facet of life on the island and has significantly helped to develop Taiwanese identity. Rather than appealing to ideology as is the case in China, the Taiwanese appeal to identity; the Taiwanese ruling class in fact has implemented legislation by appealing to the sport of baseball.[19]

Little League baseball is, perhaps, a significant part of Taiwanese culture[20] as the game has grown throughout the territory. This was done despite being missed by Albert Spalding's World Baseball Tour in 1888-89.[21] Nonetheless, through the Japanese and the Americans, baseball grew and flourished on the island. It, in time, became revered and popularized through competition and success against international teams. As their success increased, however, it was not without its share of political concerns.

Even in international baseball, Taiwan has been forced to compete under the name of Chinese Taipei in order to satisfy the Chinese government and their "One China Policy." This shows that despite Taiwanese assertions of independence through sport, they are still limited by political factors. Nonetheless, participation in events, such as the WBC, as an entity independent of China shows that they have retained at least a modicum of international representation through sport.

It was not always easy, however, as Taiwan had difficulty even entering the Baseball Federation of Asia in 1977 after refusing to give up the name "China."[22] Another important factor in Taiwan's ability to even participate against the Chinese was the decision in 1987 to lift the ban on sporting exchanges between China and Taiwan.[23] Fortunately, Taiwan has incrementally participated more and more in international competition, allowing them to assert claims of nationalism on the world stage. Baseball highlights just how precarious their political situation has been.

Taiwan, in many ways, has a peculiar relationship with the international community. As Yu-ming Shaw asserts, Taiwan was a founding member of the United Nations; yet since 1971 has not been a member state of the organization. Furthermore, it retains relationships with over 140 states, mainly through unofficial linkages.[24] This is where nationalism through baseball may be particularly important because, even if a state is unwilling to overtly recognize Taiwan, it can participate in cultural exchanges with the territory. Baseball also serves to assert an understanding of Taiwan which allows people from all over the world to know of and think about Taiwan and their political situation.

For political reasons alone, there is much cause for celebration when Taiwan was allowed to participate in the WBC. It was probably never questioned as to whether they would actually be allowed to play given their reputation and prowess as a baseball power. Yet, in other sports, participation is limited based on political concerns.

Taiwan at the World Baseball Classic

The 2006 WBC started as an attempt to increase the international profile of baseball and to start a competition that could be thought of as a legitimate global tournament like soccer, basketball, cricket, and rugby each have. Despite the dire predictions by some in the media that the WBC would flop, the tournament was an overwhelming success and showcased baseball on the international stage.

Moreover, and more importantly to this chapter, the 2006 WBC provided a forum through which Taiwan could compete on the international stage against other teams from across the world. Of the sixteen teams in the competition, only one other team, Puerto Rico, was not a recognized member of the international community. This meant that the WBC allowed Taiwan and Puerto Rico to compete and be recognized in an event that provided them equality with other *de jure* states like the United States, Japan, and all the others. The WBC, like other events such as baseball in the Olympics, provided the territory with another opportunity through sport to showcase itself.

The inaugural WBC in 2006 featured sixteen teams from across the world but was mainly limited to the Americas and East Asia.[25] It is unique amongst the major world competitions in sport because the others have only had one host or two co-hosts from a specific region. In contrast, the WBC in 2006 was played in the United States, Puerto Rico, and Japan which meant that the tournament was hosted in two very different parts of the world.[26]

It is, therefore, noteworthy that the WBC unlike other major international sporting competitions is played in multiple countries. Soccer's World Cup has been co-hosted, as in 2002 with South Korea and Japan, but never has it been played in varied parts of the world. The WBC was interesting in a sense because each pool was played in a more localized geographic area before the final stages were held in the United States. Japan hosted one group, Puerto Rico another, with the other two being played in the United States. This delineation had much to do with travel concerns and political issues.

In the case of Taiwan, however, travel was the major issue and being closer to Japan made sense. It did, nonetheless, open up a political issue. Taiwan, playing in Japan in the Asian section, competed against China, an event that gave them some sense of political achievement to be thought of differently from China. Put simply, if the "One China policy" infers Chinese jurisdiction over Taiwan, then competing against them in a global tournament infers at least a tacit level of international recognition. The game itself did not attract a massive audience but gave Taiwan an overwhelming victory over the Chinese. Unfortunately, for Taiwan it was the only victory they would achieve in the tournament, and subsequently they failed to qualify for the next phase of the tournament.

Taiwan did not advance past the first round but, perhaps more importantly, did get to play against China. This served, in many respects, a large political purpose of participating in the WBC. It was an extremely important game for political reasons in Taiwan. It is, however, important to recap what happened in the group phase before discussing the political contentions of a Taiwan versus China game at the WBC.

In their first game, Taiwan lost narrowly to Korea 2–0.[27] This game, in many ways, was decisive for Taiwan as the Japanese were largely expected to win the group. While they actually failed to do this by coming in second to Korea, they did end up exacting revenge on the Koreans by beating them in the semi-final and went on to win the inaugural WBC. In their second game, Taiwan was soundly defeated by the Japanese 14–3 in a game that was called early after seven innings on the mercy-rule. With their fate decided, Taiwan played China in their final game and won convincingly by a score of 12–3. All games featuring Japan were well attended, leaving only small crowds for the other games in Pool A. With smaller attendances at the other games, political dissent was kept to a minimum, and Pool A was decided before Taiwan and China even got to play. The political contention between the two, however, had significant implications for the WBC.

Prior to the start of the tournament, two significant political issues came to light.[28] The first issue, relating to Cuba, threatened to derail the tournament if the Cubans were not allowed to play in the United States. The American government, however, relented, and Cuba was allowed to participate.[29] The second major political issue had to do with Taiwan. Originally, Taiwan was allowed to use the name Taiwan for the competition and to raise its own flag and play its own anthem. MLB, however, was challenged by China not to allow this, and MLB relented, asserting that Taiwan could only compete under the name Chinese Taipei. Moreover, the Taiwanese were not allowed to play under their own flag and had to use the Chinese Taipei Olympic flag instead. This has significant political ramifications and continues to show China's ambitions over Taiwan. Their decision to utilize sport to achieve this end frustrated Taiwan supporters across the world including U.S. lawmaker Tom Tancredo.

Tancredo, in a letter to MLB commissioner Bud Selig, implored the commissioner not to effectively serve as China's "designated hitter" allowing the country to politically dominate Taiwan at the WBC.[30] Tancredo blasted China's ambition, arguing that for over twenty years China had held Taiwan down and making the parallel to Puerto Rico that the United States does not stop the territory from using its own name, flag, or anthem in the competition. Tancredo went on to say that China "restricts the freedom and insults the dignity of the 23 million people in Taiwan" through the restriction of using the name Taiwan during the tournament. Selig, even in the face of Tancredo's comments, surrendered to China's demands. To be fair to the commissioner, hosting the inaugural WBC was supposed to be more about promoting the sport of baseball rather than delving into major global political issues. Nonetheless, sport often becomes embroiled in political issues, and the future of the WBC will likely feature other political concerns.

The next WBC will be held in 2009 and then will proceed to rotate every four years rather than three (for example, in 2013, 2017 and so on). The decision to hold the next tournament in three years rather than four was to offset it from competing with soccer's World Cup to be played in South Africa in 2010. In this way, baseball may be able to generate greater excitement. Taiwan, as a result, will again be able to put forth a team to play in the tournament and will continue to project a global identity on the world stage that is recognizable even if their political status is not.

It will be extremely important for Taiwan to keep playing in the WBC and other international sporting events because this act, in the short term, protects their *de facto* independent status even if it does nothing to assure *de jure* sovereign recognition. Fortunately, Taiwan will remain in the WBC for 2009, once again playing their games in Tokyo. The 2009 hosts are even broader than in 2006, making the tournament truly global in that respect with hosts coming from Canada, Mexico, Puerto Rico and Japan; although, the semifinals and final will again be played in the United States.[31]

Furthermore, Taiwan will once again play China in 2009 and, in many respects, every time China plays against Taiwan there is a tacit level of recognition on their part. After all, how can you compete against a team you do not, on some level, recognize? Furthermore, if the game means something, it can be expected that the game will generate more political protests.

Beyond 2009, MLB may expand the WBC to include twenty-four countries and territories.[32] In this way, Taiwan will remain part of the WBC if it continues to play. It will be integral for Taiwan to retain the status quo in the face of the "One China policy" and to retain their *de facto* independence. Moreover, it will be important for non–UN members like Puerto Rico and Taiwan to continue to compete in these events lest they be outlawed if MLB capitulates to only allowing internationally recognized entities from competing as China would like as it seeks to advance its claims over Taiwan.

Discussion

Regions of the world with *de facto* independence face many difficulties when it comes to global recognition. As the case of Taiwan evidences, the region has to resort to numerous measures to gain international recognition, even if it may never receive the full benefits of widespread recognition from the UN.

The WBC, in a small way, upholds the current position of Taiwan even if the team plays under the moniker of Chinese Taipei. This tacit sporting recognition of the island prevents China from asserting control of the territory, at least in the short term. However, does not alter the limbo type status of Taiwan. While gaining full international recognition replete with UN membership may be extremely difficult for Taiwan, it is integral for them to retain their autonomy. Participating in the WBC allows them to do this because they are tacitly recognized by the rest of the world at the WBC.

The United States, while backing Taiwan, is unlikely to provide anything more than threats of sanctions against China which falls short of international recognition.[33] As China continues to increase its economic, military, and, eventually, political clout, Taiwan will need to do whatever it can to circumvent the "One China policy."

Baseball, as an avenue of international recognition, continues to be used by *de facto* independent territories like Taiwan whom the international community has failed for not correcting their status limbo. Other regions like Kosovo can learn valuable lessons from the case of Taiwan at the 2006 WBC. While they were not allowed to use their own name, fly their own flag, or play their own anthem, their presence did much to secure international recognition. FIFA, the world governing body of soccer, has already decided to only let internationally recognized members of the UN participate with the exception of the British "Home Nations" and colonies that have the permission of their national state (For example, Guadeloupe is allowed to compete internationally with the permission of France.).[34] The WBC, in contrast, does allow non-recognized territories like Taiwan to participate so it is important for the territory to take advantage of this and to stay on the international radar by continuing to play and assert itself through the WBC.

Notes

1. The author would like to thank John Sutcliffe and Andrew Richter for their discussions of nationalism and sport as drawn from earlier work on soccer.

2. Shelly Rigger, "Machine Politics in protracted transition in Taiwan," *Democratization*, 7 (2000): 135–152.

3. Walker Connor, "When is a Nation?" *Ethnic and Racial Studies*, 13 (1990): 92–103.

4. Anthony D. Smith, *National Identity* (Reno: University of Nevada Press, 1991).

5. Benedict Anderson, *Imagined Communities: Reflections of Origins and Spread of Nationalism* (New York: Verso, 1983).

6. Ernest Gellner, *Nations and Nationalism* (Ithaca: Cornell University Press, 1983).

7. John Breuilly, *Nationalism and the State* (New York: St. Martin's Press, 1982).

8. Allen Sack and Zeljan Suster, "Soccer and Croatian Nationalism: A Prelude to War," *Journal of Sport and Social Issues*, 24 (2000): 305–320.

9. Jeremy MacClancy, *Sport, Identity and Ethnicity* (Herndon, VA: Berg, 1996), 2.

10. Gerry Finn and Richard Giulianotti, *Football Culture: Local Contests, Global Visions* (Portland, OR: Frank Cass, 2000).

11. *Ibid.*, 256.

12. *Ibid.*, 258.

13. Alan Bairner, *Sport, Nationalism and Globalization: European and North American Perspectives* (Albany: State University of New York, 2001).

14. *Ibid.*, xi.

15. Eric Hobsbawm, *Nations and Nationalism since 1780: Programme, Myth, Reality* (Cambridge: Cambridge University Press, 1992), 143.

16. Ron Briley, *Class at Bat, Gender on Deck and Race in the Hole: A Line-up of Essays on*

Twentieth Century Culture and America's Game (Jefferson, NC: McFarland, 2003), 55–56.

17. Andrew Morris, "Baseball, History, the Local and Global in Taiwan," in *The Minor Arts of Daily Life: Popular Culture in Taiwan*, ed. David Jordan, Andrew Morris, and Marc L. Moskowitz (Honolulu: University of Hawaii Press, 2004), 176.

18. *Ibid.*, 177.

19. Junwei Yu and Dan Gordon, "Nationalism and National Identity in Taiwanese Baseball," *Nine* 14 (2006): 27.

20. J. T. Sundeen, "A 'Kid's Game'? Little League Baseball and National Identity in Taiwan," *Journal of Sport and Social Issues*, 25 (2001): 251–265.

21. Thomas Zeiler, *Ambassadors in Pinstripes: The Spalding World Baseball Tour and the Birth of the American Empire* (Lanham, MD: Rowman and Littlefield, 2006).

22. Junwei Yu, *Playing in Isolation: A History of Baseball in Taiwan* (Lincoln: University of Nebraska Press, 2007), 74.

23. Junwei Yu and James Mangan, "Dancing Around the Elephant: The Beijing Olympics—Taiwanese Reflections and Reactions," *International Journal of the History of Sport*, 25 (2008): 826–850.

24. Yu-Ming Shaw, "The Future of Taiwan: The View from Taipei," *Foreign Affairs*, 63 (Summer 1985).

25. Barry Bloom, February 19, 2008, "World Baseball Classic Field Selected: Expansion Weighed for '13 as MLB Boasts International Growth," http://mlb.mlb.com/news/article. jsp?ymd=20080219&content_id=2379216& vkey=news_mlb&fext=.jsp&c_id=mlb (accessed 15 June 2008).

26. *Ibid.*

27. All WBC scores come from the official site of MLB.

28. There were other political issues that arose *during* the tournament such as the protest of Hugo Chavez, the current President of Venezuela.

29. William Kelly, "Is Baseball a Global Sport? America's 'National Pastime' as Global Field and International Sport," *Global Networks*, 7 (2007), 189.

30. "Tancredo: MLB is not China's Designated Hitter" can be found at http://tancredo. house.gov/PRArticle.aspx?NewsID=1136.

31. Barry Bloom, March 23, 2008, "Venues set for World Baseball Classic: Japan, Mexico, Canada and Puerto Rico to Host first round in '09," http://mlb.mlb.com/news/article.jsp? ymd=20080323&content_id=2452760&vkey= news_mlb&fext=.jsp&c_id=mlb (accessed 15 June 2008).

32. *Ibid.*

33. A. Cooper Drury and Yitan Li, "U.S. Economic Sanction Threats against China: Failing to Leverage Better Human Rights," *Foreign Policy Analysis*, 2 (2006): 307–324.

34. Taiwan is a FIFA member but plays under the Chinese Taipei name, and this is legitimated as both Macau and Hong Kong are allowed to participate separately from China also.

CHAPTER 14

Bud Selig's Use of "Smart Power"
Robert F. Lewis

Joseph S. Nye, Jr., Dean of the Kennedy School of Government at Harvard University, has developed a geopolitical "smart power" model, used in this essay to characterize the nine Major League Baseball (MLB) commissioners. Particular focus is on Judge Kenesaw Mountain Landis, the first, and Allan H. "Bud" Selig, the current one. While intended to assess America's use of power in global politics, Nye's model is generally applicable in any leadership evaluation.

Nye first describes "power" as "the ability to influence the behavior of others to get the outcomes one wants."[1] Since the commissioner era began in 1921, that ability has varied, as MLB evolved from pre-union/free agency to actively contested and negotiated times. As a result of the owners overreacting to the Black Sox scandal and the 1922 Supreme Court decision affirming MLB's antitrust exemption, Landis secured virtually unchecked power over the game during his twenty-three-year tenure. Selig, however, not only must contend with government and the owners, but also with arguably the most powerful labor union in the country as well as the media who, unlike earlier, consider themselves primarily critics rather than promoters of the game. For each commissioner, therefore, both form and use of power necessarily differed.

In his model, Nye simply divides power into two contrasting subcategories: hard and soft. For Nye, "hard power" is typically military or economic in the form of threats ("sticks") or inducements ("carrots"). He observes that unilateral nations, such as the United States, tend to consider themselves exceptional and to rely primarily upon hard power to accomplish their national interests. Nye contends that the U.S. has recently practiced a foreign policy that "combines unilateralism, arrogance, and parochialism."[2] Outside

Nye's geopolitical context, hard power tends to be economic, but its dominant use also correlates more with organizations self-defined as unilateral and exceptional. MLB has historically been such an organization, supported by its antitrust exemption and mythology. While commissioners' hard power generally has economic elements, it can also reflect an autocratic adherence to the mystique of baseball, without material economic implications, as Landis often displayed in ruling "in the best interests of the game," as authorized in the 1921 MLB constitution.[3]

"Soft power," Nye observes, "is the ability to get what you want through attraction rather than coercion or payments. It builds upon the appreciation for a country's culture, political ideals, and policies" and co-opts others.[4] Therefore, nations which rely primarily upon soft power tend to be multilateral and collaborative in their approach to issues. In MLB "country," supported by its own culture, ideals, and policies, a commissioner has multilateral options to persuade fans, media, and owners as well as players and their union by improving the attraction of the game. Co-optive rather than coercive marketing has become a significant element of soft power in MLB. Credibility, Nye observes, is a crucial resource and important source of soft power.[5] It has therefore been important that MLB maintain credibility while addressing such challenging issues as gambling and steroids.

To Nye, "smart power" is ultimately neither exclusively hard nor soft. It is both, varying in proportion according to the situation. Over the years, commissioners have variously tried to balance their authoritarian hard economic power of a protected institution with the soft power of a business leader preserving and marketing the mythological attraction of the game. Commissioners have succeeded most when they have balanced their hard and soft power capabilities. Nye's smart power geopolitical critique of former MLB owner George W. Bush is based on the observation that, as U.S. President, he has relied too much on unilaterally based hard power in a global arena which benefits from more multilateral, collaborative soft power practices. The same criticism could apply historically to MLB commissioners. As MLB continues to globalize, effective use of smart power becomes more important in relations with other nations' baseball organizations, players, and fans as well as at home.

MLB is a hybrid, quasi-governmental organization, possessing an antitrust exemption that has been partially diluted by legislation (Curt Flood Act of 1998) and ever encroaching entertainment market competition. While it lacks the degree of absolute power possessed by a government, MLB's antitrust feature differentiates it from a typical free market participant and enables it to exercise more hard power clout. Former commissioner Bowie Kuhn titled his 1987 autobiography *Hard Ball* to describe his power-struggling tenure, while James Quirk and Rodney Fort used the same title in 1999 to criticize abuse of power in professional sports. In this paper, I view (and judge) MLB through its nine commissioners, with particular emphasis on Landis and Selig, in relation to the smart power model. While the observations and conclusions regarding MLB may have indirect applicability to U.S. President Bush, a former owner of the Texas Rangers, that is not the purpose of the paper.

The issue of power was central to the creation of the commissioner position and selection of its first occupant, Landis, in November 1921. The office's use of power by the nine commissioners has varied and ultimately evolved as a function of changing environments and attitudes of the incumbents and their relationships primarily with MLB owners and secondarily with other constituents. As a result, so have MLB's fortunes and relative position in the burgeoning entertainment industry. MLB has attempted to balance continuing strong emphasis on its rural mythology and embedded fundamental values with diminishing cartel-like leverage over its internal and external constituents. Crucial to that balance has been the attitude and activities of its commissioners, observed herein within the context of the smart power model.

Recognizing that the optimal proportion of hard and soft power execution should vary by situation and that smart power generally balances soft and hard power, I suggest the following relative positioning of the commissioners along a soft-to-hard power axis: Eckert, Frick, Chandler, Ueberroth, Selig, Vincent, Giamatti, Landis, Kuhn. Stated another way, Eckert, Frick, and Chandler tended to rely too much on soft power; Kuhn, Landis, and Giamatti, too much on hard; and, Ueberroth, Selig, and Vincent, the most on a balanced blend.

While balance is vital, MLB's circumstantial "ideal" has generally shifted somewhat from the harder to the softer over its history. A significant cause of that shift was the post–Landis change from a relatively independent commissioner to one primarily answerable to the owners. In a new National Agreement, adopted two months after Landis's death, the owners made three changes to reduce commissioner power:

1. Stipulated that the commissioner could not declare an action consistent with baseball rules and regulations to be detrimental to the best interests of the game. Landis had been arbitrary in his use of the "best interests" clause.
2. Required a three-quarters rather than a simple majority to (re)elect a commissioner.
3. Gave the owners the right to take the commissioner to court if they disagreed with his judgment.[6]

Therefore, it became more important that subsequent commissioners utilize soft power tactics to temper the owner hard power influence and to satisfy multiple constituencies whose relative power has increased. This argument resembles Nye's assertion that America, as world leader, needs to be more collaborative, i.e., softer, in dealing in a dynamic global environment.

Judge Kenesaw Mountain Landis (1921–1944)

Landis's background presaged his performance as commissioner. A Midwestern progressive Republican lawyer, Landis benefited from family political connections to secure Washington and Federal bench appointments. His experience, however, caused him to have no respect for titles or authority.[7] As judge of the Northern District of Illinois, he presided over three cases that helped to define his ongoing behavior as commissioner. Perhaps most famous was his imposition on Standard Oil of a $29.24 million judgment, which, despite being later overturned, demonstrated his disregard for corporate power.[8] Another, reflecting his penchant for publicity, was the trial of 113 members of the Industrial Workers of the World, the largest number ever tried in a U.S. criminal case.[9] Finally, his "strategic inaction" in delaying a decision on the Federal League lawsuit against organized baseball reflected his unequivocal love of the game and enabled the parties to reach a settlement that preserved MLB.[10] Andrew Zimbalist observes that Landis's "chief characteristic on the bench was caprice, blended with strong antipathy to any view to the left of Teddy Roosevelt, an abiding emotionalism, a flair for the media and the dramatic, and a foul tongue."[11]

Landis initially defined the role of the commissioner as he shifted from the role of Federal judge. He took advantage of owner panic resulting from the 1919 "Black Sox" gambling scandal and internal conflict swirling around Byron Bancroft "Ban" Johnson, head of the American League (AL) and commissioner "wannabe." Using that situational hard power leverage, Landis essentially dictated the terms of his contract and secured "a grant of unprecedented power over the game."[12] His early actions, a legally correct ruling against the aggressive Branch Rickey on a player (Phil Todt) contract[13] and summary banishment from baseball of eight Black Sox players, despite their court acquittal, solidified his position. As former Pennsylvania governor Dick Thornburgh notes in his foreword to David Pietrusza's biography of Landis, the decisive Black Sox action "saved baseball from joining boxing as a perpetually discredited enterprise."[14] Landis had "an inflexible hatred of gambling," reflected in decisions he had made from the bench as well in his banning another fourteen players by 1927.[15] Landis's genuine love of and respect for the game partially helped to mitigate his autocratic, self-promoting tendencies.

Larry Moffi temperately describes Landis the commissioner as a "czar with a conscience."[16] As an outspoken fan of baseball and its players, Landis became an icon who controlled MLB owners effectively. He was generally "benevolent toward players and surly toward owners,"[17] reflecting his penchant for public approval. Historian Benjamin Rader notes, however, that "Landis treated the questionable actions of the owners far more gingerly than he did those of the players."[18] He was forthright in taking on Babe Ruth, the most popular player in MLB history, specifically suspending him for barnstorming and, implicitly, for his ostentatious and immoral behavior. But, he overruled his adversary, Ban Johnson, who wanted to ban future Hall of Famers Ty Cobb and Tris Speaker for gambling activities that preceded Landis's commissionership. Landis used that decision process to force Johnson's retirement.

Unfortunately, Landis displayed too much of his leadership in the reactive role of judge. "Do it and I'll rule on it." And, sometimes, as he had done from the bench in the Federal League case, he chose to avoid ruling. Without proactive leadership from Landis, MLB "remained substantially static during the Judge's tenure." After twenty-three years, it had the same sixteen teams in the same cities; there were no consequential rule modifications; there were minimal changes in the ballparks; and, the sport remained segregated.[19]

Zimbalist concludes that Landis nevertheless provided "the illusion of a supreme being" who faithfully protected the game, but this illusion, coupled with essentially no competition in either product or labor markets, masked a vulnerability that later fell prey to competition and unionism.[20] Landis generally served well as a committed, independent administrative judge of the game, but poorly as a market-oriented business leader. His fundamental hard power approach was only partially mollified, however, by his demonstrated soft power reverence for the game.

Albert B. "Happy" Chandler (1945–1951)

Armed with the above-mentioned National Agreement changes, the owners sought a different type of commissioner as successor and hired former Kentucky Senator Albert B. "Happy" Chandler. Incorrectly assuming him to be merely an affable caretaker, the owners got someone who presided over twice as much change in his five-year tenure than Landis did in his twenty-three years. "Everyone—players, owners, fans—did better under Chandler than under Landis."[21]

Baseball remembers Chandler most for authorizing the signing of Jackie

Robinson and breaking MLB's tacit but long-enforced color barrier. Owners incorrectly assumed that this Southern politician would maintain the white game. Chandler labeled some owners "pocketbook racists," in noting that they feared integration would lower attendance from a predominantly white fan base.[22] Later commissioner Peter Ueberroth commended Chandler for his "unbridled enthusiasm when he felt something was right," noting he "wasn't afraid to make the difficult decisions."[23] Chandler fully supported Branch Rickey in the signing and Robinson in his playing. Conversely, Chandler imposed a controversial, one-year, gambling-related suspension on Dodger manager Leo Durocher a few days before Robinson's debut and incurred Rickey's and others' wrath, including being booed on Babe Ruth Day at Yankee Stadium a few weeks later.[24] Chandler later claimed that Rickey didn't give him credit for approving and supporting the Robinson signing.[25]

Almost as significant in Chandler's tenure was the Mexican League-Danny Gardella episode. In early 1946, Chandler banned for five years eighteen players, including Gardella, who had jumped to the Mexican League for considerably more money. Led by millionaire industrialist Jorge Pasquel, the Mexican League sought to exploit the post-war turmoil of returning veteran players and to compete with MLB. After three years that included court activity, Chandler reinstated all players who no longer had suits against MLB. Gardella ultimately secured a circuit court judgment that reversed the 1922 Supreme Court antitrust exemption. Before an appeal was heard, MLB and Gardella reached a settlement of $60,000 (of which he netted $29,000) that preserved MLB's monopoly status by avoiding a higher court ruling.[26]

The Mexican League competition and a near-strike by Pittsburgh players spurred the 1946 founding of the American Baseball Guild, a fledgling union headed by labor lawyer Robert Murphy. Although the guild floundered soon thereafter, Chandler, with executive Larry McPhail and player Marty Marion, negotiated an agreement that provided a package of player benefits, including the first pension plan. Feeling too much was conceded, the owners refused to renew his contract. Moffi concludes, "The greatest mistake ownership ever made was voting Happy Chandler out of office."[27] The soft power negotiating skills that had served him well in the Senate also did so in MLB, but the owner constituency wanted hard power absolute victory, not mutually beneficial soft power compromise. So, they chose an insider they felt they could control more effectively. Chandler acknowledged that his poor relations with owners and writers led to the selection of Ford Frick, a former sports writer and current NL president. Chandler sarcastically observes, "The owners had a vacancy and they decided to continue it."[28]

Ford Frick (1951–1965)

Counting his time as a sports writer and ghost writer for Babe Ruth, Frick spent forty-three years in baseball, but had remarkably little influence on the game. Sports writer Red Smith politely labeled him a "reluctant leader."[29] He served seventeen years as National League (NL) president and another fourteen as commissioner. As NL head, he was supportive of the Robinson signing. In thwarting a racist St. Louis Cardinal strike, he asserted, "I don't care if half the league strikes. Those who do will ... be suspended, and I don't care if it wrecks the NL for five years. This is the United States of America, and one citizen has much right to play as another."[30]

Perhaps responding to increasing owner dominance instead of its call for more aggressive marketing in a May 31, 1951, memorandum from Cubs owner Philip Wrigley, Frick became relatively passive in his commissioner role, often declining to rule on an issue by claiming it was a "league matter."[31] While publicly declaring that preserving the integrity of the game was a principal commissioner function, as Landis had done, Frick did not curtail Yankee owner Del Webb's casino ventures nor Webb and Yankee co-owner Dan Topping's collusive real estate and player trade arrangements with Kansas City Athletics owner Arnold Johnson.[32]

He did oversee unprecedented expansion and relocation of teams, which had remained static for a half century. Eight new cities acquired teams, but he assured that an existing city would retain at least one team. He also helped to negotiate a TV package that overcame the owners' prior criticism of Chandler for selling out for too low a price.[33] Nevertheless, as TV was becoming a major factor in sports promotion, Frick did little to capitalize on its marketing implications. Indicative of his inadequacy in this area was his decision to shift voting for All-Star game participants from the fans to players, managers, and coaches in 1958.[34] As a result of his passivity, baseball lagged behind football in capturing fans, as noted in a poll which indicated that Americans' favorite sport shifted from 34–21 percent baseball to 36–21 percent football from 1961 to 1972.[35]

David Bohmer characterizes Frick as a typical CEO of the era, one who came up through the ranks, shunned publicity, delegated significantly, and worked behind the scenes to accomplish goals pragmatically.[36] He was neither "old" nor "new," as evidenced by his controversial decision to continue parallel recognition of Ruth's hallowed thirty-four-year-old home run record after Roger Maris's sixty-one-homer performance in a longer 1961 season. Rather than any commissioner activity, he viewed his NL activity in establishing the Hall of Fame as his major contribution and was rewarded by election to that institution in 1970, before his more deserving predecessor Chandler.[37] His long tenure as commissioner was also a reward for not rocking the boat, but demonstrated within the Nye model the fallacy of relying too much on soft power. In their next selection, the owners found an even softer, almost non-existent, example of power.

William "Spike" Eckert (1965–1968)

Recommended by Tiger owner John Fetzer allegedly for his business acumen, Lt. Gen. Eckert was the least effective commissioner. He was comptroller of the Air Force when he retired, then an executive for several electronics companies before his commissionership. When critics questioned the selection, an unsubstantiated story circulated that MLB owners had intended to appoint Gen. Eugene Zuckert, a former secretary of the Air Force, but confused the name. One New York columnist dubbed the new commissioner the "unknown soldier."[38]

He lasted less than half of his seven-year term before the owners dismissed him. The Milwaukee Braves moved to Atlanta and the Kansas City A's to Oakland, both violations of the rule imposed by Frick that no single-team city should be vacated, and apparently Eckert played no substantive role in the processes. Neither did he order MLB to recognize the assassinations of Martin Luther King or Robert F. Kennedy, thereby committing a public relations gaffe.[39]

Perhaps the most notable occurrence during his tenure was the 1966 selection of Marvin Miller to head the Major League Baseball Players Association (MLBPA). Future MLB commissioners would exercise relatively little soft power as the union developed a hard power strategy and battled, generally successfully, with MLB over the next quarter century.[40]

Bowie Kuhn (1969–1984)

When Bowie Kuhn became commissioner on February 4, 1969, it meant a return to an insider as well as a compromise in the selection process. He beat out Lee McPhail, general manager of the Yankees; John McHale, Montreal Expos president; and Chub Feeney, San Francisco Giants vice-president. Kuhn, who had served as National League counsel, emulated his hero, Judge Landis, in a first-year confrontation with four team owners who had invested in a development company involved in Las Vegas casinos that reputedly had mob connections. Three of the owners divested their investments and one left baseball.[41] Despite substantial environmental changes, Kuhn continued to use Landis as his role model, without the former's success. Marvin Miller, MLBPA executive director and Kuhn's long-time adversary, observes that Kuhn was "plagued by the ghost of ... Landis."[42] Kuhn's record illustrates the fallacy of overreliance on hard power, much of which was simply fronting for the owners.

After some success in his first year, including peaceful negotiation with Miller to resolve pension funds and vesting issues and the orchestration of a White House-led commemoration of baseball's 100th anniversary, he entered a hard power war with the MLBPA that changed the business of baseball. Curt Flood's 1970 suit culminated in an open confrontation that led to final offer arbitration and removal of the reserve clause that had shielded owners since the professional game had formalized.

His tenure, third longest behind Landis and Selig, was a marathon contest between Kuhn and Miller, with Miller emerging as the clear winner. In calling him "the most effective union organizer since John L. Lewis," author Studs Turkel observes that Miller "brought an end to the age of innocence" by changing baseball.[43] Kuhn describes Miller as "an old-fashioned nineteenth-century trade unionist who hated management generally and management of baseball specifically." But, he acknowledges that he was a "superior communicator," whose "ability to cultivate the press was perhaps his greatest talent."[44] That talent enabled Miller to blend effectively soft power attraction with traditional union hard power tactics.

Miller's opinion of Kuhn did not acknowledge any talent. Observing that Kuhn had "role confusion" because he thought he represented players, Miller sardonically concludes that Kuhn was "the most important contributor to the successes of the Players Association."[45] While the commissioner's charge was to represent all aspects of the game, including players, the emergence of the union had significantly strengthened the pro-owner bias of the office. Miller concludes that Dodger owner, Walter O'Malley, was "baseball's real czar."[46]

An early example of this opposition came in 1972, the first strike in professional sports history, lasting thirteen days (nine in season) and canceling eighty-six regular season games. Miller, who says he didn't expect the strike to occur, claims that the owners lost $5.2 million and the players $600,000 as a result. Noting that the health and retirement issues at stake were relatively small, Miller concludes, "The real issue was power."[47] For the remainder of Kuhn's tenure, power, particularly hard power, was a theme.

Ironically, Kuhn decided not to pursue a hard power opportunity when Andy Messersmith and Dave McNally filed a joint free agency grievance after the 1975 season. While Kuhn could have legally ruled on the action as a complaint, instead of an arbitration grievance, Kuhn declined to do so, rationalizing that denying the players' pursuit of free agency would have provoked a strike.[48] In retrospect, since the arbitrator ruled for the players; thereby paving the way for removal of the reserve clause, Kuhn perhaps squandered an opportunity to preserve this critical hard power resource, which had been historically supported in court cases.

Significant examples of hard power exercises included an owners' lockout during spring training in 1976, perhaps spurred by the judgment which upheld the free agency arbitration decision. Another, which was the most significant of Kuhn's tenure, was the players' strike in 1981 that cancelled over 700 games and likely prompted the owners' decision not to renew his contract. The trigger issue was what compensation a team could receive for a free agent. This had been festering since the last-minute negotiated Collective Bargaining Agreement (CBA) a year earlier had passed it on to a study group. Miller claims that Kuhn told him just before 1980 negotiations that the owners needed a "victory."[49]

Miller describes the 1981 strike as "the most principled strike" he had ever participated in and "the Association's finest hour,"[50] while Kuhn, calling Miller "a prisoner of his own ego above all things," considers the strike "an inexcusable miscalculation by Miller of the clubs and me."[51] A key to MLBPA's dominance of the owners in bargaining was Miller's soft power effect upon the press and the public. It strengthened the union's bargaining position and outflanked Kuhn and the owners, who chose not to curry public favor.

Peter Ueberroth (1984–1988)

Given Kuhn's experience with the job, owners had difficulty recruiting an insider who would be their next whipping boy. Emerging from the search, however, was new American hero, Peter Ueberroth, a highly successful marketing-oriented entrepreneur who had built the second largest travel agency in the country before leading the 1984 Los Angeles Olympic Committee to a $200 million profit and becoming *Time* magazine's man of the year. In a favorable bargaining position, he negotiated a salary twice that of Kuhn's, a reorganization that gave him broader control over the leagues, and an increase in fining authority from $5,000 to $250,000. He quickly acted to settle the umpires' strike within a week of taking office by giving them more than they asked for; thereby asserting his authority over the league presidents on their traditional turf and over the owners and incurring their disfavor.[52]

Recognizing the value of celebrity marketing while upstaging his predecessor, in March 1985, he reinstated popular Hall of Famers Mickey Mantle and Willie Mays, whom Kuhn had banned from baseball-related activities for associating with casinos. As a soft power marketer, he brought MLB belatedly into the twentieth-century business world with a profitable corporate sponsorship approach similar to what he had used in the Olympics. The relatively dormant MLB Promotions Corporation, established as MLB's marketing arm in 1968, produced only $640,000 ($40,000 per team) in licensing and merchandising revenue in 1984. Within five years, Ueberroth had increased that total to $36 million. On the hard power side, however, he took punitive action against players with drug issues and tried to institute a comprehensive drug-testing program that the union stone-walled until 2002.[53]

When the players struck in August 1985, he dictated a settlement without owner approval that confined the strike to two days. In failing to include salary containment items that the owners wanted, Ueberroth set the stage for the biggest mistake of his tenure: owner collusion on player salaries that ultimately cost the owners $280 million in damages and a further calcification of the hard power adversarial relationship between players and owners that would continue for another decade.[54] In calling the collusion "baseball's original sin," Fay Vincent contends that Bud Selig, then head of the Milwaukee Brewers, and Jerry Reinsdorf, owner of the Chicago White Sox, were "the two ringleaders of collusion among the owners."[55]

Ueberroth was first and foremost a businessman who didn't have any particular affection for the game. He was also the only commissioner to leave office on his own terms, having announced after less than four years that he would not complete his five-year term. He proceeded to groom A. Bartlett Giamatti, who had been recruited by Selig to be NL president in 1986. When he left office, Ueberroth summed up his performance as "a lot of substance and not much style," reflecting the increase in profitability of MLB during his tenure.[56]

A. Bartlett "Bart" Giamatti (1989)

A classics scholar who became president of Yale University at age forty, Giamatti loved baseball as much as Landis had. Giamatti's *New York Times* op-ed piece calling for players to break the 1981 strike helped credential him as an owner candidate for commissioner.[57] He was the first choice of Selig's 1983 search committee to replace Kuhn as commissioner, but Giamatti couldn't leave Yale at the time because he was embroiled in a rancorous labor dispute.[58] Three years later, with Ueberroth ensconced as commissioner, Giamatti became NL president and heir apparent. In his two-plus years in the limited NL job, he distinguished himself as a player disciplinarian who strove to uphold the integrity of the game. That experience prepared him for the most notable act of his six-month commissionership — and one that he shared with his newly appointed deputy commissioner, Francis T. "Fay" Vincent, a business leader who had worked at the Securities and Exchange Commission, Coca-Cola, and Columbia Pictures. Giamatti focused on policy and external affairs; Vincent, on internal legal and operational matters.

Ueberroth had passed on to them allegations that Pete Rose, MLB's all-time hits leader and then Cincinnati Reds manager, had been betting on baseball games, including those involving the Reds. Giamatti, who personified the soft power mythological love of the game, undertook hard power actions to preserve the game's integrity. Armed with conclusive evidence after an exhaustive and expensive investigation, Giamatti and Vincent met with Rose and offered a settlement of first a ten- and then a seven-year banishment from the game. On August 23, 1989, they agreed on a "permanent suspension," with opportunity to apply for reinstatement after a year. Eight days later, Giamatti died of a heart attack at age 51. Nearly three decades later, Rose is still on suspension.

Francis T. "Fay" Vincent (1989–1992)

Less than two months after Giamatti died, successor Vincent got a very visible test of his power when an earthquake hit the Bay Area as the Oakland A's and San Francisco Giants were preparing to play the third game of the 1989 World Series. The next day Vincent appropriately suspended the series, asserting that "our modest little game is not a top priority."[59] He resumed the series ten days later, and MLB received plaudits for its soft power handling of the situation. That might have been Vincent's finest moment in what would be an owner-reduced three-year tenure.

When owners locked out players during 1990 spring training to push their agenda in CBA negotiations, Vincent took direction from high revenue owners and pushed through a settlement on March 20 that reopened camps, but angered many of the other owners. Vincent had hired as deputy commissioner Hall of Famer Hank Greenberg's son, Steve, who used a long-standing positive relationship with MLBPA head Donald Fehr to reach a conciliatory CBA.[60]

Vincent suspended Yankee owner George Steinbrenner for two years for associating with mob-connected gambler Howard Spira, thereby making an enemy of "the Boss." He also unilaterally decided to include former Negro League players in the MLB health plan without consulting the owners. These hard power decisions added to increasing owner dissatisfaction. Culmination came when NL and AL owners were unable to agree upon a financial settlement to compensate existing teams for the addition of two NL expansion teams in 1993. Vincent reluctantly intervened and alienated AL owners with his decision to give AL teams only 22 percent (less than the NL was proposing) of the expansion fees, but require them to contribute a proportionate 54 percent (AL had fourteen teams and NL, twelve) of the players to the expansion draft.[61]

The owners signaled their dissatisfaction by first hiring Dick Ravitch to head the owners' labor arm, the Players Relations Committee (PRC), at a higher salary than Vincent's and then by requesting that Vincent significantly limit his involvement in the bargaining process. His failed attempt to shift the Chicago Cubs from the NL East to the West division, his push to have Chicago and Atlanta superstations contribute more TV revenue to offset MLB's reduced revenue opportunity, and his reneging on an agreement to let San Francisco relocate to Tampa all created various owner enemies. The result was a no-confidence vote on September 3, 1992, Vincent's resignation five days later, and the naming of Selig as "interim" commissioner.[62] Selig had been campaigning for the job for almost a decade, and Vincent recognized it. George Vecsey of *The New York Times* called Vincent "the last commissioner" in recognition that Selig was an owner, not an independent.[63]

Allan H. "Bud" Selig (1992–Present)

Like Landis, Selig kept his "day job" when he became interim commissioner. Unlike Landis's, his prior job was a clear conflict of interest: owner of the Milwaukee Brewers. The "interim" label, which lasted almost six years, failed to mask the fact that Selig clearly represented the owners, not baseball. The owners blatantly clarified that in early 1994 when they named him permanent chair of the PRC and rescinded his powers to act unilaterally "in the best interests of baseball." Selig maintained his Brewers ownership until 2005 — and even borrowed $3 million for the team from a bank affiliated with Twins owner Carl Pohland in 1995.[64] He did put his Brewers holdings in a blind trust when he became permanent commissioner in 1998, but his daughter took over as Brewers CEO for four years and remained as chairman until the sale.[65] Despite this hard power enablement by the owners, Selig has generally relied more on his soft power skills with the owners and other constituents throughout his career. Zimbalist concludes that Selig, who admired the collaborative "league think" of the National Football League, "was the right person to shepherd this transition" of baseball to a competitive business.[66] Citing his skills in conciliation, particularly among owners, Kuhn calls Selig "baseball's Henry Clay."[67]

His first major test, however, soon descended into a traditional union-management hard power war and resulted in a MLB-worst player strike that canceled the last two weeks of the 1994 season and World Series—and delayed the start of the next season. There had been a seventeen-month owner delay in opening negotiations on the new CBA and a hard power push to include a salary cap, which the MLBPA strongly resisted. As a result of the 1994 changes in the commissioner's role and divided opinions among the owners, confusion ensued about what Selig could and could not do in the bargaining process.

President Clinton even got into the act, appointing Bill Usery, former Steelworkers head and a prominent negotiator, to mediate. Usery was able to shift the primary bargaining issue from a salary cap to revenue sharing, but he could not secure an agreement. President Clinton then proposed binding arbitration, but the owners refused. The old CBA was reinstated on March 31, 1995, in order to resume play, but agreement on the new CBA didn't occur until after the 1996 season.[68]

The new agreement did include substantial reforms that would enable MLB to move toward more collaborative governance: revenue sharing, luxury tax, Industry Growth Fund to spur global promotion, and agreement to seek a partial lifting of the antitrust exemption (which culminated in the 1998 Curt Flood Act).[69] Opportunities for soft power tactics increased, and the fans gradually reinstated their loyalties as the games began and continued. There has been no work stoppage since.

Selig has had his share of successes and failures during his tenure, now expected to last until 2013 as a result of a contract renewal. While they don't simply reflect soft or hard power emphasis, a case can be made for the successes being more a function of soft power and the failures of hard power. Two years after making him the permanent commissioner, the owners enhanced his power by amending MLB's constitution to eliminate the AL and NL presidents, put the leagues directly under Selig for most governance purposes, and included revenue-sharing procedures, within CBA constraints, as part of his "best interests" authority.[70]

Selig's fan-oriented changes—three divisions with wild card designation, interleague play, and league realignment—have been generally successful. Vince Gennaro calls the wild card "his single biggest stroke of genius" because of its enhancing September competition for playoff berths and resultant fan interest.[71] Conversely, his future-oriented Blue Ribbon Panel, which did not include a player representative, was ineffective and generally disregarded. And his failed attempt to impose team contraction, which prompted legal action in Minneapolis and a general player grievance, was a public relations disaster.

Perhaps MLB's greatest financial boon has been Major League Baseball Advanced Media (MLBAM), which MLB created in 2001, five years after Selig hired its first marketing director, reviving a focus that Ueberroth had initiated a decade earlier. Not only has it become "the sports industry leader in Internet services and sales," but it has stabilized the minor league system through its provision of consistent, quality marketing support, contributed greatly to centralized revenues that help balance MLB teams' financial positions, and helped to spread the game and market the MLB brand globally.[72]

The steroid issue has demanded a delicate blend of hard and soft power responses—and the jury is still out on its long term effect on the game. After Ueberroth's failure to implement a drug testing program two decades ago, MLB/MLBPA leadership generally floundered both in its admission of the problem as well as in its agreement on solutions. Contributing to the failure was a traditional hard power union-management stalemate that focused on parochial win-lose rather than the problem. Congress, the Mitchell Report, Jose Canseco, and other self-appointed spokesmen have provided needed external stimuli for collaborative action. Belatedly, Selig has taken positive steps, first unilaterally in the minors and, more recently, multilaterally with the MLBPA to exercise at least partial control and prevention measures. On April 11, 2008, MLB/MLBPA jointly announced agreement on positive Joint Drug Agreement modifications that respond to the Mitchell Report recommendations.[73] While falling short of complete enactment of the report recommendations, the agreement is another positive step in attempting to curtail MLB's drug problem. In having to respond to adverse publicity, both MLB and MLBPA experienced the value of soft power collaboration in addressing the issue.

Soft power multilateral collaboration was evident in the planning and implementation of the first World Baseball Classic (WBC) in 2006. MLB and MLBPA coalesced in a win-win partnership, and they at least tempered the potential leverage of their sponsorship to involve other countries, notably Japan, in the development process. Japan is slated to play an even greater role in the 2009 WBC. MLB/MLBPA was also able to convince the Bush administration to amend the American embargo and allow Cuba to participate, thereby assuring that all the best teams played in the 2006 inaugural. The WBC has demonstrated the potential to be a continuing soft power vehicle for enhancing popularity and profitability of the game globally.

Selig continues to grow in the job and has generally used his increased power in the best interests of the game by mollifying the hard power owner approach with soft power collaboration.

Conclusion

With Selig having evolved into a more multilateral leader relying significantly upon soft power tactics, MLB appears better positioned to survive and thrive in the highly competitive domestic and global entertainment economies. Among suggestions for continued enhancement are:

1. Build upon current successes in MLBAM in internet marketing and minor league operational/marketing support to strengthen the baseball brand while allowing the minors room to flourish locally. Pursue collaboration with and/or absorption of independent leagues to help protect the brand.
2. Provide more junior college baseball scholarships, avoiding competition with four-year colleges that favor football and basketball. Use them to increase African American recruits from enhanced inner city baseball programs.
3. Increase multilateral, collaborative control of Caribbean recruiting and development practices. Develop more balanced partnerships with local governments and businesses.
4. Leverage the World Baseball Classic success into closer relations with Cuba and increased involvement with lesser WBC participant countries as well as Russia. Expand/modify WBC participants and format as warranted and reinforce through MLBAM activities.
5. Enhance the possibility of a 2012/2016 return to the Olympics by committing MLB player participation on the USA team with a balanced contribution from each team and minimal adjustment of regular season schedule.

While each of these smart power initiatives possesses both hard and soft power elements, they depend significantly on multilateral, collaborative actions reflecting judicious use of soft power. Hard ball is the game, but soft ball is increasingly the business of baseball.

Notes

1. Joseph S. Nye, Jr., *Soft Power: The Means to Succeed in World Politics* (New York: Public Affairs, 2004), 2.
2. Nye, *The Paradox of American Power: Why the World's Only Superpower Can't Go It Alone* (New York: Oxford University Press, 2002), xii.
3. Andrew Zimbalist, *In the Best Interests of Baseball? The Revolutionary Reign of Bud Selig* (Hoboken: John Wiley & Sons, 2006), 22.
4. Nye, *Soft*, x.
5. Nye, *Paradox*, 67.
6. Zimbalist, 49–50.
7. David Pietrusza, *Judge and Jury: The Life and Times of Judge Kenesaw Mountain Landis* (South Bend, IN: Diamond Communications, 1998), 29.
8. *Ibid.*, 49–61, 79–89.
9. *Ibid.*, 119.
10. *Ibid.*, 157.
11. Zimbalist, 39–40.
12. *Ibid.*, 174.
13. *Ibid.*, 176.
14. *Ibid.*, vii.
15. *Ibid.*, 33.
16. Larry Moffi, *The Conscience of the Game: Baseball's Commissioners from Landis to Selig* (Lincoln: University of Nebraska Press, 2006), 39.
17. Pietrusza, 387.

18. Benjamin G. Rader, *Baseball: A History of America's Game* (Urbana: University of Illinois Press, 1992), 110.
19. *Ibid.*, 431.
20. Zimbalist, 47.
21. Moffi, 141.
22. Alfred B. Chandler with Vance H. Trimble, *Heroes, Plain Folks, and Skunks: The Life and Times of Happy Chandler: An Autobiography with Vance H. Trimble* (Chicago: Bonus Books, 1989), 226.
23. Moffi, 45.
24. *Ibid.*, 126–127.
25. Chandler, 229.
26. Moffi, 129–136; and Zimbalist, 53–54.
27. Moffi, 142.
28. Chandler, 241.
29. Moffi, 50.
30. John Thorn, Pete Palmer, Michael Gershwin, and David Pietrusza with Matthew Silverman and Sean Lahman, eds., *Total Baseball*, 6th ed. (New York: Total Sports, 1999), 150.
31. Moffi, 48; and Zimbalist, 60–61.
32. Zimbalist, 69–70.
33. Thorn, 150.
34. Moffi, 215.
35. Zimbalist, 68.
36. David Bohmer, "The Pragmatic Change Agent: A Reconsideration of Ford Frick as Commissioner," 2008 Cooperstown Symposium on Baseball and American Culture, Cooperstown, NY, June 5, 2008.
37. *Ibid.*, 63.
38. Zimbalist, 72; and Moffi, 51–52.
39. Zimbalist, 74.
40. Moffi, 217.
41. Zimbalist, 75 and 79.
42. Marvin Miller, *A Whole Different Ball Game: The Inside Story of the Baseball Revolution* (Chicago: Ivan R. Dee, 2004), 293.
43. *Ibid.*, x.
44. Bowie Kuhn, *Hard Ball: The Education of a Baseball Commissioner* (Lincoln: University of Nebraska Press, 1997), 77, 79, and 80.
45. Miller, 106, 91.
46. *Ibid.*, 75.
47. *Ibid.*, 203–221.
48. Kuhn, 157–158.
49. Miller, 293.
50. *Ibid.*, 301.
51. Kuhn, 346.
52. Moffi, 220; and Zimbalist, 90–92.
53. Zimbalist, 92, 95.
54. Zimbalist, 92–95.
55. Fay Vincent, *The Last Commissioner: A Baseball Valentine* (New York: Simon & Schuster, 2002), 278, 186.
56. Paul Dickson, ed., *Baseball's Greatest Quotations: An Illustrated Treasury of Baseball Quotations and Historical Lore* (New York: HarperCollins, 2008), 562. Comment comes from an interview with Richard Justice, *Washington Post*, March 10, 1989.
57. Miller, 401.
58. Zimbalist, 95–96.
59. Vincent, 157.
60. Zimbalist, 103–104.
61. *Ibid.*, 104–106.
62. *Ibid.*, 107–110.
63. Vincent, xi.
64. Moffi, 83.
65. Zimbalist, 144–145, 178, 199.
66. *Ibid.*, 212.
67. Kuhn, 412.
68. Zimbalist, 146–150.
69. *Ibid.*, 150–152.
70. *Ibid.*, 159.
71. Vince Gennaro, *Diamond Dollars: The Economics of Winning in Baseball* (Hingham, MA: Maple Street Press, 2007), 238.
72. Zimbalist, 190–191.
73. MLB.com, "Major League Baseball and Players Association Modify Joint Drug Agreement," April 11, 2008.

CHAPTER 15

Commodore Selig: The Importance of Japanese Baseball Players in Major League Baseball
Mathew J. Bartkowiak and *Yuya Kiuchi*

From the 1970s well into the 1990s, the influx of Japanese economic interests into the American business sector drew casual criticism to outright expressions of nativism and fear on American streets. Such reactions, however, seemed a distant memory on April 5, 2007. The eyes of the United States and Japan focused on a young pitcher recently signed to the Boston Red Sox, Daisuke Matsuzaka. Having attracted the attention of both American and Japanese baseball fans since the end of the previous season, Matsuzaka reflected an increasing presence of and fascination with Japanese baseball players in the major leagues on both sides of the Pacific, that began ten plus years ago with the arrival of pitcher Hideo Nomo.[1] Since then, names like Ichiro and Hideki "Godzilla" Matsui have opened the floodgates of media exposure, endorsement deals, and focus on Japanese baseball players.

What then happened in this short period of time? Are the presence and proven talent of these players creating an effective program of cultural diplomacy? What is the significance of baseball diplomacy in what Mike Mansfield, the longest serving American ambassador in Tokyo, repeatedly referred to as the "most important bilateral relationship in the world" between Japan and the U.S.? Have Japan's financial woes in the forms of recessions during the last decade of the 1990s neutralized the threat felt by some Americans; opening a door of acceptance for these players? All of these questions demand discussion, but it is one factor that overwhelmingly has assured the current state of acceptance and reception of Japanese players in Major League Baseball, the progressive march of transnational capitalism.

The attention paid to these questions extends far beyond player's athletic abilities. Not to detract from their performance in the Majors, but these players are representative of much larger economic powers looking to extend financial interest and gain across the Pacific. Additionally, it also reflects American interests in capitalizing globally, attaining available human and cultural resources for its own benefit. Current Japanese players in baseball are not only potentially individual cultural diplomats breaking down racism and bigotry, but are also foot-soldiers for corporate expansion and the extension of brand identities internationally including that of Major League Baseball, individual teams, and the corporations involved in the process. Furthermore, as much as American baseball teams aim to capitalize on the economic values of these players, the Japanese economy strives to generate profits by taking advantage of their individual symbolic value. There is also a sense in Japan that their resources have been taken advantage of, if not stolen, by American power. It is in these larger structures of transnational capitalism and consumer cultures that the real "acceptance" of one of Japan's most celebrated imports have come.

Due to this intricate flow of trans–Pacific capital, an examination of obvious and eye-catching signs of global capitalism does not suffice to understand the nature of this new type of cultural diplomacy. For example, the fact that the Red Sox spent over $103 million during the negotiation with Matsuzaka drew in a curious public's general attention. What is more important, however, is why the team was willing to spend so much money. The Red Sox were aware that if Matsuzaka successfully brought six extra wins to the team and helped win the pennant, his presence would enhance the annual profit in advertisement of the New England Sports Network by approximately $12.5 million. Consequently, the broadcasting station's value increases by the same amount. Since the Red Sox own 80 percent of its stocks, the team can make an extra $10 million only with advertisements at a local broadcasting station. Once other profits from broadcasting, merchandising, player placements in media, and others are calculated, there was more to win for the Red Sox than to lose. This is nothing but just one example of the vastness and dynamics of how the cultural exchange has become consequential in international business.[2]

Although a single article has no way to replicate the width and depth of this role of baseball diplomacy in global capitalism, an exploration in the major league marketing — both in a traditional "business" sense and a more contemporary "cultural" sense — will show that baseball is a cultural exchange between Japan and the U.S. and that this global economy functions around the players. From the American perspective, Japanese baseball players in the Majors show how an influx of non–American resources no longer signifies a disadvantage for the American economy and culture. This is a different situation than earlier economic concerns like automobile trends between the two countries when as the number of Japanese cars imported to the U.S. increased, the American automobile industry suffered. In this type of exchange based on culture, an increase in the number of Japanese players does not bring a decline of the American baseball industry. In reality, it boosts the economy of the major leagues via merchandizing, broadcasting rights, etc.

It is also important not to romanticize this cultural exchange. From the Japanese perspective, export no longer brings profits. While the outflow of baseball talents to the U.S. is beneficial for some industries such as broadcasting, advertising, and traveling, it is concurrently damaging to the Japanese baseball industry. Fewer games are broadcast on television. The fan base weakens. As described later, many Japanese fans perceive the outflow of talented Japanese players as the threat to Japanese "yakyuu [baseball]." Examining some of the recent developments in this baseball-driven trans–Pacific flow of capital allows us to observe some of the more recent characteristics of what Walter LaFeber calls the "new global capitalism" both of economy and culture.

Looking to Japan from the United States

In 1992, writer David Boaz released an article in the *Wall Street Journal*, entitled "Yellow Peril Reinfects America: U.S. Hostility Turns to Japan." The article ran down the economically and racially motivated anti–Japanese rhetoric present in the United States that had resulted from an influx of Japanese business interest in the United States, and the increasing competition coming from Japanese auto and technology companies. Boaz shares that the anger took many forms, including "Presidential candidate John Connally warned the Japanese they had 'better be prepared to sit on the docks of Yokohama in your little Datsuns and your little Toyotas while you stare at your own little television sets and eat your mandarin oranges, because we've had all we're going to take!'"[3] Fifteen years after the article was written an Associated Press piece lauded the fact that although Mike Lowell was the Series' MVP, "Boston had plenty of candidates. Especially in a year in which Japanese stars Daisuke Matsuzaka and Hideki Okajima helped put the world in World Series." Obviously the discussion of American "Japan-bashing" and Matsuzaka's rise to fame are both subjects that are complex and are equally worthy areas of study in themselves, but it is fascinating to see how a nation that has exhibited both fear and fascination with Japan has so successfully adopted Japanese baseball players into its most historically regarded game in these last ten years.

The presence and acceptance of these players is much more than a tale of an increasingly welcoming and less racially-focused world. The reality of the situation has much more to do with a significantly larger system of global capital and the vested corporate interest in the marketing and promotion of a global sports entity. Much of the internationalization of baseball, especially in regards to the rise and presence of Japanese talent in Major League Baseball, is a story of what Walter LaFeber calls the "New Global Capitalism." Like his examination of Michael Jordan and the internationalization of the NBA, similar corporate power structures are at play in the utilization of names like Daisuke Matsuzaka, Ichiro, and many others to break down international boundaries of consumption.

LaFeber describes the immediacy and reality of a rapidly interconnected world through media and technological innovation:

> As revolutionary technology thus integrated Americans into the rest of the world, many of them feared the strangeness and challenges that they encountered. Americans had feared the strangeness and challenges of other peoples since the seventeenth century, but never before had such dangers been so instantaneous, so immediate, as they were in the new, tightly wired world.[4]

LaFeber measures these new challenges to American identity and assures us that the march to global capitalism will eventually, even if at the expense of individual cultural identities, overcome these strange feelings: "In this developing battle of capital versus culture, capital will ultimately win."[5] This process seems to be at work surrounding this latest round of interest in the rise of Japanese baseball players into Major League Baseball culture; capital is providing a new vision of Japan and its role in the global economy.

Part of this new vision involves a marketed sense of "cool." In an article for *Foreign Policy*, Douglas McGray discusses the rise of Japan's "Gross National Cool" and its connection to the world economy. McGray stipulates that Japan's decade long-recession essentially cut out notions of the country being an immediate economic threat. The opening created by this economic downturn has created a greater sense of openness and in some cases, fascination, with the country by Americans. Japan, as the author postulates, has "succeeded not only in balancing a flexible, absorptive, crowd-pleasing, shared culture with a more private, domestic one but also taking advantage of that balance to build an increasingly powerful global commercial force. In other words, Japan's growing cultural presence has brought a mighty engine of national cool."[6]

Taking into account LaFeber's model of international capital, we can consider McGray's article as a bridge linking capital and culture in a succinct fashion. The leveling of international boundaries in favor of the spread of global capitalism allowed Japan to effectively sell a less economically threatening vision of itself internationally. This is especially true for consumers in the United States; a country that only years before had at times been embarrassingly outspoken about its views towards the Japanese.

In regards to Major League Baseball, these contingencies of international capital and the selling of Japanese culture and identity need to be taken into account when dealing with the reception of, and media attention to, key Japanese players like Ichiro and Matsuzaka in the United States. One can see that *especially* in terms of media coverage, that race and national ascriptions of character seem to have much less of a harsh focus when compared to the reception of Hideo Nomo and Hideki Irabu in the 1990s. Instead, what can be witnessed is an extremely lucrative and widespread campaign to mold "America's Pastime" into an international entity. Baseball is to be a game that exists beyond national boundaries, and that speaks the international language of capital.

The very systems of international capital that are being used to describe the outwardly well-seamed baseball of the twenty-first century were cited by many critics as forces that were creating discord for baseball in the 1990s. Reception to the expansion and use of players in Major League Baseball from Asian countries in the 1990s was seen by David Tokiharu Mayeda as much more racially focused. Mayeda cited players like Nomo as being in a racial limelight in the media and within the American populace. He states,

> Hard working and self-sacrificing, and quiet as (he was rarely quoted in newspapers), Nomo reaffirmed to readers that Asian nationals and Asian Americans were model minorities. It should be noted here that although Hideo Nomo is a Japanese national and not Asian-American, he and Hideki Irabu can still affect the way mainstream America views Asian Americans.[7]

Along with the "model-minority" concern, Mayeda focuses on the previously discussed focus on the Japanese as economic threat. This threat is the one that according to McGray's article on "Japan's gross national cool" has changed so drastically in the last few years. Mayeda saw press coverage of Nomo and Irabu as indicative of this economic fear: "What readers can potentially digest, however, is another Japanese entity that is financially threatening an American institution. Irabu's Japanese heritage and national status were displayed prominently by the *New York Times* and therefore a cultural sensitivity should have accompanied any articles, positive or negative, on Irabu." He continues later that in regards to the *Times*, "both Japan and Irabu were depicted as economic dangers."[8]

Obviously, Matsuzaka's contract with the Boston Red Sox created a similar focus. Yet, compared to the cultural insensitivity that Mayeda had seen with players in the 1990s, something had fundamentally changed in regards to the theme of economic threats. This discrepancy, as was alluded to, became one of the main protagonists for these studies when comparing media coverage of Japanese players in MLB in the 1990s versus the 2000s. As Robert Whiting in his *The Meaning of Ichiro* describes, Japanese baseball players at the turn of the century had seemingly shed stereotypes of economic imperialists.

> Americans liked them because of their belief, generally speaking, in the team ethos and their commitment to the idea that playing baseball was first and foremost its own reward-monetary considerations coming later. They were welcome additions to a game that seemed increasingly consumed by greed and ego.[9]

Although a wonderful sentiment, this welcoming seems to be more dependent on two important themes Whiting unmasks: first, domestic economic gain, and second, marketing.

Whiting shares several estimates that prove the economic worth of the further internationalization of baseball as a product, including insight into the economic weight that Ichiro brought with him to Major League Baseball and Seattle specifically. He cites ticket sales, hotel and airline reservations, souvenirs, and advertising as bringing in "over $100 million into Seattle's economy over a five-year span."[10] A good deal of this money is coming in from Japanese tourists and was the case with other teams across the nation as well.

Whiting proposes Hideki Matsui's "most important contribution may have been financial, as he single-handedly created new ways for tourists to blow their money in New York. Sales of Yankees tickets to Japanese tour groups went through the roof, as did sales of Matsui goods." He continues, "According to one estimate, the intense Japanese interest in Matsui brought in roughly 500 million much-needed dollars for the city's economy."[11] Similar stories have abounded around Matsuzaka's rookie year in MLB for fans here and abroad. From advertising in Fenway Park, to local hotels, to the sales of seventy-two Matsuzaka products available through MLB retailers nationally, the economic impact on baseball has been massive.

The marketing responsible for this recognition of MLB as an international product has astutely been able to keep up with, and in many ways, shape this reception. One only needs to look at the *Major League Baseball International Business Review* to see how consumption has created, and directed programs of international acceptance for American fans in the Pacific Rim as well as in Latin-American countries. Major League Baseball currently broadcasts in 229 countries and territories, bringing numerous broadcast deals, event sponsors, licensing agreements, player development centers, marketing promotions, local advertisers, and international events like the Japan All-Star Series along with it. With rapid growth in the Asian and European markets, MLB is experiencing robust growth as an international entity.[12]

Hence, the ideas of national boundaries are not something that MLB would consider a restraint. Attention paid to Japanese baseball players in the recent years is a larger reflection of widening markets for sports entertainment. These individuals who, as LaFeber states, could transcend race, are also "less of a person than 'something of a 24-commodity.'"[13] The reception and career of these individual players is receiving so much media focus, not because of cultural progress, but because of immense commercial progress. Keith Reed sees the exorbitant fees paid for Matsuzaka's contract as an investment in a new market versus solely an individual player: "Sox executives believe there is a big market in Japan and locally for endorsements involving the team and Matsuzaka, and that their new pitcher will boost the team's popularity in Japan past that of a certain pinstripe-wearing rival with a Japanese player of its own." He continues by quoting Red Sox senior vice president Sam Kennedy, "We want to be the team of Japan. The Yankees are very popular over there because of [Hideki] Matsui, but now we think we can get in over there as well."[14] To keep up with this hope the marketing machine of MLB, numerous corporations, and teams have reacted swiftly. Ads for Japanese companies have sprouted up in stadiums across the nation: some with Japanese language signage. Numerous American companies have translated their signs into Japanese as well, including Dunkin' Donuts and Lumber Liquidators.[15]

Whiting chronicles that such investment has been a standard with several of the current Japanese players including Matusi who had numerous "endorsement contracts for Upper Deck sports cards, Lotte ice cream, a Mizuno sports drink and Japan Airlines."[16] Ichiro inspired a "30 percent jump in ticket sales" when a bobblehead doll with his likeness was given away at Safeco Field as a promotional giveaway.[17] This was complimented by the creation of sushi stands at Safeco selling "Ichirolls" and the sales of headbands with Japanese lettering.[18] Japanese players, far beyond their athletic capabilities, are becoming symbols of the possibilities of internationally focused marketing for a supposed "American" product in MLB.

A looming question remains though. Even though in terms of market forces and the largely positive press that has surrounded more recent Japanese players like Ichiro and Matsuzaka; has anything really changed in regards to Americans views of the Japanese culturally and within the major league? The massive amount of merchandise that has been sold, points to some kind of, at least, consumable acceptance of Japanese players in MLB by Americans. This is the case even though these players only represent a small fraction of total players—even when compared against other international representatives in MLB like the Dominican Republic. As we have seen a great deal of investment in branding and creating internationally marketable images of baseball has created an "It's a Small World After All" aesthetic where harmonious page after page of the MLB *International Business Review* points to a rainbow of players: each respected and part of an international community.

Hence, do these economic realities reflect a real cultural shift? If this is the case, issues central to Mayeda's study of Nomo and Irabu have been pushed into the shadows by the media in favor of the financial discussions that these players have generated. Simply put though, the march of international capital has not killed American xenophobia. To get to the heart of the matter, MLB's business office was criticized by a former MLB employee "for fostering an environment in which anti–Asian hostility thrived." The Associated Press reported on October 16, 2003, that the employee stated that she was "repeatedly subjected until her May termination to an 'unreasonable, offensive and demeaning anti–Japanese and anti–Asian hostility that pervaded the entire International Department.'"[19] Major League Baseball is far from immune to such commentaries; discussions concerning race are ever-present and have followed the League whether in regards to considerations of minorities in coaching positions or numerous other concerns.

Such occurrences that have come and that will be sure to arise as Major League Baseball continues to reach and compose itself of an international community, are important to keep in mind as the juggernaut of transnational capitalism continues to roll in the twenty-first century. Yet, one must marvel at the immense power and sense of peace created in the media that has come through the marketing of these players as international capital-generating machines. That sense of peace and fascination exists because so much is financially dependent on sports diplomacy to continue to generate the capital to which Major League Baseball has become accustomed. In the meantime, we can see how larger economic relations shape the reception and use of cultural events like the latest media focus on Japanese players in baseball. Japan's economic life, whether at its pinnacle or in the recovery from recession; the domestic benefit of Japanese players in a competitive sports-entertainment industry; and the marketing done to ensure economic benefits to all involved, shapes reception.

Looking to the United States from Japan

Watching Japanese baseball players play a vital role in their teams' victories in the U.S. is a pleasure for many baseball fans and non-fans in Japan. It may even nurture a sense of nationalistic pride when Matsuzaka strikes out an American slugger or Ichiro hits more than 200 hits per season against American pitchers. For some industries, MLB's popularity in Japan is a great business opportunity. This trans–Pacific capital flow enabled this appealing market to generate large profits for MLB-related clothing sales. Baseball diplomacy, however, does not always bring entertainment to those sitting in front of a television set or business opportunities like it does to Japanese travel agencies organizing a weekend trip to Boston or Seattle only to watch a game.

On the other side of this excitement about Ichiro, Matsui, Matsuzaka, and many other Japanese baseball players in the Majors, there is a strong sense of fear and concern about the gravitational force that Major League Baseball possesses. In addition, many fans have expressed their ambivalence about a cultural crash between Japanese collectivism and American individualism. A continuing outflow of talented players to American teams over the last decade has become a cultural and economic threat in the minds of fans and the industry. While cultural imperialism would take place when a dominant culture exercised its centrifugal force over a less powerful one in the past, American centripetal force has caused ripple effects under the new global capitalist framework.

Tomonori Iijima reports the sense of threat that surfaced at the professional baseball owners' meeting on July 18, 2007. Keizi Oyashiro, the owner of the Nippon Ham Fighters and the chair of the meeting, admitted at the succeeding press conference that team owners had agreed that Nippon Housou Kyoukai (NHK), Japan's government-run television station, had broadcast too much about MLB. Earlier in the year, Masayoshi Son, the owner of the Fukuoka Softbank Hawks, problematized NHK's televising policy by claiming that the broadcasting station "disproportionately" emphasized MLB in its program content. NHK audiences, indeed, had more opportunities to watch a MLB game than a Japanese domestic league game in 2007. While it broadcast 127 Japanese games, it broadcast 260 MLB regular season games and 30 post season games. Compared to the previous year, the number of games broadcast for Japan's league was increased by one game, whereas broadcast games for MLB increased by fifty-five.[20] This disproportionate amount of interest in MLB by NHK is particularly significant since it is the only government-owned television station in Japan.

The decline of broadcasting stations interest in the domestic league, however, is not an isolated case for NHK. Nippon Television Network Corporation, the broadcasting station owned by Yomiuri Shimbun, or the parent company of the largest and most popular Japanese baseball team, the Yomiuri Giants, curtailed the number of broadcasted Giant's games by approximately 40 percent in 2007. Additionally, unlike in the past when television stations continued to broadcast the game until the end even after the scheduled broadcasting time was over by delaying the start of the following shows or canceling them, most channels adhered to the original broadcasting schedules and left some avid baseball fans dissatisfied. The Nikkan Sports News, one of the leading newspaper companies in sports, is unsympathetic to the team owners' claims. They summarize these unsatisfied owners' comments by claiming they are looking for scapegoats. The undercurrent of team owners' concerns is the fear that the Japanese leagues will eventually lose most of the talented players and dedicated fans to MLB.[21]

MLB has been successful in exposing Japanese fans to American baseball through various media in addition to newspapers. MLB's objective in Japan is to make a shift from player-driven hype to a more general fan-base that appreciates the game as a whole. In other words, despite the current popularity of MLB in Japan, most fans only watch games in which Japanese players play. They turn their television on to see Matsui, or because of Matsuzaka. If Matsuzaka and Okajima were to leave the Red Sox, the team would be very likely to lose popularity amongst Japanese fans. One of the ways in which MLB's Japan office is attempting to pull fans into the sport itself is to place its players in magazines. Ryan Howard appeared in *G.Q. Japan*, David Wright in *Men's Non-no*, and Joseph Mauer in *Goethe*. Bronson Arroyo appeared on MTV's "World Chart Express" which was also broadcast in Japan.[22] Through these media exposure activities, MLB aims to attract Japanese fans not only to Japanese players but also to non–Japanese players. Additionally, the league aims to educate its Japanese fans about the culture of baseball so that the league would have a more secure and stable fan base through which it can generate profit.

Another example of such efforts is to expose Japanese fans to the history and culture of MLB. "SPORT," a nightly sport news program on the Fuji Television Network features a short weekly feature called "West Side Story." In this sub-program, audiences learn about the history of MLB, the history of ballparks, the rivalry between the New York Yankees and the Boston Red Sox, and many other fundamentals about American baseball culture.[23] A similar effort took place in newspapers and on web sites. Before the 2007 season started, MLB Japan conducted an online popularity poll for all MLB teams. It was one of the promotional efforts to nurture a sense of fandom for a particular team and possibly replicate a geographical rivalry between the two cities on the other side of the Pacific.[24]

MLB has also been successful in attracting women as a new demographic group. In the past, Japanese baseball attracted adult males. With the arrival of MLB to Japanese living rooms, middle-aged housewives began to cheer for Japanese players in the U.S. This new phenomenon is mostly due to the fact that because of the time difference, the games are on television in the late morning in Japan when housewives traditionally spend time cleaning the house and doing the laundry with their television on.[25]

The next target for MLB is females between the ages twenty-eight and thirty-five. While they tend to have a relatively large disposable income, they have traditionally not been baseball fans. The strategy is to market MLB apparel to this demographic. Since cultural difference between the U.S. and

Japan makes it difficult to sell baseball jerseys, t-shirts, and caps to females in Japan, MLB came up with a new product portfolio which is more acceptable in the mind of young Japanese females. Located in Harajuku where young people gather on weekends, "LB-03," one of the most popular apparel shops in Tokyo, agreed to sell such items.[26] Similarly, Akira Machida, the store manager of the "MLB Club House Store," explains that now that the major league is one of the most popular sports in Japan, consumers are willing to spend more money on baseball-related apparel. In the past, a majority of the store's sales came from Matsuzaka and Matsui-related items that cost around twenty-five to thirty dollars. Machida now predicts that customers are more likely to purchase more expensive items. As an attempt to take advantage of this commercial opportunity, the store now sells replica jerseys for women, even though the line only included ones for men and children in the past.[27]

These capital-driven marketing efforts in Japan have so far been successful. As President Bush mentioned at the Japan-U.S. summit meeting on November 18, 2006, the transpacific flow of talent may be beneficial to the Japanese economy in some cases. Even so, if LaFeber's aforementioned prediction that capital wins at the expense of culture is true, what are the possible cultural consequences of baseball diplomacy?

As the capital-based American baseball culture interacts with Japanese culture, an inherent and traditional difference between Japanese and American culture is particularly highlighted. Although essentialism never does justice to the complexity and diversity within culture, as past sociologists and anthropologists including Edward T. Hall and Ruth Benedict have analyzed, Japanese society has prioritized collective good over individual benefit. On the other hand, American society has been characterized as individualistic by various Japanese cultural scholars. This fundamental difference between group-oriented Japanese culture and individual-oriented American culture seems to explain how differently Japanese baseball fans and media consider the success of Ichiro and Hideki Matsui. Many fans have expressed ambivalence about Ichiro's pursuit after individual-achievement while showing a sense of empathy to Matsui's collective idealism.

Although "Americanized personality" is too strong an expression to describe Ichiro's professional attitude, Ichiro has emphasized his personal achievement more than his team's success. Some of his comments reflecting this philosophy include: "I am happier when I hit four hits in a game and my team loses than when my team wins and I hit none" and "When I meet players who are playing just to win, that angers me." Although these quotes do not mean Ichiro cares less about winning, individual achievement is a major benchmark for his career. Shigenori Matsushita concludes that it was partially because of this idea that Ichiro decided to play for the Mariners when he could have obtained free agency to transfer to the Yankees or the Red Sox where he could partake in the World Series. He argues that there was something more important for Ichiro than winning the championship. Matsushita claims that something was the five-year contract that included $90,000,000, as well $32,000 annual residence fees, an SUV, four first-class round trip tickets for him and his family between Japan and the U.S. annually, guaranteed personal trainer and interpreter, etc.[28]

Matsui, on the other hand, is a collectivism-oriented player. He questions, "Baseball is a team sport. What is the point of competing on an individual basis within the team?" While Ichiro sets his target as 200 hits per season, winning the world championship is Matsui's target. Many Japanese fans and baseball analysts recognize the proximity to traditional Japanese value systems expressed in Matsui's baseball philosophy. To express his admiration, Matsushita quotes Matsui: "I am fine even if I could achieve nothing as long as my team achieves something."

Such ambivalence about capital and individualism-driven culture in MLB also appears in Japanese media reports on seasoned players attempt to join MLB from Japan. Takashi Saito, with the Dodgers, was once thought to be at the end of his career in Japan. But now he is successful as a closer in Los Angeles. Masumi Kuwata signed a contract with the Pirates as a Minor League player. Hideo Nomo and Shingo Takatsu attended spring training in 2008. Several Japanese players around the age of forty have crossed the Ocean to make it to the major leagues. When media reports about these players, they portray them as the embodiment of non-capital driven dream seekers. As *ZAKZAK*'s article title "There Is More to the American Dream Than Money" shows, "there is nothing new about young players signing expensive contracts."[29] This new and older demography of Japanese baseball players coming to the U.S. with a very small signing fee reflects how they began to test their individual talent in a new environment. Instead of focusing on "playing for the team," these seasoned Japanese players play to challenge their own limits.

Conclusion

Baseball diplomacy that operates within the framework that LaFeber terms as "new global capitalism" has different consequences, both positive and negative, compared to product and material based trans–Pacific exchange in the 1980s and before. A see-saw like understanding of globalization is no longer valid. In the past, when the Japanese auto-industry did well, American industry suffered. In the new global capitalism, both parties may suffer or benefit. Some of the examples have shown how Japanese major league players have allowed both American and Japanese corporations, baseball organizations, and other relevant entities to generate profits. Such economic-based arguments, however, do not suffice to understand the new trend. Although LaFeber suggests that capital gain is more emphasized over cultural consequence, this study has shown that the nature of cultural exchange is more complex than concepts such as "domination" or "loss of culture" can explain.

An increasing number of non–American players in MLB results in an outflow of baseball talents from non–American baseball leagues. While increasing economic interest in the game, this process still can potentially challenge, for some, the "American-ness" of MLB. These players, largely though, have seemingly found a much warmer reception than other products of the Japanese industrial-entertainment complex.

In addition, unlike the material and product export business, the intricacy of talent-based capitalism is that the outflow of resources may result in loss of money in the exporting market. Although relevant industries in Japan, MLB's Japanese office, and the Japanese professional baseball league try to identify various ways to generate profit through Japanese baseball players in the U.S., it has not been successful erasing the common idea that the trans–Pacific baseball diplomacy resulted in the loss in Japanese culture and sport.

The preceding pages have not sought to successfully diagnose and understand every aspect of the complex cultural and economic exchange that is reflected in the rise of Japanese baseball players in the major leagues. The subject continues to evolve each season and with each acquisition or trade. The subject also continues to evolve as these players create seemingly permanent residencies in a sport that has found great economic success in the last several years. Just as it is an exciting/problematic time for those financially invested in the baseball world around the globe, it is the same for fans as well as cultural critics who look to the future of the sport in national and international consciousnesses. Keeping an eye on these relationships of culture and capital can only help us understand the competitions both on and off the field in the life of baseball as an international presence.

Notes

1. Masanori Murakami became the first Japanese major league player in 1964. Kunikazu Ogawa and Yutaka Enatsu also tried to play in the Majors in 1978 and 1985, but they never made it to the field. Nomo's debut, therefore, signaled the start of the influx of Japanese players.

2. Russell Adams, "Is Ichiro's Annual Salary Too Much or Too Little? New Scoring Method to Evaluate Players Based on Profits," trans. in *Courrier Japan*, July 2007, 57.

3. Datsun is now known as Nissan. Ben Walker, "Red Sox Sweep World Series," *Toronto Star*, October 29, 2007; and David Boaz, "Yellow Peril Reinfects America: U.S. Hostility Turns to Japan," *Wall Street Journal*, April 7, 1989.

4. Walter LaFeber, *Michael Jordan and the*

New Global Capitalism (New York: W. W. Norton, 2002), 21.
    5. *Ibid.*
    6. *Ibid.*, 53.
    7. David Tokiharu Mayeda, "From Model Minority to Economic Threat: Media Portrayals of Major League Baseball: Pitchers Hideo Nomo and Hideki Irabu," *Journal of Sport & Social Issues,* 23. 2 (1999): 211.
    8. *Ibid.*, 213.
    9. Robert Whiting, *The Meaning of Ichiro: The New Wave From Japan and the Transformation of Our National Pastime* (New York: Warner Books, 2004), 205.
    10. *Ibid.*, 30.
    11. *Ibid.*, 251.
    12. Major League Japan, "MLB in Japan," Promotional Material, Tokyo, (2007): 5, 16, 24–26, 38–41.
    13. LaFaber, 16, 85.
    14. Keith Reed, "Dice-K is Already Pitching for Sox — in Japanese Ads," *Knight Ridder Tribune Business News,* Dec. 30, 2006.
    15. *Ibid.*
    16. Whitening, 251.
    17. *Ibid.*, 29.
    18. *Ibid.*, 30.
    19. Associated Press, "Woman Says Complaint Got Her Fired," 16 Oct. 2003.
    20. Tomonori Iijima, "Stop Broadcasting the Major Games," *Nikkan Sports,* July 19, 2007.
    21. *Ibid.*
    22. Major League Japan, "MLB in Japan."
    23. Hiroko Kato, interview by author, MLB Japan Office, August 3, 2007.
    24. Major League Japan, "MLB in Japan."
    25. Kato interview.
    26. *Ibid.*
    27. Akira Machida, "MLB Targets Japanese Market," *Senden Kaigi,* June 1, 2007, 53.
    28. Shigenori Matsushita, "Individualist Ichiro and Collectivist Matsui," *President,* September 3, 2007, 21.
    29. ZAKZAK, "There Is More to the American Dream than Money," http://www.zakzak.co.jp/spo/2008_01/s2008012114_all.html.

CHAPTER 16

Major League Baseball, Welcome Back Veterans, and the Rhetoric of "Support the Troops"

Michael L. Butterworth

"There is nothing more emblematic of what the American way of life is than baseball."—Navy Vice Admiral John G. Morgan, Jr.[1]

Like millions of other Americans, I made baseball a part of my Fourth of July weekend activities in 2008. July 3 was a family outing to the Class A Kane County Cougars game in St. Charles, Illinois. There, military personnel presented the American flag as the national anthem was performed and the hometown Cougars took the field in star-spangled jerseys. On July 4, I noted that the Chicago White Sox were uniformed in jerseys patterned in camouflage. Similar jerseys were worn by the Cincinnati Reds when I checked in on them July 5; that same evening, the Minnesota Twins wore caps marked with the letters of the Army, Navy, Air Force, and Marine Corps. Then, watching the Chicago Cubs play the St. Louis Cardinals on July 6, I heard TBS announcer Chip Caray explain to viewers that special baseball caps had been worn throughout Major League Baseball (MLB) during the holiday weekend. Each cap was navy blue, regardless of the team's colors, and inside the team emblem appeared the stars and stripes of the American flag.

In just a few days, then, I experienced the "national pastime" in all of its patriotic glory. Yet these events featured more than the traditional hallmarks of baseball patriotism — red, white, and blue bunting, flags, dramatic performances of the national anthem, and so on. Indeed, "patriotism" during the 2008 Fourth of July weekend was largely reduced to "militarism," as the majority of the holiday tributes were mostly about or for the U.S. Armed Forces. The centerpiece of these displays was the special caps, which had been produced by MLB in conjunction with its newest charity venture, Welcome Back Veterans (WBV). According to the WBV website, the organization is "designed to raise public awareness about issues facing today's veterans, and to raise funds to support programs and services that these returning soldiers need to repair and restore their lives."[2]

It is not as if militaristic and patriotic rituals are new to baseball. The national anthem, after all, was performed as early as 1862 and was installed as a pre-game fixture during World War II in order to demonstrate the patriotism of the American game.[3] More recently, in response to the American military presence in Afghanistan and Iraq, MLB ballparks have routinely been used as sites for bolstering the cause for war. Nevertheless, baseball officials insist that such performances are *apolitical* and that they merely reaffirm baseball's role as a cultural institution. Speaking of his post-9/11 directive that all teams play "God Bless America" during the seventh-inning stretch, MLB Commissioner Bud Selig maintained, "I don't honestly think that politicizes the issue. After all, we do have troops in Iraq and Afghanistan."[4] Thus, the relationship between MLB and WBV should come as little surprise.

On the one hand, the aims of WBV are admirable. Thousands of Americans have returned from military service during the "war on terror" to substandard physical and mental health care. Many struggle to readjust to civilian life. Some turn to crime or even suicide. Thus, any program that might remedy some of these ill-effects of war merits praise. Yet on the other hand, MLB's involvement with WBV warrants a more critical attitude, as the 2008 promotional efforts serve as rhetorical cover for the shortcomings both of MLB and the U.S. government. In this chapter, I argue that the Welcome Back Veterans program is an expressly political initiative masked in apolitical language.

As a rhetorical critic, I examine the contradictions between MLB's statements and actions. In particular, I contend that the WBV program is problematic for at least three reasons. First, it positions MLB as a protector of the U.S. military even though it has spent much of the previous seven years as a leading advocate for George W. Bush's self-proclaimed "war on terror." Second, it offers services to veterans that should be provided by the U.S. government, thus short-circuiting more critical deliberations about the Bush administration's failure to "support the troops." Third, by conflating the Fourth of July holiday with the memorialization of September 11, it further reduces patriotism to militarism and, in the process, lends tacit consent to the perpetuation of the "war on terror."

Baseball and the Military

The central aim of rhetorical criticism is to examine the use of symbols by humans to induce cooperation among one another. Traditional forms of criticism primarily understand rhetoric as an instrument of persuasion. Thus, rhetorical scholarship is designed to reveal the effectiveness of persuasive appeals. In recent decades, however, rhetorical critics influenced by cultural and linguistic turns have taken a more constitutive view of rhetoric. In the words of Maurice Charland, constitutive rhetoric is the process by which a rhetorical expression "calls its audience into being."[5] From this view, rhetoric has ideological and political dimensions that require critical judgments. Moreover, these dimensions have the capacity to constitute audiences into particular ways of seeing the world. As Charland explains, "Ideological rhetorical practice is not restricted to explicitly political public address, but can include a range of aesthetic practices, including music, drama, architecture, and fashion, that elicit new modes of experience and being."[6] Similarly, sport should be understood in these terms. Indeed, the symbolic uses of sport are common resources in the rhetorical production of culture.

If sport contributes to the rhetorical construction of an audience, or what rhetorical critics would term "a people," [7] it does not necessarily do so in equal terms. What is required, then, is an approach to rhetorical criticism that attends to and critiques discourses of power. This approach is most commonly termed "critical rhetoric," which Raymie McKerrow defines as the attempt "to undermine and expose the discourse of power in order to thwart its effects in social relations."[8] Critical rhetoric does not apply a "method" in the strict sense; rather it cultivates an attitude toward critique that actively engages rhetoric's relationship to politics. In other words, it is primarily invested in seeking better, more *democratic* ways of living. This is especially relevant for the study of an institution like baseball, which celebrates its purported embodiment of democracy even as it maintains that it has no investment in politics. Thus, as Kenneth Burke insists, "Whenever you find a doctrine of 'nonpolitical' esthetics affirmed with fervor, look for its politics."[9]

It is not difficult, of course, to find the influence of politics throughout the history of Major League Baseball. As I have argued elsewhere, for example, the post-9/11 ritual performances of "God Bless America" were deeply political.[10] Far from providing a distraction from the developing "war on terror," such demonstrations of patriotic fervor offered constant reminders of the political exigencies in the United States. Moreover, the pervasiveness of these performances limited the range of democratic expression and effectively bolstered the aims of the Bush administration. Selig's claim that baseball was apolitical, therefore, was a diversion not from politics, but from the reality that MLB played a legitimizing role in the rhetorical production of the "war on terror."

Just as many attempt to divorce sport from politics, others will attempt to divorce politics from war. As a result, the history of baseball is rife with militaristic expressions and celebrations, most of which are masked in the language of "patriotism." Academics across multiple disciplines have acknowledged that sport and war are the metaphorical expressions of one another. Political scholar Michael Shapiro, for example, notes the intertextual relationship between sport and war that symbolizes international relations; historian Wanda Ellen Wakefield traces the development of an explicit relationship between sports and the American military; and sociologists Sue Curry Jansen and Don Sabo reveal the metaphorical slippage between the languages of sport and war.[11] These studies and others confirm the familiar axiom that war is politics by other means.

The rhetorical linkage between baseball and war dates back to the game's earliest days. Jules Tygiel explains, for instance, that as a "symbol of reunification" after the Civil War, baseball was hailed as a metaphor for community and democracy.[12] By the early twentieth century, baseball leaders promoted this metaphor through public ceremonies for American troops. During World War I, for example, major league owners provided servicemen with free tickets, sponsored military parades, urged fans to buy war bonds, and, in the American League, ordered players to participate in military drills.[13] The war also led to the now common tradition of paying tribute to fallen military heroes. The New York Giants dedicated a memorial at the Polo Grounds to Eddie Grant, and in 1921 the American League created "Hospital Day." The theme, "Lest we forget," was designed to honor war veterans.[14] Nearly a century later, baseball echoed this phrase when it memorialized 9/11 victims in 2002 by declaring, "We shall not forget."

It was World War II, however, that solidified the relationship between MLB and U.S. military efforts. Numerous major leaguers were drafted into service, and many expressed doubts about whether or not baseball games should be played during a time of war. When Commissioner Kenesaw Landis wrote to Franklin D. Roosevelt prior to the 1942 season, the president responded with his famous "Green Light Letter," in which he declared, "I honestly feel it would be best for the country to keep baseball going."[15] The symbolic importance of baseball was summarized in a letter to FDR that stated, "Don't let Hitler kill baseball. Baseball is essential to our country's victory. The soldiers want it, defense workers need it. Need we say more?"[16]

Decades later, politicians attempted to use baseball to smooth over more controversial military efforts such as the war in Vietnam. By the late 1960s, explains Ron Briley, MLB sent prominent players to boost morale in Southeast Asia. During one such trip in 1969, Ernie Banks declared, "While you can take American boys out of the United States, you can never take baseball out of an American boy."[17] In 1973, President Richard Nixon insisted that freed prisoners of war should throw out ceremonial first pitches at major league openers.[18] Thus, when Bud Selig declared in 2003, "I'm very proud of the role baseball played after 9/11 and through the World Series. It was magnificent. And I believe strongly that in its own way, baseball will be good for our country [during the war in Iraq]," he was invoking a familiar tradition in which the national pastime is perceived as a symbol of unity and democratic strength.[19]

During the "war on terror," MLB and its franchises sponsored efforts to express support of American military personnel. From "Military Appreciation Day" to September 11 anniversary memorials, major league ballparks became sites for public affirmations of the U.S. Armed Forces. In the context of an ongoing war, the rhetoric of "support the troops" easily slips into a rhetoric of "support the war." Nevertheless, ballplayers willing to speak on the issue typically reproduced the attempt to separate the two. As pitcher Braden Looper said in 2003, "We need to support our troops, no matter if you're for [the war] or against it."[20] None of this is to suggest that everyone involved in baseball favors war, or that one cannot be both a baseball fan and an opponent of war. Moreover, even when baseball lends its overt or tacit support to military causes, there is no guarantee that such efforts will translate to greater support for war among the American public. Nevertheless, MLB's allegiance to the American military is cause for concern, especially in the context of the "war on terror." By 2008, U.S. troops had been in Iraq for over five years, and public support for the war had reached new lows. An opinion poll released shortly after the five-year anniversary of the Iraqi invasion revealed that 63 percent of Americans believed the war to be a mistake.[21] At the same time, Americans were coming to terms with startling statistics: over 4,000 dead, tens of thousands wounded, and more than half a trillion dollars spent.[22]

Welcome Back Veterans

In his history of the American military, Michael Sherry writes, "War created the United States."[23] Such a stark declaration may seem contradictory for a nation that purports to favor democracy, freedom, and peace. However, the very essence of American identity has often been equated if not directly with war, then indirectly with a culture of militarism. Cecilia O'Leary argues that the origins of this equation can be found in the years between the Civil War and World War, a period during which American patriotism was bound to the memorialization of war and military heroes. In addition, patriotic expression was condensed to visible symbols such as the American flag. "Consecrated in the blood of battle," notes O'Leary, "soldiers and citizens alike began to look at the Stars and Stripes as the symbolic repository of their patriotic sentiments."[24] In the decades since, the flag has become the "totem" of American nationalism, what Carolyn Marvin and David Ingle describe as the embodiment of the "shared memory of blood sacrifice."[25]

Thus, if patriotic displays are rhetorical expressions that depend on war and the military, then it should come as little surprise that the years since 9/11 have so dramatically featured war-based themes. Numerous critics have noted that the militarism already entrenched in the United States has only intensified during the "war on terror."[26] What makes this especially problematic is that the manifestations of war are so fully woven into the daily fabric of American life that they are nearly impossible to see. As Robert Ivie explains:

> War is ritualistically memorialized in any number of public media from carefully staged and regularly televised presidential encomiums to towering statues in central parks of capital cities throughout the land, patriotic performances in baseball stadiums, fulsome coffee-table books, glamorizing Hollywood films, stirring popular music, and awe-inspiring displays of weaponry in war museums.[27]

Much of this militaristic rhetoric is presented through the ubiquity of yellow ribbons and the common use of the phrase "support the troops." Marita Sturken explains that the yellow ribbon had once been used by both supporters and opponents of war. During the Persian Gulf War of 1991, however, spectacles such as Super Bowl XXV reconstituted its meaning. She argues, "The yellow ribbon was transformed from a personal expression into an avowal of faith in the imagined national community, a means by which consent was created, and a symbol of America's renewed confidence in its role as a world power."[28] Douglas Kellner adds that these expressions, alongside declarations to "support the troops" and chants of "USA," promote a form of "empty patriotism."[29] It is clear, however, that for millions of Americans, these symbols have material significance. As a consequence, as Robert Jensen suggests, the insistence to "support the troops" may as well be synonymous with "support the war."[30]

Commercial sports in the United States have been a prominent site for extending the "support the troops" rhetoric. In addition to the baseball rituals noted earlier in this essay, sports fans have witnessed near-constant tributes to the U.S. Armed Forces through military appreciation events, increased recruitment efforts through new television advertisements, prominent displays on NASCAR vehicles, elaborate ceremonies at arenas and stadiums, and even newly named events that feature the military, such as the Bell Helicopter Armed Forces Bowl. Taken individually, these moments can easily be described as patriotic and admirable. Collectively, however, they constitute an audience of spectators who are hailed as patriotic citizens *only* through their unquestioned support of the U.S. military.

Because of its history, and because it has the benefit of being played every day during its season, baseball is arguably the sport most suited for the rhetorical performances of patriotism and militarism that have been prominent during the "war on terror." In addition to formal rituals organized by MLB, individual players have aligned themselves with patriotic causes. In 2005, for example, pitcher Barry Zito founded Strikeouts for Troops, an organization designed to raise money for wounded veterans.[31] In 2007, three players from the Washington Nationals toured the Pentagon. Of the troops, pitcher Chad Cordero said, "They're out there maintaining our freedom. They're out there making sure we still have all of our rights that we know and love."[32] Then, the "Heroes of the Diamond Tour" sent four retired MLB players to Bagram Air Base in Afghanistan. In the words of former pitcher Mike Remlinger, "We wanted to come and show how much we support [the troops]."[33] Much good surely has resulted from these efforts. However, as evidenced by Cordero's comments about "maintaining freedom," such initiatives offer support for the people of the U.S. Armed Forces without raising any questions about the mission for which the troops are being given support. Moreover, through repeated declarations that supporting the troops has nothing to do with politics, these programs lent tacit support to the war effort itself. Meanwhile, if there were major league players involved with anti-war movements, they went unreported by the mainstream media.[34]

On June 23, 2008, Major League Baseball announced that it would add to this support of the military through the organization Welcome Back Veterans. In the words of Commissioner Selig, "Major League Baseball also has a long and proud history of supporting our troops. For generations Baseball has undertaken patriotic activities to acknowledge veterans and current members of the military who serve and have served our country."[35] Originally conceived of by New York Mets Chairman and CEO Fred Wilpon, the aim of WBV is to raise $100 million and provide 100,000 jobs to veterans returning from Afghanistan and Iraq. Wilpon argues there is a need to "tell all Americans that we're not sharing in the sacrifice of our armed forces. We should all realize that. They're burdened with the sacrifice — although they don't call it a burden — for our freedom and our way of life."[36] Like many others, then, Wilpon defines all military service as *necessarily* a contribution to freedom and democracy. Such a perspective contributes to the erasure of the more questionable actions taken during the "war on terror."

The June 23 announcement also included appearances and statements from high-profile players. David Wright of the New York Mets stated, "We as players are extremely proud ... to represent and pay our respects to our returning veterans." Added New York Yankees outfielder Johnny Damon, "When it comes to supporting our troops, everyone in Major League Baseball is on the same team."[37] Although Damon is credited with this statement, it appears to be official language used by MLB. Evidence of this is found elsewhere on the Welcome Back Veterans website, where Wright is quoted as saying, "This is a cause that transcends everything, so I encourage all baseball fans to join us over July 4th weekend and on September 11 in supporting Welcome Back Veterans. *When it comes to supporting our troops, everyone in Major League Baseball is on the same team.*"[38] The notion that everyone is on the "same team" only reinforces my contention that "support the troops" programs, while not overt endorsements of war, serve to endorse the war effort by closing off the possibility for dissent. The rhetorical relationship between sport and the military provides a persuasive metaphor for citizenship. Good fans are loyal and support their team (win or lose). Similarly, good citizens are patriotic and support their country (right or wrong). In a political culture constituted by George W. Bush's demand, "You are either with us or you are with the terrorists,"[39] who could wish to be on the wrong team? Thus, the language used to introduce Welcome Back Veterans constitutes baseball fans and observers as political subjects who must be prepared to choose sides.

Very few fans were likely to have seen MLB's announcement or to have read any of Wright's or Damon's comments. They were extremely likely, however, to watch baseball on the Fourth of July, a holiday almost synonymous with the national pastime. Accordingly, MLB made the holiday weekend a showcase for the charity. The most visible component was the special caps containing the colors of the American flag. In addition to being worn by major leaguers during the games, fans were able to purchase their own caps produced by New Era and available on MLB team websites. Originally, MLB officials announced that a portion of the proceeds would go to WBV. Paul Lukas, author of the sports blog *Uni Watch*, asked during a press conference what percentage of sales would go to charity during an MLB press conference. As he reports:

> The reason I ask is that some fans—including many who have already expressed their opinions to me as news of this initiative leaked out over the weekend—may view this program as just another merchandising program to move product and generate revenue. So what portion of the cap proceeds will go to the charity? And if it's not 100 percent, why not?

According to Lukas, MLB Public Relations head Rich Levin responded tersely, "The answer is that it hasn't been determined yet. This is a charity initiative—it isn't about generating revenue."[40] Ultimately, MLB determined that 100 percent of the revenues would go directly to WBV.

It was not unreasonable to question MLB's promotional motives. In recent years, corporations in the United States have increasingly used social causes as a means for improving their images and boosting their sales. Samantha King describes the phenomenon as "cause-related marketing," which occurs when a corporation "packages generosity as a lifestyle choice through which individuals can attain self-actualization and self-realization" by knowing that a portion of their purchase will help a worthy charity. Among the examples featured in her book, *Pink Ribbons, Inc.*, is the 1999 campaign by the National Football League to raise awareness for the importance of the early detection of breast cancer.[41] As King reveals, the NFL's alliance with the Susan G. Komen Breast Cancer Foundation developed in the wake of a survey that discovered 40 percent of the league's weekly television viewers were women. Thus, even as NFL officials were surely interested in helping women stay healthy in general, they were specifically interested in keeping them healthy so they could continue to watch football.

The NFL is far from the only organization involved in breast cancer philanthropy. Indeed, as Phaedra Pezzullo explains, there is a fully developed industry which is dedicated to the cause of early detection. The pioneer of this industry is the pharmaceutical company AstraZeneca, the creators of National Breast Cancer Awareness Month. Although Pezzullo acknowledges the benefits of informing women about the benefits of early detection, she objects to a rhetorical strategy that focuses only on the cure, not the cause, of breast cancer. In particular, she critiques AstraZeneca because it contributes to the environmental causes of breast cancer by using certain toxins and it profits from treating breast cancer patients through production of the medication Nolvadex. As Pezzullo summarizes, "AstraZeneca has profited from the entire cancer cycle from cause to detection to treatment."[42]

To a degree, Major League Baseball is guilty of using a similar strategy. In the aftermath of 9/11, the "national pastime" was routinely used as a rhetorical resource to cultivate support for the "war on terror." Particularly problematic has been MLB's endorsement of the war in Iraq. Years after the 2003 invasion, considerable evidence makes it clear that the war has been waged under at best faulty, and at worst false, pretenses.[43] Nevertheless, baseball's support for the military has only grown. Programs such as Welcome Back Veterans certainly provide much needed help for military personnel struggling to return to civilian life. However, the language used to celebrate the cause fails to account for how these men and women were wounded and scarred in the first place. Thus, MLB has created a charity designed to assist those whom it helped send into a highly questionable war. One might ask then, if major league officials are so interested in the health of the U.S. Armed Forces, why have they so eagerly acquiesced to the aims of the Bush administration, even in the face of mounting evidence that the war has been disastrous?

Welcome Back Veterans does not ask such questions. Instead, it features ritualistic displays of patriotism that make it all too easy for observers to dissociate the charity from the war. In addition to the star-spangled caps, MLB installed numerous ceremonies both over the July 4 weekend and on September 11. Veterans were invited to throw out ceremonial first pitches. "Welcome Back Veterans" was displayed prominently in all ballparks. In Cincinnati, all veterans were admitted without admission; in Philadelphia, a giant American flag was displayed along with flags for each of the fifty states and P.O.W. flags; and in Atlanta, an Iraq Army veteran served as an honorary captain as the stadium presented a "Salute to America Fireworks Spectacular." Of the elaborate festivities, Mark Newman declared, "It's not a war rally or demonstration, it's a tangible way of starting to really help those who are going to need it — returning troops and their families."[44]

As I have made clear thus far, in contrast to Newman's insistence, it is reasonable to view such ceremonies as an endorsement of the war. Yet if a first concern with Welcome Back Veterans is that it dissuades fans from questioning MLB's own support of the "war on terror," then a second concern is that it similarly distracts those fans from the failures of the Bush administration. By the time WBV was introduced in the summer of 2008, the U.S. military had been pushed to unreasonable limits. Despite a decline in enlistments and an increased number of troops who had fulfilled their commitment, Bush insisted on a "troop surge" policy in late 2007 and early 2008 that required extended tours of duty. In previous years, the administration exercised a "stop-loss" policy which enabled the military to retain personnel beyond their original enlistment period.[45] Meanwhile, inadequate equipment limited the armed forces in Iraq and benefits were reduced for veterans back in the United States.[46]

Although each of these decisions raises questions about the U.S. government's treatment of its military personnel, the most egregious case is surely the scandal at Walter Reed Army Medical Center. Some of the most seriously wounded soldiers from the wars in Afghanistan and Iraq were sent to the hospital to recover from their injuries. In many cases, they were greeted by bureaucratic inefficiencies, insufficient medical staff, and unsanitary conditions.[47] President Bush and those in charge at Walter Reed faced fierce criticism, especially in light of the consistent refrain of "support the troops." Army Secretary Francis Harvey ultimately resigned, and the neglect of so many veterans of the "war on terror" served to undermine the credibility of the presidential administration. Remarkably, however, despite embarrassments such as Walter Reed or the prison abuse scandal of Abu Ghraib,[48] and despite revelations that the administration inflated or invented the details in the "heroic" cases of Jessica Lynch and Pat Tillman,[49] few have been able to hold the president accountable for the overuse and exploitation of the U.S.

Armed Forces. Thus, each time an organization like Welcome Back Veterans raises awareness and money on behalf of the military it deflects even more attention away from those who should bear the burden of providing benefits to veterans.

A final concern of the MLB-WBV relationship is the conflation of veterans with the victims of September 11. As noted above, major league ballparks featured militaristic ceremonies on the anniversary of the terrorist attacks. I should note that I do not object to memorializing those who were killed on 9/11. However, it is fair to point out that the nearly 3,000 who lost their lives in New York, Washington, D.C., and Pennsylvania were not necessarily *veterans*. Thus, by using 9/11 to spotlight the charity, MLB equated the victims of terrorism with those veterans who have been charged with fighting against it. In this way, 9/11 becomes a distinctly *militarized* occasion. Indeed, it becomes the very moment that precipitated and thus *continues to justify* the ongoing "war on terror." I argue, therefore, that by spotlighting the relationship between 9/11 and the military, Major League Baseball and Welcome Back Veterans have constituted an attitude toward contemporary politics that supports veterans even as it continues to support the cause for war.

Coming Home

Given the rhetorical consonance between the Bush administration and Major League Baseball, it is likely that military expressions will continue at ballparks around the country throughout the duration of the "war on terror." Even should that conflict come to an end, there is little in baseball's history to suggest that militarism will end with it. The rhetorical analysis in the preceding pages should not be read as an attempt to assign malice to the leaders of MLB. Nor is it to suggest that patriotic performances or ceremonies that honor the military are always or necessarily misguided. However, when such displays become excessive, and I contend that in the years since 9/11 they have been so, or when they become disingenuous expressions in favor of war, fans and scholars alike should resist the politicization of the "national pastime."

In the case of Welcome Back Veterans, the rhetorical strategies used by the league's representatives run the risk of overlooking MLB's complicity with the start and continuation of the war. Moreover, by shifting attention away from the government's responsibility to provide basic care for its veterans, WBV helps the president in his rhetorical effort to "support the troops" even as he denies important material benefits. Finally, the conflation of the Fourth of July with September 11 erases important differences between the

U.S. Armed Forces and the victims of 9/11, thus contributing to an increasingly militarized culture. Alongside these rhetorical consequences, MLB enjoys the public relations benefits of "cause-related marketing."

As a baseball fan, I have learned to expect patriotic performances and military spectacles at major league games. Yet as a rhetorical critic, I am committed to examining the political significance of these rituals. In particular, the Welcome Back Veterans program and marketing campaign are problematic both for what they do and for what they do not do. Viewed as a rhetorical text, the charity campaign constitutes audiences in terms that are favorable toward war. Moreover, consistent with baseball's attitude since 9/11, no dissent from war is imagined, especially since with regard to the troops, everyone is supposed to be "on the same team." Meanwhile, in the official public service announcement and the promotional materials on its website, WBV emphasizes the baseball-inspired trope of "home." As one soldier sincerely describes, being in combat is not so much about politics and warfare. "I just wanted to get home," he said.[50] Here, then, is the chief failure of Major League Baseball and Welcome Back Veterans. For while the charity may help many soldiers readjust to home, it fails to ask how and why they ever had to leave in the first place.

Notes

1. Quoted in "Major Leaguers Tour Pentagon," Regulatory Intelligence Data, July 30, 2007.
2. The Welcome Back Veterans website, <http://web.welcomebackveterans.org>.
3. Harold Seymour, *Baseball: The Early Years* (New York: Oxford University Press, 1989), 49.
4. Quoted in William C. Rhoden, "Delgado Makes a Stand by Taking a Seat," *New York Times*, July 21, 2004.
5. Maurice Charland, "Constitutive Rhetoric: The Case of the Peuple Québécois," *Quarterly Journal of Speech*, 73 (1987): 134.
6. Ibid.
7. Michael C. McGee, "In Search of 'The People': A Rhetorical Alternative," *Quarterly Journal of Speech*, 61 (1975): 235–249.
8. Raymie E. McKerrow, "Critical Rhetoric: Theory and Praxis," *Communication Monographs*, 56 (1989): 98.
9. Kenneth Burke, *A Rhetoric of Motives* (Berkeley: University of California Press, 1969), 28.
10. Michael L. Butterworth, "Ritual in the 'Church of Baseball': Suppressing the Discourse of Democracy after 9/11," *Communication and Critical/Cultural Studies*, 2 (June 2005): 107–129.
11. Michael J. Shapiro, "Representing World Politics: The Sport/War Intertext," in *International/Intertextual Relations: Postmodern Readings of World Politics*, eds. James Der Derian and Michael J. Shapiro (Lexington, MA: Lexington Books, 1989), 69–96; Wanda Ellen Wakefield, *Playing to Win: Sports and the American Military, 1898–1945* (Albany: State University of New York Press, 1997); and Sue Curry Jansen and Don Sabo, "The Sport/War Metaphor: Hegemonic Masculinity, the Persian Gulf War, and the New World Order," *Sociology of Sport Journal*, 11 (1994): 1–17.
12. Jules Tygiel, *Past Time: Baseball as History* (Oxford: Oxford University Press, 2000), 13.
13. Benjamin G. Rader, *Baseball: A History of America's Game*, 2d ed. (Urbana: University of Illinois Press, 2002), 124.
14. Richard C. Crepeau, *Baseball: America's Diamond Mind 1919–1941* (Orlando: University Presses of Florida, 1980), 3.
15. Quoted in John Odell, ed., *Baseball as America: Seeing Ourselves through Our National Game* (Washington, D.C.: National Geographic, 2002), 60.

16. Quoted in Ron Briley, *Class at Bat, Gender on Deck and Race in the Hole: A Line-Up of Essays on Twentieth Century Culture and America's Game* (Jefferson, NC: McFarland, 2003), 33.
17. Ibid.
18. David Q. Voigt, *America through Baseball* (Chicago: Nelson-Hall, 1976).
19. Mike Klis, "Baseball Must Go On During Trying Times," *Denver Post*, March 30, 2003, C13.
20. Quoted in Joe Capozzi, "Marlins, Astros Support Bush," *Palm Beach Post*, March 19, 2003.
21. Susan Page, "Disapproval of Bush Breaks Record," *USA Today*, April 22, 2008, available at <http://www.usatoday.com/news/washington/2008-04-21-bushrating_N.htm>.
22. Sholnn Freeman, "U.S. Deaths in Iraq War Reach 4,000," *Washington Post*, March 24, 2008; Bryan Bender, "Cost of Iraq War Nearly $2 Billion a Week," *Boston Globe*, September 28, 2006, available at <http://www.boston.com/news/world/middleeast/articles/2006/09/28/cost_of_iraq_war_nearly_2b_a_week/>.
23. Michael S. Sherry, *In the Shadow of War: The United States Since the 1930s* (New Haven: Yale University Press, 1995), 1.
24. Cecilia Elizabeth O'Leary, *To Die For: The Paradox of American Patriotism* (Princeton: Princeton University Press, 1999), 22.
25. Carolyn Marvin and David W. Ingle, *Blood Sacrifice and the Nation: Totem Rituals and the American Flag* (Cambridge, UK: Cambridge University Press, 1999), 4.
26. For examples, see Andrew J. Bacevich, *The New American Militarism: How Americans Are Seduced by War* (Oxford: Oxford University Press, 2005); Chalmers Johnson, *The Sorrows of Empire: Militarism, Secrecy, and the End of the Republic* (New York: Metropolitan Books, 2004); and Nick Turse, *The Complex: How the Military Invades Our Everyday Lives* (New York: Metropolitan Books, 2008).
27. Robert L. Ivie, *Dissent from War* (Bloomfield, CT: Kumarian Press, 2007), 77.
28. Marita Sturken, *Tangled Memories: The Vietnam War, the AIDS Epidemic, and the Politics of Remembering* (Berkeley: University of California Press, 1997), 141.
29. Douglas Kellner, *The Persian Gulf TV War* (Boulder, CO: Westview Press, 1992), 256.
30. Robert Jensen, *Citizens of the Empire: The Struggle to Claim Our Humanity* (San Francisco: City Lights Books, 2004), 19–35.
31. More information is available at <http://www.strikeoutsfortroops.org/index.htm>.
32. Quoted in "Major Leaguers Tour Pentagon."
33. Quoted in "Retired Baseball Players Visit Troops in Afghanistan," *U.S. Fed News*, May 16, 2008, available at <http://web.lexisnexis.com/universe>.
34. I refer here to anti-war activism outside of the ballpark. Baseball fans will recall that Carlos Delgado protested the seventh-inning stretch performances of "God Bless America" during the 2004 and 2005 seasons. He agreed to participate in the ritual after signing a free agent contract with the New York Mets before the 2006 season. For more on his protest, see Rhoden.
35. "Message from Bud Selig," available at <http://web.welcomebackveterans.org/article/bud_selig.jsp>.
36. Quoted in Mark Newman, "MLB Announces Nationwide Initiative," available at <http://web.welcomebackveterans.org/article/halstead.jsp>.
37. Ibid.
38. Quoted in "Major League Baseball Launches National Campaign for 'Welcome Back Veterans,' in Support of Returning American Veterans, Over July 4th Weekend," June 23, 2008, available at <http://web.welcomebackveterans.org/article/press_release_06232008.jsp>.
39. George W. Bush, "Statement By the President in His Address to the Nation," White House Press Release, September 11, 2001, available at <http://www.whitehouse.gov/news/releases/2001/09/20010911-16.html>.
40. Quoted in Paul Lukas, "Cat(alog) Scans," *Uni Watch*, June 24, 2008, available at <http://www.uniwatchblog.com/2008/06/24/catalog-scans/>.
41. Samantha King, *Pink Ribbons, Inc.: Breast Cancer and the Politics of Philanthropy* (Minneapolis: University of Minnesota Press, 2006), 15–23.
42. Phaedra C. Pezzullo, "Resisting 'National Breast Cancer Awareness Month': The Rhetoric of Counterpublics and their Cultural Performances," *Quarterly Journal of Speech*, 89 (November 2003): 353.
43. There are far too many sources that detail the deceptions that enabled the war in Iraq. For a particularly good rhetorical analysis, see Stephen J. Hartnett and Laura A. Stengrim, *Globalization and Empire: The U.S. Invasion of Iraq, Free Markets, and the Twilight of Democ-*

racy (Tuscaloosa: University of Alabama Press, 2006).

44. Mark Newman, "July 4th Weekend Events in MLB Stadiums," available at <http://web.welcomebackveterans.org/article/july4.jsp>.

45. For more on this, see Monica Davey, "8 Soldiers Sue Over Army's Stop-Loss Policy," *New York Times*, December 6, 2004, available at <http://www.nytimes.com/2004/12/06/national/06soldiers.html?_r=1&ei=5006&en=15ff21cb12d1c9d4&ex=1103000400&adxnnl=1&oref=slogin&partner=ALTAVISTA1&adxnnlx=1215767427-4z1K8+w5V6NkW9KbNwePGA>.

46. For more on this, see Dave Lindorff, "Dishonorable Discharge: Bush Administration Slashes Veteran's Benefits," *In These Times*, November 26, 2003, available at <http://inthesetimes.com/comments.php?id=465_0_2_0_C>.

47. For more on this, see Dana Priest and Anne Hull, "Soldiers Face Neglect, Frustration at Army's Top Medical Facility," *Washington Post*, February 18, 2007, available at <http://www.washingtonpost.com/wp-dyn/content/article/2007/02/17/AR2007021701172.html>.

48. See Seymour M. Hersh, "Torture at Abu Ghraib," *The New Yorker*, May 10, 2004, available at <http://www.newyorker.com/archive/2004/05/10/040510fa_fact>.

49. Glenn Greenwald, "The Pat Tillman and Jessica Lynch Frauds," *Salon.com*, April 25, 2007, available at <http://www.salon.com/opinion/greenwald/2007/04/25/tillman_lynch/>.

50. The PSA is available at <http://web.welcomebackveterans.org/index.jsp>.

About the Contributors

Lisa Doris Alexander is an assistant professor of Africana studies at Wayne State University in Detroit. Her research focuses on race, class, gender, and sexuality in baseball.

Mathew J. Bartkowiak is an assistant professor of English at the University of Wisconsin–Marshfield/Wood County. He is an editorial advisory board member for the *Journal of Popular Culture*. His areas of focus are popular culture studies, popular music, social change and development, the 1960s counterculture, and, as of late, the literature of sport. He is the author of *The MC5 and Social Change: A Study in Rock and Revolution* (McFarland, 2009) and editor of *Sounds of the Future: Essays on Music in Science Fiction Film* (McFarland, 2010).

Ron Briley is a history teacher and assistant headmaster at Sandia Preparatory School in Albuquerque, New Mexico, where he has taught for thirty-two years. He is the author of *Class at Bat, Gender on Deck and Race in the Hole* (McFarland, 2003) and co-editor *of James T. Farrell's Dreaming Baseball* (Kent State University Press, 2007) and *All-Stars and Movie Stars* (University Press of Kentucky, 2008).

Michael L. Butterworth is an assistant professor and associate director in the School of Communication Studies at Bowling Green State University in Bowling Green, Ohio. His work focuses on the overlapping emphasis on contestation found in rhetoric, politics, and sport. His book *Baseball and Rhetorics of Purity: The National Pastime and American Identity During the War on Terror* is forthcoming. His scholarship can be found in *Communication and Critical/Cultural Studies*, *Communication Studies*, *Critical Studies in Media Communication*, the *Western Journal of Communication*, and the *Journal of Sport and Social Issues*.

Russ Crawford is an assistant professor of history at Ohio Northern University in Ada. He taught high school social studies and coached football in South Dakota for five years and taught high school Spanish and coached wrestling and football in Iowa for three years before earning a Ph.D. at the University of Nebraska–Lincoln in 2005. He has contributed numerous book reviews and encyclopedia entries on sport history, and in 2008 published *The Use of Sports to Promote the American Way of Life During the Cold War: Cultural Propaganda, 1946–1963* (Edwin

Mellen Press). Among the classes he teaches at Ohio Northern are 20th century American sports, baseball in American culture, and football in American culture.

Glen M.E. Duerr is a Ph.D. candidate in the Department of Political Science at Kent State University. He has recently published in *CEU Political Science Journal* and *Carte Italiane* in addition to encyclopedia entries on sport and politics. His major research interests, broadly speaking, include nationalism and sport in North America, Europe, and Asia.

N. Jeremi Duru is an associate professor at Temple University's James E. Beasley School of Law. In a joint-degree program at Harvard University, he received in 1999 a master's degree in public policy from the John F. Kennedy School of Government and a J.D. from Harvard Law School, and then served as a law clerk to the Honorable Damon J. Keith of the United States Court of Appeals for the Sixth Circuit. Much of his work involves challenges to discriminatory employment practices in professional athletics. The National Bar Association honored him with its 2005 Entertainment and Sports Lawyer of the Year award. In 2008 he was recognized as Temple Law School's Outstanding Professor of the Year.

Robert Elias is a professor of politics and chair of legal studies at the University of San Francisco, where he teaches the course "Law, Politics and the National Pastime." His baseball writing has appeared in *Nine: A Journal of Baseball History and Culture*, the *Exquisite Corpse*, the *Minneapolis Review of Baseball*, the *Berkeley Voice*, the *Big Bad Baseball Annual*, the *USF Magazine*, and the *Christian Science Monitor*. He is the author of eight books, including the baseball mystery novel *The Deadly Tools of Ignorance* (Rounder), *Baseball and the American Dream* (M.E. Sharpe), and his latest, on baseball and U.S. foreign policy, *The Empire Strikes Out* (New Press).

Robert Engvall, a professor of justice studies at Roger Williams University, Bristol, Rhode Island, holds Ph.D. and J.D. degrees from the University of Iowa. His research interests focus upon various marginalization and social justice issues within higher education. He has presented papers at numerous academic conferences on topics ranging from public-sector unionization to parental involvement in public schools. He has written three books and several articles and book chapters on similar topics.

Joshua Fleer is a Ph.D. student in American religious history at Florida State University. He has written and presented on baseball and religion with articles and reviews appearing in such publications as *Nine: A Journal of Baseball History and Culture* and *The Journal of Popular Culture*. His essay in the present work grew out of a concept originated in his M.A. thesis at Pepperdine, and a working version of it was presented at the Nineteenth Cooperstown Symposium on Baseball and American Culture, 2007.

Michael J. Haupert is a professor of economics at the University of Wisconsin–La Crosse. He has written extensively on the financial history of professional baseball teams both in the major leagues and the Negro Leagues. He is currently working on a book on the labor history of baseball.

Yuya Kiuchi obtained his Ph.D. in American studies at Michigan State University. His dissertation, "The Black Image in the Black Mind: The History of African Americans' Access to Cable Television in Boston and Detroit, 1963–1989," reflects his research interests in black representation in media and African American community building, identity formation, and empowerment. He has translated six books from English into Japanese, including Barack Obama's first autobiography, *Dreams from My Father.*

Wendy Knickerbocker is an independent scholar in American cultural history. She became interested in Billy Sunday as an undergraduate in the American Studies program at Colby College, and is the author of *Sunday at the Ballpark: Billy Sunday's Professional Baseball Career, 1883–1890* (Scarecrow Press, 2000). She was an academic librarian for twenty years, and now she is a writer, indexer, and cataloger living in Castine, Maine, who lives and dies with the Boston Red Sox.

Robert F. Lewis, hooked on baseball since player-manager Lou Boudreau led the Cleveland Indians to its last World Series victory in 1948, continues as an ardent fan of the Athletics, Boudreau's last American League stop. Following a thirty-five year career in "corporate America," Bob returned to school and earned a doctorate in American studies at the University of New Mexico. A modified version of his dissertation, "Smart Ball: Marketing the Myth and Managing the Reality in Major League Baseball," is forthcoming as a book.

Scott D. Peterson is a lecturer and a Ph.D. candidate in American literature and culture at the University of Maine. His scholarship has appeared in a recent volume of *Baseball/Literature/Culture* (McFarland, 2008). Until a few short years ago, his conversion from Cubs to Red Sox fan was very much a lateral move.

Bryan C. Price is a Ph.D. candidate in the Political Science Department at Stanford University and an active duty officer in the U.S. Army. As a baseball team captain and U.S. history major at the U.S. Military Academy at West Point, he combined two of his passions—baseball and history—to complete his senior thesis on baseball's influence on politics and the homefront during and after World War II.

Raymond I. Schuck is an instructor in the Department of Interpersonal Communication in the School of Communication Studies at Bowling Green State University. His research focuses primarily on critical and rhetorical analysis of popular culture, with particular emphasis on the cultural meaning and significance of sport.

Jessica Skolnikoff, an associate professor of anthropology at Roger Williams University, Bristol, Rhode Island, received her Ph.D. degree from American University in Washington, D.C. Her research interests focus upon youth and physical activity level, the role that sports play within the lives of college students, and marginalization issues for individuals with learning disabilities. She has presented papers at numerous conferences on topics ranging from physical education, social justice, and learning disabilities within educational settings to the impact of high stakes testing upon individuals with learning disabilities.

John A. Tures is an associate professor of political science at LaGrange College, the oldest liberal arts college in Georgia. In addition to frequently attending Atlanta Braves baseball games, he has published articles in twenty journals on such subjects as international politics, Middle East conflicts, East European politics, economic development, public opinion, and the War of 1812. He publishes a weekly column in the *LaGrange Daily News* and *Southern Political Report.*

Index

Aaron, Hank 20, 87
Abele, Homer "Pete" 14–15
Albuquerque Dukes 16
Aldredge, Victor 11
All-Star game 201
Altamirano, Porfi 162
Alyea, Brant 169n41
Amaechi, John 77
American Baseball Guild 200
American Dream 118–20, 157, 158, 166–67, 179
American National Baseball Congress (NBC) 151–53
Anson, Adrian Constantine "Cap" 9–10, 26–27
antitrust exemption 196, 200, 208
Arce, Bill 148–49, 155n7
Arroyo, Bronson 221
assimilation 4–5, 126–27, 177, 179
Atlantics 126–27
Ausmus, Brad 3, 72

Baker, Dusty 163
Baker, Frank "Home Run" 34
Banks, Ernie 87, 229–30
Barricada 162
baseball academies 5, 172, 173–74, 177–81
baseball cards 10
Baseball Federation of Asia 189
Baseball for Peace tour 163–64
Baseball Hall of Fame 9, 157, 201
baseball writing 42–43, 51–54
Bean, Billy 71–72, 74
Bellan, Esteban 138
Bennett, Charlie 34
Berg, Moe 53, 134
Birmingham Barons 84, 91
Bishop, Cecil "Runt" 11
Black Codes 104
Black Sox scandal 41, 198
Blue Ribbon Panel 208

Boers 158
Bolack, Thomas "Tom" 16
Borges, Tomas 162
Borghese, Prince Steno 147
Boston Beaneaters 11
Boston Red Sox 100–102, 212, 213
Boyd, Bob 87
Brooklyn Dodgers 57–58, 61–63, 69n19, 101
Brown, Bobby 85
Brown, Fred 11
Brown, Pat 58
Bulkeley, Morgan 10
bullfighting 137–38
Bunning, Jim 13
Bush, President George H.W. 164
Bush, President George W. 16, 141, 196, 233, 235–36
Butler, Gen. Smedley 159

California 16
Campanella, Roy 87, 90
Campaneris, Bert 160
Campbell, Charles M. 15
Cannon, Raymond J. 11, 47
Canseco, Jose 209
capitalism 46, 51, 177, 212–24
Cardenal, Ernesto 161
Carter, President Jimmy 161
Cass Baseball Club 12
Castro, Fidel 138
CBA *see* Collective Bargaining Agreement
Cedeno, Cesar 159
Chadwick, Henry 39–40, 129
Chamorro, Violeta 165
Chandler, Albert B. "Happy" 16, 197, 199–200
Chapman, J. Wilbur 29
Chevez, Tony 160
Chicago Cubs 15, 178, 207, 226
Chicago University 131–32
Chicago White Sox 226

245

Chicago White Stockings 9, 128
Chichigalpa ballpark 163
China 148, 184, 187–89
Chinese Taipei 189, 191
Cincinnati Buckeyes 100
Cincinnati Reds 226
civil religion 4, 111–13, 119, 145, 180–81
Civil Rights Act of 1866 104
Civil Rights Act of 1964 83
class 49–50, 126–27
Clemente, Roberto 160, 163, 164–65, 172–73
Cleveland Indians 101
Clinton, Hillary 59
Clinton, President Bill 208
Cobb, Ty 120n1, 199
Cochrane, Mickey 121n10
Collective Bargaining Agreement (CBA) 204, 206, 208
colonialism 5, 176–77; see also imperialism
Comerica Park 111, 112–13
commissioners 2, 16, 72, 197–200, 202
Communism 12, 43–45, 144, 148, 154, 184
Connecticut 10
Conner, Martin Sennett "Mike" 12
contracts 87–91, 92, 218
Contras 161–65, 168n26
Convention of Kanagawa 129
Cookson, Capt. Charles 152
Cordero, Chad 232
Crawford, Sam 121n10
cricket 127–28
Cronin, Joe 50, 53, 101
Crowe, George 87
Cuba 5, 134–39, 160, 167, 209
culture: American and Japanese 222–23; assimilation 4–5, 126–27, 177, 179; capitalism 213–24; cultural capital 59–63; and identity 58, 60, 65–68, 171, 179–80, 185; imperialism 175; MLB in Japan 221; myth 41–43, 54–55, 113, 116–18, 128–29; Nicaraguan 162, 166–67; socialization and performance 171, 175–76, 179; values and beliefs 67, 157, 158; war rhetoric 230–33, 236–37
Curt Flood Act of 1998 196, 203, 208
Czechoslovakia 149, 154

Daily Worker 38
daimyos 129
Daisies 84
Damon, Johnny 78–79, 233
Dantos Sports Factory 162
Davis, Eric 74
Dawson Pact 158
Dean, Jay Hanna "Dizzy" 45, 46
Dean, Paul 53
Delaware 15
democracy 142–45, 154
Detroit race riots 113–16
Detroit Tigers 113, 117
DiMaggio, Joe 52, 127

discrimination: employer 92; and globalism 219; "Jethroe Claim" 103–8; and pension funds 99–100; and sexual orientation 72–77; types of 82–83
Doby, Larry 87, 127
Dole, Bob 57–58, 62–65
Dominican Republic 138, 159, 172–74, 176–78
Doubleday, Abner 128–29
drugs 205, 209
Dryden, Charles 40
Durocher, Leo 153, 200

Eagles (Nicaragua) 159
Easter, Luke 87
Eastern Shore League 15
Eckert, William "Spike" 197, 202
Eckstein, David 20
economy: capitalism 46, 51, 177, 212–24; commodities 177; Communism 12, 43–45, 144, 148, 154, 184; globalization 6, 172, 217; in Japan 221–22; and marketing 218–19
Eduardo Green Award 165
Eighteenth Amendment 35
Eisenhower, Dwight D. 147
embodiment 175, 179
employer discrimination 92
Enatsu, Yutaka 224n1
endorsement discrimination 83
Equal Pay Act 83
ethnicity 126–27, 133, 173; see also race
European Baseball Federation 145, 147
Excelsiors 126–27

fans: and citizenship 233; as consumers 215–18; gender of 221, 234; and homosexuality in sports 79; Japanese 214, 219–24; and patriotism 232; and Selig 208; and Sunday 29–34
Feeney, Chub 202
Fehr, Donald 206
Fehring, William 160
Feldman, Jay 163
Fetzer, John E. 117, 202
Filibusters 135–36
Finley, Charley 1–2
Flint, Frank 32
"The Flying Dutchman" 10
Fort Wayne Capeharts 151–52
Franco, Julio Cesar 159
Frankhouse, Fred 47
free agency 19
Frick, Ford 48, 52, 153, 197, 201–2
Friend, Bob 14
Fukuoka Softbank Hawks 220

gambling 26, 200, 201, 202, 205, 206
Gardella, Danny 200
Gehrig, Lou 46, 47
Gehringer, Charlie 112
gender 31, 32, 221, 234

Georgia 16, 20
Germany 145–46
Geronimo Robles Stadium 164
Giamatti, A. Bartlett "Bart" 197, 205–6
globalism: and baseball diplomacy 171; and baseball politicians 20; and capitalism 212–14; and economics 6, 172, 217; and Japan 215–24; and nationalism 187; and soft power 5–6
"God Bless America" 227, 228
Gomez, Lefty 47
Gonzales, Marco 164
Gore, George 27
Gorman, John 47
Grant, Eddie 229
Green, David 162, 163
Greenberg, Hank 112, 120n1, 127
Greenberg, Steve 206
Griffey, Ken, Jr. 79
Grimm, Charlie 53, 102
Guillén, Ozzie 3, 73
Gwynn, Tony 20

habitus 175
Ham, Clifford 159
Hamilton, Duncan 148
Hansack, Devern 166, 167
Hansen, Ron 160
hard power 195–96, 199, 203, 205, 207–10
Harvey, Francis 235
Heilmann, Harry 121n10
Helmig, Claus 155n18
Hendricks, Elrod 161
Hercules club 131
Hernan Tomares Ordonez Amateur League 162
Hernandez, Willie 121n10
Heroes and Martyrs of September Stadium 163
"Heroes of the Diamond Tour" 232
Hilldale club 84, 91
Hiroshi, Hiraoka 130–31
holdouts 44, 45–47
Hornsby, Rogers 50
Horton, Willie 4, 113–20
House Un-American Activities Committee 12
Houston Astros 171
Howard, Ryan 221
Huckle, Wilbur 23n41
Hughes, Harry Roe 15
Hurley, George S. 11–12

IBC see International Baseball Congress
Ichiro (Susuki) 216, 217, 218, 222–23
identification 42–45, 48–50
identity 58, 60, 65–68, 171, 179–80, 185
Ilitch, Mike 117
Illinois 11, 15
immigration 126–27, 173
imperialism 5, 41, 133–35, 175; see also colonialism

Inchon landing 151
Indiana 11
integration: age of players 89–91, 102; and Chandler 200; first years of 101; and the Negro League 86–87; and Rodney 44, 45; salaries after 86–87, 93, 95; salaries prior to 84–86, 91–92; see also segregation
International Baseball Congress (IBC) 152
International World Series 151–52
Irabu, Hideki 216
Irvin, Monte 87, 90
Italy 146–48
Iwakura Mission 130, 131

Jagger, Bianca 164
Japan: after WWII 143–44, 149–53; fans 214, 219–24; and globalism 215–24; international competition 138–39; and nationalism 5; westernization 129–34
Jenkins, Fergie 160
Jennings, Hughie 121n10
Jethroe, Sam 4, 101–8
"John Barleycorn" 35
Johnson, Arnold 201
Johnson, Byron Bancroft "Ban" 198, 199
Johnson, Walter "Big Train" 10
Jordan, Joseph 147

Kaat, Jim 160
Kaline, Al 120n1
Kansas City Athletics 201, 202
Kansas City Monarchs 84
Karros, Eric 63
Kell, George 121n10
Kelly, Edward Austin 11
Kelly, Mike "King" 28, 32, 127
Kennedy, Sam 218
Kentucky 13, 16
Kerry, John 58
Kieran, John: on class issues 50; interviews 53; on labor 45–46; his rhetoric 3; vs. Rodney 38–39, 54; and U.S. Congress 48
Kishi, Prime Minister Nobusuke 153
Kissinger, Henry 184
Korean War 150–53
Kosovo 183–84
Kralick, Jack 160
Krich, John 163–64
Kuhn, Bowie 196, 197, 202–4
Kuwata, Masumi 223

labor: antitrust exemption 196, 200, 208; contracts 87–91, 92, 218; disposable workforce 172; and Kieran 45–46; and myth of baseball 55; and Rodney 43–45; strikes 203, 204; and Sunday 37n24; talent "hunting" 174–75, 178–79; unions 200; and U.S. Congress 47–48
Landis, Kenesaw Mountain 6, 39, 195, 197–99, 229
Lardner, Ring 40

Lasker, Albert D. 22n17
Lausche, Frank 11
Lazzeri, Tony 44
legal ethics 105–7
Lemon, Brendan 74
Little League World Series 139
Llanio, Col. Pedro 137
Looper, Braden 230
Lopez, Narciso 135–36
Los Angeles Dodgers 57, 177
Lucas, Scott W. 11

MacArthur, Gen. Douglas 150
Machado, Eduardo 137
Maciá, Maj. Carlos 137
Major League Baseball Advanced Media (MLBAM) 208–9, 210
Major League Baseball Player's Association (MLBPA) 72, 73, 202, 203–4
Malcolm X 114
Mantle, Mickey 204
Manush, Heinie 121n10
Marichal, Juan 165
Marine, Joseph E. 16
Marion, Marty 200
Mariotti, Jay 73
Maris, Roger 201
marketing 31, 205, 234, 237; see also media
Marquat, Maj. Gen. William F. 150–53
Martí, José 137
Martinez, Dennis 160, 161, 164–67
Martinez, Pedro 179–80
Maryland 10, 15
Masaya Stadium 163
Mason, William B. 132
Massachusetts 77
Mathewson, Christy 39, 50
Matsui, Hideki 176, 217, 223
Matsuzaka, Daisuke 134, 212, 213, 216, 217, 218
"Matties" 39
Mauer, Joseph 221
Mays, Willie 87, 204
McCahey, James B. 22n32
McCain, John 59
McGowen, Roscoe 3, 46, 53–54
McGraw, John 133
McHale, John 202
McKenney, Frank E. 22n32
McLain, Denny 120n10
McNally, Dave 203
McPhail, Larry 200
media: in Japan 220–21, 223; and the national pastime 142–45, 154; newspapers 40–43; and politicians 41; regulating behavior 76, 80; and soft power 204; and Tadano 77
Medina, Julio 163
Meiji Restoration 130
Messersmith, Andy 203
Mexican League 200

Michigan 12
militarism: and Fourth of July 233; and patriotism 6, 227; and September 11th 230, 236; and sport 229, 231–32; "support our troops" 231–33; and war rhetoric 230–33, 236–37
Millar, Kevin 78–79
Miller, Marvin 202, 203
Mills, Col. A.G. 128
Mills Commission 128
Milwaukee Braves 202
Milwaukee Brewers 207
Minnesota Twins 226
Mirabelli, Doug 78–79
Mississippi 12
Mitchell Report 209
Mizell, Wilmer "Vinegar Bend" 14
Mizuno 131
MLBAM see Major League Baseball Advanced Media
MLBPA see Major League Baseball Player's Association
Monaghan, Tom 117
Moody, Dwight 29
Morgan, Joe 171
Most Valuable Player Award 120n1
Muchnick, Isadore 101
Mundt, Karl 153
Mungo, Van Lingle 43, 47, 51
Murakami, Masanori 224n1
Murphy, Robert 200
Mussina, Mike 3, 75
myth 41–43, 54–55, 113, 116–18, 128–29

narrative 42, 43–45, 48, 53
National Agreement 197
National Anthem 154, 227
national pastime: and the Civil War 125–26, 229; evidence for 127–28; and immigration 126–27; and September 11th 141, 230, 236; and values and beliefs 157, 158; and World War II 229
nationalism: and assimilation 4–5; international recognition 184; and Japan 129–34; and patriotism 185, 231; portrayed 185–86; promoting 138–39; and sport 186–88; in Taiwan 5, 183, 184, 188–93
NBC see American National Baseball Congress
Negro League: after integration 86–87; age of players 89–91; development of 100; health plan 206; opportunity cost 85–86, 91, 94; and owners 88–89; and Rodney 52; salaries 84–86, 91–92
New Hampshire 11
New Mexico 16
New York Giants 229
New York Yankees: baseball academies 178; and baseball politicians 12, 15, 16; in Nicaragua 160, 164–65; salaries before integration 84, 91–92; and Sunday 34

Newark Giants 84, 91
Newcombe, Don 87
Newhouser, Hal 120n1
Newman, Mark 235
Nicaragua: and baseball diplomacy 5, 167; Contras 161–65, 168n26; and Samoza 159–60; Sandinista revolution 161–65; Third Democratic Way 165; U.S. occupation 158–59; values and beliefs 162, 166–67
Nicaraguan Baseball League 167
Nicaraguan National Guard 159
Nicaraguan National League 159
Nicaraguan Professional Baseball League 160
Nikkan Sports News 220
Nippon Ham Fighters 220
Nippon Housou Kyoukai (NHK) 220
Nippon Television Network Corporation 220
Nixon, President Richard 160, 184, 230
Nomo, Hideo 57–58, 212, 216, 223
North, Col. Oliver 161

Oakland Athletics 1–2, 163
O'Doul, Lefty 150
Ogawa, Kunikazu 224n1
Ohio 11, 12
O'Loughlin, Frank "Silk" 12
Olympics 210
Opstein, Kenneth 147
Ortega, Daniel 164, 165, 166
Ortega, Humberto 163
Ostend Manifesto 135
O'Sullivan, John L. 136
Oyashiro, Keizi 220
oyatoi 131

Padilla, Vicente 167
Pafford, Robert 16
Paige, Satchel 52, 87, 90, 92
Panama 158, 164
Pasquel, Jorge 200
Pastoriza, Capt. Manuel 137
patriotism 6, 185, 227, 231, 232, 233
pedestalization of baseball 5
Pegues, J.J. 131–32
Pennsylvania 10, 14
pensions 99, 103, 200
Perry, Commodore Matthew 129
Pettitte, Andy 72
Piazza, Mike 75
Pinella, Lou 160
Pittsburgh Pirates 10, 11, 14, 28–29
Player's League 10
Players Relations Committee (PRC) 207
politicians 9–21, 41, 66–68
Pomares, "Danto" 162
Powell, Jake 43
power: and Eckert 202; and Kuhn 203; and Landis 199; and rhetoric 228; and Selig 207–10; soft power vs. hard power 5–6, 195–96; and Ueberroth 205
PRC see Players Relations Committee

Prohibition 30–36; see also Sunday, William Ashley "Billy"

Queer Eye for the Straight Guy 78–79
Quiroz, Alexi 178

race: Black Codes 104; and civil religion 113–16; ethnicity 126–27, 133, 173; and gender 76–78; interracial play 138; and Japan 132, 214; and a "Jethroe Claim" 103–8; and Lewis 51; and marketing 218–19; and pension funds 99–100; see also integration; segregation
Ramirez, Sergio 161
Ravitch, Dick 207
Reagan, President Ronald 161
Regan, Phil 160
Reinsdorf, Jerry 205
religion: civil religion 4, 111–13, 119, 145, 180–81; and gender 31, 32, 131; God and America 116; and immigration 126–27; in Japan 129; Muscular Christianity 30, 31, 131; and theology 30
Relucido, Eric 178
Remlinger, Mike 232
reserve clause 84–85, 203, 204
rhetoric: anti-Japanese 214; baseball writing 42; and capitalism 46; and Communism 43–45; and ideology 228; and oppositions 59, 68n16; see also militarism
Richardson, Bobby 13–14
Rickey, Branch 45, 46, 198, 200
Rigoberto Lopez Stadium 163
Ripken, Cal, Jr. 20
Robinson, Jackie 87, 90, 100–101, 127, 199–201
Rocker, John 3, 72–73
Rodney, Lester 3, 38–39, 47–52, 54
Rome, Jim 74
Rooker, Jim 14
rookies 83, 90, 177
Roosevelt, President Franklin 142
Rose, Pete 206
Rounders 128–29
Ruppert, Jacob 44, 47
Ruth, Babe 40–41, 59, 198, 201
Ryan, Nolan 20

Sabourín, Emilio 137
SAC see Shinbashi Athletic Club
St. Louis Browns 101
Saito, Takashi 223
sakoku 129
salaries: after integration 86–87, 93, 95; containment 205; discrimination 4, 83, 87–91; for Negro League 84–86, 91–92; pensions 99, 103; and the reserve clause 84–85
San Francisco Giants 163, 207
Sandino, Augusto Cesar 157, 159
Schilling, Curt 59
Schwert, Pius 11

Scott, George 160
"Section 1981" 103–5
segregation 52, 55, 85–86, 94, 100; *see also* integration
Selig, Allan H. "Bud": and collusion 205; and "God Bless America" 227, 228–29; vs. Landis 195; and Rocker 73; on sexual orientation 3; type of power 6, 197, 207–10; and the WBC 191; on Welcome Back Veterans 232
sexual orientation 3, 72–77, 79; *see also* discrimination
Shimbun, Yomiuri 220
Shinbashi Athletic Club (SAC) 130
Smith, Al 59
Smoltz, John 20
Sockalexis, Louis 127
soft power 5–6, 196, 202, 204, 205, 208
Somoza, Anastasio, Jr. 160
Somoza, Luis 160
Somoza García, Anastasio, Sr. 159–60
Somoza Stadium 163
Son, Masayoshi 220
Soto, Enrique 179
Soviet Union 153
Spalding, Albert G. 26–28, 127–29, 130, 131
Speaker, Tris 199
Spira, Howard 206
sportspage 40
steroids 205, 209
Steinbrenner, George 206
Strikeouts for Troops 232
Suitiki, Matsuda 132
Sunday, William Ashley "Billy" 3, 25–36
Suppan, Jeff 20
Sweeney, Mike 20
Swoopes, Sheryl 79–80

Tadano, Kazuhiro 76–78
Taft, Charles Phelps 12
Taiwan 5, 183, 184, 188–93
Takatsu, Shingo 223
Tancredo, Tom 191
Tavárez, Julian 3, 73
Tejada, Miguel 179
Tener, John K. 10–11
Thirteenth Amendment 104
Thompson, Helen "Nell" 29
Thompson, Sam 34
Thorpe, Jim 127, 133
Throneberry, Marvelous Marv 160
Tiant, Luis 160
To Bury Our Fathers 161
Todt, Phil 198
Tokugawa Shogunate 129, 131
Topping, Dan 201
Tribbitt, Sherman 15
Trouppe, Quincy 87
Troy Haymakers 138

Trujillo, Rafael 159

Ueberroth, Peter 16, 197, 200, 204–5
Under Fire 161
United Nations 189
U.S. Marine Corps Hymn 162
Usery, Bill 208

Valentine, Bobby 74
Varitek, Jason 78
Venezuela 172, 177–78
Versalles, Zoilo 160
Vietnam War 229
Vincent, Francis T. "Fay" 197, 206–7

WABC *see* World Amateur Baseball Championship
Wagner, Honus 10
Wakefield, Tim 78–79
Walker, William 135, 158
Walter Reed Army Medical Center 235
Ward, John Montgomery 85
Waseda University 131–32
Washburn, Leonard Dana 40
Washington 11–12
Washington Nationals 232
Washington Senators 10
WBC *see* World Baseball Classic
WBV *see* Welcome Back Veterans campaign
Webb, Del 201
Weiss, Joseph M. 12
Welcome Back Veterans campaign (WBV) 6, 227, 232–37
White, Jesse 15
wild card designation 208
Williams, Albert 161, 162
Williams, Marvin 100
Williamson, Ed 32
Wilpon, Fred 232
Wilson, C.J. 20–21
Wilson, Horace 131
Wisconsin 11
World Amateur Baseball Championship (WABC) 160
World Baseball Classic (WBC): and cultural performance 176; future of 210; and identity 186; inaugural 139; and Nicaragua 166–67; and Selig 209; and Taiwan 5, 189–93
World War I 142
World War II 229
Wright, David 221, 232–33

YCAC *see* Yokohama Cricket and Athletic Club
yellow ribbon 231
Yokohama Cricket and Athletic Club (YCAC) 132–33
Yomirui Giants 220

Zito, Barry 232